PATTERNS OF
REFORMATION

PATTERNS OF REFORMATION

by
GORDON RUPP

Dixie Professor of Ecclesiastical History
in the University of Cambridge

EPWORTH PRESS
LONDON

© *Gordon Rupp 1969*
First Published in 1969
by Epworth Press
(Book Steward
Frank H. Cumbers)
Set in 12/13 pt Van Dijck
and printed and bound
by W & J Mackay & Co Ltd
at their works in Fair Row
Chatham

SBN 7162 0048 1

CONTENTS

Acknowledgements	ix
Select Bibliography	xi
Preface	xiii
Introduction	xvii

PART I
JOHANNES OECOLAMPADIUS
The Reformer as Scholar

1.	Student into Divine	3
2.	Divine into Reformer	23

PART II
ANDREW KARLSTADT
The Reformer as Puritan

3.	Ambitious Young Man	49
4.	The Champion of St Augustine	55
5.	The Great Consult	65
6.	The Wittenberg Movement 1521-2	79
7.	The Vicar of Orlamünde	111
8.	Confrontation and Dialogue	131
9.	Karlstadt's Eucharistic Rebellion	141
10.	Shallows and Miseries 1525-41	149

PART III
THOMAS MÜNTZER
The Reformer as Rebel

11.	Beginnings	157
12.	Zwickau	163

CONTENTS

13.	Prague	169
14.	The Prophet of Allstedt 1523-4	185
15.	Allstedt Writings	209
16.	Mühlhausen	221
17.	The Peasants' War	231
18.	Frankenhausen	237
19.	The Gospel According to Thomas Müntzer	251
20.	Thomas Müntzer's Liturgical Experiments	305
21.	Thomas Müntzer, Hans Huth and the 'Gospel of All Creatures'	325

PART IV

A SIXTEENTH-CENTURY DR JOHNSON AND HIS BOSWELL

The Reformer as Layman

22.	Vadianus and Johannes Kessler of St Gall	357

Appendix: 'Of the Mystery of Baptism' 379

Index 401

ACKNOWLEDGEMENTS

These studies in secondary figures of the Reformation are an expansion of the Fernley-Hartley Lecture given at the Methodist Conference in Manchester in 1955. In the interval the manuscript, like its author, seems to have put on weight. When he put the finishing touches on the initial discourse in a Methodist manse in Stockport, he little knew that his host, the Rev. Gordon Wakefield, would as a kind and long-suffering Connexional Editor receive the final version. Some of the added material was delivered as the Tipple Lectures in Drew Theological Seminary, New Jersey, in 1965, amid great kindnesses from Dean Ranson and his colleagues, despite the sombre preoccupation of the campus with the death of God. Diverse portions, in sundry manners, have been given as lectures in the Universities of Bonn, Oslo, Mainz and Strasbourg and of Otago, New Zealand. The essay on Vadianus was prepared for an international symposium to be presented to Professor Roland Bainton of Yale, a project which, through no fault of the authors, was allowed to fall through. I find some consolation in saluting him at the beginning of this book, as the *doyen* of English-speaking Luther studies, a great teacher and one of the most remarkable, gallant and Christian spirits of our age. A French version of this paper was given as a lecture in the University of Strasbourg, and printed in the *Revue d'histoire et de philosophie religieuses* (No. 4: 1962).

Two works have appeared too recently for me to take them seriously into account: H. J. Goertz *Innere und Aeussere Ordnung in der Theologie Thomas Müntzers* (Leiden 1967), and Friedel Kriechbaum *Grundzüge der Theologie Karlstadts* (Hamburg 1967). About the former I have a few reservations, while recognizing its distinction. Dr Kriechbaum's published dissertation seems to me very sound, and I am only sorry I was not able to pillage his ideas.

ACKNOWLEDGEMENTS

I have to thank Mr Ronald Hall and Dr Taylor, Librarians of the John Rylands Library, Manchester, for unfailing kindness and for permission to browse at will among the magnificent Crawford Collection of Reformation first editions. The Librarian of Manchester University Library, Dr F. W. Ratcliffe, gave me much good counsel about pre-Reformation Bibles, on which he is an authority, and Mr Webb, the head of the University Library photographic service, has helped me often, and always with efficiency and courtesy.

The world of learning is fortunately indivisible, and I acknowledge the pleasing gift of a microfilm from the University Library at Budapest, and the painstaking kindness with which the Archivist of Dresden and Dr Steinmüller, the Archivist of Zwickau, opened to me their treasures and later supplied valuable photostats. I also received much help from the Archivists of St Gall and of Augsburg, and from the Librarian of the Bayerische Staatsbibliothek, Munich.

I acknowledge also microfilms from Bern, Augsburg, St Gall, and the University of Yale. I thank the Oxford University Press for permission to quote from an article on 'Andrew Karlstadt' which I wrote for the *Journal of Theological Studies*, and the John Rylands Library for permission to reprint my lecture on *Thomas Müntzer, Hans Huth and the 'Gospel of All Creatures'*, which was printed in their *Bulletin* vol. 43, no. 2 (1961).

Among my debts of gratitude, an outstanding one must be to Mr Herbert Rees for kindly and meticulous care in helping to prepare the MS. for publication. I count myself fortunate in having had such scholarly help, which has snatched me from the brink of innumerable crevasses. The Rev. John Taylor has helped me greatly with the difficult German of 'Of the Mystery of Baptism'; and my secretary, Miss Linda Shepherd, and my wife, with typing the MS.

SELECT BIBLIOGRAPHY

Certain of the main sources consulted are here included. In the text they are referred to by the short titles given below.

ARG   *Archiv für Reformationsgeschichte*

Barge   Hermann Barge *Andreas Bodenstein von Karlstadt* 2 vols, Leipzig 1905

Br.u.A.   *Briefe und Akten zum Leben Oekolampads* (*Quellen und Forschungen zur Reformationsgeschichte* **10, 19**) ed. Ernst Staehelin, 2 vols, Leipzig 1927, 1934

CR   *Corpus Reformatorum* ed. Breitschneider & Bindseil, Halle 1834–60

Franz   Thomas Müntzer *Schriften und Briefe* Kritische Gesamtausgabe, ed. Günther Franz, with the collaboration of Paul Kirn (*Quellen und Forschungen zur Reformationsgeschichte* **33**) Gütersloh 1968

Freys-Barge E. Freys & H. Barge *Verzeichnis der gedruckten Schriften des Andreas Bodenstein von Karlstadt* (reprint) Nieuwkoop 1965

Hertzsch   *Karlstadts Schriften aus den Jahren 1523–25* 2 parts, ed. Erich Hertzsch, Halle (Saale) 1956–7

Hinrichs   Carl Hinrichs *Luther und Müntzer: Ihre Auseinandersetzung über Obrigkeit und Widerstandsrecht* (*Arbeiten zur Kirchengeschichte* **29**) Berlin 1952

Jäger   C. F. Jäger *Andreas Bodenstein von Carlstadt* Stuttgart 1856

JRL   Crawford Collection of Reformation Tracts, John Rylands Library, Manchester

Kähler   *Karlstadt und Augustin* Der Kommentar des Andreas Bodenstein von Karlstadt zu Augustins Schrift *De Spiritu et Litera* (Hallische Monographien **19**) ed. Ernst Kähler, Halle (Saale) 1952

SELECT BIBLIOGRAPHY

Lebenswerk Ernst Staehelin *Das theologische Lebenswerk Johannes Oekolampads* (*Quellen und Forschungen zur Reformationsgeschichte* **21**) Leipzig 1939
LW *Luther's Works* (American Edition): vols 1–30, ed. Pelikan, Concordia Publishing House, St Louis; vols 31–55, ed. Lehmann, Muhlenberg Press, Philadelphia
MQR *Mennonite Quarterly Review*
Näf Werner Näf *Vadian und seine Stadt St Gallen* 2 vols, St Gallen 1944, 1957
Oek.-Bibl. Ernst Staehelin, 'Oekolampad-Bibliographie', in *Basler Zeitschrift für Geschichte und Altertumskunde* **17** (Basel 1918), pp. 1–119
Theol. Z. *Theologische Zeitschrift*
TLZ *Theologische Literaturzeitung*
WA *D. Martin Luthers Werke* Kritische Gesamtausgabe, Weimar 1883–
WA, Br. *D. Martin Luthers Werke* Briefwechsel, Weimar 1930–48
ZKG *Zeitschrift für Kirchengeschichte*

PREFACE

It is part of the glorious liberty of the children of wisdom that everyman may be a freeman of the world of learning, free to go where he will, to ponder whatever seems to him profitable or intriguing, to pause, to take up a subject and put it down again, and if he likes, to turn back and return to his first love. Long may that liberty continue! There are signs it may not continue very long, especially in our Universities.

Such as they are, these studies were born free. Their author, having begun with the English Reformation, turned to Luther studies and after a space came face to face with the question, 'What do they know of Luther, who only Luther know?' – with the realization that it is not enough to look through any one pair of eyes at the 16th century. To take one's stand in the fair city of Basle, or the little town of Allstedt, or by the green banks of the Saale, might be refreshing, salutary, disconcerting. For some of us the most exciting period of the Reformation is its beginning: Luther before there were any Lutherans, only Martinians, which is not the same thing; Protestants before Protestantism – the time of the pioneers, when as yet the map-makers and the road-makers had not appeared.

To vary the figure, it is a time when all is molten, white-hot, teeming with ideas and intuitions arising from a rapidly changing and revolutionary situation – many of the new ideas dying as soon as born, some of them stifled and aborted, many more 'cabin'd, cribb'd, confin'd' by the attempt to compress truth into confessional definition. I do not suggest that the later period, say, beginning 1550, may not be equally important and engaging. I will only confess for myself how luminous it has been to ponder the Reformation in the first decade of its origin, to see how very swiftly the patterns of Reformation open up, of which Luther's is the dominant but not the only one. By 'pattern' I mean that it is not simply a question of churchmen or theologians differing from one another, as they have always done and always will, but that there are new coherences, proportions of faith, in which Christian truths are differently related to one another: there is a Karlstadt and a Müntzer pattern right on Luther's doorstep, and perhaps it is best just to look at it and eschew labels and typology.

Then there are the cities, a main ingredient in the great, emerging coherence which we call the Reformed, as distinct from the Lutheran, tradition. This pattern, in its early stages, is of extreme interest. Bernd Moeller's brilliant essay on the Imperial Free Cities, *Reichstadt und Reformation* (1962), shows us the importance of this form of Reformation, with its machinery of guild and council, and the tensions of various layers of opinion. The microcosm of little St Gall, and the macrocosm of prosperous Basle, help us to understand the more complex problems of Reformation in Zürich and in Bern, and the even more difficult problems of Strasbourg and Augsburg.

Much of what I have written must seem sadly commonplace to German and American historians. But here in England, Reformation studies still move slowly, and even in the field of English Reformation study we are cramped by unawareness of what had happened on the Continent. I could see no way of helping, without giving what for many must seem an overdose of citations and gobbets. Karlstadt they will just have to swallow, for there is no academic spoonful of sugar to make that tart medicine go down. Müntzer is like Luther at least in this, that the style is the man, that translation drains the blood away, and all one can do is, after his own example, translate more after the meaning than the words.

Finally, despite the sociologists and the Marxists and the political historians, there is still room for the consideration of people, and for historical biography. The historian, like the conjurer, does it with mirrors. His is a looking-glass world where everything is the wrong way round. For he looks back through time, back through the recent articles and contemporary monographs, through the older historians, and through them at the chroniclers and archives, seeing causes only in the light of results, and peering through hindsights at the long-vanished springs of action.

With biography, the difficulties are increased. For the dead have

PREFACE

buried their dead under a mass of documents, letters, treatises, official correspondence; and only an occasional and casual reference brings the human occasion for a second to life – as a mummy disintegrates on reaching the air. Portraits, even the good ones, of Cranach, Dürer or the younger Holbein help a little more: which cannot be said of the 16th-century engravings of which 16th- and 17th-century books are so full and which are still reprinted. They are as stereotyped as Famous Last Words in the evangelical age; and the pictures of the Reformers are all repulsively and grimly alike save that, quite haphazard as it seems, here a beard has been added or withdrawn. Not that we need capitulate to scepticism. In his more despondent moods the historian knows that all he has, at the end of thirty years, is a box of puppets, with which he plays and which move, at least for him – and who knows if they have any resemblance at all to the truth? But in his more optimistic moments he knows that there is more than this. There are those whose mind he begins to understand, whose ways of thought he begins to know, and almost to anticipate. And at the end of the day there may be a few whom he can name as his teachers and his friends, whose company he prefers to Professor What's-his-name and Dr Thingummy-bob. And if he comes that close, then through him those dead voices may speak, the only voices, as Kierkegaard says, which are impossible to silence.

GORDON RUPP

CAMBRIDGE
Feast of St Augustine 1968

INTRODUCTION

The men of the Oxford Movement, seeking to redress the balance of the sorry new age of liberalism by recalling the brave old world of the first centuries, did not imagine that they were returning to a first principle of that Protestant Reformation which it was a point of truth and honour for them to despise. Yet in the first period of the Reformation, though the authority of Scripture was primary for the Reformers, the appeal to the 'old Fathers' was of genuine importance.[1] In this they were the direct heirs of Christian humanism.

In the later Middle Ages, patristic studies seem to have languished, and MSS. grew rarer and more neglected, until the humanists in Italy, Germany, France and England began to rummage them out. The invention of printing was a turning-point. First the Italians, then the northern printing houses, began to turn out the writings of the Fathers. Erasmus – it is not the least of his significances – seems to have grasped the urgent, faster rhythm of the new medium, to have sensed that these studies could no longer be left to cliques of scholars handing round rare manuscripts, but that the new printed texts must be got out quickly, however defective the haste might make them, into the hands of the rapidly widening class of the theologically literate.

The printers, among them Aldus, Amerbach, Frobenius and Cratander, the scholars, among these Le Fèvre, Beatus Rhenanus, Erasmus, Oecolampadius, produced a great series of editions for

[1] D. Gorce, 'La Patristique dans la Réforme d'Érasme', in *Festgabe Joseph Lortz* ed. Iserloh, 1958, i, 233ff.; S. L. Greenslade *The English Reformers and the Fathers of the Church* 1960; Peter Fraenkel *Testimonia Patrum: the Function of the Patristic Argument in the theology of Philip Melanchthon* Geneva 1961; R. Peters *Unio Dissidentium and the Fathers* in *Studia Patristica*, ed. Cross, ix, Berlin 1966

INTRODUCTION

over thirty years.¹ Elsewhere individual scholars, scattered through universities and princely courts, a Hedio, a Spalatin, a Copernicus, a Sir John Cheke, might try their prentice hand at some individual patristic text and edit it for friends or pupils. Such theological writings were for the humanists only part of a great flood of reprints from antiquity, and often, like Conrad Peutinger, they stressed the value of the Fathers as exemplars of a superior classical style. The typical scholarly work of the 16th century, therefore, is peppered with classical allusions and garnished with patristic quotations. By the middle of that century this new availability of the patristic evidence had given a new edge to the appeal to primitive Christianity.² The Reformation began under the influence of humanist reaction against late scholasticism, seeking to go back, behind the synthesis of Fathers and Scripture in Peter Lombard, to the earlier dogmatic norm of a theology untouched by the infiltration of the philosophy of Aristotle. Martin Luther and his colleagues at the young university of Wittenberg, meeting in Andrew Karlstadt's rooms, re-planned theological studies along these lines before the Church struggle began; and this was not just the perennial addiction of all dons for tinkering with a syllabus, but a deliberate concentration of their teaching on the Bible, Augustine, the 'old Fathers'.³

We can indeed, a little guardedly, use the phrase 'biblical theology' to describe what went on in Wittenberg, Zürich, Basle, Strasbourg, in the 1520s. There was the appeal to the Bible, with a new method of exegesis, new tools of linguistic study, a new way of lecturing and preaching.⁴ There are times, it seems, when the Bible

[1] Among many editions of classical and medieval writers, Le Fèvre published writings of John of Damascus, the Clementine Homilies, Athenagoras, Hermas; Rhenanus, translations of Gregory of Nyssa and Basil, and the *editio princeps* of Tertullian (1521). Erasmus was associated with editions of Jerome (1516), Cyprian (1520), Arnobius (1522), Hilary (1523), Irenaeus (Lat. 1526), Ambrose (1527), Augustine (1528), Chrysostom (Lat. 1530-1), Basil (Gk. 1532), Origen (1536).

[2] P. Polman *L'Élément historique dans la controverse religieuse du xvie siècle* Gembloux 1932

[3] Luther to Lang, 18 May 1517, *WA*, Br. I, No. 41

[4] No disparagement of medieval biblical scholarship is necessary. But the kind of hum that rose from contemporaries about the biblical lectures of

itself becomes a self-sufficient dogmatic norm, when its world of thought and its imagery, themes and categories, speak freshly and vividly for themselves. Such periods – the 16th century and the 20th are among them – come rarely and do not last long. There can never be a purely biblical theology: Luther's reference to the Apostles' Creed as his 'little Bible', and the debt of the Reformers to the theology of creeds and councils generally, show that the Bible needs for its interpretation the dogma it has helped to create.[1] Despite an early violent reaction against philosophy, the Reformers soon learned that men reject its help at the peril of being at the mercy of the unconscious habits of mind and presuppositions of their own age, for it is perhaps the de-mythologizing, not so much of the past as of one's own age, which is the real problem for the biblical theologian.

There were, then, new tools. There was the revival of the sacred languages, Greek, Hebrew, a renovated Latin, be it said with papal encouragement and carried through by Catholic scholars. No doubt much of this new knowledge was amateurish and uncritical. It could hardly be otherwise when a local Jewish rabbi, or some wandering Greek scholar, was the only chance of direct instruction, amid a dearth of grammars, dictionaries and philological commentaries. Modern scholars have made the point that the humanists' Latin was not all that they thought it was, and have compared it unfavourably with the best of the Middle Ages, but there would be no point at all in the satire of the *Letters of the Obscure Men* had there not been a barbarous theological Latin which offered scope for caricature. There is the testimony of the Cambridge reformer, Thomas Bilney, that he bought the Erasmus NT in its Latin version, 'allured rather by the Latin than by the Word of God' – a fateful purchase, for it brought him eventually to the fire.

Luther and Zwingli and the preaching of Capito and Oecolampadius seems to prove that some novelty had occurred which impressed itself on hearers as being a more direct appeal to the Bible itself than that of contemporary orthodox exposition.

[1] H. Østergaard-Nielsen *Scriptura sacra et viva vox: Eine Lutherstudie* Munich 1957, p. 114; *WA* 37, p. 55, line 12: 'Hie habe ich ein klein büchlin, . . .'; J. Koopmans *Das altkirchliche Dogma in der Reformation* Munich 1955

INTRODUCTION

Side by side with the new tools was a new hermeneutic which put the exact philological meaning above a traditional theological explanation, and which stressed the importance of a text based on the most ancient and faithful MSS. Thus Antonio Lebrixa, boldest and most brilliant of the Alcalá team which produced the lovely Complutensian Polyglot, had said:

> Every time we are faced with variant readings in the Latin manuscripts of the New Testament, let us go back to the Greek MSS.: every time there are disagreements between the different Latin MSS. or between the Latin and the Greek MSS. of the Old Testament, let us seek the rule of truth in the authentic Hebrew source.[1]

In the previous century Laurentius Valla had declared:

> There are people who believe that theology is not subservient to the rules of grammar. But I say that theology must observe the usage of the spoken and especially of the written language.[2]

It was a great moment, therefore, when in 1505 Erasmus discovered these neglected *Adnotationes* of Valla and published them.[3] It was even more important when, on these principles, he gave priority to a new text of the Greek NT, collating the best MSS. he could find, and putting alongside it his own new Latin version.[4] Of less importance, but similarly hailed as a new tool, was the beautifully printed *Quincuplex Psalterium* of Le Fèvre (1509).

In four ways the Fathers were of importance. Erasmus, with his skill for rapidly gutting texts, used them as authorities for the various readings of his NT. They were valued also as exegetes of Scripture. They provided an armoury of quotations for polemical controversy, and, a little belatedly, they were valued in their own right as doctors of the Church. It is true that, as time went on, the cry 'The Old Fathers' was muted in some directions. Perhaps a significant date is 1528 when, at the Bern Colloquy, the President

[1] M. Bataillon *Érasme et l'Espagne: Recherches sur l'Histoire spirituelle du xvie siècle* Paris 1937, p. 32

[2] W. Schwarz *Principles and Problems of Biblical Translation* Cambridge 1955, p. 133

[3] ibid., p. 132   [4] ibid., p. 142

of debate ruled that only Scripture might be taken down in evidence. One wonders how far the debate with the Anabaptists concentrated attention on the Scriptures. Certainly it is, among the radicals, from Sebastian Franck and his friend Campanus who regarded themselves, in the long march of the Christian Church through history, as the only two in step, that the first really derisory remarks come: 'Foolish Ambrose, Augustine, Jerome, Gregory – of whom not even one knew the Lord, so help me God, nor was sent by God to teach. But rather all were the apostles of Antichrist.'[1]

The new tools, the new texts, crude as they were, uncritical and slipshod as their editors might be, made possible a concentration on the Bible the results of which were startling and practical enough. The Reformers of Wittenberg, Zürich, Basle, Strasbourg, St Gall, knew what they were doing when they devoted a high proportion of their energies in the 1520s to lecturing on the books of the Bible in turn, and publishing commentaries on the basis of them. These Latin works of Luther, Melanchthon, Oecolampadius, Capito, Bucer, Lambert of Avignon, had for the most part little survival value. The Greek and Hebrew characters into which some of them break out rather self-consciously at every turn must have aroused admiration rather than comprehension on the part of their readers. But there is evidence how, in distant Cambridge and Oxford, the younger scholars went to great pains because of them, and sought dangerously and eagerly these tools of the new Biblical learning.[2] They laid the foundations of the religious, theological Reformation. Thomas Garrard the book-agent, not Thomas Cromwell the politician, struck the tinder that lit Master Ridley's candle.

In English, the patristic studies of Thomas Cranmer, Nicholas Ridley and Sir John Cheke were a link not only with the Catholic humanism of More, Fisher, Tunstall, but with a whole second generation of Reformers who included Philip Melanchthon, Urbanus Rhegius, Wolfgang Musculus, and above all, John Calvin. Martin Bucer at Cambridge, and Peter Martyr at Oxford, taught their

[1] A Letter to John Campanus by Sebastian Franck (1531), ed. G. H. Williams, in *Spiritual and Anabaptist Writers* Library of Christian Classics 25 (S.C.M. Press, London 1957), p. 151

[2] Foxe *Acts and Monuments* (ed. Pratt), v, App. VI

INTRODUCTION

pupils to use and reverence the Fathers, and the patristic knowledge of John Jewell, John Foxe, Richard Hooker, marks an emergent Anglican tradition in which the appeal to the first centuries and to the Fathers would be a normative element.

Almost all the Reformers, from the humanists to the Anabaptists, appealed to the primitive Church, though there might be controversy as to how far – to the 2nd, the 4th, or even the 9th century – the penumbra of apostolicity extended.[1]

Luther claimed that the evangelicals were 'the true, old Church', which had never ceased to be, but which had been hidden, 'like the sun behind the clouds'.[2] Richard Hooker used the same argument to answer the taunt, 'Where was your Church before Luther?', and he seems to approve the argument that 'the first state of things was best, that in the prime of Christian religion faith was soundest, the Scriptures of God were then best understood by all men, all parts of godliness did then most abound'.[3] There was common agreement that the fountain stream of tradition was purest at its head, for no Newman arose to turn the argument by directing attention rather to the broad, deep, wide river well along its course, though Beda did criticize Le Fèvre, Erasmus, Luther, for pretending

> that they drink of the streams which flow nearest to the source of divine wisdom, and not of the little streams which being more remote from this source have degenerated: that is, they have in their hands Origen, Tertullian, Cyprian, Basil, Hilary, Chrysostom, Ambrose, Jerome, and others of that kind, instead of Peter Lombard, Alexander, Albert, Thomas, Bonaventura, Ockham etc.![4]

Of the association between humanists and Reformers, of the importance of patristic studies, and of the part it played in the biblical theology of the cities, the career of Johannes Oecolampadius is an

---

[1] F. H. Littell *The Anabaptist View of the Church* rev. ed., Boston 1958; F. W. Kantzenbach *Das Ringen um die Einheit der Kirche im Jahrhundert der Reformation* Stuttgart 1957

[2] 'Wider Hans Worst' (1541); 'Of Councils and the Church' (1539)

[3] *Of the Laws of Ecclesiastical Polity* III, i, 10; IV, ii, 1

[4] cited by D. P. Walker, 'Origène en France au début du xvie siècle', in *Courants Religieux et Humanisme à la fin du XVe et au début du XVIe siècle* Presses Universitaires de France, Paris 1959, pp. 111f.

INTRODUCTION

illumination. He was himself near the centre of the Erasmian movement, the pupil of Reuchlin, the collaborator of Erasmus. He played a leading part not only in the production of patristic texts, but in directing attention especially to the Greek Fathers. His career raises interesting questions about the relation between scholarship and reform in the Church and illustrates some of the interplay between personal and impersonal pressures in the Reformation. It is also of interest as a human story, the story of a sensitive, introverted academic forced by events to become a leader in a very rough ecclesiastical struggle; of a good man, one of the most attractive of the Reformers, whose high character was a byword and whom Luther and Calvin called 'the noblest of men'.

Part I
Johannes Oecolampadius of Basle
The Reformer as Scholar

CHAPTER ONE

STUDENT INTO DIVINE

Johannes Oecolampadius[1] was a Swabian, born at Weinsberg in Württemberg, and he spent his youth in the lovely, swelling, forested hills between the Rhine and the Neckar, about Heilbronn and Heidelberg. His father was a merchant who was content that his son be bred up to trade. His mother was more of a character: a member of a well-known Basle family, the Pfisters, known for her practical charity as well as for her pious devotion, and she seems to have pleaded that her son should try his hand at letters.

He attended the Latin school at Heilbronn, creeping like snail unwillingly to lessons which began at 5 in the morning in summer, and at 6 in winter, with an eight-hour day. It was the usual grammarian's grind, rooted in that rhetorical tradition which the Middle Ages drew from the classical world. There were the usual textbooks, the *Doctrinale* of Alexander de Villa Dei, the *De octo partibus orationis* of Aelius Donatus, and the *Summulæ Logicales* of Petrus Hispanus (later to be Pope John XXI). He matriculated in the University of Heidelberg, 20 October 1499.[2]

Here two great dialectical patterns were side by side, the *via antiqua* pursuing the way of exposition, while the more recent *via Marsiliana* (Ockhamism writ teutonic by Marsilius of Inghen) took

---

[1] The major sources for his life are: E. Staehelin *Briefe und Akten zum Leben Oekolampads* 2 vols, Leipzig 1927, 1934; E. Staehelin *Das theologische Lebenswerk Johannes Oekolampads* Leipzig 1939; J. J. Herzog *Das Leben Johannes Oekolampads und die Reformation der Kirche zu Basel* 2 vols, Basle 1843. The name Oecolampadius is derived, humanist-wise, from a pun on his German name, Huszgen, Huss-schein, Haus-schein; *Br. u. A.* 1, pp. 605ff.

[2] *Br.u.A.* I, No. 1

the 'way of the questionists'. The one course shared by both sets of students seems to have been the Nicomachean ethics of Aristotle, with its exposition of the Hellenic concept of 'Justice' so fateful for another student in another place, Martin Luther.

More important than its schoolmen were its humanist associations, for it touched a great series of circles of scholarly intercourse, the *sodalitas litteraria Rhenana* of the Rhineland and Alsace, with its links with the humanists of Paris, Le Fèvre and his friends, with the cities of south Germany, Switzerland and distant Vienna, with north Italy, and with numbers of scholarly correspondents scattered among universities, printing houses and princely courts. It is difficult to assess the real influence and importance of this intellectual *élite* on the changing temper of the age, and modern scholars seem alternately to underrate and overrate them. Many of them were old fellow students who had remained friends (though their correspondence is littered with tiffs and spleeny academic rows and spinsterish innuendoes of the kind at which Erasmus excelled). The Rhineland circle was of great moment for Oecolampadius: it joined Wimpfeling and Reuchlin of the older generation with Melanchthon, Brenz and Bucer of the new. Between the two generations – an older humanism fretfully loyal, and the young men soon to be in the van of rebellion – stood Oecolampadius, who like Zwingli and Vadianus of St Gall, was within months the contemporary of Martin Luther.

Jacob Wimpfeling is the first outstanding personal influence on Oecolampadius' thought and a rather precious epigram about him is his earliest literary effort to survive.[1] With Wimpfeling had been associated two churchmen, the great popular preacher Geiler of Kaysersberg[2] (whose sermons on an escaped lion at Strasbourg reveal him as the Latimer of the Rhineland) and Christopher von Utenheim,

---

[1] *Br.u.A.* I, No. 2; J. Knepper *Jakob Wimpfeling 1450–1528: sein Leben und seine Werke* 1902 (reprint 1965); L. W. Spitz *The Religious Renaissance of the German Humanists* Harvard University Press, Cambridge, Mass. 1963, Chap. III, 'Wimpfeling Sacerdotal Humanist'

[2] E. J. D. Douglass *Justification in late mediaeval Preaching: A study of John Geiler of Keisersberg* (Studies in Mediaeval and Reformation Thought, ed. H. A. Oberman), vol. i, Leiden 1966

This portrait of Johannes Oecolampadius by Hans Asper
is in the Kunstmuseum in Basle

bishop of Basle and author of the reforming ordinances of 1503, whose summons to ecclesiastical office had broken the dream of these friends that they might (as More and Colet also sometime hoped) go off and form a retreat for scholarship and contemplation. Many humanists, as Cassirer has pointed out, found lodgements at court, and one such princely centre was provided at the court of Landgrave Philip I of the Palatinate with a group of scholars who included Agricola, Conrad Celtis, Trithemius and the great John Reuchlin.

Reuchlin was the giant of the south German humanists, the greatest scholar north of the Alps until Erasmus challenged and took over the pre-eminence. He had been a champion of the sacred[1] languages and of a new critical method, and above all of the importance of Hebrew studies, involved in a bitter fight against the forces of obscurantism and antisemitism in the person of the converted Jew Pfefferkorn and the theologians of Cologne, until the Reuchlin affair (like *l'Affaire Dreyfus* of a later day) became a matter which entangled great and powerful vested interests. Nor was it all obscurantism which opposed Reuchlin. His platonizing, his dabbling in the 'Cabbala', which he shared with the Florentine Academicians, had traces of a mystic eclecticism which had entered northern humanism powerfully in Nicholas of Cusa. In the clash Reuchlin was almost ruined, but when he retired to Stuttgart in 1512, his house and library, with its fine collection of MSS., became a point of reference for scholars passing up or down the Rhine, while he was always ready to welcome any guests brought along by his great-nephew, Philip Melanchthon.

At Heidelberg, Oecolampadius proceeded B.A., 1502, and M.A., 1503. At this time, like many another in his position, including Martin Luther and John Calvin, he toyed with the idea of a legal career and may indeed (as Capito says) have gone to Bologna for a short time, until his health gave way. If so, this was one of several occasions when mental frustration seems to have brought on physical disease. However it may be, he returned to Heidelberg and then in 1506 became tutor to the sons of the Landgrave Philip. But he did not like courts and went back to Heidelberg, until in 1510 family

---

[1] W. Schwarz, op. cit., Chap. IV; G. H. Tavard *Holy Writ or Holy Church: the Crisis of the Protestant Reformation* London 1959, pp. 74ff.

influence secured his appointment by the town council as Preacher in Weinsberg.[1] Such preacherships were a late medieval institution which deserve study,[2] for they were a way of securing preaching when benefices were filled by absentee incumbents, and in many ways they anticipate the Puritan lectureships of 17th-century England. This one committed the holder – Oecolampadius must have

---

[1] *Br.u.A.* I, Nos 7–9

[2] The subject of late medieval preacherships awaits a monograph. Apart from an essay, inaccessible to me, by the late Rudolf Hermann, the best discussion is to be found in Theobald Freudenberger *Der Würzburger Domprediger Dr Johann Reyss* Münster 1954, pp. 8ff.: 'Das Predigtwesen im Bistum Würzburg in der Vorreformationszeit'. It seems that the increasingly articulate lay piety of well-to-do citizens which in other times and other places (e.g. England) was shown in the endowment of chantries turned in the 15th century in south Germany to the endowment of preacherships, in part, perhaps, to supply the lack of this kind of service from absentee incumbents. Nuremberg may have begun with a preachership in the Neues Spital (1385), in St Sebaldus (1391) and St Laurence (1423), followed by Speyer (1410) and Bamberg (1415). Preaching was included in the duties of cathedral priests, but in 1416 it seems that Heinrich Zinck was appointed specifically as cathedral preacher. Soon afterwards money was set aside for a preacher, at least a Master or a Bachelor of Theology, who should fulfil the office of reading and preaching, including some theological lecturing. Cathedral preacherships generally included what we would now call higher educational responsibilities. Of such the preaching appointment in Augsburg was typical. More interesting was the foundation of preacherships in smaller towns, whether by clerical instigation or lay patronage. These increased in numbers at the beginning of the 16th century: Schwäbisch Hall in 1502, Öhringen in 1506. The installation at Weinsberg by the family of Oecolampadius, with their son in mind as preacher, is to be seen against this background. Collegiate churches had special opportunities and recognized responsibilities for a preaching and teaching office. The modest objective of such sermons was sometimes to keep the laity out of mischief, sometimes a concern for their education and edification, and generally there seems to have been trouble taken to get the best man in education and eloquence for the job. No doubt fuller research will show that this movement, which was much older than the Reformation, is of importance in the story of the Reformation, where the number of preachers in so many towns is striking and significant. It is a movement which has so many similarities with the lectureships which played so important a role in 17th-century Puritanism in England that a full investigation must recognize similarities and inquire into possible, though perhaps not probable, cross currents.

been already ordained priest – to preach on Sundays and many festal occasions. It is from this time that he began to use the humanist form of his name, Oecolampadius.¹

A series of his sermons, 'On the Passion of the Lord', were published in 1512. His early sermons are not impressive; but he was not the kind of preacher who rushes into print at the slightest provocation, for there is evidence that he was a preacher of remarkable ability and John Faber thought that he and Capito heralded a new and better method of preaching, a judgement based on his hearing them preach in Basle, and not on the more scholarly form of their printed addresses.² These discourses are in the medieval tradition, with much division and sub-division (the 'seventhly, brethren' suggestive of English Puritanism), and he begins with the allegorical significance of seven Bells: the Golden Bell, which is the eternal decree of the Father by which Christ became our redeemer; the 'campana baritona' – 'hoc est gravis, festiva et sonora' – which is the will of Christ to suffer on our behalf. The betrayal by Judas is the fire and alarm bell. Then follows an exposition of Christ as type of the sevenfold preparation of the preacher, and the elucidation of the Seven Words from the Cross.

Educated religion in the 15th century still awaits technical analysis. But it seems that the 'modern devotion' had become transmuted by contact with new minds, like those of Nicholas of Cusa, and Jean Gerson, and by an infiltration from German mysticism through the writings of Suso and Tauler. Thus the early sermons of Oecolampadius show stresses similar to those of Staupitz and Andrew Karlstadt. No doubt Staehelin is right when he says: 'It is the world of Augustine, Hugo, Bernard, Richard, Gerson and Wimpfeling in which Oecolampadius' thoughts move.'³

---

¹ The German name seems to have meant 'house light', and his enemies later spoke of him slightingly as 'Caeco-lampadius' (dark-lamp). The citizens of Basle complained of 'Oecolampadius' as a mouthful, and gave him the nickname of 'Claus Bader' (Nick-out-of-the-bath). He was also called by opponents – like the Duke of Wellington and for the same reason – 'Old Nosey'.

² *Br.u.A.* I, No. 58; *Oek.-Bibl.* No. 2

³ *Lebenswerk* p. 53; cf. also Capito's judgement quoted on p. 32: 'Post Thomam vero Richardum inter scholasticos praecipue amplexus est. Gersonem trivit non indiligenter'; see *Br. u. A.* 2, No. 971, p. 744

But the restless curiosity for learning did not leave him, and, though still the Preacher of Weinsberg, he went to Tübingen[1] where he matriculated on 9 April 1513.[2] Here, an older student than most, he rubbed shoulders with a thin wisp of an undergraduate, yet with a brow of Wordsworthian proportions, Philip Melanchthon, through whom he came into contact with Reuchlin, and had access not only to inspiration (he may have had Greek lessons from him) but to the fine library and to MSS. which might be read and borrowed. By great diligence, and at the price of an unsettled life, Oecolampadius achieved something rare, and which brought him moderate renown – he mastered the three 'sacred languages' as they were called: Greek, Hebrew, the renovated Latin. He was not supreme in any one of them, and no doubt in all of them he must not be judged by later standards. Wimpfeling and Erasmus far outclassed him in elegant Latinity. But he was almost as good as Erasmus with Greek, and an infinitely better Hebraist though, again, outmatched in this by Pellicanus, Capito, Münster or Reuchlin.

He returned to Heidelberg, and began to hold Greek classes, with a grammar which he himself constructed and which, revised, became one of the better textbooks of the next decades. His pupils included two who became famous, Billicanus and John Brenz. At this time began his friendship with Wolfgang Capito, the Preacher at near-by Bruchsal. 'One was the sharer or author of all the counsels of the other', said Capito, and they shared books and enthusiasms and, at last, a wife; or at least Mrs Oecolampadius became Mrs Capito on the third stage of her matrimonial peregrinations.[3]

The printing houses offered a new kind of employment for scholars, and especially those like Aldus in Venice, and Frobenius and Oporinus in Basle, who were printing books with Greek and

[1] G. Ritter *Studien zur Spätscholastik* II: *Via antiqua und via moderna auf den deutschen Universitäten des XV Jahrhunderts* Heidelberg 1922, p. 133; E. Iserloh *Gnade und Eucharistie in der philosophischen Theologie des Wilhelm von Ockham: ihre Bedeutung für die Ursachen der Reformation* Wiesbaden 1956, pp. 9ff.

[2] *Br.u.A.* I, No. 15

[3] Wibrandis Rosenblatt became in turn the wife of four Reformers: Cellarius, Oecolampadius, Capito, and lastly Bucer (as his second wife). Her offspring represent a history of the Reformation in several volumes.

Hebrew in them: for here were new, technical problems about which expert advice was hard to come by. The work was drudgery and poorly paid, and often the last resort of an impoverished exile (as John Foxe made it in the house of Oporinus). But for it Oecolampadius had unique qualifications. So it was that, when in the summer of 1515 his learned friend Capito went to Basle as Preacher in the Münster and as professor of theology, Oecolampadius followed in a mechanic capacity, though notable enough, to assist in the launching of the New Testament of Erasmus, to whom by name he was already known.[1]

The great man was pleased. He had reason to be, for no other young scholar had the technical equipment to supply Erasmus' needs, and in a quiet way (and Oecolampadius' modesty was notable enough to arouse comment) his deficiencies. He came with a good testimonial from Sapidus.[2] The first task was to supply notes of philological explanation. So much polemical use has been made of the marginal glosses in the first Bibles of the Reformation that it should be noted that such notes, often of an acidly vehement character, are to be found already in the New Testament of Erasmus. But notes of some kind were a necessity in an age where there were no commentaries embodying the new method, and not enough grammars and dictionaries to go round.[3] References to Greek and Hebrew words, translations into a vernacular often itself unstable and unconsolidated, demanded a constant explanation of phrases, expressions, parts of speech.[4] A large number of the Hebrew *adnotationes* came from Oecolampadius, perhaps over a hundred, a high proportion in the Gospel according to St Matthew. He might know more Hebrew than most of his fellows, but his knowledge was not magisterial and no doubt he sometimes took refuge in a scholar's guess (which did not always come off, as later critics were to show). Then, with his fellow assistant, the jurist Nicholas Gerbel, came

---

[1] *Br.u.A.* I, No. 10   [2] *Br.u.A.* I, No. 17

[3] Examples are given by J. A. Froude *Life and Letters of Erasmus* London 1895, p. 129.

[4] See the attempts of N. Ellenbog to borrow from Peutinger Hebrew and Greek Bibles; *Konrad Peutingers Briefwechsel* ed. König, Munich 1923, letters 60, 122

the job of seeing the text through the press, the tiresome intricacy of the proofs. It is perhaps a comment on the unscientific ways of the age that at a late stage Erasmus found to his horror that his assistants had preferred one MS. (borrowed from Reuchlin) to his own authorities, and were inserting their preferred readings into the critical apparatus! Not unnaturally it aroused the Erasmian spleen,[1] and after a dust-up he corrected the rest of the proofs himself. He never did get over his disgust with Gerbel, but Oecolampadius he soon forgave and paid tribute to him as a true theologian. Nor, when the inevitable happened, and a storm of abuse against his New Testament came from the Englishman Edward Lee, the Fleming Latomus, the Spaniard Zuñiga, did Erasmus abandon his assistant. He blamed not his incompetence, but the haste of the enterprise. But why this work which had been planned and prepared for several years had to be so rushed at the last is another question, the more pointed since so many other works of Erasmus were finished at this headlong pace. No doubt the new rhythm of the printing age has something to do with it, or perhaps the well-known failure of nerve which besets scholars, leading them to jeopardize the patient research of years in a last frantic attempt to 'get the thing out'. At any rate Oecolampadius was warmly admiring and grateful: he had been a scholar of Reuchlin and a colleague of Erasmus, and thus in personal contact with the two finest luminaries of the new learning. Nor did he neglect his reading and his theological studies. He matriculated at Basle, October 1515, and fulfilled the degrees until that of Licentiate within a year. In 1518 he was to proceed D.D.

He learned, said Capito, chiefly from 'dumb masters', that is, from books, and more than most men seems to have been influenced by them, so that the world of thought was luminous for him, and the time would come when the exhortations of the Fathers would outweigh the counsels of his friends. The contact with Erasmus no doubt stimulated his existing interest in the Fathers, and enlisted his collaboration in the Erasmian edition of Jerome, the great nine-volume edition which appeared 1515–16, and for which Oecolampadius later (1520)[2] provided the Index. From this time on, the

[1] *Br.u.A.* I, No. 74, p. 113, note 5   [2] *Br.u.A.* I, No. 77

Fathers were a consuming interest for him. We have seen that the appeal to them was a consequence of the humanist revulsion from late scholasticism, and was in part the attempt of the new learning to find a dogmatic norm in the period before the infiltration of philosophy, and especially of Aristotle, into theology.[1] The dogmatists were drawn rather by Augustine and Ambrose – it is interesting to find John Eck siding with Luther as against Erasmus, here – while the exegetes gave pride of place to Origen. No doubt Erasmus had direct, personal influence on Oecolampadius, with whom he must have had many conversations on this theme. Erasmus had skimmed an enormous number of writings of the Fathers, and some he had deeply pondered. In a famous passage in his 'Ratio seu Methodus compendio perveniendi ad veram theologiam'[2] he discusses the relative merits of Origen, Tertullian[3] and Cyprian. And he ranks in the exegetical hierarchy, after the great Alexandrian Fathers, Basil, Nazianzen, Athanasius, Cyril, Chrysostom, Jerome, Ambrose, Hilary, Augustine. His tract on Ecclesiastes, written at the end of his life, includes a page on 'How to read the Fathers' which Renaudet has well described as a course on patrology.[4] Not that we must exaggerate the originality of Erasmus here: in this and much else he was less a pioneer than a focus, a temperature reading. Le Fèvre and Beatus Rhenanus were at least as concerned, and perhaps before him in this field.[5] Conrad Peutinger (with whom,

---

[1] For the decline in interest, and so in editions of the Fathers in the 14th–15th centuries, see the quotations in the interesting essay by D. Gorce already quoted above (*Festgabe Joseph Lortz* i, 236ff.).

[2] Erasmus *Ausgewählte Werke* ed. Hajo Holborn, Munich 1933, p. 295; D. Gorce, op. cit., p. 249; A. Renaudet *Études Érasmiennes (1521–1529)* Paris 1939, p. 31

[3] But penetrating also is Luther's reference to Tertullian as 'a proper Karlstadt'.

[4] A. Renaudet, op. cit., p. 32, note 3; D. Gorce, loc. cit.

[5] A. Renaudet *Préréforme et humanisme à Paris pendant les premières guerres d'Italie (1494–1517)* Paris 1953, pp. 507ff. and Index. The library of Rhenanus, marvellously intact at Sélestat, includes the 11th-century MS. from which he made the *editio princeps* of Tertullian (published by Frobenius, 1521); the copy, bearing the marks and notes made by Rhenanus in getting it through the press, is a rare and splendid example of the best humanist patristic scholarship. That the writings of the Fathers might be explosive material was

and with whose famous library, Oecolampadius was soon to come into direct contact) had long ago discussed the various merits of the Fathers.[1]

Oecolampadius himself was drawn towards the Greek Fathers. His own mastery of the Greek language drew him towards the work of translating their writings, for which the times were propitious. But he must have found them surprisingly congenial to his own temperament. Himself a devoted preacher, an austere moralist, mystically inclined, he found much that harmonized with his own tastes in the world of the 4th and 5th centuries and in Chrysostom, Basil and the Cappadocian Fathers. Nor did such studies lead him away from the contemporary Church. Like the men of the English Oxford Movement in the 19th century, he found that here in the writings of the Fathers were ample quotations with which to garnish tracts for the times in which he lived.[2]

For much of the time, 1516–18, he was back in Weinsberg, a little unsettled by criticism of his preaching to which perhaps he was hypersensitive. There had been complaints that he was too earnest, had no humour in his sermons, did not speak enough on 'topics'. He himself deplored the levity introduced by popular preachers, many of them from the mendicant orders, and the kind of buffoonery introduced into the church at Easter time. He wrote a rather solemn denunciation of frivolity, 'De risu paschali',[3] and perhaps at the same time delivered a forceful though hardly cory-

---

sensed, and most of these editions (certainly those of Rhenanus, Erasmus and Oecolampadius) contain some disclaimer in the preface; see D. P. Walker, op. cit., in *Courants Religieux et Humanisme* p. 108f.

[1] *Konrad Peutingers Briefwechsel* letter 123 (p. 208): 'Legant rogo isti qui vix nominandi sunt sophistae Dionysium Areopagitam ... Tertullianum ... duos Gregorios ... Basilium ... Origenem ... Lactantium ... Cyprianum et Augustinum ipsum et Hieronymum, Ambrosium, Rufinum, Leonem'. It is important too that Peutinger commends them as examples of a purer classical style.

[2] In the light of Capito's statement that Oecolampadius tried his hand at turning the lives of the saints into verse, we might think of him as the John Keble of the early Reformation.

[3] *Br.u.A.* I, No. 35

bantic homily himself on 'True Easter Joy'.[1] He was short-listed for the professorship in Hebrew at Wittenberg, and the story of the Reformation might have been strangely altered had he gone there and been drawn into the orbit of Luther, rather than of Zwingli, by the gravitational pull of a stronger personality than his own. Instead he became Penitentiary in the Münster at Basle, a mysterious affair which looks like one of those arrangements which enable a useful young man to remain in a university town. But he exercised pastoral care of souls, and in 1518 produced four translations from Greek divines, all one way or another concerned with Christian discipline.[2]

He now found a new circle of humanist friends: those of Nuremberg, Veit Bild, Christopher Scheurl, Willibald Pirckheimer; and of Augsburg, Bernard and Conrad Adelmann, and Conrad Peutinger. They were critical of Rome, favourable to reform, and at this time on the side of Luther and against his enemy, John Eck, who at the moment was bumbling noisily about in the university of Ingolstadt. They were impressed, indeed rather excited, by their new theologian, with the result that he was asked to preach 'with a view' in the cathedral of Augsburg.

The sermon, delivered on 24 October 1518, was no doubt an agreeable occasion, the interview afterwards satisfactory, in contrast to the grim consultation in which Martin Luther had been involved in the same city, four days earlier, with the Cardinal Cajetan. Oecolampadius was appointed Cathedral Preacher, and in the next days took his D.D. at Basle. For this was a theologian's post, and if the preaching duties were similar to those at Weinsberg, there were now theological lectures to attend to at certain seasons, and the setting, with a cultured nucleus among his audience, was more demanding.[3] In this great Imperial city were many families of wealth and intellectual eminence. Notable among them was the family of Conrad Peutinger. Peutinger, town recorder, lawyer, scholar, diplomat, was a kind of Teutonic Sir Thomas More.[4] He had a great library, a

---

[1] *Br.u.A.* I, No. 36; *Oek.-Bibl.* No. 11
[2] *Br.u.A.* I, No. 38   [3] *Br.u.A.* I, No. 43
[4] The two men had met on embassy at Bruges. Peutinger's handling of Anabaptists is sadly reminiscent of More's dealing with heretics.

famous collection of coins, maps, and antiquities, and he kept a parrot from the New World much as More had his ape at the bottom of the garden. His wife and daughters were bluestockings. His wife, Margaret (of the banking family of Welser – but when Peutinger courted her, her little Latin counted as much as her large dowry) was learned enough to argue exegetical points, in print, with Erasmus. Constance could write an elegant, witty letter in Latin like the one to her father, absent on embassy to Bruges, about his books: 'What quarrels there are about you! As often as I go into your library all your books cry out – especially the Erasmus, Pliny, Jerome – "When is our master and patron coming home?" '

Felicitas Peutinger was meditating entering religion, and in February Oecolampadius turned into German for her benefit a tract by Gregory Nazianzen on the virgin state.[1] In the middle of the year she entered the nunnery of St Katherine, and it may have been there that Oecolampadius preached, on the patronal festival, a sermon on St Katherine – the theme, 'The Wise Virgin' – for both works were published together with a third sermon.[2] This last is evidence of further contact with devout women, for it was delivered in the Brigittine house at Altomünster, a double house, but ruled by an Abbess. This sermon was entitled 'On the harmful and fruitful winds which blow in the garden of the soul'.[3]

A good deal of the important mystical literature of medieval Germany had been preached in nunneries, and these sermons, though unremarkable, are pleasing examples of what we have already noted, the conflation of the modern devotion and German mysticism. The sermon about the garden of the soul is based on the Song of Songs. Two winds blow from two opposite directions – one from the land of the Creatures, the other from the land of the Creator and from God. The sermon on 'The Wise Virgin' is longer and livelier, and begins with an historical section about the Helens and Cleopatras of this world, taken from the church historian Socrates.

[1] *Br.u.A.* I, No. 53
[2] *Br.u.A.* I, No. 67; two copies of these rare writings are in the Munich library – Rar. 1509 and Rar. 1510.
[3] Photostat, Munich Library; *Oek.-Bibl.* No. 14

Divine wisdom, in the manner of the 'modern devotion', is contrasted with human knowledge.

> Such comes not from Metaphysics or Astrology, or the analysis of the virtues, or from reading books, but only from the Spirit of God ... nobody can be called a true theologian or sage in any other way, even though he had read all the Scriptures inside and out, before and behind.

Weightier was his translation of a famous sermon of Gregory Nazianzen, 'De Amandis Pauperibus'.[1] This was indeed a tract for the times, for it may have been originally preached at the opening of St Basil's hospital at Neocaesarea, and there may well be a connexion with the opening of the great almshouse built by the Fuggers in Augsburg in 1519. Other sermons of Gregory were translated and printed by Oecolampadius in the next months.[2]

Meanwhile, ugly clouds of dark smoke from the Luther explosion drifted over the south German landscape, and the humanists found themselves implicated in the polemic of John Eck. In a marginal sneer at 'Canonici indocti Lutherani' he was supposed to have been getting at the Adelmanns, and some kind of common reply was concocted, edited, it seems, by Oecolampadius. It was able enough to infuriate the irascible Eck who tried in vain to get it burned by the hangman at Ingolstadt.

Soon his friends were buzzing venomously about Oecolampadius, 'the three-headed Cerebus' (a hit at the sacred languages). Eck had to be content to wait, and to add the name of Bernard Adelmann to the bull against Martin Luther in the following year.

Oecolampadius was unsettled again. Adelmann described him as 'homo inconstans', and perhaps there is here a flaw in his character, though something must be allowed for a man of great gifts who approaches middle life without having found the best outlet for his talents. At any rate he seems to have been discontented by the little room for study allowed by his ecclesiastical chores, and by criticism of his preaching, of his soft voice, and what he somewhat mysteriously calls his 'lack of civil prudence'. He grumbled a little ungratefully to Adelmann that his job was like working at a

---

[1] *Br.u.A.* I, No. 52   [2] *Br.u.A.* I, No. 59; *Oek.-Bibl.* Nos 25, 26

treadmill. He began to sigh for a more retired life, of which his beloved Eastern Fathers were so eloquently full, the life of study and devotion. No doubt a little romantically, with a touch of that 'accidie' which makes all clerics sure they would be happier anywhere else but where they happen to be at the moment, he began to think of the Brigittines at Altomünster, an order which at this period seems to have specialized in late and scholarly vocations. Then suddenly, without consulting his friends at hand (a sure sign that he felt they might dissuade him), he entered the house at Altomünster, on 23 April 1521.

Many Catholic humanists had little use for the religious orders: Colet, More, Gardiner, Erasmus, Adelmann, Pirckheimer, could be devastating about them. That Oecolampadius could enter religion as late as April 1521 tells us perhaps more about Oecolampadius than about the Reformation. Adelmann wrote in disgust to Pirckheimer: 'the monastery lacks even necessary things: it is thoroughly scruffy and, as you know, run by women!' – as for Oecolampadius, 'when he was with us he moaned about a treadmill; let's hope he doesn't find himself imprisoned for life!'[1] The Brigittines were as accommodating as they could be to this pike among the minnows. They welcomed him, along with what the monastic chronicle lists as 'all his household utensils, clothes, bedding, carpet, cushions, coffers, tablecloths and 46 fl. in gold'. Moreover, he brought with him a valuable part of his library of Latin, Greek and Hebrew books.[2] His superiors went out of their way to accommodate his scruples, for he would find nothing which need conflict with his loyalty to the Word of God, and when he asked about preaching, he was reassured that it was a privilege of the Order that its members might go out into the world to combat heresy.

When, a few months later, Adelmann visited his friend he found him trying to make the best of a growingly unhappy lot. He got him a pair of spectacles that he might pore over books by candlelight. John of Damascus, the Gregories, Basil the Great on 'Usury', were among the authors whose tracts he translated and published during

[1] *Br.u.A.* 1, No. 78
[2] *Br.u.A.* 2, No. 986; he may have left some behind with his parents at Weinsberg.

these months. But his withdrawal from the world did not mean his lessening interest in its affairs and he had already made himself something of a 'special correspondent' about Luther. He now wrote for his friends a private 'Judicium'[1] on him, which was so outspoken that its indiscreet publication inevitably involved him in trouble. But he followed this with a tract on 'Confession, and how it ought not to be burdensome to Christians'. His was always the faith of a moralist and he had seen something at first hand in Basle of the abuse as well as the use of the penitential system. This work caused a sensation in the Catholic camp, especially in the north where the Louvain theologian, Latomus, added Oecolampadius to the name of Erasmus on the list of dragons to be slain. Aleander described Oecolampadius as one of the great 'satraps' among the more learned Reformers, and this particular writing as worse than Luther.

As usual with his anxious temperament, mental stress brought physical strain, and he had to be excused vigils and mortifications and some of the communal devotion. His writings began to cause opposition and the house of quiet study began to loom darkly, as a prison confined within which he would be at the mercy of his enemies. It should be said that his friends were the first to persuade him to leave and that he withstood them for some time. His criticisms of the 'Rule of the Saviour', which was the Brigittine adaptation of an Augustinian rule, did not endear him further to his fellows, but with the rumour that his Prince would take action against him and that he was to be arrested, Oecolampadius was moved to decision. He addressed the brethren and reminded them of the clause in the rule by which brethren might expel a member to avoid contagion of heresy, and begged them to regard him as highly contagious. He then took his leave, departing with a group of friends who waited with a spare horse outside. He left behind not only a good many worldly possessions – this would not have greatly troubled him – but his precious books. Later, when Pellicanus in 1525 also left his order, Oecolampadius wrote bitterly: 'To enter a monastery is not so serious; but to go out, to be ridiculed as apostate and heretic, to have no sure home or employment – that is not without pain (*non caret agone*).'[2]

[1] *Oek.-Bibl.* No. 22   [2] *Br.u.A.* I, No. 267

He found a haven of sorts in the castle of the Ebernburg, the Adullamite headquarters from which Franz von Sickingen in 1522 plotted the desperate rising of the German knights. Here Martin Bucer and Oecolampadius acted as chaplains, and, if the venture seems eccentric, we might remember that the knights lost their battle, and that it could have seemed hardly less chancy than the plots and stratagems in which George Wishart and John Knox were similarly involved in Scotland. It seems that Oecolampadius had something to do with the insertion of vernacular readings in the Mass, for he preached on the theme, and wrote a simplified order of service 'The Testament of Jesus Christ', which seems to have circulated in Germany and Holland.[1] Here, as best he could, he got on with his studies, but the hurly-burly of an armed camp could hardly have been more restful than his monastery or his cathedral. It may be that von Sickingen himself sensed that things were going badly, and that he encouraged Oecolampadius to leave. So, in November 1522, he went off to Basle, bearing his sheaves of MSS. with him, the first-fruits being seventeen of forty-three translations from the writings of St John Chrysostom. They were among the most notable of his translations, and came in for a good deal of Catholic criticism.[2]

In these months, the future must have seemed uncertain, and he could hardly have guessed that he would remain in Basle for the rest of his days, still less that in a few years he would one day be its most eminent figure. Wackernagel has vividly described how fine a city Basle[3] was at this time, with its colony of scholars and artists, its

---

[1] It is printed in J. Smend *Die evangelischen deutschen Messen* Göttingen 1896 (reprint 1967), pp. 51–7. Smend is doubtful (pp. 60–2) of Oecolampadius' authorship.

[2] *Br.u.A.* 1, Nos 123–33; *Oek.-Bibl.* Nos 68–72, 74, 75, 79, 80, 81

[3] On the cities generally, see Bernd Moeller *Villes d'Empire et Réformation* Geneva 1966, a revised edition of his *Reichstadt und Reformation*; also F. Rörig, 'Die europäische Stadt', in *Propyläen-Weltgeschichte* ed. Walter Goetz, iv: *Das Zeitalter der Gotik und Renaissance 1250–1500* (Berlin 1932) Eng. trans., F. Rörig *The Medieval Town* (London 1967); H. Mauersberg *Wirtschafts- und Sozialgeschichte zentraleuropäischer Städte in neuerer Zeit* Göttingen 1960. For Basle, see the classic study of R. Wackernagel *Geschichte der Stadt Basel* Basle 1907–24, 3 vols; *Register* Basle 1954

rich men furnished with ability. A city which faced Germany on the one hand and France on the other was bound to draw to itself refugees and reformers of the most varied kinds along the highway of the Rhine. At first, Oecolampadius lived with the publisher Cratander, and began soon to teach, which as a doctor of the university he had a right to do. In the spring of 1523 he began to lecture on Isaiah, and the lectures were an immediate sensation as he rang the changes on the three sacred languages with striking virtuosity, lecturing also in German, so that the usual audience of priests and students was swollen by some 400 of the citizens of Basle. The lectures themselves became the foundation of the commentary which he published in 1525[1] and which was highly praised by Luther and by Calvin. From this time on, Oecolampadius became a name which counted, and Erasmus with his *prima ballerina*-ish acerbity said in a few months, 'Oecolampadius is reigning here.' A few months before, Oecolampadius had seemed in danger of running to seed, an introverted, unsettled recluse. Now, like his friend Bucer in another place, he was to become the soul of the Reformation in a great city. He had found his vocation as teacher and preacher, and like Luther could teach in the pulpit and preach in the lecture room.

In June he and Pellicanus were appointed to vacant chairs in theology. For this he received annually £60, his one regular income in the following years, though later augmented from other sources. But the new professor was not content to remain a remote and ineffectual don. Within a few days, he had sent to the press a tract on poor relief: 'De non habendo pauperum delectu'. Not for nothing had he devoted thought to translating the Cappadocian Fathers on this theme, and Conrad Peutinger, an important and experienced authority in this matter, judged the work important enough for him to translate into German.[2]

Scholarship and reform were to go hand in hand. In August he

[1] *Oek.-Bibl.* Nos 109, 110

[2] The parallel between Oecolampadius' career and Bucer's is close. Bucer arrived unemployed in Strasbourg in 1523. His first writings were concerned with practical charity. But there was no university in Strasbourg, where the Reformers trod on one another's heels in search of jobs.

published a translation of sixty-six homilies on Genesis by St John Chrysostom.[1] But in that month too he had flung down the gauntlet by offering four theses for public disputation. In Zürich, Ulrich Zwingli had turned academic disputation into a formidable weapon of reformation, into an occasion of public decision. Oecolampadius' theses are not in this class (he could not do alone in a few months what Zwingli had planned over four years).

None the less, they were seen to be a public challenge by the authorities, as is proved by the measures they took to stop the disputation. The council was prepared to allow the debate; but the bishop sent a personal appeal to Oecolampadius to withdraw, while the Rector of the university tried to stop the proceedings on the quibble that Oecolampadius was not a recognized professor (he did not receive his first stipend until September). Despite all this, the disputation took place and Oecolampadius defended his four theses: the first asserting the prime authority of Christ, in comparison with which the teachings of the philosophers and doctors are contemptible. (He was to get into trouble for the reference to 'doctors', for the rumour spread that he despised the Fathers.) The second thesis asserts justification by faith ('which gives nothing to the creature, but all to the divine mercy'); the third attacks the invocation of saints; the fourth treats Christian liberty and asserts that all Christians are 'brothers, kings and priests'.[2]

During the illness of the people's priest, Oecolampadius began to act as vicar in the church of St Martin, which became the inner citadel of the Basle Reformation. In the course of preparing the Erasmus NT, Oecolampadius had found among the MSS. of the Basle Dominicans a codex containing the commentary on the Gospels of Theophylact, the 11th-century archbishop of Achrida in Bulgaria.[3] These he now published in translation. He also published a series of sermons on 1 John, one of which got him into trouble for the Erasmian sentiment that it was diabolical to speak of a 'just war' among Christian men.

[1] *Br.u.A.* I, Nos 165, 166; *Oek.-Bibl.* No. 104
[2] *Br.u.A.* I, Nos 166–72
[3] Hence he is often called Bulgarius, and sometimes Vulgarius; *Oek.-Bibl.* No. 45.

From December 1522 he had been in contact with Ulrich Zwingli, though they did not meet until some months later. An alliance between the reformers of Zürich and Basle was inevitable, but it became also a loyal friendship. Oecolampadius may have found in Zwingli's gifts of clarity and decision, and his political interest, that quality of 'civil prudence' which he himself lacked. He seems to have leaned on the stronger personality, much as did Melanchthon on Luther. Later, Luther was to compare him with Icarus, led to disaster by the Daedalus of Zürich.

In this fateful decade, before Geneva was captured for reform, Basle was the *point d'appui* for the French reformers. Hither came William Farel. This explosive person reverberated like an interminable jumping cracker as he bounced among the cities in the next months, in an aura of theological sparks and smoke. His Gallic ebullience was at the opposite pole from Dutch phlegm; Erasmus could not stand him, and asserted that even Oecolampadius had been tried beyond endurance by Farel's dinner conversation, which consisted in vitriolic attacks on all and sundry.[1] But Oecolampadius was a good friend to Farel, and kept up an amicable correspondence with him for years, though not without an undertone of references to the virtues of meekness and humility. Through Farel, Oecolampadius came into contact with other Frenchmen, with gentry like Anémone de Coct, Morelet du Museau, son of the French ambassador, and with the Le Fèvre circle at Meaux, while in the next months editions of his own patristic writings were published in Paris.[2]

Oecolampadius' growing reputation is reflected in the widening circle of his correspondents. There is a sad interest in the letters of these months: not much longer could he address in terms of friendship Erasmus, Pirckheimer, Adelmann, Luther, Brenz. Yet in one point, Oecolampadius could still enter the lists for Luther, for when it became known that Erasmus was publicly to attack Luther on the doctrine of Free Will, Oecolampadius began to make remarks in sermons which Erasmus took personally, and which he did not forget; nor was Erasmus better pleased when at the end of 1524 Oecolampadius published a catena of passages from Prosper,

---

[1] *Br.u.A.* I, No. 192   [2] *Br.u.A.* I, Nos 188–9, 203–8; *Oek.-Bibl.* No. 97

Augustine, Ambrose (mainly from spurious works) which made for Luther's position.

Then, in the autumn of 1524, came the first mutterings of the great storm, the eucharistic controversy which split irretrievably the common evangelical front.

CHAPTER TWO

DIVINE INTO REFORMER

The great division between the Reformers about the Eucharist[1] has first (like other controversies, about baptism, about faith and works, etc.) to be seen in relation to their common opposition to Roman doctrine and practice, to the Mass, and to transubstantiation. Even Luther admitted that a doctrine of a spiritual presence, which gave but symbolic virtue to the elements, would be a convenience for polemic, as being plainly opposed to the doctrine of transubstantiation. In the autumn of 1524 such a doctrine was in the air. From the Netherlands came a scholar, Hinne Rode, bearing a letter for Zwingli from a Dutch reformer, Cornelius Hoen, in which a symbolic meaning was given to the consecrated elements. It is possible that Oecolampadius took advantage of the odd manners of the day, and read the letter while it was still on the road. Certainly when Veit Bild wrote in September asking about the Eucharist, Oecolampadius sent a guarded reply which stressed the spiritual character of the holy symbols.[2]

Then, at the end of October, Gerhard Westerburg, disciple and brother-in-law of Andrew Karlstadt, arrived in Basle, bringing with him a number of tracts in which his kinsman made an all-out attack on the doctrines and methods of Wittenberg. This clutch of addled polemical eggs obviously needed careful handling and the printers drew the line at the tract on baptism, which disappeared; they printed the rest, and were promptly put under arrest, whereupon

---

[1] The indispensable study of the eucharistic controversy is the massive two-volume work of Walther Köhler *Zwingli und Luther* i, Leipzig 1924; ii, ed. Kohlmeyer–Bornkamm, Gütersloh 1953.

[2] *Br.u.A.* I, No. 217

they excused themselves on the ground that Oecolampadius himself had been publisher's reader and found nothing amiss in them. Which is perhaps not so much a comment on Oecolampadius' theology as on the perennial temptation of publishers' readers to regard MSS. as written that he who runs may read.[1]

There seems to have been a meeting between Oecolampadius and Zwingli about the Eucharist, and by the end of November it was known that Oecolampadius shared with Zwingli a spiritual interpretation of the eucharistic presence. That in this there is a link with Erasmus, as Köhler suggested, is possible, but if there is, it is not so much in any direct teaching of Erasmus as in the widespread spiritualism of the humanists, shared by John Colet, Le Fèvre, and the Florentine Platonists. In the next months, slightly deflected by the rise of the Anabaptists and the Peasants' War, controversy, misunderstandings, and invective multiplied.

It was perhaps natural, but baneful, that Luther saw all this through the eyes of Andrew Karlstadt, and dismissed all those who denied the Real Presence as fanatics (*Schwärmer*). In the case of Oecolampadius, a series of minor accidents made the charge more plausible. First Karlstadt himself arrived in Basle, though he departed without seeing Oecolampadius. Then Thomas Müntzer was given dinner by Oecolampadius, who was ignorant of the identity of his visitor, was impressed by his edifying discourse about the Cross, and was only disillusioned and horrified when his guest began an attack on Luther so venomous that he guessed his identity.[2] In the next months other radicals seemed to have some link with Oecolampadius. He corresponded with friendliness with Balthasar Hubmaier, on the eve of his conversion to radicalism. Hans Denck had been a pupil of Oecolampadius, and Denck's future ally, Ludwig Hätzer, was to be for many months the chief instrument for translating Oecolampadius' works into German, a trusted member of Oecolampadius' own household until he got one of the maids with child and hurriedly departed.[3]

---

[1] *Br.u.A.* I, No. 226

[2] *Br.u.A.* I, No. 227; 2, No. 465, p. 21

[3] J. F. Gerhard Goeters *Ludwig Hätzer, Spiritualist und Antitrinitarier* Gütersloh 1957, Chap. VIII

There is probably some truth in Oecolampadius' statement that he tried to keep silence, for the sake of peace, but that he was bombarded by so many questions from correspondents and members of his congregation that he had to take up pen and paper and enter a conflict in which Luther and Zwingli were already engaged. The opening round was a battle of exegesis, concerning the meaning of 'This is my Body'. Luther took the words simply to mean what they said, and insisted that no trope should be read into Scripture where the context did not demand it. Karlstadt had affirmed that by 'hoc' (τοῦτο) Christ had intended his own physical body, and that the words 'This is my Body' were a kind of hiatus, unconnected with what he had said immediately before and after. Zwingli took 'est' to be a trope, and to be better rendered as 'significat'. Oecolampadius characteristically fastened on a patristic phrase, in which Tertullian took 'body' to be 'figura corporis'.[1] Here, then, was Oecolampadius' contribution to the controversy, to bring his patristic learning to bear, and to appeal to a spiritual interpretation of the presence which could be found in the writings of the Fathers.[2]

In the summer of 1525 he published a treatise which became an important handbook in the controversy, 'De genuina verborum Domini: "Hoc est corpus meum" juxta vetustissimos authores expositione liber'.[3] He was cautious enough to have it printed in Strasbourg rather than in Basle, but imprudent enough to dedicate it to the preachers of Swabia, the most notable among whom was his friend and pupil, John Brenz, a devoted disciple, however, of Luther in this matter. The Strasbourg theologians did their best to mediate, and Bucer, in a flurry of fuss, wrote to all and sundry. The Swabian preachers wrote a reply in which they hinted that Oecolampadius was in some ways worse than Karlstadt, though far more learned; although they spoke to him with respect and even affection.[4] Soon there came attacks from the Catholic side. Erasmus, it is true, sent an amazingly mild report to the Council of Basle in

---

[1] see *Br.u.A.* I, No. 235. The reference is to Tertullian *adv. Marcionem* IV, xl; Köhler, op. cit., i, 123, note 4.

[2] For a discussion of some of the patristic elements, see C. W. Dugmore *The Mass and the English Reformers* London 1958, part i.

[3] *Br.u.A.* I, No. 261; *Oek.-Bibl.* No. 113   [4] *Br.u.A.* I, No. 289

which he described the work as learned: 'adderem etiam pium' – 'if that can be godly which fights with the teaching and consensus of the Church'.[1] But the book was censured by the university of Paris, and to Oecolampadius' chagrin publicly attacked by his old friend, Willibald Pirckheimer.[2]

In a letter to Hubmaier (January 1525) Oecolampadius describes the kind of liturgy he would like to see, and makes interesting use of periods of silence to stress the spiritual, meditative, inward character of the rites:

> After the confession, gospelling, hymns and prayers and after the Trisagion, I would have a period of silence appointed in which each might fervently meditate within himself on the Passion of the Lord. Then the words of the Lord's Supper appointed for the rite should be read publicly and intelligibly, and when these have been read, again a great silence for meditation and the giving of thanks. Afterwards should come the Lord's Prayer and, when this is over, the communicants should be summoned to the Lord's Supper, having first been admonished by the minister that each shall examine and judge himself. And if anybody is present who has been admonished by the Church the second or third time according to the Lord's command he should be repelled from the table until there is sure proof of his penitence, and he is reconciled. Then when they have received communion with the exhortation to charity and care of the poor, the congregation might depart in peace.[3]

Oecolampadius' eucharistic doctrine awaits its monograph, and cannot here be treated in detail.[4] When he defends Zwingli, it is with a view to emphasizing the positive values of his doctrine. Thus against Luther's complaint that Zwingli put our Lord in some remote, spatial heaven, 'like a stork in a tree top' or 'like a bird in a cage', Oecolampadius denies that in fact the Lord is seated for ever on his throne listening to endless angelic symphonies. In an interesting aside, he suggests that Luther it is who puts our Lord in a cage, by imprisoning the sacred humanity once again in history,

---

[1] *Br.u.A.* I, p. 411, note 294   [2] *Br.u.A.* I, Nos 280, 318
[3] *Br.u.A.* I, No. 239: 18 Jan. 1525
[4] There is an important discussion of his influence on the English Reformers in Peter Brooks *Thomas Cranmer's Doctrine of the Eucharist* London 1965.

time and space, in this sinful, fallen world. However negatively some of Zwingli's statements might sound, Oecolampadius is concerned to stress a true, spiritual presence. In an important summary of his teaching which he sent to John Haner in 1527, he makes the following points:

> I believe the natural body of Christ to be in one place, namely heaven: otherwise there would be no true body.
>
> I freely confess the Body of Christ to be present in the bread [*adesse pani*] in that mode in which it is present in the Word itself, through which the bread becomes a sacrament and a visible word.
>
> Through faith the Body of Christ which is as absent as it can be [*absentissimum*] is as present as it can be [*praesentissimum*] to the soul.
>
> This presence of the flesh of Christ is profitable [*utilis*] indeed: but profitless and far from the manner of faith it is, if we say that bread is the substantive body or that the body of Christ may be in many places at once.
>
> Those who reject a trope in the words of the Lord's Supper declare themselves to be contentious, and interpret the scriptures otherwise than by the analogy of faith.
>
> They speak well and religiously, who say that they come to the Body of the Lord, or eat his Body; profanely and contemptibly, who declare that they only receive the bread and a sign; for they declare their unbelief . . . if they say they have eaten the sign only and not also the thing signified, which the sign means [*si solum sacramentum et non etiam rem, quam sacramentum signat, manducasse dicatur*], the one with the mouth, the other with the mind. . . .[1]

Here, then, a true spiritual presence is affirmed, and the relation to the elements is such that the nature of a sacrament is kept. It must be remembered that the view attacked by Oecolampadius here, which would think of bread and wine as bare signs, is not that of Zwingli, but of the Anabaptists and radicals. At any rate, these stresses of Oecolampadius would be preserved among other Reformers as Bucer and Peter Martyr, and would become an element in the later Reformed doctrine.

[1] *Br.u.A.* 2, No. 470

We have already noticed Oecolampadius' interest in liturgical matters, about which he had his own ideas, and concerning which he was quite independent of his friend, Zwingli. At St Martin's he had refused to say Mass when there were no communicants, and from All Saints' Day 1525 had celebrated with a simplified liturgy.[1] Copies of this were circulated in manuscript, and published in 1526 in the name of 'certain preachers of Basle', with an interesting preface stressing the need for experiment and diversity as a branch of Christian liberty. The order included forms for baptism and communion, and for the visitation of the sick (Oecolampadius had composed a Litany for the sick and dying while at Altomünster, and a simplified form of this was published in Basle).[2]

Meanwhile, the growing menace of the Catholic powers, the threat of political and military action against the Reformers, led to closer and more frequent correspondence between the evangelical leaders. The Swiss in particular were driven, both Catholics and Reformers, to look beyond the Confederation for allies. In this period, the links between Basle and Strasbourg were strengthened and to some extent offset the alliance with Zürich.

Dr John Eck, who after his debate with Luther and Karlstadt in Leipzig in 1519 seems to have felt himself the holder of the European title for verbal prize-fighting, wrote at the end of October 1525 offering the Swiss cantons to debate with all and sundry, but mentioning specifically Zwingli and Oecolampadius; and on any subject, but mentioning the Eucharist. The matter was postponed, but revived in 1526. Disputations in public had been a useful technique of the Swiss Reformers, but for once the evangelicals were badly outmanœuvred and perhaps it is not too much to see behind it the unusually able Catholic counter-planning directed by John Faber. The place for disputation was fixed at Swiss Baden, where the authorities were firmly on the Catholic side. When it became clear that the affair would be one-sided and, indeed, dangerous, the Reformers began one by one to make excuses, and the city council refused to let Zwingli go.

The result was that when Oecolampadius and a group of Basle pastors arrived in Baden at the end of May, they found themselves

[1] *Br.u.A.* 1, No. 298 [2] *Br.u.A.* 1, No. 356; 2, No. 569

outnumbered, outranged and outgunned by the Catholics, who included the formidable trio, Eck, Faber and the publicist Thomas Murner. Eck himself was a theologian of parts, with humanist equipment, eloquent, flamboyant, violent, with a great memory and a vast supply of low debating cunning – rather like the mental image some Catholics have of Martin Luther. He had spent some time recently getting up the theology of the Reformers and had published in May 1526 a *Handbook of commonplaces of the Lutheran heresy* which included many gobbets from Zwingli and Oecolampadius.

The disputation began in the usual leisurely, courteous way, and the two opponents drew near like sailing ships wafted on their syllogistic breeze. The preliminary discourses were unexciting, and indeed tedious. As the judges wilted towards the end of a three-hour oration from Oecolampadius, he amiably suggested an adjournment until midday, 'for I too am a little weary' – which the judges amended with alacrity to a recess until one o'clock. But even this did not satisfy the audience and, after some lunchtime lobbying, somebody from the floor suggested that there be a two-day respite – ostensibly for the arrival of reinforcements which both sides expected. There were eighteen rounds in all between Oecolampadius and Eck, and the affair ended with a kind of exhibition bout in which Eck took on single-handed and one at a time half-a-dozen reforming preachers in turn.

The debate had its moments. Eck roared and rampaged and danced all round his opponent, asserting and distinguishing and, when pressed, taking refuge in his authority. At one point, John Faber produced unexpectedly a manuscript of Irenaeus which seems to have disconcerted Oecolampadius. At another point it was Oecolampadius who defended patristic authority, while Eck came near to asserting: 'The Bible, I say the Bible only, is the religion of Catholics.' In the taverns and refectories of the city the debate went on at another level and with writers like Thomas Murner and Nicholas Manuel there was scope for both the higher and the lower witticism. The vote was a farce in the circumstances, and on the whole the Reformers had little to be pleased about in the whole affair, which was a public setback for their cause in Switzerland and led to a notable hardening of opinion in the Catholic cantons of Switzerland against the teaching of Zwingli, whom they openly impugned as a heretic. But Oecolampadius had nothing to be ashamed of. His learning and sweet reasonableness had more than offset the rumbustiousness of his opponent. More important, he had for the first time taken the strain of leadership, and had acquitted himself manfully. He was growing.

The situation in Basle was complicated (in comparison with Zürich, Strasbourg or Bern) by the presence of a bishop, of a cathedral chapter, and by the persistence of an influential Catholic core in the inner council of the city.

It was part of the technique of the Reformers in the cities to secure, fairly early on, a mandate from the magistracy enjoining scriptural preaching. Such an edict was passed in Zürich, perhaps as early as 1520, and a similar ordinance was enacted in Basle in May 1523, but with little evident effect. It does seem as though Basle might have been carried by assault early in Oecolampadius' ministry there, but the situation was allowed to bog down, and a long struggle resulted. Oecolampadius had a group of loyal preachers in the city, Markus Bertschi of St Laurence's, Wolfgang Wissenburg of the Spital, his deacon Jerome Bothanus, Johannes Luthard, Thomas Geyerfalk – and he was in touch with a more disparate group of pastors in Basel-Land. The Catholics were strongest in the Münster, in St Peter's and St Theodore's, and in Klein Basel over the Rhine. Their theologian was Ambrosius Pelargus and their preacher from 1525 onwards, Augustinus Marius. After his first sermon, Oecolampadius had waited on him with an eirenical letter urging that they might confer amicably together.[1] But Marius and his friends refused all contact with heretics, and conducted a campaign of such virulence as to bring protests from his own side, in a city where for once the phrase 'divisive preaching' referred to immoderate polemic from the Catholic side. On 16 May 1527 the Council asked both sides to justify their attitude to the Mass from Holy Scripture, and to submit memoranda.[2]

The cathedral authorities warned the Council that the decision to abolish or not to abolish the Mass rested with the spiritual and not

[1] *Br.u.A.* 1, No. 309   [2] *Br.u.A.* 2, No. 492

the temporal power. In the late summer there was a compromise. The evangelicals might worship in St Martin's, St Laurence's and the Augustinian house, and none should be compelled to hold or hear Mass there, but elsewhere there should be no innovation. It sounds like a victory for the Reformers but in fact led to a crop of expulsions and resignations among the evangelicals in Basel-Land.

The Reformers had pondered the lessons of the Baden disputation, which were that they should dispute only in cities where the reforming party was strong and where sufficient safety was assured for them to come in force. The result was the Bern Colloquy of 1528.[1] This time the Reformers left nothing to chance. Zwingli, Bucer, Capito, Oecolampadius and his party all attended and this time the Catholics consisted of theological rag-tag and bobtail. From St Gall came Vadianus whom Zwingli described as the leading layman of Switzerland, and he was one of the presidents of debate. A number of evangelical theses were propounded, of which the first was notable and memorable:

> The Holy Christian Church, whose only head is Christ, is born from the Word of God, remains in the same, and does not listen to the voice of strangers.[2]

The sermon-tasters had an orgy, and passed from church to church listening to the leading Reformers. Characteristically, Oecolampadius chose as his theme 'Of the love of God for his Church [*Gemeinde*]'.

The disputation had immediate consequences for Bern, where great reforming mandates followed. The Basle contingent went home disgruntled, chagrined that now their own city lagged behind Zürich and Bern, to say nothing of St Gall, Constance and Strasbourg.

In the Council the policy of procrastination was maintained by a Catholic core in the inner Council, all of them high officers in the four merchant guilds. In February 1528 an edict was passed 'that every man should abide in his own faith', a feeble attempt to peg

---

[1] *Br.u.A.* 2, Nos 535, 537–48
[2] K. Guggisberg *Bernische Kirchengeschichte* Bern 1958, pp. 101ff.

down events which now had their increasing momentum. At Easter there were disturbances and image-breaking in town and country Basle, and members of the spinners' guild broke images in St Martin's and the Augustinian church, the ringleaders being arrested but swiftly released.[1] It was clear that increasing pressure was being brought to bear by the craft guilds. At the end of the previous year the evangelical preachers had been invited as guests at the annual guild feasts, while Catholic clergy had been ignored.[2] In pulpit and press, pamphlets and sermons increased the tension and it was felt to be an aggravation when works by Pelargus and Eck were published in the city.[3] At the end of the year it was evident that a crisis was near. The Reformers now had a programme, a leader and a party. There was available a massive precedent from Zürich and other cities about how the godly magistracy should exercise its *jus reformandi*. The Basle preachers had their own liturgy with its simplified rites of baptism and eucharist. It seems likely that psalm singing had been introduced on the Strasbourg precedent – it found more favour with Oecolampadius than with Zwingli.

Oecolampadius' leadership was all-important in these months, especially from the pulpit, and we hear no more about a weak voice or lack of civil prudence. His outspoken references to public matters, to usury, to bribery and corruption were worthy of a Zwingli or a Latimer, and led to frequent consultation with the Council before whom he was respectful but firm, as when he refused to give the authorities the names of those whose crimes he had denounced. His biblical expositions show a concentration worthy of Luther or Calvin, as he lectured on Haggai, Zechariah, Malachi, Daniel (this commentary was one of his major works), Jeremiah and Ezekiel. There followed lectures on Lamentations, Job, Hebrews, the Fourth Gospel, Hosea, Amos, Obadiah, Jonah, Genesis and Matthew. No wonder that his health began to suffer and his enemies gibed at him as a walking corpse.

In March 1528 Oecolampadius had decided to marry. His native Weinsberg had been razed to the ground in reprisal for the 'Weinsberg massacre' of the Peasants' War, and his parents had come to

[1] P. Roth *Durchbruch und Festsetzung der Reformation in Basel* Basle 1942
[2] *Br.u.A.* 2, No. 570   [3] *Br.u.A.* 2, No. 563

live with him in Basle. His mother had died soon after his return from the Bern Colloquy, so there were two men to be looked after in his house. For some months now his professional stipend had been augmented with regular income from St Martin's, so that he was better able to support a family. But Oecolampadius was in his forties, no doubt a rather donnish bachelor with set ways, so that there was room for hesitation, in addition to the opprobrium with which his Catholic opponents would surround the match. Erasmus' letters buzzed with gossip – but he made one famous comment to the effect that it was time to stop talking about the Lutheran tragedy, for it was much more a comedy, which always ended in a wedding![1]

Wibrandis Rosenblatt was the merry widow of Ludwig Keller; she was aged 26, personable and cheerful. She needed to be, in an age when 'Reformer's wife' was a dangerous and precarious occupation. She was to be in turn the wife of Oecolampadius, of his friend Capito, and of his friend Bucer. Oecolampadius' misgivings were soon allayed, and he wrote to Capito in some relief:

> My wife is what I hoped all along. She is neither quarrelsome, talkative nor flighty and she looks after the home.

He took well to his domestic life, tragically short though it was to be, and there are references in his letters to the coughs and sneezes of the three children whom he characteristically named Eusebius, Irene, and Aletheia.

But he had not let go of his patristic studies. In August 1528 Cratander published a new edition of the works of Cyril of Alexandria in three volumes. He had based his earlier edition of 1524 on existing Paris editions, but the new collection was much enlarged with new translations by Oecolampadius.[2] He may also at this time have finished other translations which appeared after his death, in 1531 and 1546. Part of this edition carried a long epistle dedicated by Oecolampadius to the Margrave Philip of Baden, in which

---

[1] *Br.u.A.* 2, No. 554
[2] E. Staehelin, 'Die Väterübersetzungen Oekolampads' *Schweizerische Zeitschrift* 33 (1916), pp. 57ff.

Oecolampadius defended himself at some length against his detractors.[1] He had no difficulty in rebutting the charge that he was an enemy of learning ('we do not pour scorn on the arts as good gifts of God but affirm that they deserve praise') or of the Fathers ('nor do we move the doctors from their rank, but we do not equate them with the apostles and prophets'). He can point to sons of eminent citizens entrusted to his care, whom he has always urged to tackle Greek and Latin. The more difficult charge was that he was an incompetent translator, who had falsified the Fathers. He had been accused by Catholic humanists of inelegant Latin and of ignorance of Greek.

More precise had been the attack upon him by Germanus Brixius, a canon of Notre-Dame. Oecolampadius had used for his translation of the life of Babylas by Chrysostom a codex belonging to the Basle Dominicans, and, perhaps after complaints by Brixius, Erasmus had published the Greek text. Brixius was able to make his own translation and, on behalf of friends in Paris, published a list of over 200 alleged errors on the part of Oecolampadius.[2] Some of the complaints against Oecolampadius were based on the assumption that the so-called 'opus imperfectum' of Chrysostom on St Matthew was his work, but in fact it had appeared in the 1524 edition in a volume with which Oecolampadius had no connexion. This, in the preface to Cyril's works, Oecolampadius now explained. What he could not have known was that Erasmus had defended him against Brixius, on the grounds that Oecolampadius suffered from haste rather than ignorance. Erasmus knew only too well the troubles of publishing at Basle: he too had been in perils of typesetters, in perils of proof readers, in perils from bad handwriting, in perils from jealous theologians. And besides, he needed Oecolampadius' help and work for his own editions. Oecolampadius did not deny that he had made mistakes, was eager to amend them. More serious were the charges of deliberate omissions. But he had often to rely on one unsatisfactory MS., like the copy of Theophylact which had a lacuna between folios 254 and 255.

In 1527 John Faber paid a short visit to England, as member of an Imperial Embassy (a visit about which students of the English

[1] *Br.u.A.* 2, No. 597   [2] *Br.u.A.* 2, Nos 555–7, 583, 597, 702

Reformation need to know more) and consorted with two humanists, the bishops John Fisher and Cuthbert Tunstall, both of whom were already ardent opponents of Oecolampadius on dogmatic grounds. In 1529 Tunstall wrote to Erasmus, begging him to keep Oecolampadius' name out of any further translation, on the ground of his ill repute as a heretic and his incompetence as a translator. Yet this Erasmus could not and would not do. It is extraordinary that in these months, when the Reformation in Basle reached its climax, and relations between the two men must have been strained, Erasmus could quietly plan to take over Oecolampadius' work, and that in 1531 Oecolampadius could finish translating the fifty-five homilies of Chrysostom on Acts, which Erasmus had begun but had abandoned, refusing to believe them authentic. And so some of Oecolampadius' work went into the 1530 edition of Chrysostom which Erasmus edited, and the fifty-five homilies were included in an appendix to a reprint in 1531. It sheds perhaps a little light on the odd fact that, unlike Glareanus, Erasmus did not in fact leave Basle until the hubbub of reformation was almost over. It is a great tribute to Oecolampadius' singlemindedness and love of learning that he kept up these studies in the crowded last months of his life.[1]

The Reformation in Basle was now much more than the leadership of Oecolampadius and a group of preachers. There was a growing body of civic opinion which found expression through the instrument of guild machinery. During Advent 1528, Marius delivered a violent series of sermons on 1 John, a long-delayed counterblast to Oecolampadius' series on the same theme. A prominent councillor announced that he would attend no more Council meetings until there was a showdown. On 23 December there was a fateful meeting of over 300 guildsmen in the Gardeners' Guild (with which Oecolampadius was connected, through his wife) and these drew up a strongly worded petition to the magistrates, demanding the abolition of the Mass, and an end to the scandal of 'divisive preaching'. It may well be that Oecolampadius had something to do with this document, which rehearsed the sorry story of procrastination and demanded that, as a mother should protect her daughter from bad company, the Council must protect the city from

[1] E. Staehelin, op. cit.; *Br.u.A.* 2, No. 702

public profanation. The manifesto seems to have been supported by all the guilds save the Bread-bakers, the Smiths, and the Sailors and Fishermen (a nice problem for the Marxist historian!).[1]

It seemed as though the bloody precedent of Magdeburg, where 500 had been killed in civic riots, might be followed in Basle, and neighbouring cities and princes sent delegates in an effort to find a peaceful solution. As they entered the city across the fortified Rhine bridges, they could not fail to note ominous signs of armed hostility.[2] Little Eusebius was born on Christmas Eve, but there could have been small rejoicing at a christening accompanied by the intermittent tramp of armed bands pacing the streets. On 5 January 1529,[3] the magistrates appointed commissioners to meet both parties, but, whereas some 3,000 armed evangelicals appeared in the Franciscan church, there were but 350 of their opponents. The Council now knew it must act swiftly. It announced its readiness to enforce the evangelical mandate of May 1523: it ordered all preachers on pain of dismissal to attend the weekly meeting of preachers. A public disputation about the Mass would be held in June. Until then, one Mass a day would be said in the Münster, in St Peter's and in St Theodore's. In an ordinance of 6 January, it was said that those who wished to do so might leave the city.

The Catholic authorities saw disaster as imminent, and the chapter began to take measures for flight, as a body, to Neuenburg. The irascible scholar Glareanus, who had long vented his spleen against Oecolampadius, began to pack his bags. The authorities had been foolish indeed to suggest an armistice until June. In fact the crisis came on 9 February after the guilds had sent an ultimatum to the Council. It met that morning behind closed doors, with armed guards, chains having been flung across the surrounding streets. At the news that the Council still hesitated, an angry crowd of some three hundred entered the Münster and tore down the images: similar scenes followed in St Ulrich's and St Alban's and in Klein Basel. On the following day, Ash Wednesday, there were bonfires of wood and paintings. We are told that the poor people

---

[1] P. Roth *Durchbruch* pp. 12–14   [2] ibid., pp. 17–18
[3] *Br.u.A.* 2, No. 629; P. Roth (ed.) *Aktensammlung zur Geschichte der Basler Reformation in den Jahren 1519 bis Anfang 1534* iii, Basle 1937, No. 333

carried off some for firewood, and we catch a glimpse of a 'goldsmith and an artist with a red beard' who rummaged for greater treasures. It is sad even to speculate what loveliness may have perished on that day, but Ash Wednesday was the day on which, in Florence, Savonarola had burned the vanities of his city, and the austere Oecolampadius, in a letter to Capito, simply commented: 'Tristissimum superstitiosis spectaculum', and wrote in real relief that in fact the affair was so swiftly and bloodlessly decided.[1] For at last the political decision was made, and the Catholic leaders were 'honourably dismissed' from the Council.[2]

Evangelical preachers were to be installed in former Catholic pulpits and this involved the transference of Oecolampadius from St Martin's to the Münster. On 18 February a lay commission was appointed to draw up new ordinances and, though Oecolampadius was not a member, he submitted many memoranda at this time.

The great reforming ordinance appeared on 1 April 1529, and it is an impressive and notable document. Though there was, no doubt, available a mass of precedents from Zürich and Bern and other cities, the theological opening must surely owe something to Oecolampadius. It begins with the sentence from Romans 1: 16: 'I am not ashamed of the gospel of Christ'. The preamble which follows in the name of the ex-burgomaster sets the whole reformation within the dispensation of the Word of God, and announces the intention to order afresh the religious life of the city, in the Name of the Holy Trinity, and in default of amendment by the spiritual authorities who might have accomplished the task so much more easily, had they been minded to do so. The first and most important section follows, entitled 'How the Word of God is to be preached', and here in simple, moving scriptural phrases the gospel of grace is rehearsed, stressing the atonement, and the offer of the grace of Christ, 'that we may walk in a new, peaceable, godfearing Christian life, as the true preaching of repentance shows forth'.

On the lines of the earlier evangelical mandate of 1523, rules are given to avoid divisive preaching by centring it on the exposition of the books of the Bible—'and yet preachers may use parables,

[1] *Br.u.A.* 2, No. 636; P. Roth *Durchbruch* pp. 55–6
[2] P. Roth (ed.) *Aktensammlung* iii, No. 371

anecdotes, natural illustrations, common proverbs and the like', so they be not against the law of faith and love. The examination of the preachers themselves is now of prime importance and to this end synods are to be held twice a year. The re-arrangement of parishes is then set out, and rules for the priests and deacons, for the celebration of the sacraments, baptism and holy communion, and for the visitation of the sick. On Sunday great prominence is now to be given to services of prayer and preaching. There would be prayers at several churches early in the morning, and sermons at 8, 12 and 4 in the Münster. On workdays there would be services of prayer in specified churches and a half-hour sermon in the Münster intended for councillors and lawyers. At 3 in the afternoon there would be the important biblical exposition (comparable with the St Gall exposition and the Zürich prophesyings). Needful regulations follow, about marriage and divorce and the setting up of a consistory court. There is a brief reference to images: 'we have in our churches no images which may lead to idolatry.' The first half of the mandate stresses the importance of schools and the need for the sacred languages to be taught in the university. The second half of the mandate deals with private and public morals.

One advantage came to Basle from the long postponement of its reformation. The mandate, when it came, could be carried out. The intricate matters arising from the secularization of church property involved the city in long-drawn-out controversy with the refugee clergy, and it became impossible to get payment of tithes from property remote from the city, and in Habsburg lands. The chapter had long since departed, and, when the fuss was almost over, Erasmus left for Freiburg, treated with honour to the last, and able to chat amiably with friends at the quayside before his boat put off. By now, Oecolampadius was the dominant figure and, for the next months, he was for Basle what Zwingli was in Zürich, and what Calvin would be in Geneva.

Oecolampadius' oration, 'De reducenda excommunicatione', to the spring synod of the Basle clergy in 1530,[1] is called by Staehelin, with good reason, 'an event of first class importance'.[2] He had always been interested in discipline from the time when he had

[1] *Br.u.A.* 2, No. 750 [2] *Lebenswerk* p. 511

been Penitentiary in 1518. He had written a tract on confession during his Altomünster days which had involved him in controversy with the formidable Latomus. He had pondered the evangelical way of dealing with obstinate sinners, and was sure that they could not simply be handed over to the magistrate. The discipline of the Church he now claimed to be part of the pastoral office of the Church, which used different means from the sanctions of public law, for the Church must be concerned not with outward actions but also with the motives of the heart. Where fines and imprisonment might make no impression, sinners could be convinced if they were publicly declared by the Church to be apostate and cut off from the Body of Christ.

In the second part of the oration, Oecolampadius sought to show that 'the time of penitence is not past'. Excommunication had become a tyrannical weapon in the Roman usage, and the discipline of the spirit had become perverted to trivial and unworthy ends. It must now be otherwise. 'We are ministers in the Church of Christ, and we must remember that we are indeed ministers – and seek not our own authority, but that of the Church.' This power cannot be handed to the congregation, which includes women and children. The true representatives of the Church ought to be, as in the early Church, Elders, 'whose judgement, as of the more prudent, expresses the mind of the Church'. It would be fitting, too, if representatives of the magistracy were joined to those of the congregation. If, therefore, the four town pastors joined four councillors and four representatives of the Church, the twelve censors could exercise the required discipline with 'gravitas', and without new clerical tyranny. The offences to be dealt with would be those affecting purity of life and doctrine. The public laws of Basle were, it was true, concerned with a Christian city, but their mixed community must include Jews and heathens. An Anabaptist might well be a citizen but not a member of the congregation. The Church cannot simply hand over its discipline to the magistracy.

In the third part, Oecolampadius speaks of the carrying out of this discipline. One of the censors should deliver first a brotherly admonition, followed, if need be, by a second from two or three. If this fails, then the whole body of twelve are to admonish and, if this fails, excommunication follows. The Council had done bravely, Oecolampadius concludes, with the reformation of the city. This would crown their work to restore the purity of the Church that it might truly be a people 'of holiness and faith unto the Lord'.

In keeping some autonomy for the spiritual power, Oecolampadius was obviously not prepared, after the example of Zürich, to capitulate to the magistracy, and he anticipates the solution later attempted by Bucer and achieved by Calvin. This was 'civil prudence' with a vengeance, and for a moment it seemed as though Oecolampadius' blueprint might be taken seriously by his own and other cities. But the empirical situation was too entangled: within the mixed community were intransigent Catholics and Anabaptists. The fortunes of the Anabaptist movement had fluctuated in Basle but had prospered rapidly in 1529, while in December a congregation of more than thirty was arrested in Basel-Land. On 29 December there was a disputation between the Anabaptists[1] and the pastors in the presence of the Council, at which the Anabaptists

[1] There had been two previous encounters between Oecolampadius and Anabaptists, in 1525 and 1527. This was the first after the carrying through of the civic Reformation, and the first, therefore, with which the city rather than the pastors had been concerned. Oecolampadius had preached against the Anabaptists in 1525 before he knew that there were any in Basle. On the first occasion of discussion, in 1525, Laurence Hochrütiner was a vehement spokesman and attacked Zwingli and Oecolampadius for their 'human wisdom which knows nothing of the Cross', while Oecolampadius took a fairly mild position, that infant baptism is not forbidden in Scripture – not himself being able to take Zwingli's more positive assertion that it is scripturally commanded. A correspondence between Oecolampadius and Hubmaier, which had begun before the latter's conversion to an Anabaptist position, turned into a series of arguments. In June 1527 a 'Brother Karlin', in jail in Basle, demanded a hearing from the city theologians. Marius and the Catholics refused to take part, when invited to do so by the Council, on the ground that Oecolampadius was worse than the Anabaptists. 'Brother Karlin' put forward four theses: three fairly vehement against infant baptism and the limitations of the authority of the secular power, the fourth the innocuous one, 'Whoso teaches otherwise than Christ has taught is a perverter of the people.' See further, John Yoder *Die Gespräche zwischen Täufern und Reformatoren in der Schweiz 1523–1538* Täufertum und Reformation in der Schweiz I, Karlsruhe 1962, pp. 63ff., 110ff., 120ff.; also Paul Burckhardt *Das Tagebuch des Johannes Gast* Basle 1945, Introduction.

showed no fear and no inclination to compromise. When one of the councillors said mildly, 'What do you think, brother?' he got the sharp retort, 'I don't recognize you as my brother.' Finally, when Oecolampadius had said in the course of the argument that the Bible did not speak of a spiritual magistracy only, the Anabaptist leader replied that, unlike Oecolampadius, he hadn't a fat living which gave him endless time to rummage through the Bible; like the first apostles he had his daily bread to earn! This cost Oecolampadius (who in the last months had been buying modest properties) a great laugh, which he swiftly rebuked with: 'Non est ridendi tempus, o clarissimi viri!'

Indeed it was no laughing matter. The sanctions against the rebel Christians were savage enough. They were to be ducked in the Rhine, then exiled, and thereafter, if caught, they would be executed. Hans Ludin von Bubendorf was the first to be executed in Basle, on 12 January 1530, and the cruelty of the punishment, and the noble fortitude of the sufferer, roused a good deal of sympathy. Oecolampadius' own tract about the Anabaptists is a rather feeble affair, but now he took the initiative with the Council, spent many hours in pleading with Anabaptist prisoners, getting one sentence commuted to a fine and, after a dramatic appeal in the council chamber, secured the release of Jacob Treyer. But the punishments continued with fearful effectiveness and, by March 1531, there were no Anabaptists left in the city.

A greater stumbling-block to the acceptance of his discipline was the distrust of the clergy by a self-conscious laity, and the fact that in practice the machinery of the twelve censors might prove difficult to operate. At any rate the other cities were lukewarm, and Zwingli showed no sign of being willing to change the Zürich set-up. At a conference at Aarau in September 1530,[1] Oecolampadius and the Basle pastors did their best to commend the scheme. Oecolampadius asked that at least Basle be given a free hand and the experiment commended. This the other cities agreed to do, for it cost them nothing and simply handed back the responsibility to the Basle Council, which soon found its own excuses. In Strasbourg too, Bucer found difficulties: a 'patristic severity' in the scheme of

[1] *Br.u.A.* 2, Nos 934, 940

Oecolampadius when what was needed was 'Pauline lenity', though how lenient the Apostle was in these matters might be questioned. In Basle, the idea of the Twelve was dropped. The pastors were to watch over one another but, if any wished to exercise the office of binding and loosing, he must report to the Church, while the secular arm and its sanctions still underlay the whole matter. Then censors were appointed and, in March 1531, Oecolampadius could write to Conrad Sam in Ulm with a modified rapture. But once again the Council ran into difficulties with non-communicating Catholics and, when Oecolampadius went off on a mission to Ulm, the Council modified his scheme still further behind his back.

The years 1529-31 brought not only triumph for the Reform in Bern and Basle but the growing menace of Catholic arms. Zürich began to build a civic league, hampered by civic particularism and the cautious neutralism of Bern. Basle was drawn closer to Strasbourg, its near neighbour. Philip of Hesse, a Protestant whose lands also were vulnerable, had these things partly in mind when he invited Lutheran and Swiss theologians to confer about the Eucharist and other theological differences in his castle in Marburg.[1] Relations between the two parties were strained and they kept Zwingli hidden for some hours so that it fell to Oecolampadius to return the official greeting. This summit conference wisely consisted of private sessions in the main, and never became a public disputation. Oecolampadius was paired with Luther (no doubt for personal reasons, but they were, after all, the two D.D.s) and Zwingli with Melanchthon. Although the conference broke down at the crucial point, other agreements were made and it did some good.

During the months that followed, Oecolampadius kept up his studies. At this time he devoted some attention to defending the Catholic faith against the novel doctrines of Michael Servetus.[2] When Melanchthon produced a catena of citations from the Fathers making for the Lutheran view of the Eucharist, Oecolampadius could not withstand this challenge, and produced perhaps his weightiest piece of theological argument, in which he cited a large number of passages from the Fathers of East and West (sometimes in Greek, more often in Latin) ranging from Irenaeus, Athanasius

[1] Köhler *Zwingli und Luther* ii, Chap. 2 [2] *Br.u.A.* 2, Nos 765, 766, 893-7

and Chrysostom to Theophylact and Hesychius, the whole set within a dialogue between himself and an imagined simple believer named Nathanael.[1]

In April and May 1531, Oecolampadius conducted an important visitation, going through Basel-Land like a true evangelical bishop, interrogating, examining and exhorting especially about the Anabaptists. From May to July he was away helping to reform Ulm, in company with Bucer and Blaurer, and returned to reorganize the theological faculty in the university where he and Simon Grynaeus lectured on the Old and New Testaments in alternate weeks. Of great importance, too, were his sermons in the Münster, 131 of which he delivered on St Mark's Gospel, while on workdays he began a series on Colossians which were broken off at Chap. 2:23 by his illness and death.

Now, though he did not know it, the sands were running out. He had so far forgotten his earlier remarks about 'just wars' as to support the policy of Zwingli, though Basle, like Bern, did so with reluctance and with reservations, inhibitions which were to play their part on the fatal day of Cappel.

We have one happy glimpse of Oecolampadius at the celebrations with which Liestal in Basel-Land celebrated its dedication feast. There were military manœuvres and a sham fight, and Oecolampadius, on horseback, inspected the men, as his enemies said, 'like a general at the head of his troops' – though, unlike the other 'Old Nosey', he came no nearer than this to any battlefield. At night, cloaked, he walked amiably and paternally among the junketing crowd.[2]

A few weeks later came the real thing, the battle of Cappel, and the death of Zwingli. Among a score of chaplains slain was Bothanus from Basle, a friend and former deacon of Oecolampadius. The disaster was a grave shock to all the Swiss Reformers, but to none so poignant as to Oecolampadius. He had been in poor health for some time and, whether it was the strain of heavy tidings or the infection of the plague then prevalent, he was taken seriously ill.

[1] *Br.u.A.* 2, No. 748, Basle 1530: 'Quid de eucharistia veteres tum Graeci, tum Latini senserint, dialogus'.

[2] *Br.u.A.* 2, No. 767

After a few days he took a turn for the better and his friends hoped that the worst was over. Then a carbuncle developed malignant and venomous power. On the evening of 21 November he called his children to his bedside to give them his blessing. Wibrandis stood by the little group of rather frightened infants, her cheerful face now pale and anxious. He spoke to them one by one, Eusebius, Irene, Aletheia, and the babes answered his questions with stammered promises they could hardly have understood. Next morning his brethren hastened silent through the streets to gather at his side. Now he could speak but faintly and had not strength to take communion. Only once, when somebody asked if the light were too strong, if they should draw the blind, did he strike his breast and murmur with a smile (perhaps remembering his name): 'Abunde lucis est' – 'here's light enough within'. Early in the morning of 23 November he entered the true presence.

It is not easy to delineate the man. The records, despite the massive collection of documents superbly gathered by E. Staehelin, have not very many personal touches.

If Erasmus' waspish picture of Cannius, in his *Colloquies*, is a side glance at Oecolampadius, he had piercing black eyes and a yellow, jaundiced complexion. Familiar, too, were his beard, his large nose, his scholar's stoop. He was not one of the great scholars of the age, but perhaps no other of the Erasmian school was so much involved in affairs as he became, and there is surely something impressive about the way in which he kept at the work of study and translation, right to the end. Given the necessity to get the works of the Fathers printed, and so out and available for the widest circle of readers, Oecolampadius is subject to the same criticisms as must be levelled at Erasmus, and his own contribution to making known the Greek Fathers is not negligible. In the sad eucharistic controversy he had his own part to play. His own mind was perhaps more subtle than Zwingli's, and he avoided some of the Zürich Reformer's rather negative lucidities, while making positive stresses which were to remain as important elements in later Reformed doctrine. His edition of patristic texts kept the Fathers in the forefront of the controversy at a time when the initial appeal to biblical exegesis was in some danger of giving way to a revived Protestant scholasticism.

It has yet to be shown how far the influence of Oecolampadius' patristic studies influenced his generation of reformers, not least in England. When it came to the working out of the reformation, his theology sustained him, for he was himself a moralist, much exercised with problems of penitence and Christian discipline, a field in which thorny, practical problems arose in Basle and the other Swiss cities in the years 1528–31.

No doubt he was much under the influence of his friend Zwingli, but he had always a mind of his own, and in the matter of excommunication he tried valiantly to set up safeguards against a possible tyranny of the godly magistrate, and anticipated the work of Bucer and of Calvin in this matter. Though we have the impression of an introverted scholar who did not take kindly to administration, he did grow noticeably in 'civil prudence' and won the respect and following of the very canny burghers of his city. Not himself dowered with a forceful personality or a gift of leadership (in this like Thomas Cranmer in England), he was forced into a position of eminence and rose manfully to the challenge of events. It is not, I think, fanciful to see his moral stature grow during these troubled, critical years. Beginning as an amiable, shy dilettante, with evident elements of instability, he was not embittered or broken by misadventures and disappointments, but came to a more and more fruitful employment of his gifts for the service of his Church. Modern research is showing how complex was the situation of reform in these Swiss cities, that the great personalities were but one element in the intricate over-all situation. But certainly in Basle Oecolampadius counted more than anybody else and was by no means the ineffectual angel that his friend Haller was in the city of Bern. His light did indeed shine more and more before his fellow men, lighting the whole house.

We glimpse the bearded scholar with pendulous nose, peering through his spectacles at some propped-up codex, by candlelight (he would do very well for Rembrandt's 'The Philosopher'); the cathedral preacher making the best of a poor voice, but taking fire beneath the burden of his message – like the baritone bell in his sermon, he was 'gravis et sonora' – and moving the hearts of his great audience; or the church leader kneeling before the Council to beg pardon for a penitent Anabaptist; the beloved father bidding farewell to those tiny children, and handing over to his solemn comrades that care of the Churches which had been his daily charge. These, it may be, are authentic lights which flicker as we peer among the shadows which hide from us the past.

Part II
Andrew Karlstadt
The Reformer as Puritan

CHAPTER THREE

AMBITIOUS YOUNG MAN

Andrew Rudolf Bodenstein von Karlstadt was born in the Franconian village of Karlstadt about the year 1477.[1] He had kinsfolk in the district, and contrived to keep in touch with them in later years, especially with his mother and his sisters. The faint impression that he may have been too surrounded by admiring females in his youth may be erroneous. Of his schooling we know nothing, and may suspect he shared the common grammatic grind of his contemporaries. He went up, rather late, to the university of Erfurt (B.A. 1502) and then on to Cologne where he read theology among the Thomists in the famous hostel, the Montanerburse. He was therefore trained as a Thomist, and specially indebted to the 15th-century popularizer of Thomist theology, Capreolus.[2]

New universities offer scope for ambitious young men, and when Karlstadt came to Wittenberg in 1505 it was no doubt because of the opportunities, and also because it was a centre of the *via antiqua*.[3]

---

[1] Jacob Grynaeus says that he was older than Luther (b. 1483) and Karlstadt, in the dedication of his edition of Augustine's *De Spiritu et Litera*, affirmed that he had been offended by Luther's youth ('Movebar Martini juventa': E. Kähler *Karlstadt und Augustin* Halle 1952, p. 4; see n. 5). This would seem to imply some years' seniority. On the other hand, he matriculated at Erfurt in 1499–1500, which seems an astonishingly senior age for the 16th century.

[2] *ob.* 1444

[3] In the present confused state of 15th-century studies one can only suggest that the distinction between *via antiqua* and *via moderna* is more blurred than older textbooks suggest. Scotus had a foot in both camps, so that it was easy for Karlstadt to move from St Thomas to Scotus, while on the other hand there were areas of theology where Scotus agreed with Ockham.

A dominant figure here was the Vice-Chancellor, Martin Pollich of Mellerstadt, a figure of fashionable humanist virtuosity in letters and medicine, but also an uncompromising Thomist. He instigated a series of Thomist studies which issued from the equivalent of a modern university press, and Karlstadt produced for it two studies in Thomist logic: 'The Intentions' (1507) and the 'Distinctions' (1508).[1]

They have the faults of a young scholar, are a little too erudite, polemical to a degree, too over-anxious to claim originality.[2] Still, such as they were, they were among the literary first-fruits of the young academy. The Rector, Christopher Scheurl, for whom indeed all Wittenberg geese were already and proleptically swans, could say with some extravagance that Karlstadt was not only skilled in the sacred languages but 'a great philosopher, a still greater

---

One complicating factor is the revival of Augustine. There is an underlying element of Augustine in almost all medieval theology, much in Peter Lombard, and even more in St Thomas, but in the later middle ages there were recurrent revivals of Augustinian doctrines, although it is important to ask which part of Augustine is revived at any one point. See G. Leff, 'The changing pattern of thought in the early 14th century' *Bulletin of John Rylands Library* March 1961, pp. 354ff.; H. A. Oberman *The Harvest of Medieval Theology: Gabriel Biel and Late Medieval Nominalism* Harvard University Press, Cambridge, Mass. 1963; *Forerunners of the Reformation* Lutterworth Press, London 1967; G. Leff *Gregory of Rimini: Tradition and Innovation in Fourteenth Century Thought* Manchester University Press, Manchester 1961. The Wittenberg interest in Augustine under Staupitz, Luther and Karlstadt has to be seen as something which looks backward to these medieval reverberations as well as forward to the Reformers.

[1] Barge, i, 31; K. Bauer *Die Wittenberger Universitätstheologie und die Anfänge der Deutschen Reformation* Tübingen 1928, pp. 5ff.; K. Aland, 'Die Theologische Fakultät Wittenberg und ihre Stellung im Gesamtzusammenhang der Leucorea während des 16. Jahrhunderts', in *Kirchengeschichtliche Entwürfe* Gütersloh 1960, pp. 302ff.; G. Bauch, 'Andreas Karlstadt als Scholastiker' *ZKG* (1898), pp. 37ff.

[2] Barge, i, 22, n. 76: 'Praecursorem in hac re non viderim'. This chimes with Luther's later comment that Karlstadt 'by nature has a strange head which always looks for that which is unusual and no one hitherto has known' (*LW* xl, 188).

theologian, but greatest of all as a Thomist', and he prophesied that, given a few more Karlstadts, Wittenberg would soon rival Paris.

Conservatism in theology did not necessarily involve antagonism to the new learning and both Pollich and his protégé made polite gestures towards it. Karlstadt dabbled in inferior Latin poetry, got up enough Greek and Hebrew to make a splash on the printed page, and was on the side of Reuchlin in his great affair. His thought moved within the scholastic framework, towards the teaching of Scotus, represented on the faculty by Nicholas Amsdorf. By 1514 Karlstadt was lecturing on Scotist theology to the Franciscans.

Into the harmonious discord between Thomists and Scotists there came an intruder, Jodocus Trutfetter, trailing clouds of Nominalism from Erfurt (seconded, in the Arts faculty, by one of his pupils, Martin Luther).[1]

Trutfetter seems to have been reluctantly imported by Pollich in order that the attractions of the university syllabus should be balanced, and the hastily amended statutes could not bear to mention Ockham, but spoke instead of the *via Gregorii* of Gregory of Rimini. But if Trutfetter posed astringently the question, 'What is truth?', he did not stay long for an answer but in 1510 went off in a huff to Erfurt, leaving Pollich to insert Karlstadt in his room as professor of theology and archdeacon of the Castle church.[2]

The university of Wittenberg, and the collegiate church of All Saints, were twin objects of the earnest and sometimes meddlesome benevolence of the Elector, Frederick the Wise. The two foundations were necessarily entangled. The Castle church had sixty-four clergy to attend to the divine offices and perform some 9,000 commemorative Masses annually. Its canons and high officers were

[1] Luther was, beyond doubt, trained within Nominalism. Neo-Thomists sometimes politely lament that he never really came into contact with St Thomas, and Protestant theologians sometimes as politely reply that he grew up in a Nominalist environment. This is to ignore the strength of the *via antiqua* in Wittenberg, and even if Luther knew no more of what went on in the lectures of his colleagues (Karlstadt and Amsdorf) than do most professors he could hardly not know the main stresses of Thomism, even though in the case of both 'ways' it was not so much St Thomas and Ockham but the epigoni, Capreolus or Biel, whose teaching was in question.

[2] Karlstadt proceeded D.D. at the end of the year.

professors in canon law or in the *via antiqua*. As archdeacon, Karlstadt was committed not only to his professorial duties, but to a round of ecclesiastical chores, a network of religious activities. Part of the income of his office derived from the living of Orlamünde, a pleasant little town on the green banks of the Saale, and this was to be for Karlstadt a fateful association. Karlstadt seems to have got on well enough with the theologians and became Dean of the Faculty in 1512[1] so that he presided when Martin Luther took his doctorate. His relations with the lawyers were not so happy. When we have made all allowances for medieval litigiousness, and for the fact that the archdeacon's office was the place where the medieval Church was 'earthed', Karlstadt had green fingers for producing ecclesiastical nettles, and his colleagues might well have reflected that, if the question whether an archdeacon could possibly be saved were debatable, there was no doubt at all that one particular archdeacon was damnable. It would need a Teutonic Trollope to do justice to his intrigues in the years following his promotion. He became involved early on in a wrangle about tithes, which turned on a debt of half a guilder, and he thoroughly upset his Prince by threatening to appeal to the Pope.

Then there was his ambition. This he openly admitted: 'I'm as keen to get on as the next fellow.'[2] The office of Provost of the Castle church was not only highly paid, but ranked third in the university hierarchy. It was known that Karlstadt had his eye on it. But it was the preserve of the lawyers. When, therefore, he asked leave of absence to go to Italy, his colleagues were suspicious. He told a good tale, how he had been robbed and wounded on a visit to relatives, how on his sick bed he had vowed a pilgrimage to the shrines of Sts Peter and Paul at Rome. They gave him leave, on condition that he attended no academic courses. He rode off to Torgau and appealed over their heads to the Elector, who gave him permission to study law in Italy. So he went off, having made elaborate arrangements for the receipt of his stipend, but only half-hearted attempts to provide an academic substitute. Now he flagrantly overstayed his leave and the long vacation began to turn

[1] He was also Dean in 1514, 1516, 1517, 1520, 1521, 1522.
[2] K. Bauer, p. 7: 'Ich habe gleich so gern ehr als ein annder'.

into a sabbatic year. Rumours filtered back to Wittenberg: he had left Rome after a disagreement with his supervisors, he had gone to Siena. There, after a few weeks, he had obtained a doctorate in both Laws, from the university of Siena.[1] The dire threat that his stipend would be stopped brought him home at last, swaggering in fine Italian clothes, to make humble peace with the Elector while wrangling fiercely with his exasperated colleagues. He was soon involved in another rumpus, this time about the living of Uhlstädt and this time he played off the chapter against his Prince. It is all rather trivial, but it is important to note how he had tired the authorities long before the Luther affair swelled into the Reformation. In 1520, when the Provost died, Karlstadt wrote a touting letter to Spalatin which ended the friendship between them. The post went to Justus Jonas.

[1] Siena was notorious for the speed with which its doctorates could be obtained and the slightness of the tests demanded of candidates. In 300 years, out of 553 German candidates in Siena there was no failure; cf. Bernd Moeller *Johannes Zwick und die Reformation in Konstanz* Gütersloh 1961, p. 38

CHAPTER FOUR

THE CHAMPION OF ST AUGUSTINE

*A living man is certain to stop talking.
But once a dead man begins calling out
(instead of keeping quiet as is the custom)
—who is to silence him?*

S. KIERKEGAARD

When Martin Pollich died in 1513, and Johannes Staupitz retired to live in south Germany, Martin Luther became the dominant figure at Wittenberg. From 1509 onwards, as his marginal notes on Peter Lombard show, he had been openly critical of the intrusion of Aristotle into theology, and more and more restive at some of the teachings of the schoolmen, the more so as he concentrated on biblical studies, using the new humanist tools and sharing their approach. Then he began to read Augustine, first in the easily available and best-known *De Civitate Dei*, and *De Trinitate*, and then the anti-Pelagian writings in the eighth volume of the eleven-volume Amerbach edition (1506). His preference for Augustine marked him off from Erasmian humanism, and led him to a much more radical antagonism to the later scholastic teachings (and especially the near-demi-semi-Pelagianism of the Nominalists). His new theological stresses became something of a programme involving, first, the concentration on biblical study and, second, the use as a dogmatic norm of Augustine and the Fathers ('ecclesiastical doctors'), leap-frogging over the later scholastics.

It was therefore of importance for the university when Karlstadt was won over to the new theology. He was now a Scotist, and a canonist, and one who accepted the teachings of authority. On

25 September 1513, Luther presided – it should normally have been Karlstadt as Dean – at a disputation on the occasion of the promotion of Bartholomew Feldkirchen to the degree of Sententiarius. In the course of it Luther attacked the authenticity of the pseudo-Augustinian tract, *Of true and false penitence*. This involved attacking the authority of the Decretals and of Peter Lombard and brought Karlstadt to his feet in angry protest.[1]

Karlstadt was probably as much offended by the impertinence of this contempt for authority as by Luther's argument. In Leipzig, in January 1517, he bought his own edition of Augustine's works (perhaps the Paris edition of 1515). He must have meditated on this, day and night, for by the spring he had bidden goodnight to the schoolmen, and had become more Augustinian than Luther himself.

It is possible that Staupitz also had something to do with his change of mind. L. Keller, in a learned but one-sided essay, suggested Staupitz as the true father of the Wittenberg Reformation, and it is true that Staupitz influenced all his friends and pupils. It can hardly be an accident that in 1518 both Luther and Karlstadt should both dedicate important tracts to Staupitz and that both refer specifically to some deeply significant saying of Staupitz (in Karlstadt's case the sentence from Ps. 119:94[2]: 'I am thine, save me').[3]

Certainly Karlstadt stood nearer to Staupitz in his theological background. For Staupitz had also been trained in Thomism in the Montanerburse in Cologne, though in his case there was the influence also of Aegidius Colonna, the authoritative teacher of the Augustinian order. Staupitz's mature theology, as witnessed by his sermons, shows clear evidence of 15th-century pietism, of the conflation of the 'modern devotion' with German mysticism, of the

---

[1] *WA, Br.* 1, No. 26, p. 65: 'illos implacabiliter offendit, praecipue Doctorem Carlstadium'; No. 30, pp. 77ff.

[2] Psalms are numbered throughout this work according to the Authorized Version, except where otherwise indicated.

[3] L. Keller *Johann von Staupitz und die Anfänge der Reformation* 1888 (reprint 1967); E. Wolf *Staupitz und Luther* Leipzig 1927, pp. 12ff.; Kähler *Karlstadt und Augustin* pp. 4, 6ff.; Th. Kolde *Die deutsche Augustiner-Congregation und Johann von Staupitz* Gotha 1879

influence of Gerson and Tauler, of such doctrines as conformity with Christ, and the virtue of resignation (*Gelassenheit*).

A strongly Augustinian sermon of Staupitz, 'Libellus de executione eterne predestinationis' appeared January–February 1517,[1] and it is just possible that it may have been this which clinched Karlstadt's conversion to Augustinianism.

It may be that Karlstadt's change of mind was apparent to his colleagues by the end of March.[2] It was certainly evident to all when in April he published 151 theses which amounted to an Augustinian manifesto, for where they were not simply quotations from the African Father, they were thoroughly Augustinian resolutions, many of them with a sharp edge against the scholastic teachers, often quite specifically against Karlstadt's former authority, Capreolus.

Luther was delighted with them. He sent a copy of them to Scheurl in Nuremberg – 'Not the paradoxes of Cicero, but of our own Carlstadt, nay rather, of Augustine, . . . Blessed be God who once again bids the light shine out of darkness'.[3]

They seem to have been put forward deliberately on the eve of the exposure of relics in the Castle church – a striking anticipation of Luther's similar action some months later. They begin by asserting the authority of the Fathers, subject to the supreme authority of Holy Scripture (Th. 1 and 4). They are, in the main, concerned with Grace and Free Will – and rebut the scholastic opinion (sometimes ascribed to Gregory of Rimini) that Augustine exaggerated when he wrote against Pelagius. They also treat the relation

---

[1] Copies were sent to Wittenberg by C. Scheurl, but perhaps not until March. Spalatin had received one at the end of January; see *WA, Br.* I, p. 94, n. 1; Kähler, op. cit., p. 4*. Karlstadt also bought Tauler's sermons in 1517, and this too may have been prompted by Staupitz. For an edition of this in English, see H. A. Oberman *Forerunners of the Reformation*.

[2] If the fragment of a letter from Luther to Lang (*WA, Br.* I, p. 33) is genuine, it must be dated 28 March 1517: 'Paratus est vel unus Carolstadius etiam cum gaudio cunctis eius modi sophistis et iuristis contraire. Et faciet et prosperabitur.'

[3] *WA, Br.* I, p. 94, lines 16ff. (6 May 1517): 'ne dicam de iis, qui ea potius cacodoxa . . . judicabunt, . . . Sunt . . . paradoxa modestis, . . . sed eudoxa et calodoxa scientibus, mihi vero aristodoxa.'

between the 'inward' and 'outward' man, and between Law and Spirit. The last theses deal with predestination and eternal life and with the problem of sin after baptism.[1]

Karlstadt intended to publish some further exposition of the theses, but never did so. Instead he put his new enthusiasm into an important course of lectures on Augustine's *On the Spirit and the Letter* which he delivered before a large audience, 1517–18. He began arrangements for printing the text as a tool for the students, in the not unusual way, but turned the work into a learned commentary. He got on quickly with the first part, which went to the press early in 1518. It was warmly commended by Luther. When Spalatin wrote asking advice for reading, Luther drew his attention to this work of 'our Carlstadt, a man of incomparable application',[2] and Karlstadt, replying to a similar request, drew attention to the work, but not immodestly.[3]

Thereafter came delays. Karlstadt was sick of a fever.[4] He found increasing preoccupations in the impact within the university of the new teaching programme, and of the Indulgence controversy which, it was now plain, could not be regarded as the private controversy of Dr Martin Luther, but as an affair in which the whole reputation of the university of Wittenberg was involved. Luther had to be content to send out the first sheets to his friends in March 1518,[5] and the rest of the work did not finally appear until February 1519. Even then it was a torso, lacking the last part.

None the less, it was a learned and, from its timeliness, an important work. In the letter of dedication to Staupitz, Karlstadt told the story of his conversion to Augustine – 'obstupui, obmutui, succensui', how he began to draw away from scholasticism and turn to the Bible and the Fathers. The body of the work is evidence of hard reading. There are numerous quotations from Augustine;

[1] There are useful comments on them in Kähler, op.cit., pp. 4*ff.

[2] *WA, Br.* 1, p. 134, lines 47ff. (18 Jan. 1518): 'Noster Carlstadius, homo studii incomparabilis, explicavit miris Explicationibus & edidit.'

[3] Karlstadt to Spalatin (*WA, Br.* 1, p. 132, lines 7ff.): 'Ego profecto librum de spiritu et litera Augustini doctissimi comperi ansam ad secretiora theologiae latibula praestantem.'

[4] *WA, Br.* 1, p. 154, lines 9f.

[5] *WA, Br.* 1, p. 154, line 4: 21 March 1518

next comes Ambrose, who is cited seventy times; then Bernard; then twenty quotations from Gregory the Great, eighteen from Jerome, thirteen from Cyprian, eleven from Cassian, and two from Origen.

At a time when Luther was beginning to criticize Erasmus as a theologian, to his friends, it is perhaps noticeable that Karlstadt speaks twice of 'our Erasmus'.[1]

But, if the work represents the new learning, his arrangement of authorities was thoroughly medieval. When Capito pointed this out, and suggested that the new method ought to lead to a new kind of exposition, Karlstadt readily agreed and promised something of the sort when he should publish the last part – another reason, maybe, why it never was done. Kähler suggests that there are undertones here which mark off Karlstadt's Augustinianism from Luther's. For Karlstadt it is the dichotomy between Letter and Spirit, Law and Spirit, rather than the Lutheran dialectic of Law and Gospel, which matters. Faith has not the same importance for Karlstadt as for Luther. There is a stress on the inward work of the Spirit – the inward Word which 'precedes all works and touches the heart' – which foreshadows, it is thought, Karlstadt's later spiritualism. There is an absence of stress on Christology – 'here is a theology of Grace, not a theology of Christ.' But, if the contrast is great between Karlstadt's commentary and the powerful theology of the Cross which Luther put forward at Heidelberg in April 1518, we must remember that Karlstadt was, after all, tied to his text. And certainly nobody noticed these nuances at a time when the two men worked side by side as comrades as never before or after.

Here then was the 'purer' theology, the return to the Bible and the Old Fathers, and the abandonment of the late schoolmen. This now became important for the whole university. In a famous letter, Luther wrote to John Lang in May 1517:

> Our theology and St Augustine go forward and, by God's work, reign in our University. Aristotle goes down more and more, and

[1] Later in 1519 Karlstadt could still speak of 'our Erasmus' – 'the principal and most eminent of all theologians, our Erasmus' ('Epistola adversus ineptam et ridiculam inventionem J. Eckii', Wittenberg 1519).

perhaps to future and lasting ruin. The lectures on the Sentences pall, and nobody can hope for an audience unless he puts forward this theology, that is, the Bible or St Augustine or some other doctor of authority in the Church.[1]

A year later, Luther could write to his old teacher Trutfetter 'from whom I first learned to place trust only in the canonical books, as the touchstone of the rest':

> I simply believe that the reform of the Church will be impossible unless canons, decretals, scholastic theology, philosophy and logic, as these things are now, are utterly uprooted and other disciplines put in their place. So sure I am in this conviction that I pray daily that God will as soon as possible allow the purest studies to be brought back, that is, the Bible and the Fathers.[2]

Luther can claim that this is not his private view:

> You know what kind of spirits we have here – Karlstadt, Amsdorf, D. Jerome [Schürpf], D. Wolfgang [Stähelin], both the Feldkirchens and D. Peter Lupinus. These firmly agree with me, nay the whole University does, with one exception.[3]

Karlstadt, in his preface to Augustine's *On the Spirit and the Letter*, addressed the students against the same background of solidarity:

> I congratulate you, fellow students, that the truth of sacred letters shines once again in our University, . . . Rejoice that you are allowed to hear, learn and understand the true Bible from Doctors of the Church and from the Bible itself, not from the schoolmen or from vanities.[4]

Here in Wittenberg, he adds, the lectures all proceed 'ex fonte' – for Martin Luther expounds Hebrews; Peter Lupinus, St Ambrose; Aesticampius, St Jerome.

Probably Luther's phrase 'purer theology' represents the aims of him and his colleagues better than the name 'new theology'. For the programme was one which could be paralleled elsewhere. Other universities, like Vienna or Louvain, had humanist disciplines at least running side by side with the traditional syllabus. The return

---

[1] *WA, Br.* I, p. 99, lines 8–13   [2] *WA, Br.* I, p. 170, lines 33–8
[3] *WA, Br.* I, p. 170, lines 22–5   [4] Kähler, op. cit., pp. 9f.

to the Bible and the Old Fathers, the rejection of late scholasticism was a thoroughly Erasmian programme. If one asks where the difference lay in Wittenberg, one can only point to the theological emphasis on Augustine, and to the personal qualities of Luther (soon to be seconded by Melanchthon).[1]

The new theological priorities demanded readjustments of the university programme which had practical repercussions through the timetable, syllabus, examination system as well as the all-important question of staff. We get glimpses of these affairs in Luther's letters in the next months to a triangle of interested friends: John Lang at Erfurt: Christopher Scheurl at Nuremberg: and to George Spalatin, a friend at court in a special sense, since so much depended on his advice as secretary and chaplain to the Elector in these matters.

Early in March 1518 there was an important conference in Karlstadt's lodgings (he was Dean of the Faculty) about the practical proposals which must be brought to the attention of the Elector.[2] Luther wrote a few days later that this would involve lectures in the sacred languages, on Pliny, in mathematics, on Quintilian, the abandonment of lectures on Petrus Hispanus, Tartaret, and some of the lectures on Aristotle.[3] This was a humanist but not a revolutionary programme, for much of it was already being carried out in such universities as Vienna, and Henry VIII's reforms in the universities of Oxford and Cambridge were to show the same emphasis on the sacred languages. Both Karlstadt and Luther agreed in attacking the intrusion of scholastic logic into biblical theology.[4]

[1] Bauer, op. cit.; Aland, op. cit., p. 283; also E. G. Schwiebert, 'New Groups and Ideas at the University of Wittenberg', *ARG* 49, 1958, pp. 60ff.; L. Petry, 'Die Reformation als Epoche der Deutschen Universitätsgeschichte', in *Festgabe Joseph Lortz* ii, 317ff., cf. 337-9.

[2] Luther to Spalatin (*WA, Br.* I, p. 153): 'Fuimus nuper apud Dominum Doctorem Carlstadium, . . . et coepimus tractare . . . de lectionibus studii nostri initiandis vel instituendis.'

[3] *WA, Br.* I, p. 155, lines 42ff. There is useful information about the university of Wittenberg in E. G. Schwiebert *Luther and his Times* St Louis, Mo. 1950, Chaps 8, 9.

[4] *WA, Br.* I, p. 143, lines 81ff.: 'Postremo dum rogas, . . . , quibus in locis logica theologiae sit necessaria, tibi respondeo: in nulla locorum, quia

These changes could not be effected suddenly. Thomist logic was the first to go, but Scotist logic remained for a time. Aristotle was never entirely abandoned in Wittenberg, but new texts and methods, such as Le Fèvre had long used in Paris, were adopted by Bartholomew Feldkirchen and Augustine Schürpf. More important were the proposals for lecturers in Greek and Hebrew, about which the Elector wrote to Reuchlin as a referee of eminence. The result was the advent of Reuchlin's young great-nephew, Philip Melanchthon, nepotism of the right kind, though few could have guessed that the slight young student would one day be denominated 'preceptor of Germany'. His inaugural address was a programme of humanist studies, and Luther soon gave his new colleague generous praise, his only concern being that this genius in their midst should not be worked to death, and that his gifts might not be wasted in academic chores.

The arrangements in Hebrew were less happy. Old Böschenstein who came in November (not so old, but he termed himself 'senex') was something of a character, but a thorough grammarian, interested only in the language ('As if we wanted to turn out orators to the Jews!' was Luther's tart comment)[1] and suspicious of those who saw in Hebrew only a tool for biblical study.[2] He grew disgruntled, took to muttering during lectures that it was time he had a holiday, stayed long enough to queer the pitch for the university, which failed to grab the brilliant young Hebraist, Dr Caesar, and finally left them all in the lurch, so that Melanchthon was fain to add Hebrew grammar to his other teaching duties.[3]

The new coherent, forward-looking programme, centred in the theological faculty, but touching all departments of the university, began to attract young men, so that in the next years the student

---

Christus non indiget figmentis humanis' (Karlstadt to Spalatin); p. 149, lines 9ff.: 'Quaeris, Quatenus utilem Dialecticen arbiter Theologo. Ego sane non video, Quomodo non sit noxia potius Dialectice vero Theologo' (Luther to Spalatin).

[1] *WA, Br.* I, p. 228, line 34
[2] *WA, Br.* I, p. 174, line 49; p. 175, n. 17; p. 203, lines 11ff.
[3] *WA, Br.* I, p. 228, line 30; p. 297, lines 1ff.; p. 298 notes

population doubled, a growth that was only to be checked by Luther's public impeachment. Karlstadt had become used to being academically No. 2 to Luther's primacy, and we have no evidence what heartburning, if any, the advent of the still younger, even more learned Melanchthon caused him, though relations between them were always cooler than with Luther, who never entirely forgot the comradeship of these perilous and exciting months.

If the church struggle which now began spoiled the Erasmian hope of a golden age of sacred letters, it also interrupted and brought to near-disaster the Luther programme of biblical theology. The Indulgence controversy came almost as a side line, was very much Luther's own preoccupation with a problem of practical abuse and pastoral care, and, if the theological roots of it were indeed deep, it did not seem evident to many of Luther's friends that it was right to raise a question which must impinge swiftly on problems of ecclesiastical authority. Karlstadt was among such friends.

In February 1518 Spalatin put to both men a question about good works preparatory to grace, and if the two answers differ notably it is perhaps because Spalatin put the question in either case a little differently.[1] Karlstadt takes the question as one of trusting in good works and is trenchantly Augustinian: the attempt to make human works divine is the highest pride and the worst vice. After a comic digression in which he rather naïvely suggests that a gift of thirty florins towards the cost of paper would make his treatment of this question in his commentary more easily available, he concludes with an eloquent section, paradoxes which might easily have come from Luther's lectures on Romans and Hebrews: 'Thine is the righteousness, mine the unrighteousness; thine the glory, mine the confusion; thine the might, mine the weakness!' Luther, on the other hand, takes the question to be one of 'intention' and discusses the subjective conditions of penitence, despair in oneself and confidence in the mercy of God.[2]

[1] *WA, Br.* I, p. 146, lines 56ff.: 'Et si hanc sententiam non tenet Noster Carlsta[dius], certum est tamen mihi, ...'
[2] *WA, Br.* I, pp. 142–3, lines 12ff., 41ff., 75ff.; p. 145, lines 13ff.

CHAPTER FIVE

THE GREAT CONSULT

Others apart sat on a hill retir'd,
In thoughts more elevate, and reason'd high
Of providence, foreknowledge, will, and fate,
Fix'd fate, free will, foreknowledge absolute,
And found no end, in wand'ring mazes lost.
MILTON: *Paradise Lost*

The two matters, the new university programme centred in the return to Augustine and the Fathers, and Luther's battle about indulgences, intersected fatefully and unexpectedly in the person of John Eck. He and Luther had struck up a mild academic friendship through their common friend, Scheurl, so that it was greatly to Luther's chagrin that he heard that Eck had attacked his theses. This he had done in a private document intended in the first place for Bishop Gabriel von Eyb, of Eichstätt. A copy of these *Adnotationes* reached Luther, probably through Bernard Adelmann of Augsburg, and Luther replied to these 'Obelisks' (as he nicknamed them) with a series of 'Asterisks'.[1] This he may have done before his departure for the Heidelberg Chapter of his order in April 1518. But he must have shown it to his colleagues, for during his absence Karlstadt suddenly and unexpectedly, and without Luther's knowledge, leaped to the defence of his leader and of 'our theology' with a vast array of 379 theses, to which he added twenty-six for good measure while they were in the press.

[1] J. Greving (ed.) *Johannes Eck, Defensio contra amarulentas D. Andreae Bodenstein Carolstatini Invectiones (1518)* Münster 1919, pp. 7ff. 'Obelisks' and 'asterisks' are printers' technical signs.

Karlstadt's reason for intervening (if the preface written later, perhaps by Capito, reflects the position) was that the attack on Luther involved 'the whole academy of letters at Wittenberg, and especially the theological faculty'. The opening theses have no direct reference to Eck at all, but deal with the authority of the Bible. 'The text of the Bible,' said the first thesis, 'when brought forward by a doctor of the Church, counts for more than the authority of the doctor who alleges it.' Thesis 12 affirms: 'The text of the Bible is to be preferred not only to one or many of the doctors of the Church, but even before the whole Church itself.' Then at thesis 101 comes a series of resolutions directly and explicitly against Eck, though only three of the 'Obelisks' were singled out. Karlstadt was in fighting trim 'wi' a hundred theses an' a', an' a''.[1] He dismisses Eck's view that, properly speaking, the Church cannot be penitent – a view of the sinlessness of the Body of Christ which still cuts deep into the differences between Catholic and Protestant ecclesiology. The theses go on to the intricate question of the relation between grace and the human will. One of Eck's statements, that the will reigns in the human soul as a king, and one of Karlstadt's affirmations, that God is the author of the whole of our good works, were to be important points of argument in coming months.[2] There follows a row of theses against the moral teaching of Aristotle, and a series about indulgences which shows that Karlstadt has in mind the recent counter-theses of Wimpina and Tetzel, and that, despite earlier misgivings, Karlstadt had come over to Luther's side.

At this time, when there was still a chance that the whole Luther affair might be hushed up, neither Luther nor Eck wanted public controversy. Luther wrote to Scheurl in real embarrassment at his colleague's action.[3] The 379 theses were apparently intended for the regular Friday disputations in Wittenberg (had a convalescent Karlstadt written them out during his enforced leisure, to get the disputational chores out of the way?). The first theses had been debated in May at the promotion of Nicasius Claji, and had then

---

[1] Barge, i, 117ff.

[2] Greving, op.cit., pp. 61 (Thesis 50), 71 (Thesis 40), and Index (p. 92) *s.v.* Bodenstein

[3] *WA, Br.* I, p. 219, lines 32ff.

been printed. At the end of May Eck wrote to Karlstadt in a tone of 'Why pick on me? Why not attack Wimpina or Tetzel?', hoping at least to prevent the printing of the theses against himself. But printed they were, in time for the promotion of Bartholomew Feldkirchen on 7 July, after Karlstadt had sent Eck a spirited reply which ended 'Long live Luther!'

But that, Luther's friends were beginning to think, was the great question. For his enemies were loudly threatening that he would soon be burned, and rumours from his south German friends were that he was to be arrested, sent in chains to Rome, thereafter no doubt to disappear in some dark hole in the Castle of St Angelo.

When Luther went off to Augsburg to meet Cardinal Cajetan, it was a moment of personal loneliness and danger more daunting perhaps than the later and more famous appearance at Worms, when half Germany was evidently at his side. But Luther himself saw quite clearly that the fate of his colleagues and of his university was bound up with his own. He wrote to Spalatin from Augsburg, on 14 October 1518:

> If I am disposed of by force, the door is open for an attack on Dr Karlstadt and the whole theological faculty [*et tota theologiae professionem*] – and, as I fear, the sudden ruin of our infant University – as Pharaoh ordered the Israelite children to be snatched from their mothers' womb and drowned.[1]

His colleagues took the point, and stood solidly behind him. In the really critical moment in Luther's career, when the Elector Frederick had to decide whether to disown his protégé, the Faculty not only addressed their Prince on his behalf, but asked Luther to write the first draft of the letter.[2]

Eck had already decided to reply to Luther and had begun to see possible advantages to himself and the Catholic cause in a public debate. He published his 'Defensio . . . contra amarulentas D. Andreae Bodenstein . . . invectiones' on 14 August.[3] At the end

[1] loc. cit.
[2] A full account of this, with the letter, is given in E. G. Schwiebert *Luther and his Times* pp. 364ff.
[3] There is a copy of this and the succeeding pamphlets between Eck and Karlstadt in the John Rylands Library, Manchester.

of the month, Karlstadt began a reply, 'Defensio contra D. Johannis Eckium monomachiam'.

Now it was Karlstadt's turn to draw back and raise objections about notaries, and about who should pay the expenses (he was generally in financial difficulties). In an interview at Augsburg, Luther haggled politely on Karlstadt's behalf. Perhaps with his tongue in his cheek he suggested Wittenberg as a suitable place, to which Eck retorted with the even wilder suggestion of Rome. Finally, the choice narrowed to Erfurt or Leipzig, and Eck promptly chose Leipzig where he had many friends, and where the disputation would be under the aegis of Duke George of Saxony.

The question was now whether this should be a straight fight between Karlstadt and Eck or a three-cornered dispute which could include Luther. There began a series of literary skirmishes in which the direction of Eck's attack turned more and more plainly towards Luther.

Early in 1519, then, Luther and Karlstadt stood side by side as champions of the Augustinian theology, the one a monk, the other a secular priest, both doctors of divinity. Both at this time show undertones of a 'theology of the Cross'. Luther had re-discovered the *Theologia Germanica*, and his lectures on Galatians, which he published in 1519, still show traces not only of Tauler, but of the mystical influence of Dionysius the Areopagite. Karlstadt had bought Tauler's writings in 1517, but it is in his tracts of 1519 that there first appears mystical terminology. His writing 'De Impii Justificatione' outlines two ways: that of death, destruction, and descent into hell; that of resurrection, deliverance, renewal, return from the dead – and stresses that this twofold way which Christ trod has its counterpart in us.[1] There is a stress on penitence, as a storm raging in the soul, which reminds us of the somewhat later theology of Thomas Müntzer. There is certainly not enough evidence to suggest that at this time, or at any time, Karlstadt underwent some inward conversion. Then, almost by chance, Karlstadt found momentary fame.

He got his friend, the famous artist Lukas Cranach, to draw for him a cartoon of two wagons: one bearing the Cross, on the way to

[1] Barge, i, 138

heaven; the other full of scholastic writings, on the road to hell.[1] Although Karlstadt disclaimed any personal intentions, vowed that the picture had no reference to any living person, the Leipzig theologians howled with rage. A copy was torn to pieces publicly in a pulpit, and young men were asked in the confessional whether they had laughed at it.

Karlstadt published in April 1519 a pamphlet of elucidation, a curious and confused composition[2] which printed in heavy type texts of scripture and some theological jingles which suggest that in this, Karlstadt's first writing in the vernacular, he was trying to get the popular ear. Here again the mystical element is noticeable, and for the first time the technical term 'resignation' (*Gelassenheit*). Meanwhile, theses for the disputation began to appear: seventeen from Karlstadt about penitence, twelve from Eck, and countertheses by Luther which now raised the critical, dangerous question of the Roman primacy. In an open letter to Karlstadt, Luther suggests that really this controversy is not worthy of Karlstadt's diversion from the great theme of grace, and deplores his own preoccupation with such subsidiary questions as that of indulgences.[3] Whether this was a warning or exculpation of his colleague or not, it is noticeable that Karlstadt's two tracts of 1519 each end with the sentence: 'we submit in all things to the judgement of the Roman Church.'

The Wittenbergers arrived in Leipzig on 24 June 1519, files of armed students flanking the two wagons, in the first of which sat Karlstadt, hugging a small library, while Luther, Melanchthon, and the Rector of Wittenberg University, Duke Barnim of Pomerania, occupied the second. As the cavalcade turned into the city gate, Karlstadt's wagon crashed. Those among the Leipzigers with an eye for omens must have been delighted to see the author of the notorious 'Wagon' cartoon precipitated into the muck. Karlstadt was badly shaken, hurt his thumb and had twice to be bled by the physicians. He was not in good physical shape for an exhausting ordeal.

[1] Barge, i, Excursus II; Kähler, op. cit., p. 51*n.
[2] 'Auslegung und Erläuterung...' (copy in JRL)
[3] *WA, Br.* I, No. 142: 4 February 1519

The disputation began at the end of June 1519 while the Wittenberg team were entering their lodgings with the printer Melchior Lotter (one of his proof readers, Thomas Müntzer, no doubt eyeing the proceedings curiously). A brief was nailed to the church door from the bishop of Merseburg, forbidding the disputation. It was torn down swiftly and thereafter ignored.[1] Then it seemed that the affair might break down, first during the long wrangle between Karlstadt, Eck and the Leipzig authorities about procedure, and again when Luther learned that behind his back it had been decided that proceedings should not be published at once but after judgement had been given by the arbiters, the universities of Erfurt and Paris. Nor, finally, was Luther much pleased when Karlstadt, not altogether unnaturally, refused to give Luther pride of place, and allow him to be the first speaker.[2]

The preliminaries were a blend of the picturesque and the tedious. There was a solemn procession to St Thomas's, to hear the first performance of a Mass in Twelve Parts, by the well-known musician George Rhau. Then came the official opening in the great hall of the Pleissenburg Castle, in the presence of the whole court. They fidgeted through a tedious oration about 'Theological debates and their procedure', delivered in Latin by the humanist Petrus Mosellanus (he kept his wit for his letters in which, among other things, he described Eck and Karlstadt as 'a pretty pair of Scotists'), and after a thrice-repeated *Veni, sancte Spiritus*, there was a welcome adjournment for refreshment.

There are many accounts of the debate, mainly from sources unsympathetic to Karlstadt. Wittenberg and Leipzig were great rivals and feeling in the town was running high (so that there were a hundred lesser disputations o' nights in the taverns, in one of which an eminent indulgence-seller was goaded into an apoplexy). Mosellanus has left an unflattering thumbnail sketch of Karlstadt, the

---

[1] Schwiebert, op.cit., Chap. 19; R. H. Fife *The Revolt of Martin Luther* New York 1957, Chaps 18–20. For Karlstadt the best theological account is C. F. Jäger *Andreas Bodenstein von Carlstadt* Stuttgart 1856, pp. 26ff.; see also Barge, i, Chap. IV

[2] The incident would be much more intelligible and interesting if Luther's request had in mind that he would debate Free Will and Grace also.

little tubby man, with his dark, almost negroid appearance, his harsh, unmelodious voice, his bad temper.[1]

The earnestness, the seriousness with which Luther and his Wittenberg friends approached these theological issues is an important trait, for it differentiated them from many of the humanists, and it makes intelligible their sustained reproach of Eck that he came to the disputation more concerned with victory than with truth.

We have seen how Karlstadt had put Augustine's doctrines at the centre of the struggle, which began with the question of the relation of the human will to grace.[2] This was a field where something of that 'unclearness' which Lortz has noted as a characteristic of contemporary theology reigned,[3] for even the Council of Trent was to account the matter too delicate and intricate for close definition. We may, if we will, look at this as one of the last of the innumerable medieval debates on this subject. We may look ahead half a century to the debates of the Calvinists in Holland and the Puritans in England – there is a diagram drawn up by Eck which is worthy of William Perkins – or to the Catholic controversies with Bajus and Jansen.

Both debaters had a tactical weakness. For Eck there was the fact that not only was Pelagianism (which included the doctrine that the human will, unaided by grace, can perform good works) notorious heresy, but semi-Pelagianism had been condemned at the Council of Orange (529). Eck himself was enough of a humanist to be not much at home with Scotus, and some of the jargon of the late schoolmen – the famous 'doing what lies within one's power (*facere quod in se est*)' – was difficult to justify without confusion and contradiction. Karlstadt, on the other hand, wished to rely on the supreme

---

[1] Mosellanus to Pflug: 'Statura est brevior, facies autem nigricans et adusta: Vox obscura et inamoena, memoria infirmior et ad iracundiam promptior' (Barge, i, p. 153, n. 66). Eck in one of his pamphlets ('Contra Martini Ludder obtusum propugnatorem Andream Rodolphi Bodenstein Carlstadium' JRL) confirms this: 'quod pronunciacio esset ei gravis aspera et hiulca: memoria esset illi vel nulla vel parva, discursus modicus'.

[2] We may keep 'Free Will' for 'liberum arbitrium' if we remember that modern Catholic theologians prefer to translate 'Free Choice'; see E. Gilson *The Christian Philosophy of St Augustine* Eng. trans. London 1961, Chap. III

[3] J. Lortz *Die Reformation in Deutschland* Freiburg 1948, i, 137

authority of Scripture but, as the later debate between Erasmus and Luther was to show, the speech of the Bible (and especially the Hebraic ways of expression of the Old Testament) is unphilosophical, so that biblical statements tended to prove too little or too much. Capito had remarked on Karlstadt's old-fashioned way of citing authorities to support a new theology, and this was to appear during the disputation. Karlstadt could not speak with the fluency and originality of Luther, whose theological development during the last five years had been at a dimension of depth beyond that of Karlstadt.

From the layman spectator's point of view, there was no comparison. Karlstadt approached his opponent like an artilleryman dealing with a besieged city, slowly drawing nearer with sappers, mines, earthworks, ravelins, until after pounding away a breach might be made. Eck was of the cavalry. No wonder that he was frustrated and furious.

Eck's memory, his ability to string quotations together fluently (if not always accurately) was a great trait. Karlstadt seemed to have no memory at all (Eck sarcastically suggested that it had leaked out when the physicians bled him). There he stood, ducking his head up and down like a nervous hen, humming and hawing, squinting now at the ceiling, now at the floor, ringed by a squad of assistants who handed him long memoranda, and then piles of books which he opened in turn, one, two, three, four, and from which he dictated to the scowling notaries. At one point Eck could stand it no longer and cried out, 'This is a debate, not a homework display! (*Actus noster est disputatio, non praelectio domi concepta*).'[1] Finally, to the relief of all, the judges ruled that there should be no reading from memoranda. There was, too, a certain amount of audience participation, and both complained that the other was receiving too many helpful notes. Two points might perhaps be added in Karlstadt's favour. Tiresome and cumbrous as his method was, he ensured that his quotations were in their true context and that they were written into the record. Second, he enunciated his own biblical principle in a way which goes deep into his theology: 'To know the Holy Scriptures does not mean reciting many authorities from

[1] Jäger, p. 31

memory but seeking the spirit from within the letter and so seeking and tasting our Lord Christ.'[1]

But when we add to these things that Karlstadt easily got worked up and lost emotional control, we can understand that Eck won the sympathy of most of his hearers, and at moments reduced his opponent to a figure of fun.

To the theologians, or at least those who kept awake, the debate was much more even. It began at 2 p.m., on Monday 27 June 1519. Eck affirmed that the sum of the contention between them was his view that 'the human will has an active causality, a productive power, is able to elicit a meritorious work, but not without the grace and spiritual help of God'. He quoted in support of this Ecclus. 15: 14–19 and a tract of Jerome (an unlucky choice, for the tract was by Pelagius). Karlstadt was committed to the view that the human will is passive, not only towards divine grace, but in the performance of a good work. He developed this in a properly Augustinian stress on the fact that the will finds its true liberty only when freed by grace, 'for this is the true theology, to know nothing save the power of Christ, and our own weakness'. Eck at one point seems to have implied that the human will had some 'natural' capacity of its own for good, apart from grace, and something to this effect was written into the record, but it was ambiguous enough ('natural' might mean different things to a Thomist and an Augustinian) and he hotly denied having admitted so much, saying that, if he had held that the will is as a monarch in the human soul, it was in relation to inferior faculties. Nor did he intend, he said, to imply that free will has a special operation apart from grace.[2]

Pressed hard, Eck asked for an adjournment which was granted. The debate resumed on some quotations from St Bernard, claimed as a support by both speakers. Karlstadt for the moment dropped his conception of passivity in so far as he would concede that the will, set free by grace, has a certain activity. It was at this point that the dispute about written memoranda occurred and there was again an adjournment. A crop of saints' days now gave both sides a breather, and the debate did not begin again until 1 July.

[1] Jäger, p. 33   [2] Jäger, pp. 34ff.

Each disputant now tried to press the admissions or inconsistencies of the other. Eck insisted that Karlstadt's admission of an activity of the human will implied a doctrine of co-operation in which the human will, though subsidiary to grace, was a factor in the performance of the good. Karlstadt still insisted that the whole of our salvation is of grace. There began another argument about St Bernard and a distinction by Eck between 'totum' and 'totaliter'. He said that it could be predicated of God that he produced a good work 'wholly', but not 'entirely'. Karlstadt attempted to dismiss this as unscriptural sophistry – the point was never decided and was to be resumed in the acrimonious aftermath in later months. There followed another respite (The Feast of the Visitation of the B.V.M.) and then a day's debate on 3 July, when Karlstadt seems to have had the worst of it.

Then came the dramatic interlude, the long-awaited, dangerous, exciting debate between Eck and Luther. It threw the rest of the proceedings into the shade. When Karlstadt re-appeared, it was before a tired audience, and it would have taken a much more gifted orator to make the new debate anything but an anticlimax. The first theme was whether, when a man does what in him lies (*facere quod in se est*), he can remove obstacles to grace. Karlstadt tried to push Eck into the apparently near-semi-Pelagian interpretations of some of the late scholastics, but Eck refused to admit that this referred to the human will unassisted by grace. The final debate was whether the just sin, even in good works, even in the act of martyrdom. In the end it just fizzled out. Having hardly begun with a bang, it certainly ended with a whimper. Luther had already left, the tireless Karlstadt could not persuade Eck to tackle yet another row of theses. Their host, Duke George, wanted to get the castle aired before the now eagerly awaited advent of a party of huntin', shootin', fishin' friends.

There followed a literary hubbub. Both sides wrote to their friends, claiming the victory (the arbiter universities, after delay, evaded pronouncing on the disputation). Eck wrote a very nasty letter to the Elector Frederick, attacking Luther and Karlstadt but praising Luther to the disparagement of Karlstadt (a clever move), hinting that some contribution to his own expenses might be forthcoming, and insolently suggesting that the Elector might publicly burn Luther's anti-papal writings. The Elector turned the letter over to his theologians, who composed a spirited joint reply.[1] Eck was swaggering about south Germany, and he had much to be pleased about. He had greatly increased his own personal reputation, not least with Rome. He had wiped the floor with Karlstadt. He had at the very least manœuvred Luther into making damaging and dangerous admissions. Luther himself was disgusted with the whole business, with its levity, its unconcern for truth, the virulent hatred of the Leipzigers towards himself. But he won much sympathy from the humanists. The Augsburg scholars, Oecolampadius and the brothers Adelmann, wrote the effective 'Canonici Indocti', and in Nuremberg Willibald Pirckheimer produced the brilliantly successful satire, *Eckius Dedolatus* ('Doctor Corner polished off').

The damage done to Karlstadt psychologically and in relation to Luther was deep. There was the beginning of evident strain between himself and Luther (though Luther dedicated his *Galatians* to him, and wrote kindly to Spalatin – 'treat him gently, he has had a rough handling from Eck').[2]

And not only from Eck, but from Jerome Emser. Nor had Karlstadt been unaware of the disparaging gossip. He could not let ill alone, as Luther was prepared to do. In October 1519 he wrote a 'Letter against the inept and ridiculous invention of John Eck',[3] in which he dug up again the argument about 'totum' and 'totaliter', sprinkled with classical allusions to impress the humanists. Such subtle distinctions could attract few readers, and Karlstadt was on surer ground in his next writing, 'On the Words of God, and with what sincerity and plainness they ought to be preached'.[4] Here, in the matter of the superiority of Scripture and the Fathers to the late schoolmen, he had all the Erasmians on his side.

Karlstadt began with a story. During the disputation, he was sitting with John Lang in the audience, when Eck came up, remarking that, if he agreed as much with Luther as he did with Karlstadt, he would be prepared to dine with Luther. Karlstadt then burst out

---

[1] *WA, Br.* I, Nos 192, 193 (August 1519), pp. 463, 502
[2] *WA, Br.* I, p. 505, lines 30ff.: 20 August 1519
[3] Barge, i, 168 (copy in JRL)   [4] Barge, i, 172ff.; Jäger, p. 70

with the complaint that, though this had appeared to be true in the disputation, where concessions had been made and agreements pronounced, Eck had in the pulpit, on the Feast of the Visitation, made the most outrageous statements, and had even adduced, as a writing of Jerome, a tract of Pelagius, after the real authorship had been declared.

Eck replied that it was not seemly to say before an unlearned audience what might properly be said in the schools. We may not sow the same seed among common and untutored Christians which we plant in the cultivated soil of the educated. It is against this that Karlstadt writes a fiery plea for the 'open Bible', quoting Erasmus (a new edition of Erasmus' *Method of Theology* had recently appeared). It is an all-out attack on the scholastic preachers, who drag their theological authorities and the heathen Aristotle into the pulpit, corrupting the Word of God with the traditions of men, putting forward their own opinions in the name of Christ, doctrines not found in Scripture ('in scripturarum locis'). He appeals to Christian men not to allow such preaching. 'Woe unto those who would rob of the knowledge of the Holy Scripture the humble and poor, the naked and simple, who, by their very poverty, are prepared for the Word of God.' It can hardly be compared, as Barge compares it, with Luther's 'Appeal to the ... German Nation' six months later, if only because it is in Latin, but it is another instance of Karlstadt's biblicism, of an emphasis on the written word. Karlstadt's 'The Bible says ...' anticipates the Reformed and Puritan tradition.

A few days later appeared Eck's writing 'Against the foolish champion of Martin Luther, Dr Andrew Rudolph Bodenstein from Karlstadt'.[1] It takes up the argument about 'totum' and 'totaliter'. It includes a 'plan of salvation' showing the stages of justification and sanctification, some of which – inspiration and justification – are from God alone, whereas to agree to inspiration and to accept it is the part of human will; while to remain in it is something to which both grace and the human will contribute. It treats Karlstadt throughout with complete contempt, deriding his personal appearance and lack of intellectual gifts, piling up derogatory

[1] 'Contra Martini Ludder obtusum propugnatorem Andream Rodolphi Bodenstein Carlstadium': JRL

adjectives. It drove Karlstadt beside himself. He must have been almost choking with rage when he went to see Luther, who wrote to Spalatin in some alarm that Karlstadt intended to call his reply 'Against that Silly Ass and self-assertive imitation doctor' and begged Spalatin to make him tone it down, but not to mention that he (Luther) had written, 'for the man is prone to suspicions'.[1] It does seem that Karlstadt did make some revision. The pamphlet is bad, but in respect of zoological and anal vocabulary it is better than some of Luther's later polemic. At any rate it was bad enough to make the author blush when he read the work in print. He kept silence for several months. Luther wrote in despair to Spalatin: 'This is where we came in. Karlstadt disagrees with Eck. Behold the fruit of the Leipzig Disputation.'[2]

Thus ended the Great Consult. The solemn disputation 'for the love of and for the sake of eliciting truth' had petered out 'in wand'ring mazes lost', and in a flood of personal abuse and schoolboy recrimination.

[1] *WA, Br.* 2, p. 30, lines 12ff.   [2] *WA, Br.* 2, p. 36, lines 22f.; Barge, i, 178

CHAPTER SIX

THE WITTENBERG MOVEMENT 1521-2

> '*Law, Brer Tarrypin!*' *sez Brer Fox, sezee,* '*you aint seen no trouble yit. Ef you wanter see sho' nuff trouble, you des oughter go 'longer me; I'm de man w'at kin show you trouble*', *sezee.*
> —*Uncle Remus*

At this point in the Karlstadt story we are perhaps in some danger of accepting the contempt of Eck and the embarrassment of Luther, and dismissing Karlstadt as an academic buffoon, not to be taken seriously. It is important to notice that now, and indeed much later, he had his disciples[1] and his circle of friends and influence.

Perhaps early in 1520 he made a successful tour of the mining district of Joachimsthal, and the dedications of his tracts in these months show that he had established friendly contact with a number of lay notables, among them Heinrich von Könneritz who sent his three sons to Wittenberg, as much for Karlstadt's sake as for Luther's. Joachimsthal had strong business links with Annaberg, and it may be that Karlstadt went on there from Joachimsthal. At any rate Annaberg was a centre of the cult of St Anne, and its relics and indulgences were the special concern of the Franciscans, of the Guardian Francis Seyler, and the Vice-Guardian, John Furcheim. At some time early in 1520 Seyler had issued a warning against those who 'run off to the new Prophets at Wittenberg who decry Indulgences', and this moved Karlstadt (in a tract of 10 August

---

[1] At this time Nicasius Claji and Matthew Hiskold; later, Martin Reinhard and Gerhard Westerburg.

1520: 'Of the Power of Indulgences, against Brother Francis Seyler'[1]) to protest, 'If I keep silence, the grass and leaves, wood and stone, heaven and earth will cry out on the day of judgement'. In the overall situation, the theme of Karlstadt's tract was rather dated, and its publication coincided with the publication of Luther's fiery 'Appeal to the Christian Nobility', which had moved far beyond the original question of the validity of indulgences, about which Karlstadt has little new to add, though in his emphasis on the need for works of love and for practical philanthropy there is perhaps a hint of his preoccupation with the practical moralism of the Epistle of St James.[2]

More important is Karlstadt's continuing biblicism:[3] 'I will know no other forgiveness of sins than Scripture teaches'—'no other word, no other holy writings, no other gospel . . . than that which the Holy Scripture contains'. When Karlstadt heard that Seyler had suggested that 'the Doctor also believes things which are not in the Bible', he answered: 'Indeed I do, as that mendicant monks love gold!' Seyler also pointed out that this biblicism meant the end of such customs as the use of holy water and consecrated salt, and this became an incentive for Karlstadt to scribble off in five days another tract, 'Of Holy Water and Salt'.[4] This proved timely and popular – it went quickly into four editions – and may have been one of the more influential of his writings. From early days in the medieval Church the blessing of things had not always been kept free from the suspicion of magic, and the prayers for the *benedictio fontis* in baptism were early casualties of Reformation liturgical change. Here Karlstadt's spiritualism is apparent, though it may be going too far to see here, with Barge, the beginnings of the anti-sacramentalism

---

[1] 'Von Vormögen des Ablas, wider bruder Franciscus Seyler parfuser ordens': Barge, i, 206ff.; Jäger, p. 70 (copy of this and the second tract against Seyler in JRL)

[2] On the preoccupation with this epistle of the later English Lollards, see E. G. Rupp *Studies in the Making of the English Protestant Tradition* Cambridge 1947, pp. 5, 50; but see also Luther's 95 Theses, 43–5, for the same emphasis on works of love.

[3] The opening chapters of G. H. Tavard *Holy Writ or Holy Church* put the opposite context: the Catholic tradition upheld by Eck and others.

[4] 'Von geweyhtem Wasser und Saltz . . .' (JRL); Jäger, pp. 80ff.

apparent in his later eucharistic radicalism. Here he does not do much more than stress the importance of faith, and make the valid distinction, thoroughly medieval, between *res* and *signum*, and protest against contemporary superstition, nourished by church customs and encouraged by some ecclesiastical vested interests.

In treating of holy water, Karlstadt stresses the importance of faith. Apart from faith, holy water is no different from bath water. Just as the children of Israel were saved by water, so Pharaoh and his host were drowned by it – 'if you believe, holy water will be holy; if not, it will be death and destruction for you.' Water in the Scriptures, says Karlstadt, means patience and persecution, and suffering for Christ's sake. There is a further meaning (John 13: 5–10) of the washing away of daily sin. This stress on the solidarity of the Church in Head and Members and on the suffering of Christians is interesting. In itself it may be paralleled in Luther's utterances 1518–20, and is not perhaps to be too sharply distinguished from his 'theology of the Cross'. But taken together with Karlstadt's main references to the use of water as signifying suffering and tribulation, there is a remarkable – possibly accidental, one cannot press it – approximation to the teaching of Thomas Müntzer, a teaching which goes on through Hans Huth into some of the early Anabaptists. We know that from early in 1519 Müntzer had been interested in Karlstadt, had been in correspondence with his vicar at Orlamünde, and was present at the Leipzig disputation. There is, thus, more than a presumption that they were at this time in friendly contact.

The third strong point in the little leaflet is the sharp rejection of papal authority: 'I don't give much for what Pope Alexander or other Popes have taught – it is the Word of God that binds me and is dear to me, that throws all the Popes overboard; and that is our faith, and none else'. This sets the key for the next months of Karlstadt's thought and writing, as he himself came under impeachment in the papal bull against Luther. If the Leipzig disputation is the high-water mark of Karlstadt's Augustinianism, in the next months the Erasmian biblicist comes to the fore. In the disputation, as we have seen, Karlstadt was not primarily concerned to argue about papal authority and indeed evaded the issue as long as he was able.

But the angry aftermath, the literary warfare, had led Eck to attack Karlstadt as vehemently as Luther, and when he went to Rome to further Luther's impeachment, it was to breathe fire and slaughter against Karlstadt also.

In these months, then, Karlstadt put forward some of the clearest statements of 'sola Scriptura' of the first years of the Reformation. No doubt in this he echoes the past, the biblicism of some of the Nominalists, and of such 15th-century theologians as Gerson.[1] There is a new, if Erasmian, stress on the ability of the laity to read and interpret Scripture and an uncompromising assertion of the sufficiency of Scripture. In August 1520 he produced his last really learned work, 'De Canonicis Scripturis Libellus'. He had worked on this for some time and it had been subject matter of his lectures. Relations with Luther had been a little strained after Leipzig and there are indications that Karlstadt was far from well. But it seems also that there were rival groups among the students, and that Karlstadt's decision to lecture on the Epistle of James had some reference to disparaging remarks which Luther had made publicly as early as his 'Resolutions' of 1519.[2]

Karlstadt seems to have believed some student gossip that Luther had declared in one of his lectures that James was written by Jerome (underlying this may be some remark like 'this is a right Jerome-ish epistle'). And though Luther is not mentioned by name, the Epistle of James and its implied detraction run like a King Charles's head through this work on the Canon. The first main point, this apart, is the assertion of the paramount authority of Holy Scripture, 'the majesty of Holy Writ', the sharp rejection of St Augustine's well-known tribute to the authority of the Church, the assertion that Scripture is superior to the Fathers and to the Councils of the Church. 'By Holy Scriptures we judge all things, she is queen and mistress judging all, but judged by none.' Those who suck in the traditions of men imbibe poison. Just as the bee draws honey and the spider poison (!) from a flower so the faithful simple heart draws nourishment from Scripture while the legalist finds no sustenance. Holy Scripture is sufficient because 'Christ lives, breathes, speaks and expounds beneath all the letters in all things

[1] Tavard, op. cit., pp. 52ff., 118ff.   [2] Barge, i, 186ff.; Jäger, pp. 92–101

(*omnibus in commune sub literis vivit*). Would that all [the reminiscence of Erasmus is plain] to whom the Lord God gives the gift of interpreting Scripture, would exercise it, whether layman or cleric, temporal or religious.' Second in importance in this tract are his discussions on the canonical authority of the various books. In regard to the Old Testament he follows St Jerome closely while about the New he keeps close to Erasmus. Though he is wooden and rigid, and not very perceptive, in comparison with Luther, he sometimes goes beyond his colleague, as in criticizing the Mosaic authorship of the Pentateuch. A German abridgement of this tract, 'What Books are Biblical' (if it came out in November 1520 and not a year later[1]), has even greater emphasis on the authority of Scripture, and the ability of the laity to handle it:

> If a peasant from his plough could show the Council by Scripture that his meaning was right and that of the Council of the Church was wrong, then the Council ought to yield to the peasant and give him honour on account of the Biblical writing.[2]

In June 1520 came the promulgation in Rome, in the Piazza Navona, of the bull against Martin Luther. But the publication of the excommunication in south Germany was entrusted to John Eck, who, with some irresponsibility, added to the proscription the names of his own personal enemies, including Karlstadt, Bernard Adelmann and Willibald Pirckheimer. Long before a copy reached Wittenberg, Karlstadt knew that his teaching was condemned, though it seems that his own name was not added until the bull was published in Meissen. By now, Karlstadt too had burned his boats, and though his own personal fate and his literary reaction to it are on another scale than Luther's, they have their own poignancy, and remind us of the still weighty personal impact of public condemnation by the Church. He wrote a leaflet of the conditions (*Bedingungen*) under which he would consent to be interviewed by Catholic authorities, stressing the lamentable warning of the fate of John Huss. Again he stresses the supreme authority of Scripture, and the incompetence in it of the higher clergy, in contrast with some of the

---

[1] Barge, i, 236 takes the later date. [2] Barge, i, 237

laity – 'A craftsman may know more of the Scripture nowadays than a bishop.'¹

A few days later (19 October 1520) he drew up a formal, solemn appeal from the papal condemnation to a General Council, and had the document attested by the notaries. (Thirty years later, in England, Thomas Cranmer was to do this very thing.) Karlstadt protests that he has been condemned without citation, that the Pope has obviously not read his books(!). Again he stresses the authority of Scripture, about which he will be instructed not only by the 'High-ups' (*grossen Hansen*) but, if need be, by a little child. 'The bull cries out, "Arise, O Lord, Arise Peter, Arise Paul" . . . but when it comes to handling our doctrines, Christ is asleep, Peter has gone on a journey, Paul is not at home, and the Church suffers great extremity.'²

This was followed by a long and undistinguished tract, 'Of the Papal Holiness', which compares unfavourably with Luther's great writings of this summer and autumn. In dedicating it to a Frankish knight, Karlstadt uses language reminiscent indeed of Luther's 'Appeal to the Christian Nobility'. The body of the work attempts to show that, far from being infallible, Popes may err and sin and commit wrongs. In this tract too there is evidence of Karlstadt's unfortunate habit of putting second things first, as when he devotes a whole section to the number of horses kept by Popes – a rather stupid wrangle. Like Luther also, at this time he speaks of the common priesthood of believers though his use of 'Pfaffen' with its slightly anticlerical overtone suggests a difference of emphasis (the beginning of the unfortunate role played by the conception of the 'Priesthood of Believers' in Protestant anticlericalism).

> All Christians are parsons, for they are built upon the one stone who makes them parsons [Pfaffen]. . . . So are they a spiritual house, a holy priesthood, to offer spiritual sacrifices. . . . From which it follows that faith in Christ makes all believers into priests or parsons, and that the parsons receive nothing new when they are consecrated, but are only chosen to the office and service.³

None the less, in these writings Karlstadt burned his boats, and

¹ Barge, i, 224; Jäger, pp. 142ff.   ² Barge, i, 229–30   ³ Barge, i, 234

made it clear that, unlike Adelmann and Spengler and Pirckheimer, he was not going to submit. What it means in such circumstances to defy public opinion, and how shocking it must have seemed to many that the chief authorities in the Church should be renounced, and what mortal perils might lie ahead – these are things which, curiously enough, are plainer to us at this time in Karlstadt's rambling prose than in Luther's magnificent German. Karlstadt was concerned at this time at the attitude of his kinsfolk. Like Sir Joseph Porter, K.C.B., whom generally speaking he did not very much resemble, he might cry, 'I snap my finger at a foeman's taunts', but in his case the corollary did not apply: 'And so do his sisters and his cousins and his aunts', for with one voice his relatives (largely female) seem to have recommended submission. The result was his 'Open Letter about the very highest virtue of resignation'.[1] In it he addresses 'my mother, brother, sisters, cousins, aunts, kinsfolk, and all dear friends in Christ'. The tract begins with his own tribulation – 'I might well say, Now, O God, my Creator, my Redeemer, my Refuge, my Body and my Life, leave me not. Depart not from me' – a situation which he naturally expresses in terms of the Psalms. He refers to the menaces of powerful enemies, of his adversary (Leo X) who is as a ravening lion. Yet where the choice is between physical death and obedience to God, and eternal death and disobedience, there is no doubt which he must choose.

> In this matter I know neither father nor mother, but I follow divine Scripture alone which cannot err or deceive me, even though at the same time I suffer shame, derision, poverty, misery. ... I know I must be resigned and that I must resign all creatures.[2] I know that I cannot be a disciple and follower of Christ unless I renounce father and mother, brother and sister and friends, my own nature, skin, and hair – all must be renounced, all within and all without me, for I know there is no higher virtue in heaven and earth than resignation [*Gelassenheit*].[3]

[1] 'Missive von der allerhöchsten Tugend Gelassenheit' (JRL); Barge, i, 225

[2] Luther also could use similar language about 'Gelassenheit', a word which lay deep in the Tauler-Staupitz vocabulary; see below, pp. 118–20

[3] Barge, i, 227–8 (JRL)

> Faith is enclosed in Holy Scripture as in a walled garden — how can I then contradict scripture to the destruction of my oath and faith?

In a reminiscence of 1 Cor. 13, he adds:

> For I know that there is no higher virtue in earth or heaven than Resignation. A man must renounce all his goods, honour, friends, body and soul. Though I burn in the flames and have not Resignation my suffering is become unprofitable — that is, if I do not love God and hold him in trust, faith and hope I am a tinkling cymbal — I must sink my will completely in the divine will and submerge my own will in all things.

This highly personal open letter is in no sense a theological exposition of the meaning of 'Gelassenheit'. To that, he was to return in a future treatise.

The months which for Martin Luther found their climax at the Diet of Worms went more calmly for his colleague. At the beginning of the year came disappointment, for the long awaited vacancy came at the Castle church, with the death of the Provost. But whatever little academic content there had originally been in Karlstadt's doctorate in law, his colleagues knew how ill fitted he was for the post. After a little half-hearted lobbying on the part of Luther, and open touting by Karlstadt himself, the post went to Justus Jonas, fully learned in law, leaving Spalatin and Melanchthon rather disgusted by Karlstadt's evident ambition.[1] But if it was a disappointment to an old hope, he could not have been greatly displeased not to have been still more entangled in the ecclesiastical chores of his cathedral offices, which on theological grounds were becoming more and more distasteful to him. During the next months he kept fairly quiet, and in some matters, as about communion in both kinds, he had an open mind.[2] He provided the usual academic theses on familiar themes, such as the authority of Scripture and the relation of grace to predestination. Only occasionally is there an interesting note — as in his insistence on the duty of fathers to read the Bible to their households.[3] Perhaps his unease

---

[1] Barge, i, 244   [2] Barge, i, 245

[3] Barge, i, 248, n. 22: 'Omnes quoque patresfamilias ad praedicandum familiaribus suis dei verbum sunt obnoxii, privato tamen officio.'

with his cathedral colleagues is reflected in the Erasmian criticisms he voiced at this time against the mechanical performance of divine service, and in his demand for a vernacular liturgy.[1]

Then in May came an unexpected diversion. Christian II of Denmark, engaged in stormy struggles with his own nobility, was planning a series of ecclesiastical reforms, and sent to Wittenberg for some gifted theological adviser. The Wittenberg authorities seem to have acted carelessly, and sent a young man, Martin Reinhard (one day to be among Karlstadt's most ardent followers). The Danish authorities were in turn surprised, irritated, amused and disgusted. The newcomer had no degree and had hastily to be matriculated. He was appointed to preach in St Nicholas' church in Copenhagen, but he had no Danish and his hearers no German, and his manners were eccentric, so that attendance at his services became a matter of amusement, and even of comic parody, among the citizens. In the end he was packed off home and told to return when he had a degree. In the days after the Diet of Worms the Wittenberg authorities had two problems, what to do with Martin Luther and Andrew Karlstadt. They seem to have toyed only momentarily with the thought that Luther might be better off in Denmark, but finally they allowed Karlstadt leave of absence to go. Wisely, his visit was more private than that of Reinhard, though it seems that he gave some lectures, and that his advice was sought by the king. He probably served on a legal commission, though it is impossible to say what, if any, direct influence he had on the measures which Christian II was preparing at reckless speed. One issue only, clerical marriage, suggests Karlstadt's influence, for there is evidence that this theme was exercising him at the moment. But the reformation in Denmark at this time misfired, and the middle of June, to everyone's astonishment, found Karlstadt back again at Wittenberg, where his presence could only be an embarrassment to the authorities. It seemed at first that he might be persuaded to return to Denmark, but he presented a list of financial demands – a sabbatical year without paying for a substitute, and the cost of

[1] Barge, i, 248. The more radical theses of 1 March, attacking private masses by implication, since he denies that prayers can benefit the dead, I should be inclined to put at a later date, possibly 1522.

carriage for his books, etc. – which were so steep that the Elector seems to have said that, after all, he had better stay.

The situation in Wittenberg that summer was delicate and explosive. It is easy to remember Luther's moral triumph at the Diet of Worms and to underestimate his opponent Aleander's tactical victory which followed in the Edict of Worms, passed by a rump Diet some days later. For it not only made Luther an outlaw, but put the Elector Frederick in a dangerous position, in which any disturbances and innovations might justify the armed intervention of his Catholic neighbours, well informed as they were about goings-on in his territory, through the watchful and hostile proximity of Duke George. And though this was primarily a question, 'What shall we do with Martin Luther?', there was also the question, '– and about Andrew Karlstadt?', since of all the Wittenberg theologians he had been named in the bull, *Exsurge, Domine*. These things may account for Karlstadt's comparative silence in the first half of 1521, and for the moderation, if not of his utterances, of his behaviour until October of that year. Of the explosiveness of the situation there could be no doubt. There had been the growing ferment in Germany over the last months, as Luther had rallied to his cause important elements in the nation, among the knights, the merchants and the common people. In his journeys Luther himself had been disquieted at the ominous signs of social and political unrest. Given the new situation arising from the Edict of Worms, there may have been wisdom as well as short-term expediency in hiding Luther in the castle of the Wartburg. And it paid dividends: some of his finest writings, and the immense German Bible derived from his Patmos. Yet he had disappeared from Wittenberg at a critical time, rather in the manner of the exit of Mark Antony in *Julius Caesar*, leaving the mob he had worked up to fever pitch:

Mischief, thou art afoot,
Take thou what course thou wilt.

For now a host of practical questions, arising from the religious and theological issues raised by Luther's acts and writings, could not longer be postponed.

Luther had sketched a programme of reform in his manifestoes of

1520. But it needs to be emphasized that until the autumn of 1521 there had been no revolutionary actions, save for the act of defiance in burning the papal bull. The laws and worship of the Church had not been contravened. These summer months were a lull while the dark clouds gathered before the storm burst. Then suddenly, things began to happen, one after another. We are certainly not to see Karlstadt in this as sole pioneer or leader. But he was one of the leaders; all his days, where trouble was concerned, he was a kind of catalytic agent. Certainly things began to move in Wittenberg almost from the very day of his return from Denmark, frustrated, with a programme in his pocket.

At first, his still seemed to be the Martinian programme, and who more fitted to initiate discussion of further change than Karlstadt as Dean of the Theological Faculty? What more fitting vehicle of such discussion than Disputations, the normal Friday weekly discussions and the more formal degree examinations, over which Karlstadt naturally presided? But it was perhaps an ominous pattern, 1518 over again: Luther away, and Karlstadt plunging into a spate of theses which pushed affairs along too rapidly. The other obvious leader was Philip Melanchthon, who had the confidence and hope of Luther, which was denied to Karlstadt. But this young layman in the Arts faculty was at some tactical disadvantage. Almost immediately the question would be raised, too, of where the *jus reformandi* lay, along lines which would subsequently have to be faced in city after city, territory after territory – Church, congregation, Prince, town council – the clergy, the godly magistrates, the Christian congregation, the mob!? From the spiritual authorities no lead in reform was to be expected: in these very months Albert of Mainz was toying with the idea of reviving indulgences, and was only prevented by some forthright spiritual blackmail on Luther's part, the threat of a deadly pamphlet which the Reformer wrote but did not in the end need to publish.[1] The appeal lay therefore to the godly Prince. But Frederick the Wise was at this time in a most delicate and dangerous position. Their territories intermingled, his kinsman Duke George was able to look over his shoulder, eagerly noting each threat to the public peace of the

[1] *WA, Br.* 2, Nos 442, 447, 448

Empire, each breach of the Edict of Worms. The dispossession of Duke Ulrich of Württemberg by his neighbours shows that the threat was not imaginary. At any rate, in critical weeks the Elector and his adviser Spalatin kept clear of Wittenberg and let their emissary on the spot, Christian Bayer, cope as best he could with their confused and often impracticable instructions.[1] The town council of little Wittenberg is not to be ignored. Wittenberg was no Augsburg or Zürich, but at least its magistracy was in touch with the Christian opinion of the town. The parish churches also count. Luther's attempt to get Melanchthon into a pulpit at this time, Karlstadt's intrusion into Luther's own church and pulpit, testify to the importance of the Christian congregation (the *Gemeinde*). There were also the two corporations: the university, and the collegiate church of All Saints. The university had been the citadel of the Martinian reformation, but its machinery was slow. With the exception of Jonas, Karlstadt and Amsdorf, the chapter of All Saints' were stubbornly against reform. Luther was to chafe and groan at this idolatrous 'Bethaven' which was to continue in their midst until at least 1524. Finally there were the angry young men, of town and gown, anticlericals, in whom turbulence and iconoclasticism were less a programme than 'doing what came naturally'.

The story of events in Wittenberg, October 1521 – March 1522, is intricate, and it is extremely difficult and delicate to assess Karlstadt's part in the ferment which has been aptly called 'The Wittenberg Movement'. In the famous controversy between Barge and Müller, both seem to have exaggerated the independence of Karlstadt in what happened.[2] To Barge, Karlstadt is the real leader, the pioneer of a lay Christian puritanism. For Müller, he is a second-rate 'awkward squad', an innovator indeed, though of undesirable changes which had to be corrected by Luther. What was good in Karlstadt's programmes derived from the Martinian programme. It seems best to outline the happenings of these fateful weeks, which are on the whole well documented, and to return to the question of Karlstadt's part in them.

[1] Irmgard Höss *Georg Spalatin 1484–1545* Weimar 1956, p. 216
[2] Barge, i, Chap. VII; Karl Müller *Luther und Karlstadt: Stücke aus ihrem gegenseitigen Verhältnis* Tübingen 1907, Chaps 1, 2

That summer, it can hardly be denied, Karlstadt raised in the university new and important questions which provoked Luther himself, first to further consideration, and then to writing and action over the new issues. Thus, on 20 June the first sighting shots were fired when Karlstadt produced seven theses for the weekly academic disputation, about marriage, not only of the secular clergy, but of widows and monks. Marriage of the clergy, however, had ceased to be a theoretical question in Germany. At the beginning of May, Bernhard of Feldkirchen married and Melanchthon wrote a pamphlet in his defence. Another priest, Jacob Seidler, got into more serious trouble when he wed, for he was arrested in Duke George's territory and thrown into prison. The authorities took no heed of a joint memorandum from Jonas, Melanchthon and Karlstadt, and Karlstadt could only write a letter of comfort to this too practical disciple as he languished in gaol, uncertain of his life.[1]

In these weeks Karlstadt turned out one or two rather trivial tracts. One, 'On receiving the Sign and Promise of the Holy Sacrament',[2] stressed the spiritual meaning of the sacrament much as he had done in his earlier writing about consecrated salt and holy water. In July he wrote on 'That the Kingdom of God suffers violence'[3] (Matt. 11:12), in which he characteristically quarrelled with all previous exegetes and ended up with his own crashing platitude, that those who enter the Kingdom must suffer. This was something that Luther had expounded from the time of the ninety-five theses in dozens of writings, but it seems that Karlstadt had his own audience, and we have evidence that some took him seriously, for Sebastian Helmann wrote about the tract to John Hess: 'The little book by Karlstadt will comfort you. For it behoves us who are of the Kingdom to enter heaven through tribulations.'[4] Karlstadt elaborated his theses on celibacy at a degree examination on 12 July. The theological arguments he hastily crammed into two writings:

---

[1] C. L. Manschreck *Melanchthon: The Quiet Reformer* New York 1958, p. 72. (Despite Manschreck, Seidler does not seem to have been executed; see Barge, i, 287, 399ff.)

[2] Barge, i, 281 [3] Barge, i, 293

[4] Nikolaus Müller, 'Die Wittenberger Bewegung', *ARG* 1908-9, pp. 176, 178

one in German, 'Instruction concerning Vows', and the other in Latin, 'Against celibacy in the clerical, widowed and monastic estates'. The first tract has a good deal of Erasmian invective against the abuses concerning vows to saints, and enough references to the all-embracing Will of God and to renunciation to show the persistence of Karlstadt's Augustinianism.[1]

More startling and ominous were his scriptural arguments, which included a long examination of Numbers 30, of 'flowers that bloom in the spring'-like irrelevance, and one or two eccentric bits of exegesis. Luther's first reaction to the suggestion that monks should marry was an amused 'Not me!' but he admitted that he had not thought the matter out. A day or so later, when he had got hold of some of the sheets of Karlstadt's tracts, he was more disturbed. With the eyes of a hostile world on Wittenberg, it was essential that reforms should have the plainest scriptural warrant: 'what is demanded of us is light, plainer than that of the sun and the stars.'[2] But if Karlstadt's exegetical moonshine was dangerous, it did at least goad Luther into making up his own mind. Luther now wrote some theses of his own about vows and sent them by Melanchthon to the Faculty of Theology, and these foreshadowed his own catastrophically influential tract, 'Concerning Vows', which he began to write in November 1521.

From celibacy Karlstadt turned to the Sacrament of the Altar, and to demand communion for the laity in both kinds. The restriction of the laity to the species of the bread had been a matter of ecclesiastical usage rather than divine law, had arisen from motives of reverence during the Middle Ages and was theologically defensible from the doctrine of concomitance, that the whole Christ is present under both species. But the restoration of the chalice had been the watchword of Hussitism, so that any restoration of the cup would provoke the charge of Bohemian heresy. This was a subject on which, six months before, Karlstadt had refused to pronounce in a letter to Spalatin.[3] It now became a matter in which he

---

[1] Barge, i, 265ff.
[2] *WA, Br.* 2, Nos 424 (1 August), 425 (3 August: p. 374, lines 20ff.): both to Melanchthon
[3] Barge, i, 245

was to prove more truculent than his colleagues. On 19 July, at a degree disputation, he asserted: 'Those are not Bohemians, but true Christians, who partake of the bread and wine. Whoso receives only the bread, in my opinion, commits sin.'[1]

There was here a deep difference, though it was not yet apparent, between Karlstadt and Luther. Luther, in his manifestoes of 1520, had declared that the withholding of the wine was wicked and despotic and had demanded communion in both kinds. But that it was a matter of necessity, on pain of sin, he did not believe.[2] Fundamental to the common Martinian front was the view that the Mass had become an error and abuse, when its sacrifice had become a work. On this Karlstadt agreed with his colleagues, but while in these weeks his stress was on communion in both kinds, theirs was on the abuse of private Mass. Yet the difference was one of emphasis. It became widely known in Wittenberg that on 29 September Melanchthon and his students communicated in both kinds.[3]

Private Mass now headed the Martinian agenda. In a letter to Melanchthon, of 1 August, Luther asserted that he would never again celebrate in this way.[4] It is possible that this opinion was made known to the Augustinians. At any rate one of them, Gabriel Zwilling, as a preacher, a fervent spell-binder hailed by his admirers as 'Another Martin', now took the lead. Anticlerical violence was in the air. Thomas Müntzer in Zwickau had been in trouble some

[1] Barge, i, 290

[2] cf. 'The Babylonian Captivity': *Works of Martin Luther* ed. Henry Eyster Jacobs, 6 vols (Philadelphia 1915–), ii, 186ff.

[3] The statement of Manschreck (op. cit., p. 72) that Melanchthon celebrated is quite incredible. The evidence is the letter of Sebastian Helmann, of 8 October: 'P.M. cum omnibus suis discipulis in parrochia in die Michaelis sub utraque specie communicavit' (N. Müller, 'Die Wittenberger Bewegung', *ARG* 1908–9, p. 177). The Catholic prebends, in their report to the Elector later in the year, mentioned two other occasions (one of which, however, could possibly refer to the Melanchthon incident). At any rate, such celebrations took place in Wittenberg and were known to have taken place before Karlstadt's famous demonstration on 25 December (Barge, ii, 547). The letter of Melanchthon printed in N. Müller, op. cit., pp. 181–3 cannot be dated at this time.

[4] *WA, Br.* 2, No. 424, p. 372, line 73: 'Sed et ego amplius non faciam missam privatam in aeternum'.

time before for inciting violence against a priest. When the hermits of St Antony came on their usual begging round on 5–6 October, they were pelted with muck by the students and their ceremonies interrupted. But the sensation of that week-end was a sermon by Zwilling which was an all-out attack on the Mass.[1] It brought a hasty deputation from the university: Jonas, Melanchthon, Karlstadt, and Dolsch. When Frederick the Wise was informed, he appointed a committee of nine under the Vice-Rector to report to the chapter and the university.[2] Once again they interviewed Zwilling, but the effect was to provoke a filibustering sermon of several hours in which once again the preacher assailed Mass, the adoration and elevation of the Sacrament, and communion in one kind.

In the next few weeks there was a flurry of dispatches between Frederick and his Chancellor, Brück, and his emissary on the spot, the lawyer, Christian Bayer. On 13 October the Augustinians, under the leadership of Zwilling, ceased to celebrate Mass. Then, on 17 October there was an important university disputation. Karlstadt presided, and the debate turned on the Mass and the need for changes to be made. The theses and the course of the debate show that Karlstadt considered that communion in one kind was a worse abuse than private Masses themselves, and it was probably much more than the impartiality of a debating president which made him put both sides of the case, against Melanchthon and Jonas who also intervened. It seems that this disputation was of the kind which the Swiss reformers were to make into a regular technique, where an academic disputation turns into a forum for testing and leading public opinion. We have the evidence of two onlookers, which agree remarkably that at this time Karlstadt counselled caution and full discussion, before any changes should be made, and that it was young Melanchthon who pressed for immediate action. Against him, Karlstadt stressed the need for consulting the magistrates of Wittenberg and obtaining the concurrence of the whole Christian congregation of the town, lest offence be given to the little

---

[1] Ulscenius to Capito: 6 Oct. (N. Müller, op. cit., p. 174); G. Brück to the Elector: 8 Oct. (N. Müller, op. cit., p. 179)

[2] C.R. i, 459–60; N. Müller, op. cit., pp. 186–7

ones.¹ Melanchthon retorted: 'We have preached enough in this Capernaum', and asked what the point of consulting the magistrates would be – 'I know your excellency is in favour of reform in these things' – to which Karlstadt replied: 'Indeed, but without violence, and without giving occasion for calumny.'

It is important to bear this in mind. Six months later, these were to be the very arguments which Luther would use about Karlstadt. We need to credit him with an attempt at moderation when the crisis first appeared, against his own material interests, which would be involved with the cessation of his festal Masses at All Saints'.²

The report of the Commission to the Elector (20 October) reflected the debate, and came down heavily in favour of reform. It pleaded for immediate communion in both kinds, but was prepared to put up with private Masses for a time, urging the Elector to give a lead, and not to be worried by the calumnious cry, 'Bohemians!'³ The report thoroughly upset Frederick the Wise and his secretary Spalatin, in residence at Lochau. They replied firmly that reforms of this kind, far-reaching in their consequence, could not be initiated in a corner, for they concerned all Christendom and must therefore be left until the meeting of a Council. Spalatin added a note on the legal and financial complications involved in the abolition of Masses. In any case, the commission must be widened; all the chapter and the senior members of the university must be consulted. (The rest of the university wisely disclaimed competence, and the Catholic prebends sent their own hostile minority report.⁴)

At this time Melanchthon composed sixty-five theses on the subject of the Mass, beginning with Justification by Faith, attacking the Mass and ending with the Priesthood of believers (Th. 62: 'Omnes enim sacerdotes sumus').⁵ Luther now wrote a drastic tract (about which the only moderate thing was that it was written in Latin): 'Of the Abrogating Private Masses'. When this

---

¹ Albert Bürer to Rhenanus (N. Müller, op. cit., p. 192); Ulscenius to Capito (N. Müller, op. cit., p. 206)

² Barge, i, 315ff.   ³ N. Müller, op. cit., p. 199; C.R. i, 469

⁴ Barge, i, 326; Höss *Georg Spalatin*, pp. 212–13; N. Müller, op. cit., p. 210; C.R. i, 471

⁵ C.R. i, 478

tract, with the even more forthright 'Concerning Monastic Vows', reached Spalatin in November, between the Elector and the deep sea of Martin's wrath, he desperately tried to halt their publication, and was rewarded with Luther's violent anger.

Two tracts which Karlstadt composed at this time are in contrast to Luther's stormy but more powerful writings. The first reflects his attempt (he was, after all, Dean of the Faculty of Theology) to maintain a mediating position. 'On the Adoration and Reverence for the Signs of the New Testament' was dedicated to the great artist, Albert Dürer. In this he insists on the Real Presence, and on the reality of the signs of the New, as distinct from the Old Testament Covenant – perhaps an attempt to correct the preaching of Zwilling.[1]

More important was the second tract: 'On Both Kinds in the Holy Mass'. As in the theses, he develops the view that the two species have a different theological significance, for the wine symbolized the passion and death of the Lord, the bread, resurrection and eternal life. There are a good many anticlerical references, to parsons (*Pfaffen*) and to the rights of the laity. On the Eve of All Saints, Jonas, as Dean of the Castle church, seems to have held the limelight for a brief moment, attacked Masses and expressed the hope that they might be abolished. On 4 November came the hostile report of the Catholic prebends, which, however, admitted that there was a case for communion in both kinds, only mentioned Zwilling by name, and spoke respectfully of 'Dr Martinus'. It reports that on All Saints' Day, a chaplain (unnamed) had communicated the laity in both kinds, in the parish church.[2]

From Communion and Mass, back to Vows. In November the Wittenberg Augustinians began to leap over the wall. Of the forty inmates, fifteen had left by the end of the month, Zwilling the last as captain of the rebels. The Prior pathetically complained to the

---

[1] Barge, i, 328. Thus, the Catholic prebends report about Zwilling: 'Solle auch bmelter Gabriel von dem hochwirdigen sacrament, wie dasselb nit anzubeten, vnd es einem regenbogen vorgleicht' (Barge, ii, 546). Whereas Karlstadt in the pamphlet explicitly says: 'Brot vnd wein seind nit allein tzeychen, wie der Regenbog war' (Barge, i, 330, n.50).

[2] Barge, ii, App. 9, pp. 545ff.; N. Müller, op. cit., p. 218

Elector that he could not safely go abroad into the streets. There was evident restlessness among the Franciscans, and among the Augustinians in Erfurt. In Erfurt there were also riotous demonstrations, and these spread back to Wittenberg at the beginning of December. A mob of town and gown invaded the parish church, seized the Mass books and drove off the celebrants. The following day a mob of about forty nailed a manifesto to the door of the Franciscan church and threatened to storm it in a few hours. An alarmed town council hastily reinforced the watch, and an angry Elector demanded that the culprits be caught, and a full investigation made.[1] The rumpus gave rise to an agitated series of memoranda to and fro between the town council and the Elector, via Christian Bayer. The reforming members of the university commission seem to have been a little cowed by the vigorous refusal of the Elector to initiate reform, and no more was heard of Melanchthon's plea for immediate change. But Luther was angry with Spalatin. He made a tip-and-run raid into Wittenberg in the first week of December. Unless the news was deliberately kept back from him by his colleagues, which is unlikely, he must have heard all about the disturbances. So that it is no doubt a deliberate defiance when he wrote to Spalatin, 'I am thoroughly pleased with everything I see and hear.'[2]

In these days Karlstadt too was busy with a tract, 'On the Word of Paul: I beseech you, brethren, that you all speak the same thing' (1 Cor. 1). This writing, like his previous writing on the violence which the Kingdom suffers, is an honest attempt to bring contemporary events into direct judgement under Scripture, and seems to have specific reference to the memorandum of the Catholic prebends, who defended the withholding of the cup with the

---

[1] Barge, i, 242; N. Müller, op. cit., pp. 268–77

[2] *WA, Br.* 2, No. 443, p. 410, line 18: 'Omnia vehementer placent, que video & audio'. That Luther should at the same time speak (line 20) of writing a warning against sedition has reference to the ferment he had noted during his journeyings that year, but may also, despite the opinion of the Weimar editors, have some reference to Wittenberg too; see Luther *Ausgewählte Werke* ed. Borcherdt (Munich 1948–), iv, 9–20, 319–23: a useful modern edition with excellent notes.

authority of Councils and Doctors.¹ Karlstadt again explicitly asserts the supremacy of Scripture against such human judgements, and places the blame for any tension and schism on those who resist the truth.

Not for nothing did Karlstadt prefix to his pamphlet 'On Both Kinds . . .': 'Printed in the Christian City of Wittenberg'. For the town council, sensitive to the Christian people of Wittenberg, now becomes important. At some date in the middle of December a deputation of members of the congregations presented a petition to the council.² They seem to have asked for pardon for the rioters. More important were articles which they adumbrated concerning the reformation of the city. They demanded that the Gospel should be freely preached; that Mass be no longer compulsory; that vigils and brotherhoods be abolished; communion administered under both kinds; that drunkenness be restrained by closer oversight of inns and that disorderly houses be abolished. These foreshadow the mandate of the city in the following month. It must surely have been drawn up with the assistance of the theologians and we must suppose that at this time both Karlstadt and Melanchthon were in consultation with members of the council. The Elector felt strongly, however, that any innovation would be dangerous and impolitic, though there is evidence that he was not unsympathetic to the views of his theologians. Taking advantage of the obvious and inevitable failure of the university and the chapter to agree, he sent word by Christian Bayer, on 19 December, that there should be no change in the Mass, but that orderly disputation about these things should continue.

Karlstadt seems to have stopped celebrating or preaching for a while, but in a sermon on 22 December he suddenly announced that on the occasion of the next festal Mass for which he as archdeacon would be responsible, on the Feast of Circumcision (1 January), he would communicate the laity in both kinds, without vestments and with a shortened service. When this was reported to the Elector, he sent word to Christian Bayer that he should prevent him from doing any such thing while this grave matter was still

[1] Barge, i, 356; ii, 550
[2] Karl Müller *Luther und Karlstadt* p. 30

under discussion.[1] The effect on Karlstadt was not what was intended. He now announced that he would celebrate this evangelical Mass on Christmas Day instead. Before dismissing this as the flagrant disobedience which heralded a fanatical campaign, it is worth considering whether, had Luther been in Wittenberg during these weeks, he might not have done the same. For certainly Luther would have disobeyed his Prince if he felt the Gospel demanded it. In the last weeks, it had been Melanchthon who had suggested reform without tarrying for any, and Karlstadt could at least claim that the magistrates were on his side. Melanchthon had indeed gone as far as a layman could, by publicly taking the sacrament in both kinds at Michaelmas. The obvious next step was for one of the leading clergy to do publicly what had been done more than once privately in the last weeks, and after all, Karlstadt was the most eminent of the Doctors in the university who held high office in the chapter.

It was a Christmas of tension. Christmas Eve saw gangs of town and gown roaming the streets, and no doubt primed for the occasion. Some of them noisily invaded the parish church, put out the lights, menaced the priests, shouted ribald ditties like 'The Maid has lost her shoe', and went on to All Saints' where they howled down the ministrants with contumely.[2] The next day there must have been a tense, crowded congregation in All Saints', when Karlstadt, without vestments, strode past his glowering colleagues and began to preach. The sermon itself was a minor revolution, for it invited communicants to come even if they had not made confession, or if they had not fasted. He then proceeded to celebrate, with a minimum of manual acts, without the elevation, and omitting all references to oblation. The words of consecration he pronounced aloud and in German (this he later defended on the ground that this was the crucial part of the service, and that something like this was necessary to intimate to the people that the moment of communion was approaching). The rest of the service was in Latin. It is true that to offer communion in both kinds was not new: in the university, the parish church and the Augustinian monastery such services

[1] N. Müller, op. cit., pp. 320ff.
[2] Barge, i, 357; N. Müller, op. cit., p. 388

had already taken place. But that it should be done on a public feast day, in witting defiance of the Elector, was an act of revolutionary leadership and was recognized as such. But he had not done with innovations. On the Feast of Stephen he took Melanchthon and Jonas with him to the village of Sagrena and there was betrothed to a young girl of about 16, Anna von Mochau, daughter of a poor gentleman, and described as 'not very beautiful'.[1] Luther was pleased and said so, for he knew the girl and her family. The wedding took place later in January, and Karlstadt did what he could to make it a public occasion, defending his action in a memorandum to the Elector, laying out a great sum on the junketings.[2] But here again we may not exaggerate the novelty, for within a week or two Justus Jonas followed his example.

Immediately after Christmas three strangers arrived, well equipped to fish in troubled waters. They were friends, perhaps disciples, of Thomas Müntzer, who had become involved in disturbances in Zwickau after Müntzer's hasty departure earlier in the year. The leader, Nicholas Storch, a weaver, was impressive with his long beard and his sombrero – and hearers were taken by the learning of this unlettered craftsman who spoke so fervently of divine colloquies and visions. The second, Thomas Drechsel, may have been lettered, and was perhaps a kinsman of a Zwickau cleric. The third, who had been with Müntzer in Bohemia, Mark Thome or Stübner, a former pupil of Melanchthon, had acquired considerable dexterity in scriptural debate. They soon flustered Melanchthon, and Amsdorf too was impressed. Indeed, after getting rather the worse of the argument, Melanchthon wrote to Luther for

---

[1] On Karlstadt's celebration, see the report of the Catholic prebends (29 Dec.): N. Müller, op. cit., p. 386; Ulscenius to Capito (1 Jan.): ibid., p. 391. For the anonymous 'Zeitung aus Wittenberg' (6 Jan.), ibid., p. 406. On the betrothal and wedding, see ibid., pp. 387, 390, 391, 410–12. Justus Jonas to J. Lang: '*Carolostadius* uxorem duxit puellam nobilem sed pauperem' (G. Kawerau [ed.] *Der Briefwechsel des Justus Jonas* i, Halle 1884, reprint 1964, p. 83; No. 74).

[2] *WA, Br.* 2, No. 449, p. 423, line 45; Barge, i, 364; N. Müller, op. cit., pp. 400–2. It was the occasion of much gossip and ridicule from his enemies, and a scurrilous and blasphemous nuptial Mass was printed in which Karlstadt appears as a 'Fisher of Women' (there is a copy of this rare tract in JRL).

advice, and sent a report to Spalatin and the Elector. It looks as though the bother of the last weeks, culminating in this new upheaval, had been too much for Melanchthon, who tended to go to pieces in a crisis.[1] In these weeks neither he nor Justus Jonas did very well, and once again, in default of Martin Luther, the initiative fell, not improperly, to Karlstadt. We have only one enigmatic reference to the association of the prophets with him; they may have stayed with him and certainly talked with him. But the fact that he soon began to speak in much more extreme and radical terms, and that he began to lecture on Malachi, suggests that he found them congenial. He had very probably been in contact with Thomas Müntzer since the Leipzig disputation of 1519, for his Vicar at Orlamünde, Konrad Glitzsch, was a friend of that stormy radical.[2] It seems likely that Karlstadt followed up his evangelical Mass at the parish church with a similar service in the parish church on 1 January.

Early in the New Year came a fateful General Chapter of the Augustinians at Wittenberg, in which they not only (on Luther's advice) endorsed the apostasy of the greater part of the Wittenberg brethren, but defended their action in two theological documents 'pour encourager les autres'. This example, and Luther's important treatise 'On Monastic Vows', naturally encouraged similar actions which now took place elsewhere.[3]

On 24 January occurred an event which Barge rightly stressed as one of the most important events of the early Reformation. The council of Wittenberg now issued 'The Ordinance of the City of Wittenberg' – an evangelical mandate which was the prototype of what was to follow in many other European towns. It embodied the reforms already foreshadowed in December, and endorsed the changes already made. Communion was to be allowed in both kinds, and the laity might take the host, and put it into their mouths. The references to oblation were to be omitted, but the words of consecration were to be in German. The elevation would be discontinued. Pictures and images were to be removed, and the altars in the parish church, where, unlike All Saints', the city had

[1] C.R. i, 535ff.; WA, Br. 2, pp. 424, 443; see also the report of Spalatin: N. Müller, op. cit., pp. 392ff.
[2] Franz, V, 2, p. 554f.   [3] N. Müller, op. cit., pp. 402ff.

some jurisdiction, were to be reduced to three plain altars. Brotherhoods were to be abolished and their moneys put into a common chest – a powerful stroke this, for there were a score of such sodalities in the little town. The begging of the mendicant orders was now prohibited, and begging missions on behalf of new buildings forbidden on the ground that 'we have more than enough churches already'.[1]

Instructions were given about a Common Chest (literally, for the number of locks was prescribed) from which loans were to be made available to artisans, and grants to be made for poor students and for the relief of the poor. Oversight of public morals was to be kept, and disorderly houses abolished. About this, and about poor relief, the mandate was to have permanent importance. The city was grappling with the universal 16th-century problem of vagabondage and poor relief, and the concern for philanthropy was to be an important stress of the Reformation, running through its story like a gold thread among all too much venality.

Karl Müller pointed out, against Barge, who would have given all the credit for this document to Karlstadt, that most of this programme was in fact Luther's and had been put forward by him in many treatises, not only the manifestoes of 1520. That at this time the Elector's representative, Christian Bayer, was elected, certainly as councillor and perhaps as mayor, shows not only the concern of the town to keep in step with the university, but also that the godly magistrates did not intend to go against the godly prince.

None the less, it seems that the mandate represents some kind of tug-of-war behind the scenes, and that it may have been a result of combined effort by the university authorities – Jonas, Melanchthon and Karlstadt among them – and the city council. They endorsed the reformation which had taken place so far, and they carried Melanchthon (with some misgivings) with them. But there is also somewhat in the mandate which bespeaks Karlstadt rather than his colleagues, and notably the reference to the removal of pictures and images. About these things Karlstadt did not keep silent. He preached fiercely, and when the council foolishly named a day when images would be removed, there was inevitable violence and dis-

[1] Barge, i, 378ff. It was a point made by Karlstadt in his autumn theses.

order. Then Karlstadt put his preached arguments into his new pamphlet, one of the most influential of his writings, 'Of the putting away of Pictures, and that there should be no beggars among Christians'.¹

Karlstadt begins with the propositions that pictures in churches are against the divine command, 'Thou shalt not have strange gods'; that carved and painted pictures on altars are even more scandalous and devilish; that they should be removed. Images and pictures, he contends, have become so much the subject of abuse that in effect they are idolatrous; they come under the insistent and repeated invective of the prophets against such things, in addition to the plain commandment of God to Moses. He deals at length with the famous statement of Gregory the Great that pictures are the books of the layman, and asserts that nobody ever learned from pictures the way to heaven: 'For the Word of God is spiritual and of use only to faith;'² 'without the Power of God nobody is made holy';³ 'all the pictures on earth put together cannot give you one tiny sigh towards God.'⁴ He has to admit how deeply ingrained is reverence to such images, and how reluctant men are to lay hands on them, but since the spiritual authorities refuse to do so, the secular power must follow the example of the righteous kings of Israel: 'the highest authorities must ordain and perform this.'⁵ To all this there is a great and obvious objection and Karlstadt could not avoid it: are not these Old Testament prohibitions part of the Old Law? are they not superseded in Christ?⁶ He answers truculently that to say so is heresy; for 'Christ stood fast in the Will and content of the Old Law',⁷ which he came not to destroy but fulfil. 'I tell you that God has not less diligently and truly forbidden pictures, than murdering, robbing, adultery and the like.' Finally, Paul denounced the pagan images in his sermon on the Areopagus. Thus Moses and Paul agree.

There was a profound difference between Luther and Karlstadt in this matter, though it was not as clear to most people in the beginning of 1522 as it was when, in 1525, there appeared the

---

¹ 'Von abtuhung der Bylder, Und das keyn Betdler unther den Christen seyn soll' (Lietzmann *Kleine Texte* 1911, p. 74). Barge, i, 386. This too bore, as imprimatur: 'In the Christian City of Wittenberg'.

² p. 9 B i   ³ p. 10 B i   ⁴ p. 16 C ii   ⁵ p. 21 D i   ⁶ p. 21 D i   ⁷ p. 21 D ii

devastating first part of Luther's 'Against the Heavenly Prophets'. That this was a living issue three years later, however, does testify to the influence of Karlstadt and the prevalence of his point of view. We are not here concerned with Luther's doctrine.[1] Suffice it to say that for Luther the Old Testament had a quite other significance than for Karlstadt. For Luther the laws of Moses were for Israel what the common law, 'The Mirror of the Saxons', was for the Germans. It was useful, but it was only binding in so far as it represented fundamental divine or moral laws. By refusing to apply univocally what the Old Testament said about images and idolatry to Christian use of pictures and statues, Luther's Protestantism, as distinct from Karlstadt's (and Zwingli's) Puritanism, left room for a whole dimension of beauty to be used in the service of God.[2] Had his view prevailed, later Protestantism, not least in the 19th century, would have been spared the cult of what the Gryphon called Uglification and the 20th-century rash abandonment of Puritanism for a secularized religiosity immersed in sentimental and second-rate vulgarity. It was, moreover, for Luther an essential point, which he would drive home in the spring of 1522, that a reform of these things by law alone or by outward violence could achieve nothing. The image must first be removed from the hearts of men – and then the superstition would disappear, and the objects of abuse would fall into disuse.

This is to be remembered, however, on Karlstadt's side. The humanists, and not least More, Colet and Erasmus, had drastically criticized superstitions about images and the invocation of saints. The Reformers in England and Switzerland were to expose instances of sordid and flagrant scandal in connexion with particular shrines. There can be little doubt that for some, the saints themselves had come to obtrude into what should have been the realm of divine intercession and redemption. In the next years, it would appear that a great weight of opinion was nearer to Karlstadt than to Luther

[1] Hayo Gerdes *Luthers Streit mit den Schwärmern um das rechte Verständnis des Gesetzes Mose* Göttingen 1955, is a useful but not always perceptive study of this question.

[2] On the first part of 'Against the Heavenly Prophets', *LW* xl, 73ff. On the Eight Wittenberg Sermons, 1522, *LW* li, 66–97

about these things, and in city after city in Germany and Switzerland the godly magistrates were to remove images, while in the England of Edward VI and of Elizabeth I, as well as in Scotland and in France, reforming voices attacked these things and not only demanded but secured their removal. This indeed became one of the differentiae between the Lutheran and the Reformed traditions.

The second half of Karlstadt's tract deals with the responsibility of a Christian city for its poor. 'It is a sure sign that a city is but weakly Christian when you see beggars about the streets' – but magistrates must suppress sturdy beggars as surely as they are bound to care for the genuine needy. As for students who earn their living by begging, it would be better to send them home to their parents, to earn an honest trade, than for them to stay and become idle layabouts, fodder for 'illiterate, popish, lying parsons'.[1] Typically, Karlstadt wrests the teaching of Deut. 15 about a sabbatic year to apply to the present Church and demands that 'Abbots, Vicars, Provincials, Ministers' should release their servants and that monks and nuns be 'permitted to go free'. But money must be found for pensions for them, and, if need be, the vestments and vessels of the Church must be sold for this purpose. Despite the odd arguments and much of the wooden proof, there is a real concern for the poor, and if Deut. 15 is remote, it was right to put at the head of this section of the tract, Ps. 41: 'Blessed is he that considereth the poor and needy'. The Reformation did not mean the end of humanitarianism, but the rise, amid much venality and greed, of a newly directed philanthropy.[2]

At some time during these months Karlstadt issued a number of theses about church music and the Gregorian chant in particular.[3] They are, again, Puritan, and among the reformers Zwingli was soon to follow in Karlstadt's steps. But there were some things of which Erasmus had made sharp complaint, and there is little here that an Erasmian humanist might not have said – had he been tone-deaf! Beginning with an orthodox enough definition of prayer as 'the raising of the mind to God', he goes on to affirm that the Gregorian

[1] p. 25 D iiii
[2] see W. K. Jordan *Philanthropy in England 1480–1660* 3 vols, London 1959
[3] They are printed in Barge, i, 492f.

chant moves the mind still further from God – to say nothing of the mumbling, the shrieking, like geese, of the choristers, and the lascivious sounds of musical instruments – the wailing of organs – 'let us leave such things to theatrical performances or the palaces of princes. Paul said, you show forth the death of the Lord, not the death of Pyramus!'

Again, there is a little to be said on Karlstadt's side. Church music had become complex; it was not only the Reformers who felt the dangers of polyphonic singing which hid the message of the Word, for some Popes were exercised about this very thing. None the less, Luther's was the more excellent way, which made Protestantism safe for music and the fine arts. At any rate, the defection of a number of singing men from All Saints' early in 1522 may have something to do with Karlstadt's polemic.

Meanwhile, at this time events were happening elsewhere which increased the pressure in the opposite direction. The Reichsregiment met in Nuremberg on 20 January, and addressed itself to the Saxon princes and to the bishops in their dominions, reproaching them for the innovations of which they had heard – communion in both kinds, marriage of clergy, apostasy of monks – and demanding that the authorities take measures (including the appointment of preachers) to enforce law and order. Pending a national council, no innovations were to be sanctioned, and all acts of rebellion must be punished.

The spiritual authorities made a half-hearted attempt to do something. The bishop of Naumburg simply read the edict. The bishops of Meissen and Merseburg attempted a visitation, but it fizzled out in the face of stubborn hostility, and from lack of support from the secular arm. The archbishop of Mainz had attempted to set up indulgences again – but Luther's furious threat to lampoon him publicly in a way that he would never forget made him at this time only too ready to keep the peace with Luther through his secretary Capito. Spalatin and the Elector took warning from these things, but Spalatin at least seems to have seen that the demand for preaching gave the reformers a loophole.[1] In the next weeks, side by side

[1] Höss *Georg Spalatin* p. 219. There began at this time a withdrawal of Catholic students from the university big enough to alarm the Elector.

with the reduction of Masses, there was an increase in preaching in Wittenberg, Jonas expounding the Psalms each day and Karlstadt preaching twice on Fridays. Karlstadt was soon to get into great trouble with Luther for leaving the pulpit in All Saints' where he had a duty to be, and intruding into what was properly Luther's pulpit in the parish church where Karlstadt had no right at all. But Karlstadt had some excuse, for the authorities had refused to appoint Melanchthon at Luther's request – he was, after all, a young layman and there were clerics available – and the chapter of All Saints' had some say in the matter, for the jurisdiction in the parish church was the usual medley of town and chapter rights.

The proceedings of the Reichstag, about which Duke George forcefully informed his kinsman, were decisive for the Elector and his advisers. If he had felt innovation dangerous in the autumn, he knew that something drastic must now be done. Very sharp and definite instructions were given to Hugo von Einsiedel who had now replaced Bayer as the Electoral representative. They were to confer with the council and the university. Von Einsiedel wrote two stiff letters. The first, to Melanchthon, told him to silence Gabriel Zwilling (he had resumed his tempestuous preaching campaign at Eilenburg). The second was a very direct request to Karlstadt himself to stop preaching – or at least to moderate his utterances – 'otherwise people will think you are far more concerned for your own glory than for the fruit of the Word of God'.[1] Karlstadt's is an agitated reply with signs of his minority complex – 'I know I have enemies; what I say is bound to give offence to unbelievers. My preaching is grounded on Scripture, which is why it gives offence.' He dodges the question of his illegal intrusion into the parish church but affirms his right to preach in the Castle church and – with a genuine and sound point – 'I may be an unworthy one, but I am, after all, a Doctor of Divinity.'[2]

Meanwhile the council sought to explain apologetically why they had carried through the reformation, and on 12–13 February an important consultation took place at Eilenburg between the Electoral officials (the Elector and Spalatin rapidly moving court elsewhere, still keeping out of things) and the university authorities and

[1] N. Müller, op. cit., p. 432; C.R. i, 543–5   [2] N. Müller, op. cit., p. 436

those of the chapter. Hugo von Einsiedel must have put forcefully the danger in which the recent happenings had put the Elector and the city in the light of the Diet at Nuremberg. The authorities seem to have been completely cowed. Melanchthon said that his first wish and that of his friends had been to refrain from innovation after the happenings of Christmas, but that the tide of events was too strong and some concession must be made.[1] Karlstadt, in one of his typical pricked-bubble collapses, promised not to preach any more, and wished he might be punished if he did. Yet the result of this was a compromise, an order which neither restored the *status quo ante*, as the Elector demanded, nor endorsed the reforms of the 'Ordinance'. The consecration was to remain in German, and communion in both kinds was to be allowed, but the sacrament was to be administered so that communicants were not to take the bread themselves, the elevation would be retained as a 'sign', on which the congregation would be instructed. None would be forced to celebrate or communicate. To this the Elector replied on 17 February expressing his displeasure that a compromise should have been accepted and demanding that matters should be restored to their old use. In expressing his displeasure, he insisted that it be made clear that he himself was not responsible for these decisions – which might entail heavy consequences. By this time, not only Melanchthon but the Elector Frederick began to look to the prisoner in the Wartburg. Philip's letters had for some time had a 'Will ye no' come back again' sound, and Frederick sent messages to him through his representative in Eisenach, apologizing for not having done more for the good cause, but explaining some of the difficulties and dangers caused by the latest edict of the Reichstag.[2]

Luther replied in a short note, ironically congratulating his Prince that he had at last managed to get hold of a piece of the real Cross and not just another relic, but telling him not to be downhearted, and in the last line promising soon to be in Wittenberg. This really did scare Frederick, who sent a swift reply begging him to do no such thing, and provoked in return Luther's most famous

[1] *C.R.* i, 558–9
[2] the Mandate of 20 Jan. 1522, demanding that all religious innovations be suppressed or nullified.

THE WITTENBERG MOVEMENT 1521-2

and finest letter in which he, the strong in faith, offered protection to his Prince.[1] He returned to Wittenberg, quietly confident. Still bearded, dressed as a German knight, he provided two undergraduates, one of them John Kessler, with the finest journalistic scoop of the century,[2] and years later Kessler wrote the splendid tale of how two shy Swiss students from St Gall met an unknown knight, reading a Hebrew Bible, with one hand on his sword, how they whispered that it must be none other than the great Ulrich von Hutten, and how the stranger stood them a drink and paid for their dinners. All this in the Black Bear at Jena, where months later Luther and Karlstadt would meet in a far less pleasant scene.

At no time did Luther seem panicked or worried – probably he was the calmest person to have been in Wittenberg for months: the fruit of his *parrhesia* of faith was the magnificent series of sermons which he preached on eight days,[3] successively, beginning on 9 March 1522. He had shaved his beard and put away his lay dress, and now, deliberately dressed in his Augustinian habit (the whole difference between Karlstadt's conception of reform and his, is in the touch), he spoke plainly yet gently to his own people from his own pulpit. In this series of masterly addresses he went to the root of the differences between the Wittenberg Movement of the last months and true reformation by the Word of God. He preached on the primacy of love over zeal, concern for the weaker brother as more important than a fiery intolerance.

> Without love, faith is nothing ... and here, dear friends, have you not grievously failed? I see no signs of love among you ... let us beware lest Wittenberg become Capernaum.[4]

He saw, and said, that it was a root error to turn the evangelical 'may' into a legalistic 'must'. The difference between reformation and Puritanism lies in this distinction, and it shows itself in a difference of method and of timing. To rush in and abolish abuses by force, without preaching first, without explaining what was at

---

[1] *LW* xlviii, letters 386–93; *WA, Br.* 2, Nos. 448, 454
[2] *Johannes Kesslers Sabbata mit kleineren Schriften und Briefen* ed. E. Egli and R. Schoch, St Gall 1902, pp. 76ff.
[3] *LW* li (sermons), 69 ff.; *WA* 10, iii, 1–64   [4] *LW* li, 71

stake to those ignorant, unconvinced and unconverted, was to do injury to weak consciences, and to carry through a reformation only in outward things.

The effect of these sermons was decisive. We must add the psychological effect of Luther's presence, at this time almost serenely confident. The situation was restored, the social measures of the 'Ordinance' were to remain, but the innovations in regard to worship were to cease for the time being, and there was an end to violence. In all this, Luther never mentioned Karlstadt's name. We do not even know if there was a private interview between the two men. If there was one, it must have been painful and angry. For Karlstadt, it was a cruel disappointment and a bitter personal humiliation.

CHAPTER SEVEN

THE VICAR OF ORLAMÜNDE

In arguing too, the parson own'd his skill,
For e'en though vanquish'd, he could argue still;
While words of learned length, and thund'ring sound
Amazed the gazing rustics rang'd around.
    GOLDSMITH: *The Deserted Village*

'Heyo, Brer Tarrypin, whar you bin dis long-come-short?'
sez Brer Fox, sezee.
'Lounjoun' roun', Brer Fox, lounjun' roun' en suffer'n'.'
    —*Uncle Remus*

There may have been a personal rebuke from Court, and Karlstadt was forbidden to preach in the Parish Church. For a few days – like Mr Toad of Toad Hall whom he much resembled – he was cast down. Then he began to prepare an answer, fiery, retracting nothing, and indeed making more extreme statements than before, including the re-affirmation that to put an image on an altar was a worse crime than adultery, since it offended against the first of the Ten Commandments. He would not name Luther, but would direct his fire with ambivalent polemic against the Catholic publicist Dr Ochsenfart who was in the vicinity and who accompanied the bishop of Merseburg on a visitation. But it was obvious what was in the wind. Was the whole affair to be now re-opened, Luther's sermons to be but another round in an interminable wrangle? Luther made it quite clear that if Karlstadt published anything like what was threatened he would reply. The authorities had even clearer ideas of what should be done, and insisted that

Karlstadt's partly printed tract and the remaining MS. should be submitted to them. When they read it, they had no doubt that it must be prohibited, and the tract and MS. were accordingly confiscated.

Outward politenesses were still observed. The Faculty kept the proprieties when visitors came, or in correspondence with the world outside. Melanchthon might refer more testily than usual to 'ABC' and 'Mr Alphabet', but there was still some consideration for an awkward colleague. Karlstadt was put down to lecture on Zechariah and was soon writing to Thomas Müntzer that 'I lecture more about dreams and visions than anyone else on the Faculty'. Luther admitted that the lectures were good, but complained that their times were unpredictable.[1] Months later, the Elector was still complaining that his two married professors, Jonas and Karlstadt, were always gadding about doing everything but what they were paid to do.[2]

The fact was that Karlstadt had found escape in the simple life, and had bought a farm at Wörlitz. He wrote a not very tactful letter to Müntzer, whose fortunes were at their lowest ebb following the unhappy issue of his Prague adventure, inviting him to come and do some digging. He himself was seen wearing a grey peasant cloak, and a felt hat, answering to 'Neighbour Andrew', loading dung on a cart, and handing round beer in the local. He who was beginning to despise the sophistries, as they now appeared, of academic life was to be seen agape at any yokel with a dream to tell. We might feel that at this time Karlstadt was a very model of a modern intellectual, since these large gestures of solidarity with the workers were accompanied by a determination to hold on to his academic and ecclesiastical stipend.[3] In notes which have survived of his lectures on Zechariah there is an interesting *locus*: 'Jugi Adami agricola ego sum'. But if he found the collegiate church a burden on his conscience, his university responsibilities began to get on his

---

[1] *WA*, *Br.* 3, No. 566, Luther to Spalatin, 2 Jan. 1523: 'quod Carlstadii sit incerti temporis' (Barge, ii, 3, n.9).

[2] Frederick the Wise to Schurf, 7 Aug. 1523; Barge, ii, 14, n.27

[3] Though he often talked about it, he did not in fact resign until August 1524.

nerves. To move easily from hobnobbing with the rude mechanicals to the pomp and circumstance of a doctoral procession involved more psychological agility than Karlstadt possessed. He startled his students by addressing them as 'dear colleagues' – for though the priesthood of all believers was by now a familiar theme, the vice-chancellorship of all undergraduates lay within the mists of four centuries ahead. Then, at a promotion of Doctors, he announced he would promote no more, that two guilders were not enough to drug a conscience now that he realized that these fooleries were unscriptural, since Christ said: 'Call no man master'. One can imagine the public embarrassment of the occasion: Luther twice made to walk out, but in the end stayed and said nothing.[1]

It is just possible that Karlstadt the Puritan might have been won round, but not Karlstadt the Contemplative as well. We know from his earlier tract on 'Gelassenheit'[2] that he was addicted to mystical notions before the coming of the Zwickau prophets. After all, the former Thomist turned Augustinian was already strongly spiritualist, and we have then to reckon with the influence of Staupitz, Tauler and the *Theologia Germanica*. But it looks as though Karlstadt's head was turned by the Zwickau prophets who were in and about Wittenberg for the first half of 1522, Stübner staying with his old teacher Melanchthon and indulging in post-prandial contemplation in an armchair – including a startling vision of St John Chrysostom in hell. Storch himself hovered in the neighbourhood. There are interesting differences between Karlstadt's and Müntzer's mystical doctrines, but one suspects a fairly widespread jargon among radical groups which may well pre-exist the Reformation and represent an inchoate and incoherent lay movement more widespread than any yet traced.

Incorporated in his archdeaconry in the collegiate church there was the living of Orlamünde, a pleasant country town on the river Saale. The vicar, Konrad Glitzsch, was unpopular and neglectful. He had sold the trees for firewood, and let the vicarage fall to rack and ruin. On the other hand, Karlstadt, who began to visit the town more and more frequently, was always well and honourably received. He now conceived the idea of becoming his own vicar, and

[1] Barge, ii, 12, n.24   [2] see above, p. 85

the notion appears to have been rapturously received by the congregation, which was more than ready for a change. An appeal was made to Duke John, who was not unsympathetic to the idea, provided that Glitzsch withdrew of his own free will, and that all parties were satisfied. He seems to have thought that some kind of agreement to this effect between Karlstadt, Glitzsch and the town council would settle the matter. At this stage nobody raised or pressed the obvious legal point that this was a living of which the nomination and patronage belonged to the university and to the Castle church. Throughout 1523 and the first half of 1524 Karlstadt stayed in Orlamünde, more and more neglecting his academic duties, and keeping away from Wittenberg as much as possible. He soon won the ears and sympathy of the congregation at Orlamünde, and his influence spread to surrounding villages. His attempts at farming seem to have been bungled or at least unfortunate. The main thing was that he was far enough away from Wittenberg to produce his programme which had already once been thwarted. Rumours circulated – that he had given permission for bigamy, that he refused to baptize infants, that he was conducting a campaign for the removal of pictures and images. He seems to have radically simplified the Mass, a name which he now repudiated, and to have conducted the service in German. He also taught the people to sing psalms which he had himself translated from the Hebrew. Nor all this time was Karlstadt without friends and disciples. The most important of them was the lawyer, Dr Gerhard Westerburg, son of a patrician and leading citizen of Cologne, and an impressionable and not unimpressive layman. He began as an ardent disciple of Storch and then became a firm ally and friend of Karlstadt, marrying a sister of Mrs Karlstadt.[1]

Foiled by the censors at Wittenberg, Karlstadt seems to have been able to get theological tracts printed at Strasbourg and early in 1523 he produced a printed sermon, 'On the condition of Christian souls, on Abraham's Bosom and Purgatory'.[2] Like most of his contemporaries Karlstadt had no belief in or hope of salvation for

---

[1] Three sisters all married Reformers.

[2] 'vom Stand der Christglaubigen Seelen von Abrahams schoss vñ Fegfeür' (Freys-Barge, No. 95).

the damned, but among reformers it was a nice and rather vexed theological problem whether souls slept after death until Judgement, or whether they went, as in traditional belief, to purgatory. Karlstadt's tract is not a very impressive contribution to the debate but he quotes Wessel Gansfort, who had given, as Tauler had also done, a spiritualized interpretation of the purging of the soul.[1] Westerburg seems to have felt it scandalous that the true, prophetic Reformation should be smothered in the valley of the Saale, and that this babble of green pastures and Arthur's bosom should be lost to posterity. He made for Cologne and there circulated a tract of his own on 'Purgatory and the state of different souls according to a Christian interpretation', which, though apparently only an abridgement of Karlstadt, became a best-seller, winning for the delighted and only half embarrassed author the nickname 'Dr Purgatory'.[2]

Westerburg had written two versions, one in German and the other in Latin, and had dedicated it to the town council of Cologne. It was therefore aimed at the learned and administrative classes. He was joined by two other enthusiastic Karlstadtians: Nicholas Symmen from Weida, who called himself (did Karlstadt borrow the phrase?) 'the New Layman'. To him was added Martin Reinhard who had come some way since his undergraduate exploits in Denmark where he had preceded Karlstadt as preacher in 1521, and who shared with his friend and master exotic memories of what had promised so hopefully in those weeks in wonderful Copenhagen. For a moment, the dazzling prospect opened of the great city of Cologne won over to the Reformation and to the Karlstadt programme (which was perhaps not so very different from the pattern of numerous cities in the next years). Westerburg was able to provoke a public disputation, but the formidable Catholic opposition marshalled swiftly and at the last minute it was all called off. Forbidden access to the theologians, they turned to the lawyers, and

[1] On this, see the interesting material in G. Huntston Williams *The Radical Reformation* London 1962

[2] I agree with G. H. Williams that this would make more sense if Westerburg wrote first and if Karlstadt made large quotations from his kinsman, as he also quoted from Gansfort's *Farrago Rerum Theologicarum* (published in Wittenberg 1522). But it seems that Barge's evidence for an earlier date for Karlstadt's tract must stand.

Martin Reinhard succeeded in getting half-way through a course of lectures when they were denounced by theological spies. It was the end. Gerhard sprang into the stirrups, and so did Martin – Nicholas came later – and so they brought the sad news from Cologne to Orlamünde, to a Karlstadt perhaps neither depressed nor elated. The truth is that his parishioners had been disappointed when their new Vicar-cum-Rector had elected silence, and was usually to be seen striding alone, head down in gentle melancholy. The fruits of his meditation were two major tracts printed in Strasbourg. It was only when Westerburg and Reinhard returned to Jena, and subsidized a printer whom they had inveigled on Karlstadt's behalf that Karlstadt woke with a start and with the odd pamphlet, 'Why has Dr Karlstadt kept silence so long?'

Apart from a curious, and in the main very innocuous sermon, 'Whether a man may be saved without the intercession of the Virgin Mary', which seems to have been printed in Wittenberg at this time,[1] Karlstadt could obviously not hope for anything controversial to be passed by the Wittenberg authorities. This is perhaps why his two most considerable mystical treatises, 'Of the Manifoldness of the one simple Will of God' ('Von manigfeltigkeit des eynfeltigen eynigen willen gottes. was sundt sey') and 'What is meant by "sich gelassen" and what the word "Gelassenheit" means and how it is to be treated in Holy Scripture' ('Was gesagt ist: Sich gelassen. Und was das Wort gelassenheit bedeut, und was es in hayliger Schryfft begryffen')[2] were printed in Strasbourg. The influence, explicit and implicit, of the *Theologia Germanica* on these tracts is plain, though it is clearer in the second. For it is the explicit intention of the exposition of 'Gelassenheit' to instruct the layman, George Schenck of Schleusingen, in the doctrine which he has learned in the 'little book, *Theologia Germanica*'.[3] The stress on

[1] Freys-Barge, Nos. 106–9. It seems to have been a fairly popular tract, running into three editions in a year.

[2] Freys-Barge, Nos 102–3, 104–5. There are copies in JRL: Crawford Tracts 482, 483.

[3] see also later in the tract: 'If you are not satisfied with this answer, read "Theologia Germanica" ' (d ii). 'Do not be worried about these little words, "I", and "self-hood", and "I-ness", for you will find them many times in "Theologia Germanica" ' (d iv).

selfishness as the essence of sin, and on the viciousness of the self-regarding pronouns, 'I', 'me', 'mine' and the adjective 'my'; on our union with God as a subordination of our will to that of God, our need to forsake ourselves and love only the divine will – all these are taken directly and uncritically from the little book which Luther had unwittingly presented to the Radical Reformation. In the background too are the writings of Tauler.[1] Under the surface there is still a good deal of Augustine – one wonders whether hermeneutically Karlstadt ever moved beyond his own lectures on Augustine's *On the Spirit and the Letter*, and whether in the end his dualism of 'flesh and spirit' is not Augustinian (and Erasmian) rather than Pauline and Lutheran. And still deeper under the surface there is perhaps more of St Thomas and perhaps even Scotus than Karlstadt ever realized, in relation to a stress on knowing God, and on the divine will. These traits are more evident in the first tract, which has as its main theme the distinction within the one will of God (for Karlstadt, like St Thomas and Augustine, stops short of two wills in God): of the eternal, loving will of God revealed in Christ and in the prophets and the Scriptures, and the fateful, providential will which moves and sustains and carries all things, even the wicked. At times the argument is obscure – but later Karlstadt plausibly put the blame on the printer. Then, too, Karlstadt has a way of arguing with himself almost in the manner of a minstrel show with himself as Mr Interlocutor – for he keeps repeating imagined objections, and at one point seems to toy with the idea that all evil must be finally regarded as good since it is within a universe which God created good.

These lines of thought may have had an interesting consequence in Karlstadt's very last academic disputation at a time when relations between himself and his colleagues were at breaking point. It was a sensational debate for in it Karlstadt brought forward the text

[1] The interesting comparison by E. W. Gritsch ('Thomas Muentzer and the origins of Protestant spiritualism', *MQR* **37** July 1963, pp. 186–8) of the spirituality of Tauler and the *Theologia Germanica* and that of Müntzer is useful, though I wonder whether in fact most of his differences and distinctions can be pressed. One would need to take Karlstadt into consideration for a verdict on some of them.

John 8:44 – which asserts that the Devil sinned 'of his own' (*Eygenthum*) – and used it to attack the hitherto complete dominance of an Augustinian monism in the Faculty: a farewell hand-grenade indeed! It was a text which Hans Denck was to take over from Karlstadt in a defence of free will.[1] The argument and the account of this last debate Karlstadt published in a tract, 'Was God the cause of the Devil's Fall?',[2] and the argument developed in a printed sermon, 'Of Angels and Devils'.[3]

Karlstadt's second tract, on Resignation ('Gelassenheit')[4] is a useful and important discussion of a key conception in the doctrine

---

[1] The relation between Karlstadt and Denck has been misunderstood by recent writers, notably by Walter Fellmann in his admirable edition of Denck (*Schriften* part 2: *Religiöse Schriften* Gütersloh 1956, p. 27) and by G. H. Williams *Spiritual and Anabaptist Writers* p. 88, n.3. Both take Denck's writing 'Whether God is the cause of Evil' to be directed against Karlstadt on the grounds that Denck is referring to a situation caused by a sermon preached in Nuremberg (on Quinquagesima Sunday 1524) by the famous Peasant of Wöhrdt, Diepold Peringer of Ulm, whom Luther describes as 'a thorough Carlstadt' (*WA, Br.* 3, No. 854: 'Rusticum illum seditiosum totum Carlstadiensem nobis longe prefert'). Both editors affirm that this refers to Karlstadt's teaching about predestination. But it is clear that the reference is to Karlstadt's assertion that invocation of saints was idolatry and that this was the theme of Diepold's sermon. Denck, on the other hand, twice refers to the Devil as sinning 'of his own' and to John 8:44, and he shares Karlstadt's devotion to the *Theologia Germanica*. I do not doubt that there are in Hans Denck as many echoes of Karlstadt as Fellmann has shown that there are of Thomas Müntzer.

[2] Freys-Barge, No. 114   [3] Freys-Barge, No. 122

[4] To the meaning of 'Gelassenheit' in Karlstadt's writings, its use in the *Theologia Germanica* is, no doubt, the most important clue. But it may be that it is Karlstadt's writings, and his two pamphlets on the theme, which are the bridge between German mysticism and the Reformation radicals. On the one hand, there is its use in the writings of the Blessed Henry Suso; cf. Ray C. Petry (ed.) *Late Medieval Mysticism* (Library of Christian Classics 13, S.C.M. Press, London 1957) pp. 245–58. Professor Petry defines it as ' "resignation", "abandon", or "joyful endurance and patience in the face of adversity" '. In *The Little Book of Eternal Wisdom* trans. J. M. Clark (Faber, London 1953), Suso himself suggests a definition: 'love bodily discomfort, suffer evil willingly, desire contempt, renounce thy desires, and die to all thy lusts. That is the beginning of the school of Wisdom, which is to be read in the open and wounded book of my crucified body' (cited by Petry, op. cit., p.

of 'inward religion' in south Germany, for it was a word much used by Staupitz and his friends before it became a catchword of the radicals. Karlstadt begins by examining its use in common speech, and we may doubt whether in fact it was as well known in many villages as bread and cheese! But he distinguishes usefully between the negative '*verlassen*' of abandonment, purely passively, and '*gelassen*' which is an active word, of positive commitment. It is plain that for Karlstadt the portmanteau word 'Gelassenheit' conveys the whole path of our sanctification, the purging from fleshly, i.e. self-centred, desires, the learning to forsake our own will and cleave to the will of God, an abandonment so complete of ourself that there must be a 'Gelassenheit in Gelassenheit'; that is, we may not make a work, or virtue, of our surrender to God. 'Gelassenheit' comes to mean all that '*Anfechtung*-Faith' means to Luther.

At times Karlstadt approaches eloquence and this is perhaps the best of all his writings:

> There is a true marriage between God and the believing soul – we must renounce all things [*gelassen*] and cling to God, becoming flesh and blood with Christ, of two made one, so that we lift our eyes to God and as it were look out and see through his eyes the things which he loves and what he would have us do or not do. In this way we are to die to our own wills and live in the divine will, and become one Thing with God, as Christ and God are one will and remain unalterably so.

What it means to be 'gelassen' is described almost entirely in terms of the *Theologia Germanica*:

---

258). J. A. Bizet *Henri Suso et le déclin de la scholastique* (Paris 1946) discusses two stresses: *Gelassenheit* as a way of renunciation for the soul seeking union with God, and as the detachment of the soul from creatures. He quotes a definition from Nietzsche which is interesting: 'jene zarte Gelassenheit, welche sich "Gebet" nennt und eine beständige Bereitschaft für das Kommen Gottes ist'. Other references will be found in G. H. Williams *Spiritual and Anabaptist Writers*, where *Gelassenheit* is defined as 'resignation' or 'yieldedness' (p. 272), and where the virtue is found in Denck, in Grebel, and finally in Ulrich Stadler in a most un-Karlstadtian form: 'It is true abandon to yield and dispose oneself with goods and chattels in the service of the saints' (p. 284).

This word 'mine' means my honour and my dishonour, my use and my misuse, my desire, my dislike, my reward, my loss, my life, my death, my bitterness, happiness, outward and inward life, everything to which 'I' and my 'I-ness' can cling – this all must go out and fade away, if I am to be 'gelassen'.

But when this 'I' and 'I-ness' fall to the ground, and I am now of no account in the eyes of men, then I come to that true knowledge of the love of God, and then I am 'gelassen', a renounced, surrendered, committed man. I have washed my feet, taken off my clothes, and I sleep but my heart is awake (Song of Songs 5). I rejoice with my inward ear – am I then to rush round preaching and teaching? I ought rather to refrain from these things until divine obedience and brotherly love drive me to it, and Christian faithfulness.

It is difficult to give a comparative assessment of all this, and perhaps a vain thing to attempt it. We can see what it meant to Karlstadt at this time: he had not a bruised conscience, but he had a bruised personality, and no doubt found comfort in the thought that the things which had happened to him in his series of humiliations and failures had fallen out to the progress of 'Gelassenheit'.

Karlstadt's quietism is in contrast to the dangerous practical mysticism of Thomas Müntzer. In his weeks of contemplative retirement in Orlamünde he was in the very mood of 'stillness' which endangered the Methodist Revival in England in the 1730s, and his piety is that of the mediocre *Gelassenheit* of an Antoinette Bourignon rather than that of a St Teresa. To the questions which Reformation moral crisis had posed at a Dostoevski-like depth, Karlstadt came up with Mme Guyon-like solutions. Three hundred years before in this very land – and one wonders whether Karlstadt, Müntzer and even Luther knew of it – in Helfta and Mansfeld, Eisleben and Hackeborn the Gertrudes and the Mechthilds of the first spring of German 'inward religion' had explored this dimension at a deeper and more poignant level.[1] We must be fair, and add that there is a good deal of Scriptural exposition in the tract, and that the stress on the imitation of Christ is not as legalistic and as much

---

[1] see Wilhelm Preger *Geschichte der deutschen Mystik im Mittelalter* Leipzig 1874, vol. i; also Gertrude d'Helfta *Œuvres Spirituelles* i, ed. Hourlier, Sources Chrétiennes, Paris 1967.

under the sign of the law as Luther in his criticism (and later Lutheranism in its dismissal of the *Imitation of Christ* spirituality) supposed. Some of it can be paralleled in Bonhoeffer's *Cost of Discipleship* and his protest against 'cheap grace'.

With the setting up of a press at Jena, at his own free disposal, a fresh stream of pamphlets, edifying, earnest, dull, came from Karlstadt's pen: sermons, answers to theological questions, and more and more polemic.[1] No doubt the practical chores of farming had taken a deal of time, and he seems to have had no gift for it at all. And he had been plunged into his own kind of *Anfechtungen*. He could not but be aware of the reproach against him of Luther, that he had left his due and lawful vocation as a university professor and as a canon of the cathedral church, to do a lay work for which he was not qualified and to exercise a spiritual ministry which belonged to another. If his premonition of lay ministry and of worker-priesthood seems to us a genuine insight, however badly carried out, it was something which, even Karlstadt realized, needed in that decade some justification. The positive worth, therefore, of his tract 'Why has Dr Karlstadt kept silence so long?' was his discussion of the nature of 'a true, undeceivable calling'.

It is likely indeed that at this time he had lost all taste for his former way of life, and that he was as unwilling to take up his duties on the theological faculty as to perform the cathedral duties which were so entangled with Popery. He admits that 'outward confession of faith' – writing and speaking the truth – is dangerous and not without a trial of the spirit, so that 'it was more profitable for me to sit still and listen to the voice of the bridegroom'. Two other reasons for his silence are given (he does not mention the fact that he has not had a printing press): the fact that contemporary polemic is full of railing and abuse; and, with a characteristic self-accusation, 'I find it difficult to write without becoming abusively personal and it might scandalize my brother, and bring me into

[1] The most important of these tracts have been published by Erich Hertzsch (ed.) *Karlstadts Schriften* part i. The tract, 'Why has Andreas Karlstadt kept silence so long?' is on pp. 3–19. There is a valuable collection of Karlstadt tracts among the Crawford Tracts in JRL, and there are some in the British Museum.

judgement'. Another reason is the incompetence of some of his printers: 'not only have sentences been muddled but in some of my books whole columns have been disordered and the meaning and content of the same books destroyed.' The rest of the booklet is devoted to the theme of the need of an inward calling. Without this, the mere outward calling (such as he implies his own previous activity to have been) is a snare and a delusion. Paul and the Apostles had such an inward calling as gave them a sure pledge of God's Spirit. If we are to witness for Christ, the Spirit must 'prepare and foreordain, comfort and invite us and we must receive our commission from God through Christ'; 'I count none for a pastor, ecclesiastic or bishop, unless he has been appointed by God.'[1] It is the clerical office to preach the Word of God, but it is needful to wait for a sure inward call. He then suggests a possible objection that God is the author of all action, outward and inward, whether we are still or silent, and plunges into one of his favourite themes, the distinction between God's fateful will which works even in the ungodly and the will of his good pleasure which he gives to those who obey his will in the Spirit. Paul intends that those who have hands laid on them shall be seen to have such an inward call; and that others can recognize such a call he takes to be shown by the fact that even Pharaoh recognized it in Abraham and Joseph, and Nebuchadnezzar recognized it in Daniel. But as Acts 2 shows, the congregation must give themselves solemnly to prayer. We do not read that the Spirit called Paul or Barnabas in dreams and visions but that he spoke to them inwardly. Karlstadt's friends therefore misunderstand when they expect him to go on writing simply because he has an outward call; whereas he had rather to go into retreat and wait until God, whom none can withstand, should move him. There follows a passage which was a favourite radical theme, of the sevenfold purging of the soul like gold or silver, and a sevenfold anoint-

---

[1] It is interesting to compare this with Luther's tract, 'Concerning the ministry', which he wrote in view of the emergency situation in Bohemia in 1523 (*LW* xl, 7ff.), and in which he stresses the competence of the congregation to choose its pastor, but says little about the inward call. There are many indications that Karlstadt may have read this and is concerned to correct what seems to him its deficient emphasis.

ing of the Spirit. Karlstadt says that such a bearing of the cross was needful for him, for in himself he found only will and desire, and contempt and hate. It is the inward joy which counts.

> It is always less dangerous to stay in than go out – it is dangerous indeed to deal inwardly with the word of God, when the soul hears it freshly from God – it is much more dangerous to break out with it and press with it through the ranks of one's enemies. None the less I must let God's will be done and the unsurrenderedness ('Ungelassenheit') and love of my own soul will become the reproach of mine enemies, and a fiery purgatory. For we must all be conformed to Christ and follow in his steps, and so I ought to preach Christ not in a corner but in the midst of the congregation.

Luther, who at this time had written to the Bohemians that in emergency fathers of households must exercise the ministry of the Word, had stressed this ultimate priesthood of Christians. Karlstadt goes even further, in a passage which reminds us of Burns's picture of the Scottish father in 'The Cotter's Saturday Night':

> God's commandment stands to all fathers, that they should teach their children and servants. Every man is bound to preach God's Word in house or at table, morning or evening, in field or barn, whether at leisure or at work, and he is to study God's Word and treat of it to those who are round him, or who belong to him. This is a universal command addressed to all who understand God's Word and God has made them all through this commandment to be priests, all men to whom he has universally revealed it. For nobody is excluded, because God's commands pertain to all men, and touch the love and honour of God and his neighbour.

'Of the Sabbath, and of Commanded Holy-days' is the last of the mystical tracts, and an important premonition of Puritanism.[1] No doubt in many ways it is thoroughly medieval, but it is also the precursor of a whole literature, beginning with Martin Bucer, on the importance of Sabbath observance, which was to become one of the frames of 17th-century English Puritan piety.[2] The legalism of this

---

[1] Hertzsch, i, 23–47; Barge, ii, 53ff.; Jäger, pp. 393–406
[2] A. Lang *Puritanismus und Pietismus* 1941, pp. 25ff.

sabbatarianism was roughly but not unjustly handled by Luther in some forthright paragraphs in his 'Against the Heavenly Prophets' where he shows it to be of a piece with Karlstadt's iconoclasticism. Luther asserted that Karlstadt and his friends had grievously misunderstood the import of the Mosaic law: the Old Testament regulations, he maintained, are binding on Christians only in so far as they express natural law, and in regard to them full freedom must be left for Christian discretion and liberty.[1] It has to be admitted, however, that in the matter of images and the observance of Sunday, large parts of Protestantism were to take a view nearer to Karlstadt than to Luther, and in the British Isles, from Puritan times onward, Protestants have taken the Christian Sunday, if not the Sabbath, more legalistically than did Luther.

Let it be conceded that Karlstadt's tract is vulnerable. It is, as Jäger complained, 'negative, abstract, dualistic'.[2] There is a lop-sidedness about it, as Gerdes says, an exaggerated inwardness joined with a pietistic legalism.[3] The pamphlet never reconciles its inward doctrine of renunciation, which presupposes a devout, spiritually-minded audience, with the nagging moralism adopted towards the rough manners of the farmers, labourers and maidservants who must have made up much of Karlstadt's Orlamünde congregation. None the less, he seems aware of some of his difficulties, makes a strenuous attempt to leave room for Christian liberty, and despite all the mystical, cumbrous and almost comic jargon, there is evident a concern for a Christian Sunday as a day not only of rest and of public worship, but of family and personal devotion. In his clumsy, rather muddle-headed way, Karlstadt was a pioneer.

How far in this tract he was dominated by an Augustinian (perhaps an Erasmian and Platonic) dualism between letter and spirit may be debatable, but he certainly aims to keep the inward spiritual meaning of the Sabbath as the prime object of its institution. The origin of the Sabbath he finds in the Book of Genesis and the account of creation. (Throughout there is no reference at all to the day of resurrection, nor does he relate his theme of 'Sabbath rest' to the Epistle to the Hebrews.) God has given commandments to men for one end, that they may be made like him, conformed

[1] *LW* xl, 92, 98   [2] Jäger, p. 406   [3] H. Gerdes, op. cit., pp. 31ff.

to his Godhead ('gleichheit seiner Gottheit', 'Gottförmig').[1] Beside this prime purpose of the Sabbath there is our human duty towards our neighbour, the responsibility of the householder for his family and servants. There are many things about the Sabbath which are variable, but from its ultimate purpose we must not budge one hair's breadth. The scope of the Sabbath extends to angels as well as men; in short, to all 'the citizens of God's city'.[2] Above all, the Sabbath is to be a time of waiting upon God, that a man may come to understand 'with a precious, fervent and mighty understanding that it is God who makes us holy'. Sabbath rest is a kind of knife of spiritual circumcision.[3]

> Rest has waiting time (*Langweiligkeit*) and drives away the thick skin and obstacle from the heart.

It is above all a time of resignation ('Gelassenheit') when a man renounces his own ways and wills and lusts, and puts on the will of God. It is therefore a time of spiritual illumination, when

> an enlightened and illuminated spirit is lit with the light which lighteth every man, and which will lift up such a spirit above all the mountains of the earth, so that it has no delight in created things, but its joy exists only in God who leads him into the light of the most high sun, and who returns bearing this reflected light into God.[4]

Whereas for Luther the importance of Sunday worship is for public preaching of the Word and administration of the Sacraments, Karlstadt stresses the importance of Christian devotion, and anticipates later hymnology, as, for instance, the lovely Sunday hymn of Benjamin Schmolck (1672–1737):

> *Light of light, enlighten me,*
> *Now anew the day is dawning;*
> *Sun of grace, the shadows flee,*
> *Brighten Thou my Sabbath morning;*

---

[1] Hertzsch, i, 23   [2] Hertzsch, i, 26   [3] Hertzsch, i, 27

[4] This echoes the older, Dionysian tradition, and it is to be noted that similar passages may be found in Luther's early lectures on the Psalms (1513–15) and were not dropped entirely from the second course, 'Operationes in Psalmos', which he prepared in 1519–21.

With Thy joyous sunshine blest,
Happy is my day of rest....

Rapt awhile from earth away,
All my soul to Thee upspringing ...

Nought today my soul shall move,
Simply resting in Thy love.

(trans. Catherine Winkworth)

From the rapt mountain tops, Karlstadt descends abruptly to the plain, in an outspoken homily (c.5: 'Of the misuse of the Sabbath').[1] He discusses in recognizably modern terms the error and sin of those who use Sunday for joy riding, for family visiting, for fun and games, and of those who overwork their kitchen staff by demanding a slap-up 'Sunday Dinner'. An employer must take care for his servants, and not only of human beings but animals too, for if it be asked whether God takes care for oxen, Karlstadt answers that he cares also for elephants and buffaloes! But above all it is faith which teaches us what to do and what to leave undone: 'for it is a mighty wisdom which tastes God's bounties, and knows how God has freed us from Egyptian bondage.'[2] Above all, the collecting of debts and the railing at debtors from the pulpit is an abuse of Sabbath (there is a marginal note: 'mark this, you rich usurers').[3]

When Karlstadt comes to treat of man's command over the Sabbath (cc. 6–7), there is greater room for liberty than we might suppose. These outward customs may be broken not only in case of necessity but in case of usefulness. 'For all outward customs are instituted for the sake of man, and the believer is Lord over them, and has power to do or not to do such things as need demands, and as his spirit understands.'[4] Thus a man may gather simples if the herbs are for his neighbour's medicine, and when a servant sees the storm clouds roll up he is to get out the horses and tend to his master's hay and crops lest they be ruined. It is not fitting for ser-

---

[1] Hertzsch, i, 30   [2] Hertzsch, i, 31

[3] Hertzsch, i, 32. Usury was at this time a 'topic' in Saxony, not only for Luther but for preachers such as Strauss, Stein and Karlstadt.

[4] Hertzsch, i, 35

vants to take their ease in the village inn while their master is left hungry and thirsty. How far he is from intending to erect a Christian Torah, is seen in his un-Jewish distinction between great and less commandments – God has ordained some great and precious matters, but others are of less importance and we are not commanded to do all things alike according to the letter.[1] 'These things I write', says Karlstadt, 'that maids and servants may not use this book of mine as an excuse for carnal liberty.' And perhaps such a sentence was intended as much for the quieting of their employers, for, like a good deal of puritan and evangelical literature, it seems aimed at the householder-employer class.

Karlstadt returns to the inner man, who is concerned with eternal things, whereas the outward man is occupied in the temporal and transitory affairs, law and custom. Here the jargon crowds in again, from Tauler, the *Theologia Germanica*, and perhaps from Suso, though one suspects he drew upon a widespread radical jargon with technical terms and a 'plan of salvation' about which we have only intriguing hints. These 'states of the soul' are almost untranslatable, and are best indicated by capital letters:

> For the Waiting Time, and the Passing of Time is a spiritual circumcision, a preparation for the reception of the work of God. A man ought to stay still and suffer the whole time. For this cause the Sabbath was instituted for the sake of the Waiting Time and that a man should learn from this Passing of Time.
>
> Good were it for a man to bury his head in his hands on the Sabbath day, and thus bowed down to recognize with pain his sins and his unholiness, for so he would hasten more swiftly to him who alone makes pure and holy.

It was not unjustly that Luther ridiculed this. Most of the rough workaday peasants and artisans could have no time or inclination to do anything of the sort, and many of them, if they sat with their heads buried in their hands, would be doing it on the morning after the night before, and for very different reasons. It was a fair reproach to Karlstadt and his like that we ought not to

---

[1] Hertzsch, i, 36

> *strive to wind ourselves too high*
> *for sinful man beneath the sky.*

It is a proper comment that some kinds of Protestants have tried to turn wayfaring Christians into second-rate mystics, and that Luther's pattern of hymns, catechism, sermons, Bible is better. Or is this perhaps to underrate the spiritual capacities of some at least among Karlstadt's lay hearers? If there were laymen who could understand the *Theologia Germanica*, was not this rather crude spiritual theology an attempt, however clumsy, to do something for Christian laymen in the world, which has behind it the honourable background of the modern devotion in its German dress? The inward use of the Sabbath is to lead us to Resignation (*Gelassenheit*) and is a passive affair – 'God works in us in a passive way [*leidender*] that is, man has to receive the divine work.'

Returning to the workaday world, Karlstadt says that while in theory any day would do, there must be a common and widely held Sabbath for human convenience, though in case of need each householder has a duty to provide a Sabbath for his household.

> For every householder has greater authority in his home to arrange and order its worship than any Pope or Bishop, yea, than a whole congregation.[1]

It is interesting to see how closely his thought is linked here with another essential of Puritanism, the godly home ranged under the head of the household for devotion and prayer (and this would include such Catholic homes as those of Sir Thomas More and Conrad Peutinger).

There intervenes a violent little section, 'On the so-called Holy Days of saints and angels'. These saints' days are institutions of the devil or his son (a marginal note explains: 'The Pope is the Devil's first-born son'). For – and is this the first *Soli Deo gloria* of the Reformation? – 'the Sabbath exists for the sole glory of God', and it is a day which God makes holy. Just as the sign of wine outside an inn is a cheat and lie if there is in fact no wine within, so is the sign of a holy day which cannot in fact make holy. 'I will say nothing of

---

[1] The close bond between the family and the Sabbath has an affinity with Judaism.

the damage which a householder suffers when the realm of his authority is diminished by the tyranny of the Parsons – through these Parsons' holy days.'

A final section refers to the divine compassion and to the person of Christ. As God has commanded men to labour from the time of Adam, so has he also provided this day of rest out of 'his fatherly love and boundless compassion'.

> But remember that Rest demands the Quiet Time (Waiting Time) so that the rester shall have a Quiet Time when he rests in God, and rests in a godly manner.

It is a time of self-examination 'for to such a consideration of our own evil will are we brought by the Rest of Waiting Time or the Waiting Time of Rest'. It is therefore better to enter the house of sadness than the house of cheer – for the Sabbath is a day of Temptation (*Anfechtung*), of Sadness and Tribulation.

In the final paragraph he seeks a more cheerful note and says that we must not forget (though he seems to have done so for most of the treatise) that the Sabbath is a time of forgiveness of sins, when we come to reconciliation with God. But this must happen through the six spirits of God – and our advent into the seventh. He promises to write a whole tract about this, and it is a pity that apparently he never did this, for the themes of the seven spirits and the sevenfold purging and sprinkling haunt us in many tantalizing references in the writings of Karlstadt, Müntzer and their radical disciples in this decade, and make us suspect a whole underground piety of which we get many hints and which the leaders of the radicals take for granted. At the very last, in his closing prayer, he touches the note of joy.

> May God enlighten all shepherds of his poor flock that we all may come with him to a true knowledge of his divine holiness and that we may be led out of all tribulation, and come at last to his eternal joy. Amen.

Karlstadt's tract is certainly no masterpiece, but it is full of interest. It was no doubt too entangled in mystical jargon with little survival value, to have much influence. But it does contain some astonishing premonitions, even when we have made allowance for all that may have been borrowed from the late medieval underworld. One wonders how far its Old Testament legalism was part of contemporary piety in regard to rest and holy days, whether the astonishing one-sidedness of this tract, in its entire absence of reference to the Lord's Day and to resurrection is a defect of a western theology of the Cross which did in fact give insufficient room for Easter and its joys. For Karlstadt, as for so much later Sabbatarianism, Sunday is 'a day of Rest – and sadness'. Even the inward, spiritual meaning of it with all the emphasis on the divine will and sanctifying energies, and the passiveness of the human heart, is preoccupied with states of the soul, and set throughout in the doleful, minor key. In the end Karlstadt's Sabbath is under the sign of the Law rather than of the Gospel.

CHAPTER EIGHT

CONFRONTATION AND DIALOGUE

Thys varyaunce endurynge betwyxte them: dyuers forsoke M. Luther and leaned to Carolstadius syde, & manye malycyous letters fraudulētly forged, were conueyed frome the one to the other, with calumnious prechinges, ye and when they met together, more ready wyth fystes than with pacient arguments to trye their cause hadde they not bene sondered.

WILLIAM BARLOWE: *A dialoge describing the originall ground of these Lutheran faccions, and many of their abuses* (1553)

Academic gossip loses nothing in the telling, and the existence of the Jena Press, and the news of Karlstadt's innovations could not but alarm and anger the Wittenberg theologians. Luther was asked by Chancellor Brück[1] to give his own reasoned opinion on advice given by Karlstadt which apparently counselled bigamy as an allowable way (no doubt on Old Testament precedent) out of matrimonial difficulties. That same week he wrote again to him about the scandal of Karlstadt's Press at Jena. In deference to the Imperial Diet at Nuremberg, which demanded proper oversight of printing and publishing, the Wittenberg faculty had complied, and agreed to submit their writings to censorship. It seemed to Luther both dangerous and offensive that Karlstadt, of all people, should be the one exception.[2] In a frank letter to Spalatin, on 14 March, Luther expressed his own reaction to the 'monstra Carlstadii' – Karlstadt's 'enormities'.[3] Modern

[1] *WA, Br.* 3, No. 702, p. 231, line 3
[2] *WA, Br.* 3, No. 703, p. 233, lines 15-25
[3] *WA, Br.* 3, No. 720, p. 254, line 6

Protestants, who perhaps pray 'for' their good causes more timidly, or at any rate less exuberantly, than their 16th-century fathers, may find it difficult to understand how important for Luther was the notion of praying 'against' anything. For Luther this was a grim, final expedient, like the cane in a boys' school of other days. So he says to Spalatin that if the worst comes to the worst he will have to pray against Karlstadt, burned up as he is 'with ambition to make a name for himself and get glory'. He suggests that Karlstadt should now formally be recalled to his teaching and preaching duties.[1] If he will not come, then we must lay a formal charge before the Prince – 'and perhaps I will also admonish him by letters'.

Karlstadt came to Wittenberg on 2 April, and was treated kindly by old comrades – so much so that he agreed to return to his long neglected academic and preaching duties. But he felt different when he got back home, and found how horrified were his friends and disciples (and no doubt Mrs Karlstadt) at the thought of his leaving Orlamünde. He now found all kinds of reasons for delay (it was his Italian trip all over again). He had put the glebe and vineyard in order at his own expense. The bad weather had spoiled the hay. Fifty loads of dung had been put on fields from which so far there had been no return. He could not hand over to another incumbent until he had his money back.[2] To Duke John he wrote in another vein, about the great success of his preaching, which brought people from afar.

On 3 May, the congregations of Orlamünde and neighbouring townships wrote to Duke John, alarmed at the rumour that their pastor might be taken from them, saying (perhaps a little too generally) that every congregation had the right to a true shepherd, one who preached the Gospel, was of good life, and full of the Holy

---

[1] Luther had put the position, as he saw it, neatly in his letter to Brück (No. 703, p. 233, lines 18f.): 'docere paratus, ubi non vocatur, ubi vero vocatur, semper tacendi pertinax': 'always ready to teach where he is not called, but where he is called, always obstinately silent'.

[2] Barge (ii, 107, n. 32) thinks that Melanchthon's comment – 'quanquam sit theologus, tamen pecuniae minime contemptor' – is unfair; but the reference is to Karlstadt's general attitude, and it does seem fair. It may be that he was simply an unpractical muddler, for he never seems to have made money at Orlamünde or elsewhere.

Ghost. This time Duke John raised the undoubted rights of the university and the collegiate church in the patronage of Orlamünde, in the nomination and confirmation of the living. To these, belatedly, the town council now addressed itself asking that this might now be done, and speaking of Karlstadt's merits in glowing terms. These turned to the Elector, who replied on 19 May – they had rather asked for it – that a suitable parson would be appointed, with all those high qualifications which the congregations had so rightly stressed as being needful. There followed another formal summons to Karlstadt to return to Wittenberg, and this he foolishly ignored. He really had only himself to blame if trouble now followed.

These were anxious and troubled weeks for the Saxon authorities. There was the Elector Frederick, ageing and not very well, perhaps the most inclined to caution and to tolerance, anxious to be loyal to his darlings, his university and his Castle church, and highly respectful of all that Luther said, but perhaps himself a little puzzled, having been truly admonished a few months ago for too much interference and having been told by Luther that it was not the office of a ruler to meddle with preaching, which pertained to the spiritual kingdom. Down in the troubled area of Orlamünde, the Saale valley, and the Allstedt area, Duke John found things even more difficult. And there were also difficulties arising from the preaching of Johann Strauss in Eisenach and his own chaplain Dr Wolfgang Stein. The young Duke John Frederick was an ardent disciple of Luther – he wrote to his old teacher, Veit Warbeck, that he was regarded by some as a kind of Grand Inquisitor but that he honestly believed that the Saxon situation might explode at any time and that the 'Satan of Allstedt' (Müntzer) was completely possessed by the devil, while Karlstadt with one innovation after another was making way for Satan's supremacy in Orlamünde too.[1]

On 24 June, John Frederick accordingly wrote to Luther asking for his help, begging him to make a preaching tour of Thuringia, especially with an eye to what kind of preachers were to be found in the various centres, with a view to the deposition of those who were

[1] *WA*, Br. 3, p. 311 Beilage

teaching false and incendiary notions; in this way, false prophets might be put away and the good ones preserved.[1]

In the next weeks Müntzer's own troubles came to a climax, following his *Fürstenpredigt*, and he began to seek active allies. He sent such an appeal to Karlstadt, who was so horrified that he tore the letter in pieces – and then went to seek advice, putting the scraps side by side on a table. The result was that not only Karlstadt but the citizens of Orlamünde very definitely and quite firmly refused to have anything to do with the programme of violent, anticlerical war. Yet Karlstadt did not disavow his friend, and he wrote him a letter[2] urging him to discontinue the 'blasphemous' elevation of the Host.[3]

Luther himself was occupied in preaching and writing, expounding the errors of the false prophets and warning authorities of the dangers inherent in the situation (the Peasants' War broke out in August). In one sermon in Wittenberg he mentioned Orlamünde by name and got in reply a very nasty letter indeed, offensive and truculent, so unpleasant in fact that he assumed it had been dictated by Karlstadt, until he learned in Orlamünde at first hand that Karlstadt had created a group of sour and awkward anticlericals in his own image, and of a type which was to persist as a yellow streak in Protestant history.

The university now considered it had found a substitute for Karlstadt who would uphold the rights and dignity of the university and yet be an acceptable and diligent preacher and pastor. This was its own Rector, Kaspar Glatz, also a Doctor of Divinity. He was eager to have the job, though he was soon aware that he could do nothing at all while Karlstadt was about the place, and he was in

---

[1] *WA, Br.* 3, No. 754, p. 310, lines 44ff.

[2] Barge, ii, 113ff.; see also Karlstadt's apologia for his role in the Peasants' War, and his repudiation of Müntzer: 'Endschuldigung', Hertzsch, ii, p. 111

[3] Franz, II, No. 56, p. 415. There is a certain amount of heavy leg-pulling in the Müntzer–Karlstadt correspondence; on hearing that the Karlstadt baby was to be called Andrew, Müntzer seems to have asked, 'Why not Abraham?' – to which Karlstadt now solemnly asks, 'What are your reasons for such a statement?' It is likely that Müntzer was tilting at Karlstadt's superannuated Judaism.

the event to find himself wearied with the task of contradicting the Saints of Orlamünde.¹

Luther was not one to run away from this kind of challenge and he accepted the invitation of his Prince and departed on a preaching tour of the Saale area, Jena, Kahla, Neustadt and Orlamünde. He was greeted with abuse and physical threats from the crowds, and probably with some deliberate discourtesy on the part of some officials. But he had a full house when he preached in Jena, outlining the errors of the false teachers in their midst, but without naming names.²

Karlstadt, present at the back of the church with a felt hat pulled over his eyes, was deeply offended and sought to justify himself in a personal interview in the Black Bear at Jena which has been reported in one of the most dramatic of all Reformation documents.³ It is not a nice scene, but it came to a dramatic climax as the two angry, middle-aged men faced one another across the table, before a small crowd of gaping peasants and Electoral officials, and Luther tossed a golden guilder at his adversary who caught it, and held it up for all to see, before carefully putting it in his purse. It seems to have been an old German custom proclaiming the two men public

---

¹ Glatz was no Martin Luther either. On 18 Jan. 1525 he wrote a rather understandably venomous letter to Luther about Karlstadt, which includes the following: 'As you know, he pretends that he has a spirit with him who makes revelations – and he has a monk with him, a nasty knave, as chaplain. When he has people in to supper, this chaplain goes round secretly throwing sticks and stones about. Then Karlstadt says, "I know what's worrying the spirit, he is cross with me for sitting here and drinking – excuse me, I will see what he wants." And after a little, he comes back from talking with his spirit (that is, the daft monk) and tells one lie after another, how that Luther's teaching is not from God and we are to beware of it like the plague and suchlike obscenities' (*WA*, *Br.* 3, No. 818, pp. 424f.). This is mostly silly gossip, but the poltergeist stuff at least is interesting, when we remember that from quite different sources a poltergeist story was told in Basle after Karlstadt's death (see Barge, ii, Excursus VIII).

² Barge, ii, 123ff.

³ The so-called 'Acta Ienensia' by Martin Reinhard (printed in *WA* 15, No. 226, p. 323) appeared in 1524 as a pamphlet: 'Wes sich Doctor Andreas Bodenstein von Karlstadt mit Doctor Martino Luther beredet zu Jena, und wie sie wider einander zu schreiben sich entschlossen haben.'

enemies, and that Luther was acknowledging, indeed challenging Karlstadt to write against him openly and in public, as an open enemy. Luther proceeded to Orlamünde and to an interview with the council, at which he refused to allow Karlstadt to be present, as he did not recognize him as the lawful incumbent. There was a long wrangle, in which one of the peasant speakers declared that there was warrant for the removal of images in the words of Jesus in the gospels, 'Let my bride come to me naked, without a nightdress', at which Luther groaned and hid his head in his hands in mock despair. As Luther left the town, the bells pealed with joy, and Karlstadt addressed an excited and devoted congregation: 'We who have heard the living voice of God beside the river Saale do not need to be taught by any monkish scribe.'

By now the authorities – not Luther, who knew of it later – had decided that Karlstadt was an incorrigible trouble-maker in a country with more than enough trouble-makers on its hands. He had repeatedly ignored the summons of his friends and of his Prince, with procrastinating tactics which they knew only too well over too many years. He had neglected his own calling, and instead had implemented the very programme of innovations and reforms which had been repudiated in Wittenberg as untimely, inexpedient and theologically unjustified. Henceforth, in fact, the secular authorities were harder on Karlstadt than Luther was (in the Reformation generally this tended to be so, and Strasbourg is another example of the magistrates coming down more sharply than the preachers on the radicals). Karlstadt was to go into exile and at once, though his pregnant wife might stay until the child was safely delivered. This she did, but when she refused to have it baptized, the rough penalty followed and she was forced cruelly soon to drag after her husband. His exact route is uncertain though he seems to have tarried in Augsburg on the way to Basle.[1]

---

[1] Hermann Rinn (ed.) *Augusta 955–1955* (Augsburg 1955): Friedrich Hermann Schubert, 'Die Reformation in Augsburg', p. 292. In the next months he was to visit many cities, including Strasbourg, Heidelberg, Schweinfurt and his home town of Karlstadt, and to wander up and down Franconia, trying to avoid peasant disturbances which pushed him again and again to the borders of Saxony, which he might not enter.

Basle was the fateful place. Thither Gerhard Westerburg preceded his kinsman, with a batch of tracts to be published.[1] One of them, on Baptism, was confiscated. But the others appeared. They were the first sour, unripe fruits of the grim challenge and the golden guilder. In them Karlstadt, wittingly or no, conscientiously or unscrupulously, did his damnedest to hurt the cause of his old colleagues, did in fact far more damage than the pitifully cruel tract which Thomas Müntzer at this time was printing against Luther. In the first place, Karlstadt not unnaturally made the most of the fact that he had been driven out 'unheard and unconvinced', and he found considerable sympathy at least in Zürich and Strasbourg and with Zwingli, Capito and Bucer. In the second place he now revived all his old arguments against Luther, and especially the never-to-be-forgotten Wittenberg sermons of March 1522. This shows plainly in his tract, 'Of the two highest commandments, the Love of God and of our neighbour'.[2] It is a strange medley of piety and invective. The first part, about the love of God, is written in warm and contemplative style, though he succeeds in saying about love almost all that Luther had said about faith. 'God puts his greatest work in the ground of the soul in which ground he lives, teaches, rests and rules.' 'Love is no use without faith, so that a true work is that of a loving faith and a believing love.' 'Love is purer than any other work, and plunges the lover deeper in God with greater unity than any other work.' God implants a tiny spark in the soul which he nourishes to a flame, a mustard seed which grows into a great tree. Thus the first half of the tract is Taulerian 'inward religion'. We might expect the second half to be concerned with philanthropy, with the fact that the Christian is a man for others. Instead there is a virulent attack on the whole theme of Luther's Wittenberg sermons. God has not commanded us to love those who believe false teaching. They are not our neighbours, but swine before whom we are forbidden to cast our pearls. We are not to give them friendly words or eat with them in our houses. The mark of real love for our neighbour is our earnestness for the truth, which grows from our hatred of evil, on

[1] Freys-Barge, Nos. 124-52
[2] Hertzsch, i, 49ff. It had been written at Orlamünde but was not printed until 1524. Freys-Barge, No. 121

genuinely 'evangelical and Mosaic grounds'! Love the poor and needy by all means, but have nothing to do with those who are un-Christian, for Christ refused to pray for those who are of the world!

The other tract in which Karlstadt attacked Luther's Wittenberg teaching was much more effective, perhaps his best polemical writing, the little 'Shall we go slow and respect the consciences of the weak?'[1] Karlstadt begins with the Lutheran cry: 'The weak, the weak, the sick, the sick, not so fast – slowly, slowly does it!' He will have nothing to do with this false compassion. If you see a child playing with a sharp knife, you snatch it away as fast as you can, and so must we do with idols and pictures and all that is against the commandment of God. It is true that in the Acts of the Apostles Paul and Barnabas preached very short sermons before calling for action – but we are not bound (!) by their example. Are we to teach God's commandments slowly, linger about the King's business? wait for the mob? Is not all this fine talk about 'brotherly love' really an anti-Christian cover for something worse even than Popery? About the middle of the tract there are three lines, indented for emphasis, which were to have a long history in Puritanism and not least in Elizabethan England half a century thence:

> Each congregation be it great or small shall make up its own mind what is right and shall do it without tarrying for any [*und auff niemant warten*].

There is a good deal which Karlstadt has said many times; images are worse than adultery, which he must have said scores of times since 1521. If we know that images and Mass are idolatrous then our congregation, and the congregation in any city, is responsible for their removal, and the time for this is always 'Now!' – at the first opportunity. In short, to add 'In good time. Care for the weak, the

---

[1] Freys-Barge, No. 138: 'Ob man gemach faren, vnd des ergernüssen der schwachen verschonen soll, in sachen so gotis willen angehn.' It had only one edition, but it chimed so exactly with the mood of the Swiss Brethren, with Conrad Grebel and his friends who took the same attitude to Zwingli as Karlstadt and his friends to Luther. The tract is to be found in Hertzsch i, 74ff. and repays careful study.

weak, the sick, the sick!' is a plain attempt to gloss the divine commandments with the words of men. No wonder that the Anabaptists of Basle liked these pamphlets and went off with bundles on their shoulders.[1]

But it was not only the Anabaptists who listened to Karlstadt though they found his programme most congenial of all the Reformers. It was not simply warm humanity which made Zwingli and Oecolampadius, Capito and Bucer feel that there was something to be said on Karlstadt's side. The pattern of civic reformation was in some ways nearer to what Karlstadt wanted than to what Luther wanted, in that there was an attack on and removal of images, a radical simplification of the Eucharist, and a plan of public reformation by edict, with a regard for the will of the individual congregation and for the town council. Karlstadt's programme is not only a premonition of the Radical Reformation, but an ingredient in the emergence of the Reformed, as distinct from the Lutheran tradition.

[1] So concerned have modern historians been to disentangle the first Anabaptists, the Swiss Brethren, from contamination with Thomas Müntzer that Karlstadt's influence on them has been obscured. That he had more in common with them than had the social revolutionary is evident from the famous 'Open Letter' addressed by Grebel to Müntzer in September 1524: 'thou and Carlstadt are esteemed by us the purest proclaimers and preachers of the purest Word of God. . . . If thou or Carlstadt will not write sufficiently against infant baptism . . . I will try my hand . . . especially thee and Carlstadt, and ye do more than all the preachers of all nations. . . . We also desire to be informed if thou and Carlstadt are of one mind. . . . We commend this messenger to thee, who has also carried letters from us to our brother Carlstadt. . . .' G. H. Williams *Spiritual and Anabaptist Writers* pp. 78–82; Harold S. Bender *Conrad Grebel c. 1498–1526* Goshen, Indiana 1950, Ch. VII and Appendix IV

CHAPTER NINE

KARLSTADT'S EUCHARISTIC REBELLION

*After thys fell a dissention betwene M. Luther and
Carolstadius, aboute the Sacramente of the aultar.
For Carolstadius denyeth in it the bodelye presence
of Christe, affyrmynge that when he spake these words:
Hoc est corpus meū he meant them of his owne corporall
bodye and not of the Sacrament.*

WILLIAM BARLOWE: *A dialoge describing the originall
ground of these Lutheran faccions,
and many of their abuses* (1553)

When, at the great Eucharistic Colloquy at Marburg, Karlstadt was refused permission to attend, Justus Jonas upheld the decision on the ground that it was a debate between the Wittenberg team and the Swiss, and that Karlstadt was 'a traitor' and a 'deserter'. In the painting in the Wittenberg parish church (1547), in which Our Lord is shown giving communion to his disciples among which is Luther, Judas is shown as a small, negroid figure much as Karlstadt is said to have been. At any rate that is how he was regarded by his former comrades and colleagues: the lost leader who had made the great refusal.

The bitterness of this owes a good deal to Karlstadt's final blow, for it pierced between the joints of the Lutheran armour. Luther had publicly acknowledged the open feud between them and challenged Karlstadt to do his damnedest; this Karlstadt now did in the batch of eucharistic tracts.

There is badly needed a full consideration of the eucharistic controversy of the Reformation in the English tongue. We also need a careful monograph on Karlstadt's specific contribution to that great debate. For his writings are obscure and contradictory, while the theme itself abounds in difficulties. We have to recognize that the doctrine of the Sacrament of the Altar had been under heretical fire for centuries, and that all manner of spiritualizing alternatives had been put forward by theologians, while among the common people plain, commonsense blasphemies were current in a score of catchwords – as among the English Lollards, 'round robin', 'Jack in the box' had been applied to the sacred Host. So that it is not easy to say how far Karlstadt was thinking alone and ahead, and how far playing to an anti-sacramentarian gallery.

At this time the notion of a symbolic, spiritual Presence was in the air. The spiritualism of the Platonist revival, discernible, say, in Erasmus, had found expression in Holland in other writings, in those of Wessel Gansfort, and in the letter of Cornelius Hoen, which Hinne Rode brought, through Wittenberg, on the way to Switzerland, where Zwingli welcomed its teaching which chimed with his own interpretation. It does not seem likely that Karlstadt was either aware of this teaching or influenced by it.[1] Despite the spiritualist emphasis of his early writings on the sacraments – on holy water, on salt, and on the sign and promise in the Eucharist – he seems to have believed the Real Presence until 1523 and I find no proof, as Barge seems to find, that he had changed his views when he wrote his tract, 'Of the Priesthood and Sacrifice of Christ'.[2]

It is not likely, in fact, that Karlstadt attacked the doctrine of the Real Presence in print before his exile. Then he fired a salvo. Without prejudice to the strength or weakness of his arguments, let us give him credit for the fact that the first round in the great eucharistic debate should concentrate on Scripture and on exegesis.

About the Sacrifice of the Mass there was common agreement

---

[1] I think the arguments of Barge (ii, 150, n.8) still stand; see also O. Clemen *ZKG* **18**, 353ff. The eucharistic treatise of Gansfort was not included in his *Farrago Rerum Theologicarum*, which was published in Wittenberg, perhaps while Luther was at the Wartburg. An English translation of Hoen's letter, with an excellent introduction, is now available in H. A. Oberman *Forerunners of the Reformation*.

[2] It is one of the Jena tracts and is dated December 1523.

among all the Reformers, from Luther to the radicals. They abolished an offertory and mutilated the Canon in their liturgies. In their preaching they denounced both popular abuse and eucharistic theory which suggested that in any sense the Mass was a repetition of what had been offered once for all on Calvary. Whether they misunderstood, or understood very well, what late medieval theory and practice intended is beside our present point. As regards the point of Sacrifice, the Reformers had driven a wedge between the doctrine of Atonement on Calvary, and the sacramental application of that offering. They not only attacked erroneous teaching at this point, as they believed, but a teaching which necessarily magnified the importance of the office of priest, as one who was commissioned to offer such a sacrifice on behalf of the living and the dead.

What Karlstadt now did was to apply this theological technique to the other half of the Eucharist, to its meaning as Communion. He also would drive a wedge between the historical death of Christ, and the sacramental conveyance of the benefits of Christ by the eating and drinking bread and wine, which were thought to be the blood and flesh of Christ himself, truly present in his sacred humanity as well as his divinity. And Karlstadt too knew that he was not simply attacking erroneous doctrine, but a teaching which necessarily magnified the office of a priest, whose prayers were answered by the miracle of transubstantiation. And here Karlstadt was attacking not only the papists but his former friends and comrades.

The first tract, 'Whether it can be shown from holy scripture that Christ, with body, blood and soul is in the sacrament',[1] begins by attacking the word 'sacrament', applied to the Lord's Supper, as not grounded in Scripture, where this word hardly ever appears. There follows an exposition of 1 Cor. 10:16 in which Karlstadt denies that the 'cup of blessing' has anything to do with consecration – it is the knowledge and remembrance of the shed blood of Christ which brings forgiveness, and this is the blood which flowed from his body, not anything in a cup; and this is effectual

---

[1] Freys-Barge, Nos. 124–5: 'Ob man mit heyliger schrifft erweysen müge, das Christus mit leyb, blut vnd seele im Sacrament sey.' Barge, ii, 151ff. Copy in JRL 178

because of the inward will of Christ to suffer on our behalf. That and that alone is the blood of the New Testament – 'it is shameful to hear men say that Christ has brought his blood secretly into a chalice and brought us some benefit there, and that this is the blood of the New Testament.' The cup has been appointed for a remembrance, that each who drinks from it may think on the Lord. Karlstadt finds no sacramental meaning in the bread and wine: they do not convey grace, nor are they the signs of grace. They are not effectual signs, they are not even bare signs (*nuda signa*) for they have no connexion at all with the body and blood of Christ.[1]

The only readable and the most explosive of the tracts is the next, the 'Dialogue . . . of the abominable and idolatrous Misuse of the Blessed Sacrament of Jesus Christ'.[2] The dialogue form gives some sort of artificial respiration to Karlstadt's normally dull style (Bucer, another tedious writer, tried the same trick once or twice). The tract takes the form of a conversation between two priests, Gemser and Victus, and a layman, Petrus. There are double undertones – one to stress the importance of the layman, and the inspiration of the Holy Spirit: good 'Storchismus' stuff this, so that it is the layman who has the last word and makes the few not very funny anticlerical jokes. On the other hand Karlstadt is aware that this is going to get him into trouble and in the first lines there is a 'chip on the shoulder' acknowledgement that he will be thought simply to be seeking novelty.

Victus begins by admitting that he is troubled about talk of sacraments generally and is not amused when Gemser reels off traditional scholastic definitions. Victus demands some clear, biblical word and asserts that the Vulgate itself has many inaccuracies when compared with the Hebrew and the Greek. After some wrangling Gemser observes (what the reader has long since understood): 'Ah, I see you are worried about whether Christ in his humanity is present in the sacrament!' For, though the parsons may huff and puff and blow themselves up, the Host remains just as small and thick as it was before the consecration. Gemser mutters

[1] Barge (ii, 170, n.63) points this out.
[2] Hertzsch, ii, 5–49: 'Dialogus . . . von dem grewlichen vnnd abgöttischen missbrauch des hochwirdigsten sacraments Jesu Christi'.

about 'mystery' but Victus retorts: 'Now you are croaking like a raven – I demand that you explain to me . . . show me one word of Christ or one letter from the Bible which says that Christ is inside that tiny Host, and I will believe.' At this point, Gemser coughs, and whispers that there is a layman present, and suggests they converse in the sacred languages. For a page or so the dialogue goes into Greek and Latin, while Gemser mutters, 'We ought not to be talking about these things in front of laymen; before we know what's happened, peasants will be as good as priests.' They begin to discuss the Greek word *'touto'* in 'This is my body' when the layman politely intervenes, Gemser hissing, 'What did I say? This clown will be sure to examine all we are saying.' He then explains to Petrus the grammatical cases of the Greek language, whereupon Petrus puts forward the view – for he too has long found it incredible that bread could be the Body of Christ – that by 'this' (*touto*) Christ intended to point, not at the bread and wine, but to his own physical body. Gemser says sceptically, 'Who taught you that idea?', on which Petrus appeals to the Spirit – 'I hear his voice, but him I see not, nor do I know how he comes and goes.' 'Who is that?' 'Our Father in Heaven.' 'Would', sighs Gemser, 'that I could be taught in such a heavenly way.' To whom Petrus replies, 'But are not you too a poor man to whom God's living voice gives creaturely form?' Gemser says, 'I was once, but am now no longer', to which Petrus replies, 'If you have a desire and a longing for righteousness and a heart which burns for it, then for you too the Greek text can be a divine medium.' Gemser then asks the ground of this assurance which Petrus has (the argument at this point is curiously reminiscent of the conversation between Christian and Ignorance) and Petrus says that, though an outward witness is needed for the edification of the weak, 'I do not need it myself, for I have the inward witness of the Spirit as Christ promised.' Gemser asks why Petrus had not spoken out before, and gets the very Karlstadtian reply: 'The Spirit had not impelled me fast enough – if he had driven me more strongly I would have concealed less, and it would have been as a fire in my bones – we have to keep secret the times of the Spirit for his honour's sake, but now the time has come for plain speaking.'

Gemser now returns to the text and admits that in St Luke the word 'this' is written with a capital letter which seems to bear out the argument of Petrus that 'This is my body' has no connexion in Our Lord's discourse with the previous or subsequent words about eating and drinking but is a completely isolated utterance. Petrus insists that to eat the body of Christ is 'to have an inward taste of Christ's sufferings', to receive Christ is to know him heartily and passionately and this knowledge of Christ is what is essential, not any sacrament. We must feed on Christ spiritually, otherwise there is no more profit than if we fed on Christ's outward body. When Gemser asks what we must do in order to feed on Christ spiritually, Victus replies we must cast ourselves on him. He who has a passionate remembrance of Christ's body as given for him and wishes to demonstrate this outwardly in the congregation, he is worthy to receive it. But it is interesting that here, in a very 'reduced' doctrine of the Eucharist, Karlstadt insists that more is involved in 'remembrance' than bare intellectual remembering. He couples together the remembering and the showing forth of the Lord's death – *anamnesis* and *kerugma*. 'You can as little remember Christ without faith and a knowledge of Christ as a man can remember his father if he has never known him. And so this remembrance is like in nature and manner to our knowledge and our faith. If our knowledge of Christ is warm and clear, then is our remembrance impassioned and plain. If it is only hearsay, then the whole thing becomes trivial.'[1] He can even add: 'the remembrance [*Gedächtnis*] justifies us.' There are a few sneers at Wittenberg[2] (taken up in one of the later pamphlets, 'Against the old and new Popish Mass'):

[1] see also in the later tract, 'Of the anti-Christian misuse of the Bread and Cup of the Lord' (Bb): 'The remembrance of Christ grows out of the knowledge of Christ, which is not a raw, cold and idle remembrance, but a fresh, warm and active remembrance that gives and creates joy – and which counts as precious the body which is given for us and the blood of Christ shed for us – treasures it, gives thanks and makes us conformed to Christ and ashamed of all that is contrary to Christ.'

[2] 'Those whom men call Doctors wear fine round and pointed caps and hoods and go in long gowns, but are really like scarecrows made out of beggars' rags.'

The sacrament is an outward thing and can neither bless us nor hallow us nor make us just and free though we adored it a thousand times. We are not to eat like sows, but we are to meditate on his sufferings, and on the gravity of our sins, and on Christ's ineffable obedience and surpassing love.

Finally he returns to an old emphasis of his on the difference between Christ's death and his resurrection and the insistence that the Eucharist is concerned with Christ's death; how we shall celebrate the resurrection, we shall only know when Christ comes again, bringing another kind of cup.

In the much slighter pamphlet, 'Against the old and new Popish Mass'[1] Karlstadt inveighs against the elevation of the Host, and of the error of 'Dr Martin and the poor Bishop of Zwickau [Hausmann]' in keeping the name of 'Mass'. The only point of interest is the defence of a vernacular liturgy with which he begins the tract.

The '*touto*' exegesis was soon famous, and familiar as the most original and eccentric contribution of Karlstadt to the controversy and Luther had little difficulty in exposing it to ridicule in his 'Against the Heavenly Prophets'.[2] But Barge is right to protest that this bit of eccentricity is by no means all that Karlstadt had to say, and that he is not just echoing older arguments, but is putting forward ideas of his own, out of his own wrestling with Holy Scripture, which were to be taken up again and again in the next years, to become part of that rationale for a spiritual Presence and a view of the Eucharist which would find acceptance by many millions of Protestants in succeeding centuries.

Luther dealt with Karlstadt in a treatise in two parts: the first dealing with the question of 'images' and Karlstadt's doctrine of the Law, the second with the Sacrament; both parts entitled 'Against

[1] JRL 178; Freys-Barge, No. 131
[2] It soon dropped out of consideration in the controversy. That Lascells, one of Henry VIII's gentlemen in England, seems to have got hold of the idea much later might be because he had hit upon it for himself. Or he may have learned of it through the curiously well-informed pamphlet of William Barlow, *A dialoge describing the originall ground of these Lutheran faccions, and many of their abuses* (1531). See A. G. Dickens *Lollards and Protestants in the Diocese of York 1509–1558* Oxford 1959, p. 33f. I think it highly improbable that Lascells got the idea directly from Karlstadt.

the Heavenly Prophets'.[1] It is a fine piece of polemic, despite occasional lapses into abuse, written with a skill and humour which put it in the top, the Sydney Smith class, for humorous polemic. Its most telling argument is its massive delineation of the relation of Law and Liberty: the Law of Moses, said Luther, was for the Jews what the Saxon *Sachsenspiegel* is for Germans; it only pertains to Christians as it embodies that law of nature which is written in the hearts of all men. To take it as literally binding, as Karlstadt does, is to have no defence against the arguments of the revolutionaries like Müntzer who urge the literal application of the Old Testament commands to slay the ungodly. Here, if anywhere, is a rationale which defends a Protestant conception of Christian liberty as against the legalism of the Puritan view. And although Richard Hooker stands magnificently alongside Luther in these matters, it must be admitted that a great deal of the Protestant reform under Zwingli and Bullinger, Bucer and Calvin (and even, in the matter of images, Edward VI and Elizabeth I of England) accepted large parts of Karlstadt's programme. During the Peasants' War Karlstadt was in that rose-red city half as old as Europe, Rothenburg ob der Tauber.[2] He was no revolutionary, but he had kept dangerous company and when almost all his associates were taken and executed in the cruel aftermath of the revolt he was saved only by a grovelling appeal to Luther, who intervened, took him and his family into his house, and procured for him permission to stay in Saxony if he kept quiet.

[1] *WA* 18, 62ff. There are useful commentaries in Luther *Ausgewählte Werke* iv: 'Der kampf gegen Schwärm- und Rottengeister'. Eng. trans. *LW* xl, 73ff.

[2] In his apologia for his behaviour there are vivid glimpses of the Peasants' War. At one point he was marched in front of armed guards and made to read publicly a peasant manifesto. At another, his wife, making her way to his mother, was arrested and her goods rifled by anticlerical peasants who exclaimed, 'Ha! parson's goods, parson's goods!' To which she replied, 'No, these were earned with our own bitter toil.' Hertzsch, ii, 105–18: 'Endschuldigung D. Andres Carlstads des falschen namens der auffrür so yhm ist mit vnrecht auffgelegt.' Luther wrote a generous preface.

CHAPTER TEN

SHALLOWS AND MISERIES 1525-41

I love my fellow creatures – I do all the good I can –
Yet everybody says I'm such a disagreeable man!
And I can't think why!
—*Princess Ida*

But Karlstadt could not resist the temptation to intrigue; he would correspond with his old associates, and at last he found the conditions so intolerable that he revoked his recantations and left Kemberg, making for east Frisia. Here there was a tug-of-war going on as to whether the Reformation should be Lutheran or radical, and Karlstadt teamed up with a radical as explosive as himself, that Melchior Hoffman with whom he shared a debate against Bugenhagen in 1529.[1]

He made a half-hearted attempt to gatecrash the famous eucharistic conference at Marburg, but Jonas said that nobody wanted this 'goose or rather crow among the swans'. In 1530 he left Frisia when armed men came to seek him out, and went to Basle and then to Zürich where the leaders, Zwingli and Oecolampadius, were kind to him. They thought him mellowed by his sufferings and singularly unlike the person they had imagined from the polemic of Luther. He became deacon in the Spital and got a job as a proof-reader. Then Zwingli made him vicar of Alstatt where for once he was plunged into an intrigue not of his own devising. October saw the disaster

[1] see Peter Kawerau *Melchior Hoffman als religiöser Denker* Haarlem 1954, p. 7, and a letter cited there which describes what must be one of Karlstadt's last writings: 'Carolstadius et Melchior adversus disputationem et Pomerani argumenta librum edunt et prelo committent.'

of Cappel which came as a deep and numbing shock to all the leaders of Protestantism in the south. It was rumoured that Karlstadt was among the score or so of parsons who lay dead on the field. But with the death of Zwingli and of Oecolampadius a few weeks later a new régime succeeded, led by Bullinger in Zürich and Myconius in Basle.

In 1534 Karlstadt was called from Zürich to Basle, to the Chair in the theology of the Old Testament, and it seemed that at last he might really settle down to lecture and dispute at his old, real trade and be content. But within a short while there was a new intrigue, with Karlstadt at the heart of it. In Basle there were four authorities in tension: the local parochial clergy, the magistracy, the university, the people. Karlstadt threw himself with energy into a plan for university reform in company with the great humanist Amerbach. But soon this began to take the form of a movement directed by the university authorities, with Karlstadt in the van, and supported by the magistrates, against the powers and position of the clergy. The excuse was that it was necessary to control an arrogant clericalism on the part of the reforming clergy (there is evidence that this was an apprehension in other Swiss cities in these years). It came to a head with Karlstadt demanding that the clergy in the city must be amenable to academic discipline, and should be on the teaching staff of the university (the very association against which in Wittenberg he had been prime rebel). He demanded that all such public teachers should take at his hands the doctor's degree. This was a hit against Myconius who was a fine teacher but who lacked any impressive academic qualifications, and a reflection too upon old Simon Grynaeus who had been the right-hand man of Oecolampadius in the great days of the 1520s. Nor were matters mended when Karlstadt suggested that in the circumstances Myconius and Grynaeus might be given a degree with exemption from disputation. And now it is interesting and sad to find Myconius and Bullinger exchanging letters and saying about Karlstadt exactly what Luther and Melanchthon had said a decade ago: 'I wish I had known: I would rather have cut off my hand than let that devil in here.' So the man who in 1523 had denounced all academic degrees, attacked a learned ministry, poured contempt on the teaching church, now demanded that all clergy in a university city be theologians, and dangerously elevated the *ecclesia docens* above the ministry of the Word and Sacraments.[1] Suddenly at the end of 1541 the plague raged in the city of Basle. Karlstadt was infected early in December and on Christmas Eve at 11 a.m. he departed this life.

There were two ghost stories about Karlstadt, circulating very soon after his death. One, about his 'demon', is obviously false. The other, about 'poltergeist phenomena', is not so easily discredited and the evidence will be found in an appendix to Barge's biography.

Among the long line of witnesses against Karlstadt we must, it seems, include his wife. We must surely pity the man, but behind him we must see the young girl of sixteen, the roses dying from her cheeks as she strove to follow her unpredictable husband through all the changes and chances of his vulnerable life, eternally traipsing the long roads, in rain and snow, up hill and down dale, until when he died she was a helpless cripple, an old woman at forty, confined to bed with arthritis and the stone, writing a terrible lament to Luther whose heart turned over that a wife could so write about her Christian husband.

This finally may be said. We too easily treat Luther as the norm of the Reformation, both in his continuity and discontinuity with the medieval Church. But there were from the first other elements, other compositions of old and new. There was much in the late medieval context, the deep anticlericalism, the uneven distribution of suffering, the failure of religion to give to common men an intelligent initiative, the acid criticisms of humanists, the exotic whisperings of sectaries and mystics, which prepared men for something much more radical than Luther, which hailed indeed his manifestoes and his bold defiance, but was baffled and disappointed by the pace and scope of the practical reformation which followed. It has often been said that Luther lost popular elements of support in the time of the Peasants' War, which had been whole-heartedly on his side; it would perhaps be truer to say that these elements moved in the years 1524–5 towards a more congenial leadership, a more radical

[1] Paul Burckhardt *Das Tagebuch des Johannes Gast* Basle 1945, pp. 38ff., 61ff., 70ff.

and austere pattern of Reformation. It was here that Karlstadt was a real pioneer.

In Luther, Zwingli and Calvin we see minds of commanding stature at work. Even they are not to be isolated from the context of the age, so that their wrestling with Holy Scripture, their pondering theological problems, is like those intellectual inquiries of all men at all times and in all places, in undertones and overtones, in part a response to the pressures of history itself. In the Karlstadt pattern of Reformation we see something equally important, not less enthralling to a historian: how second-rate minds and 'awkward squads' may also have insights, penetrate new truth, rank therefore also among the pioneers, since the subtle pressures of human life have brought them too, close to the frontiers, and across into a no-man's-land between received tradition and new orthodoxies.

It is amazing how much of Puritanism is anticipated in Karlstadt's turgid and long-winded pamphlets, one or two of which, *Ob man gemach faren . . . soll* and his eucharistic dialogue, came home with forceful influence in the German and Swiss cities, and were echoed by such men as Ludwig Hätzer, Hans Denck, Conrad Grebel, and Sebastian Franck. Luther by no means understood the whole of Karlstadt: but some he did understand. It is easy to read the story, as Barge reads it, as though Karlstadt's hopeful and forward-looking lay Puritanism was ruthlessly ironed out only by force, in the rigid application of a Wittenberg party line. It is easy to point out that the lack of much that was thereby excised was to be a permanent defect of Lutheranism: how defective much of Protestantism has been in the kind of 'inward religion' to which Karlstadt's mystical theology corresponded: how badly Germany has suffered from not having the kind of Puritan freedoms which the English Free Churches have bred, with their emphasis on the power of the congregation and their large place for lay initiative. But it is part of the tragedy that these ideological encounters never happen in a vacuum, and that the whole situation was bedevilled by a personal equation. Moreover, much of Luther's criticism was deep and penetrating and is still cogent: he knew, as Karlstadt did not, what it means to begin with the bruised conscience which needs peace with God, and how immense is that Christian liberty which comes through living faith in Christ. His reading of the relation of law and Gospel, and of the meaning of law in the Christian life left room for liberties and beauties which might have perished: he made the Protestant Church safe for the music of John Sebastian Bach, and for that greatest son of the Saale valley, George Frederick Handel. Those of us who, with Martin Luther and Richard Hooker, are Protestant but not Puritan can still turn gratefully to Luther's profound rationale in seeking to combat the petrifying moralism into which Protestantism so dangerously falls, in defying that sectarianism which imperils the return to Christian unity.

Andrew Karlstadt might have been an honoured figure in the Lutheran reformation, might have held the place which in his default was filled by Bugenhagen. In his age, he might have been a great figure in the Swiss reformation, a pattern of life and doctrine nearer to his heart. He was not a buffoon or a scoundrel. But there was in him a dreadful element of what the Bible means by 'folly'. For religious men, the story of Andrew Karlstadt must be, in the main, a cautionary tale.

Part III
Thomas Müntzer
The Reformer as Rebel

CHAPTER ELEVEN

BEGINNINGS

In the church of St Catherine, Zwickau, there survives today one small fragment of its medieval glass, a figure of St Stephen, that angry young man of the Primitive Church, whose fiery diatribe against the elders of Zion provoked his violent death. That is perhaps how Thomas Müntzer, sometime preacher in that church, would have seen himself, though it is hardly the image which has prevailed in Protestant history. There he has been, for most of the time, Luther's 'arch-devil of Allstedt', while even among his former followers, in the radical and Anabaptist camps, the effect of the shock of Frankenhausen was for Müntzer's name to be whispered in undertones, a kind of Saxon Guy Fawkes.

Today the pendulum oscillates. At one end, the Mennonite historians, in their proper attempt to free the history of Anabaptist origins from the myth of Melanchthon and Bullinger, have underlined the fanaticism of Müntzer.[1] At the other end, the Marxist historians,[2] and notably E. A. Kosmincki and M. M. Smirin, have

[1] On the Protestant myth and its fallacies, see Heinold Fast's able study *Heinrich Bullinger und die Täufer* Weierhof (Pfalz) 1959; also H. S. Bender *Conrad Grebel*; and 'Thomas Müntzer und die Täufer' *Theol. Z.* 1952; Torsten Bergsten *Balthasar Hubmaier* Kassel 1961, Prolegomena, chap. 1; R. Friedmann, 'Thomas Müntzer's Relation to Anabaptism' *MQR* April 1957.

[2] On Marxist-inspired studies of Thomas Müntzer as a revolutionary, see Friedrich Engels *The Peasant War in Germany* (English translation) Moscow 1956; M. M. Smirin *Die Volksreformation des Thomas Münzer und der grosse Bauernkrieg* Berlin 1956; A. Meusel *Thomas Müntzer und seine Zeit* Berlin 1952; E. Bloch *Thomas Müntzer als Theologe der Revolution* Berlin 1961; G. Zschäbitz *Zum mitteldeutschen Wiedertäuferbewegung* 1958 (this last a useful and perceptive study).

depicted him as the real hero of the real 'People's Reformation' while Luther becomes the effete apostle of bourgeois reaction.

There has, however, been a more serious rehabilitation.[1] In one of his great luminous essays Karl Holl claimed for Müntzer more originality than for all the other radicals put together, and, though recent research has produced a great number of interesting radical figures of great interest, perhaps Holl's comment ought to stand. He fascinated another great historian, and Heinrich Böhmer's comments on Müntzer are always to be taken seriously as among the most weighty contributions of a very great scholar to 16th-century studies. Meanwhile, a number of careful monographs and essays mount up. If Annemarie Lohmann's analysis of Müntzer's life and development is an overrated work, and indeed to be received with much reserve, she marshals a great deal of evidence. More recently, essays by Franz Lau and Walther Elliger have added judgements of real perception to the interpretation of Müntzer, and the hardly accessible essays of Mehl on Müntzer's Liturgies and the studies by Hinrichs on Müntzer's political ideas have illuminated other important aspects. But while it is fairly clear that his social and political ideas are always theological and that he cannot be interpreted in Marxist terms – M. M. Smirin's study is at least a serious attempt by a Marxist to do justice to this fact – there is still much that is mysterious: intriguing questions which we cannot answer, and about which we shall only offer one or two guesses in the pages which follow.

Thomas Müntzer was born in Stolberg, in the Harz mountains of

---

[1] cf. Karl Holl *Gesammelte Aufsätze zur Kirchengeschichte* Tübingen 1927, No. 7, pp. 420–67: 'Luther und die Schwärmer'; H. Böhmer *Studien zu Thomas Müntzer* 1922; and *Gesammelte Aufsätze* 1927; Annemarie Lohmann *Zur geistigen Entwicklung Thomas Müntzers* (*Beiträge zur Kulturgeschichte d. Mittelalters und d. Renaissance* **47**) Leipzig/Berlin 1931; O. J. Mehl *Thomas Müntzers Deutsche Messen und Kirchenämter mit Singnoten und liturgischen Abhandlungen* Grimmen 1937; Carl Hinrichs *Luther und Müntzer* Berlin 1952; (ed.) *Thomas Müntzer: Politische Schriften* (*Hallische Monographien* **17**), Halle 1950; G. H. Williams (ed.) *Spiritual and Anabaptist Writers* (Library of Christian Classics **25**), London 1957; *The Radical Reformation* London 1962; W. Elliger *Thomas Müntzer* Berlin 1960

Saxony, about the year 1491.¹ His family may have moved about between Stolberg, Quedlinburg, Halberstadt and Halle, though we know almost nothing about them.² It seems certain that it was he who matriculated in 1507 in the university of Leipzig, and in 1512 in the quite new university of Frankfort on the Oder. At some time and place he was ordained priest (there is perhaps a medieval tension between the two seculars, Müntzer and Karlstadt, against the religious, whether orthodox Franciscans or the great Augustinian hermit, Luther). He took the higher degree of Baccalaureus Biblicus.³

His education seems to have bred in him a real zest for learning, he was a good Latinist, had some slight acquaintance with Greek, was an accomplished Hebraist, above all, a voracious reader. At some date unknown he was priested, and like many another bright young scholar had a number of short-term posts. He commenced usher at the Gymnasium at Aschersleben, a post which would have involved him in preaching at St Stephen's church.⁴ It is significant that as a very young man he seems to have been in trouble for organizing some kind of conspiracy against Bishop Ernest of Magdeburg⁵ (d. 1513). He became provost of a nunnery at Frohse in 1516.

---

[1] The attempt by Hermann Goebke ('Neue Forschungen über Thomas Müntzer', in *Harz Zeitschrift* Bad Harzburg 1957) to demonstrate that he was in fact much older (b. about 1466 and the same age as Erasmus!) and an Augustinian monk must be regarded as historically almost worthless, nor are his attempts to construct a family pedigree much more convincing. Goebke has a better essay, 'Thomas Müntzer familiengeschichtlich', in Brendler (ed.) *Die frühbürgerliche Revolution in Deutschland* Berlin 1961.

[2] We hear of a sister, of his mother (who left him some furniture and some sort of church income) and of his stepfather, with whom he quarrelled; see Franz, II, Nos 17, 22, 26, 28, and especially 14.

[3] Franz, p. 537; the evidence is clearly stated in an official greeting composed by Müntzer and addressed to the town authorities in Zwickau.

[4] Goebke, op. cit., p. 15

[5] The evidence is to be found in his confession under torture that 'Zu Aschersleben und Halla do habe er in der jugent, als er collabrator gewest, auch eyn verbuntnus gemacht. . . . Ist widder bischoven Ernsten hochloblicher gedechtnus gewest' (Franz, p. 548f.). Historians have questioned such an early date, and if 'Gegend' had been misread as 'jugent' the difficulty would be removed. But there is no evidence for this, and the explicit reference

He already had some reputation as a theologian, for a respectful letter from the Rector of the Martin School at Münster wrote asking his opinion of the scope and theology of indulgences, in the summer of 1517.[1] For a time, in 1519, he became assistant and supply preacher to a devoted Martinian, Franz Günther of Nordhausen, who as a preacher at Jüterborgk was engaged in battle against the local Franciscans.[2]

Superficially, Müntzer seemed just another Martinian, and though he did not belong to the charmed circle of 'Wittenberg men' it was on Luther's recommendation that he received his most promising appointment to date, that of supply preacher at Our Lady's church, Zwickau.[3]

This preachership was another of those late medieval foundations intended to supply the lack of service of absentee incumbents. The preacher at Zwickau at this time was the Erasmian humanist, Sylvius Egranus (1485–1535), who had himself taken a long leave to visit Erasmus and other scholars in the Rhineland and in south-west Germany. Zwickau itself was a flourishing, restless community, near the mining areas and with a strong weaver element, with perhaps sharper class distinctions than elsewhere. In Stephen Roth, its recorder, it possessed a citizen of renown, whose magnificent library became a prized civic inheritance. He too was an Erasmian and a patron of Egranus.

Müntzer's arrival was heralded on 28 April 1520, and he may have preached his first sermon on Ascension Day (17 May).[4]

---

to Bishop Ernest seems to suggest that the confession must be taken as it stands.

[1] Franz, II, No. 2, p. 347

[2] Franz, II, No. 7; at Easter 1519, Müntzer preached in Jüterborgk.

[3] That he did not lack friends or influence is suggested by a letter from a (possibly inebriated) friend, the Archdeacon of Elsterberg, ending, 'Farewell, my dear old sausage' (Franz, II, No. 10, p. 356).

[4] P. Wappler *Thomas Müntzer in Zwickau und die 'Zwickauer Propheten'* (Wissenschaftliche Beilage zu dem Jahresbericht des Realgymnasiums mit Realschule zu Zwickau, 1908; reprinted in 1966 as No. 182 of the *Schriften des Vereins für Reformationsgeschichte*); the town treasury reports: 'x. gr. eyne Boten gen weysenfels, dem Newen predinger Mgro. Thomas Montzer Zweene tage vorharret' (Wappler, op. cit., p. 20, note 71).

BEGINNINGS

That Müntzer was a fluent and powerful preacher we have ample evidence. We can endorse Hubert Kirchner's statement that he was 'wholly preacher, wholly theologian'.[1] It is a great pity that his writings are almost all of them polemical, for he may have preached much more solidly than we know of, about the common substance of Catholic Christianity as it was accepted in his day. (We are encouraged in this thought by the beauty of his liturgical writings, and his devotion to Tauler.) The surmise is strengthened by the discovery, among the papers of Stephen Roth in the Zwickau archives, of a fragment of a sermon, apparently notes made by Roth, and labelled 'Thomas'. This was a sermon preached on the Nativity of the Virgin Mary and follows the line of Bernardine devotion, with a strong biblical and Christological reference, and a reference to Mary as 'mediator between God and man'. Appended to it are some remarks by Müntzer about the difficulty of chastity for many people, and a protest against too early acceptance of boys into the monastic life.[2]

No doubt by reason of influential friends, Müntzer did not need to leave the city on the return of its preacher, but became preacher in the church of St Catherine. There is some plausibility in reading the story from here on, on Marxist lines, and the Soviet historian, M. M. Smirin, makes the most of it. It seems to be true that there were social disparities in Zwickau and tensions more marked than in other towns, that there were those who had prospered through trade, and that there was a poorly paid proletariat, of which the artisan weavers' guild was something of a focus. It is true that St Catherine's was their church and that Müntzer found in them a more sympathetic audience than in the very mixed assembly of the church he had left. It is true that Egranus was a humanist, who

[1] H. Kirchner *Johannes Sylvius Egranus* Berlin 1961, p. 56

[2] I am grateful to the Zwickau archivist, Dr Steinmüller, for copies of these. They have now been printed by H. Kirchner, 'Neue Müntzeriana' *ZKG* 1961 (see also Franz, pp. 517–18). I think one must be tentative about these fragments, which might be mislabelled fragments of sermons by Egranus. There is also an impressive Christological fragment among Müntzer's papers, formerly in Dresden, now in Moscow, of which the Dresden Hauptarchiv have facsimiles. This is an able piece of orthodox Christological argument (printed in Franz, III, 4 (c), pp. 520–2).

probably liked to do himself well: he went preaching in the even more prosperous Joachimsthal neighbourhood, and, though the reproach comes from his enemies, there may be truth in the pasquil which claimed that

> *You like best to sit among the fine ladies,*
> *They give you presents of wine,*
> *You have to be among the Top People.*[1]

Yet we must not over-simplify this picture of Egranus as 'Slave of the Thick Penny' and Müntzer as the eager prophet of class war. St Catherine's church was also the official *Schlosskirche*, and he was in contact officially with notables. Moreover, as a receipt recently discovered proves, he went from Our Lady's church to St Catherine's for double his former stipend as supply preacher – and probably to a much larger congregation.[2]

---

[1] Du sitzt auch gerne bey den schönen Frawen
   Den kanstu woll Die ohren krawenn
   Das sie Dir schencken ein kandell mitt wein
   Du wiltt nür bey den Grossen Hansen sein.
   —Seidemann *Thomas Münzer* Beilage 5, p. 111

[2] I am indebted to Dr Steinmüller for copies of the receipts for Müntzer's stipend; they are printed in Franz, p. 564.

CHAPTER TWELVE

ZWICKAU

Soon there was discord between the two preachers, who had noisy followers. Egranus' discourses seem to have been moralizing and Pelagian, and his learned arguments about the lost end of St Mark's Gospel may have seemed tame indeed against Müntzer's anticlerical fireworks. Certainly Müntzer now attacked Egranus from the pulpit and got in return a contemptuous note: 'I write in German [Müntzer was a thoroughly competent Latinist] because I see that your Spirit has no use for sound learning or for Holy Scripture' and he bitingly adds: 'No doubt you are instructed by the Spirit about whom you boast so much and whom as I hear, you have created out of Water.'[1]

There are extant, in Müntzer's handwriting, a series of theological propositions attributed to Egranus.[2] The German critics have made rather heavy weather over them, as to whether they are genuine, or just a caricature.

Obviously some are caricature: 'There has been nobody more learned than Egranus these forty years. He himself is Apostle No. 1 in Zwickau', and the final comment: 'These propositions I will dispute against the whole world, and especially against that Ass Thomas Müntzer.' But other propositions are exaggerations of

[1] Egranus to Müntzer, February 1521: Franz, II, No. 20, p. 367. Egranus' own complaint, 'That you bawl and bedevil me from the pulpit I must put up with . . .', is confirmed by the Zwickau annalist: 'Solche und ander unarth durch Magister Thoma und seine handhaber gesterckt, hat Magister Egranus uff der Canzel gestrafft mit vornunft und Fuglicher weise.'

[2] Franz, III, 3, pp. 513-15

authentic statements, such exaggeration being an all too common feature of contemporary polemic.

Judging from these propositions (which may have been written after Müntzer and Egranus had left Zwickau and when Egranus had found lodgement in Joachimsthal) the divergences between them were the Martinian theology, as it was at this time still obviously linked with the theology of the Cross. There seems to have been argument, perhaps misunderstanding, about Christology, and Egranus is accused of belittling the sufferings of Christ, and of playing down the necessity of Christians also partaking in the sufferings of temptation, and the agony of faith. There was division too about the salvation of all the elect, and the extent to which under the Old Covenant men were saved, and whether by grace or by works of the law, and hence about the whole meaning of the Old Testament for Christians. Egranus was accused too of overstressing the historical sense of Scripture, and of saying that the 7th Chapter of Romans had the Jews in mind, and therefore did not pertain to the Christian experience. Here are Martinian doctrines reversed, though there is a hint here and there of a stress on the present guidance of the Holy Spirit which was to become a hallmark of Müntzer's own theology. There is something, therefore, of special significance in Müntzer's claim that his opponent denied the power and leadership of the Spirit in the Church, after the time of the Apostles.

None the less, Müntzer was less and less able to keep a bitter anticlericalism from his sermons. In this too he was no different superficially from other Martinians: not only Luther himself but almost all his abler subordinates were becoming involved in controversy at this time, not least with the fiery dogmatists of the religious orders. The Franciscans had already become a target for Müntzer while assistant to Günther. Now the preachings of the Minorite, Tiburtius from Weissenfels, on visits to Zwickau, drew Müntzer's intense indignation and led to charges against him being brought to the attention of the local bishop of Naumburg. In this new crisis, Müntzer turned for comfort to Luther himself, 'my father in God' – 'lantern and emblem of the friends of God'.[1] He complains

[1] Franz, II, No. 13 (13 July 1520), pp. 357–61

of the rage of his enemies against him, 'for I spare nobody, religious, secular, priests and laity – all are to blame.' None the less, he claims: 'My Cross is not quite complete – for all the magistrates are on my side, and almost the whole city.' He gives examples of the shocking teaching of Tiburtius and his crew, matters which cut across the Martinian stress on 'inward religion', on predestination and the assurance of faith, and the distinction alleged by Catholic theologians between precepts and counsels of the gospel. 'With all my power I warned him . . . he threatens with his whole order to destroy me, and climbs his wagon like a champion raging with furious oaths.' It may be that Müntzer subscribed the letter with a phrase similar to that which appears in a receipt for his preacher's stipend that year: 'Thomas Müntzer qui pro veritate militat in mundo'.[1]

It may very well be that, in the months while Egranus was away, Müntzer had the sympathy of the magistracy and of much of the town. But a new situation had arisen with the return of Egranus, though we need not suppose that it was only the notoriety of Müntzer's goings-on which drew Egranus home. Certainly, a clash was inevitable, and Agricola in a friendly letter warned Müntzer not to become involved with Egranus, 'a man without a scrap of humanity'. At first sight, this seems strange, for John Eck had added the name of Egranus to those impeached in the bull against Luther, in this very summer. This may have simply been an example of the levity with which Eck implicated his own personal enemies, or it may be that Egranus' modernist, Erasmian preaching had caused a stir, and notably his attack on the received version of the story of St Anne who, as patroness of miners, was much in vogue in these mining areas, and his attack on the legend of her three marriages. At any rate, the matter was put right in a personal interview and Egranus' name erased by Eck. What is clear is that both Luther and Agricola at this time were suspicious of Egranus, whose theology cut across the Martinian doctrines at a time when the Tauler emphasis on 'inward religion' had not yet crystallized out from Luther's doctrines of Faith and of Justification. So that, apart from

[1] The receipt, vastly magnified, is painted on the walls of the town hall of modern (Communist) Zwickau.

his own personal acidity, Müntzer in the next months again appears as a defender of Martinian theology.

How far, by the end of 1520 and the spring of 1521, Müntzer had moved from Martinian theology in a new direction cannot be more than guessed. But it seems clear that he was now associated with revolutionary and radical elements within the city which probably coalesced round him. We shall examine more closely on a later page the possibility that this radical teaching was not new for him, that it underlay the Martinian surface of his mind, and that it found reinforcement in his mystical reading during the period when he was most associated with nunneries, themselves in regions with a long tradition, and indeed a noble heritage, dating back to the Thuringian nunneries of the 12th century. But at this point begins his close association with the men who were to become famous as the 'Zwickau prophets'. Their leader was a layman, a weaver, Nicholas Storch, who perhaps exaggerated his own simple and unlettered background. At any rate, Müntzer is said to have extolled Storch's profound and visionary piety from the pulpit. We know that another of this group, Mark Stübner, a former student of Melanchthon at Wittenberg, was Müntzer's close comrade. Another, Drechsel, may have belonged to a priestly family.

Contempt always brought up the bile in Müntzer, who now uttered bloody-minded threats all round. A number of pasquils circulated on both sides while clerical windows were shattered by Müntzer's party. Among the lampoons against Müntzer is the significant sentence: 'Oh, Thomas Müntzer, thou bloodthirsty man'.[1] This chimes remarkably with another letter from Agricola, this time full of stern warning: 'People are saying that you breathe nothing but fire and slaughter'.[2] Truth comes out in anger, and there may be some truth in the charge against Egranus (whose income must have trebled Müntzer's 41 fl. a year) of loving ease, of sucking up to the great ones, and encouraging the fine ladies to give him gifts of wine.

Although the contrary has often been suggested, I think it far

[1] J. K. Seidemann *Thomas Münzer: eine Biographie* (Dresden/Leipzig 1842), Beilage 5, p. 108
[2] Agricola to Müntzer: Franz, II, No. 21, p. 368

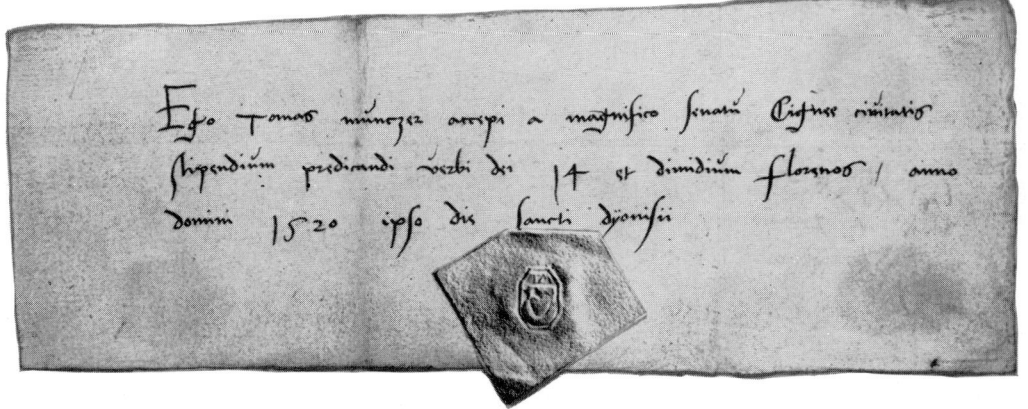

(Top) Thomas Müntzer's receipt for his stipend as supply preacher in the church of Our Lady at Zwickau (see page 160)

Ego Tomas Munczer accepi a magnifico senatu Cignee civitatis stipendium predicandi verbi dei 14 et dimidium florenos, anno domini 1520 ipso die sancti Dyonisii

Note Müntzer's coat of arms, a sword in a heart

(Bottom) Thomas Müntzer's receipt for his stipend as preacher in the church of St Catherine, Zwickau

A senatu Cigneo accepi vigintiquinque florenos post dominicam que Misericordia domini dicitur quod protestor manu mea propria
Tomas Munczer qui pro veritate militat in mundo

Note the characteristic signature (see page 165)

more likely that Müntzer led, rather than that he was led by, these men. Certainly in the spring of 1521 there was a beginning of civic crises which continued after Müntzer's own departure and before the end of the year were to eject the Zwickau prophets in the direction of Wittenberg.

Before this, however, Müntzer was involved in more serious trouble on his own account. St Stephen the Martyr may have had a fascination for Müntzer (we have noted that there was a stained glass of him in St Catherine's church). At any rate on St Stephen's Day 1521 Müntzer launched an incendiary and anticlerical diatribe. He provoked the congregation to attack one of its members, a local priest, who was driven from the church in an uproar, was pelted with stones and dung, and only escaped with his life through hasty flight. There were official complaints to the bishop by members of the town council, and Müntzer seems only to have been saved by influential counter-measures from his own patrons. Müntzer was now the centre of an agitated ferment and complained that attempts were being made to poison him, and that his windows were broken on the eve of Lent by angry opponents.[1]

The uproar reached its climax in April 1521 (at the very time when Luther faced the great ones of the world in the Imperial Diet of Worms). There seems to have been an attempt at civic revolution. After it failed, Thomas Müntzer indignantly denied any part or lot in these unsavoury proceedings; he had a perfect alibi ('I was in the bath at the time') and, but for him, there would have been very bloody goings-on. It was a little too pat, and the authorities had had enough alarms and excursions from Thomas Müntzer. He had to get on the move again and now left Zwickau, at this time still a Martinian, still able to defend theological theses written by Melanchthon and to describe himself enigmatically as 'aemulus Martini'.[2] Egranus, a true Erasmian in being thin-skinned, touchy, and unable to put up with hubbub, had gone off to the more prosperous Joachimsthal. Müntzer's radical friends were able to linger, but at the end of December 1521, in order to avoid arrest,

[1] Seidemann, op. cit., Beilage 5, p. 107
[2] 'Aemulus' does not necessarily mean 'rival', and could mean 'successor' or 'follower' – it is a word Müntzer uses several times.

they too fled, to fish in the troubled waters of a Wittenberg dominated by Andrew Karlstadt.

The draft of a letter from Egranus to Luther (18 May 1521), congratulating Luther on his happy escape from 'the tyrants' at Worms, makes a fitting epilogue to the rumpus between Egranus and Müntzer. Egranus, now in the Joachimsthal, sums up for Luther all the ills he has received since the advent in Zwickau of 'Thomas tuus' (confirmation of the fact that Thomas had come to Zwickau with Luther's commendation). Though Luther himself would not be predisposed to take Egranus' words at their face value, there were comments here which were to find echoes in Luther's own thoughts in coming months, in the light of the Wittenberg activities of the Zwickau prophets. 'The impudence of the man who would neither follow the counsels of his friends or the authority of Scripture! but who relying on his own spirit roused only factions'; and then the phrase which might have been the epitaph on Müntzer of all his enemies: 'homo ad schismata et hereses natus' – 'a man born for heresies and schisms'; there is the definite allegation that he had roused conspiracies among the rabble and gathered them into conventicles – 'this most lying of men'![1]

[1] *WA, Br.* 2, No. 412, p. 345f.

CHAPTER THIRTEEN

PRAGUE

In April 1521, Thomas Müntzer left Zwickau, after the crisis in the city which he may have provoked but which may have boiled up unexpectedly – so that his own indignant alibi may have justification. Elsewhere in Germany also, dramatic events were taking place. Martin Luther had appeared at the Diet of Worms: the Edict of Worms had been passed, declaring him an outlaw and imposing the menacing sanctions of Imperial authority against religious innovation. Then came the dramatic disappearance of Luther himself: for some months hardly anybody knew that he was the Prisoner in the Wartburg, and we know that many, among them Albert Dürer, believed that Luther had been killed. What was to happen now to the Martinians, their leader gone? What of the protection which the evangelicals had enjoyed because Frederick the Wise had come obstinately to be the patron and guardian of Luther? One part of the answer may be that some of the Martinians turned to Melanchthon (whose immensely influential *Loci Communes* appeared at this time) – and we shall see evidence of a Melanchthonian phase among Thomas Müntzer and his radical friends. But with Luther gone, there was no obvious centre for reform in Germany. Little wonder that Müntzer should be attracted by the thought of an appeal to Bohemia. In Zwickau he had been in a city with many links with the not too distant Czech cities. It was notorious that here were strong opposers of the Roman Catholic hierarchy, not only in the Utraquist ranks, but among more radical groups and parties. Moreover, there were known to be Martinians in Prague with whom contact might be made.

How far Luther's possible death influenced Müntzer's thoughts about his own fate, we cannot tell. It may not be just the persecution complex of the Left which made him talk of 'secret plots against me which at last burst out into the open' or of the rumour that he had been poisoned. Certainly in the letters of these months, he shows a sense of possible disaster, the fact that 'I wander in all the world on behalf of the gospel' being bound up with his possible martyrdom.

Once he had decided to visit Bohemia, he sought for companions and arranged some domestic affairs.[1]

Among his radical associates, it seems that Nicholas Storch refused to come, but that he found an important companion in Mark Thome, or Stübner (the word denotes his father's occupation, which was that of bathhouse keeper, which he maintained in Elsterburg). Stübner had been a student at Wittenberg under Melanchthon (matr. Wittenberg, 26 May 1518) and may also have debated with Melanchthon at Wittenberg in the spring of 1521.[2]

From a letter to Stübner we learn that Müntzer was arranging for the care of furniture and goods left him by his mother and by his friend Maurice Reinhart, while he wrote to Michael Gans about correspondence.[3] He wrote a letter to Nicholas Hausmann, the new parson in Zwickau, upbraiding him for leaving him in the lurch, for not attacking Egranus, warning him against any attempt to undo Müntzer's own work among his parishioners, and claiming that he was visiting Bohemia 'not for money or glory' but in expectation of his own death.[4]

An attempt to get a Bohemian disciple – 'Hans Lebe der pheme' –

---

[1] I do not find the evidence enough to support the view that he made repeated visits to Bohemia, or that after a tip-and-run raid to Saaz in May he returned to Saxony for a few weeks in June – views held by Lohmann, Böhmer and Husa; cf. Franz, II, Nos 22–25, pp. 369–73.

[2] Franz, II, No. 22, note 2

[3] Franz, II, No. 24

[4] Franz, II, No. 25. The use of 'visitasse' is a problem, since it seems to suggest that Thomas Müntzer had already visited Bohemia and returned by June. Husa suggests that Müntzer went to Saaz in April 1521 and made a short trip home in June. I prefer to believe that the past tense might imply 'that you may know I did not visit Bohemia . . .'.

with two companions, Klapst and Hans von Freistat, seems to have failed.¹

Václav Husa, in his valuable but often highly conjectural study of Müntzer's visit to Bohemia,² makes the interesting suggestion that Müntzer, after leaving Zwickau and before visiting Bohemia, followed Egranus to Joachimsthal. This, as he says, would account for the lampoon against Egranus, which dates from the time of his Joachimsthal preaching, and for the propositions which Müntzer drew up against Egranus and which, he suggests, might now have been published to draw Egranus into ridicule. We know that something startled Egranus into leaving Joachimsthal at this time. There is evidence also of the arrest of certain citizens for public disturbances. All this sounds like Müntzer at work, but there is no direct evidence at all, and it seems better to abstain from more conjectures about these months than the facts would support.

In September his old family friend, Hans Pelt, wrote from Halberstadt of rumours that Müntzer was now preaching publicly in Prague with the help of two learned interpreters.³

Husa produces some useful Czech evidence about Müntzer's stay in Prague.⁴ There is a report from the Bohemian humanist Jan Hodejovsky (only known through a 17th-century Jesuit work) that he heard Müntzer preach at this time in the Corpus Christi chapel, and in Latin in the famous church of John Huss, the Bethlehem chapel. From another Czech source we learn that he preached in the Utraquist church of Our Lady in the Old City and may have celebrated, administering in both kinds. Moreover, the Czech chronicle of Bartos states that Müntzer was guest for three months in the house of an influential citizen (an 'eye of the city') and Husa plausibly suggests that this was the lawyer Burian Sobek from Kornice, a former Wittenberg student, one who arranged for the publication in Prague of some of Luther's writings and was in 1521 recorder of the city.⁵ Husa's list of radical Czech leaders in Prague is purely conjectural: if they were at that time in the city, Müntzer

¹ Franz, II, No. 23: 'pheme' = 'Böhme' ('Bohemian') perhaps.
² Václav Husa *Tomáš Müntzer a Čechy* Rozpravy Československé Akademie Věd. Ročník 67. Sešit 11, 1957
³ Franz, II, No. 28, p. 377   ⁴ Husa, op. cit., pp. 116-17   ⁵ loc. cit.

may have met them. But it seems to be going well beyond any evidence to suggest that it was in such Czech radical circles that the denial of infant baptism, and the later Anabaptist teaching of Stübner in particular, arose.

There is real, though late, evidence[1] that Müntzer went first to the town of Saaz,[2] which had many links with Zwickau, and which had a strong radical ferment. It may be that Müntzer would also have contact there with a former Wittenberg student and Martinian, Artemisius.

The next piece of evidence seems to be a set of theses headed, 'Questio M Tome Munczer disputanda'.[3] There follow a set of

---

[1] Husa, op. cit., p. 40, quotes Cochlaeus (1565): 'Thomas ille intravit Bohemiam ad Socenses, ab illis missus fuit Pragensibus, salvo tamen conductu, ibi vero predicabat adiutorio interpretis: paucis tamen diebus ab eisdem capitur, et 40r custodibus in una domo, ne evadat aut exeat, custodiae traditur.'

[2] Fabricius (quoted by Melchior Adam *Vitae Philosophorum* Frankfort 1706, p. 72) says: 'Müncerus profugit in Boëmiam ad Satienses: inde proficiscens Pragam, in carcerem conjicitur et quatuor custodibus elusis evadit, et in Hercinios veniens, Alsteti munus docendi suscipit.'

[3] L. Müller *Der Kommunismus der mährischen Wiedertäufer* (*Schriften des Vereins für Reformationsgeschichte* 142) Leipzig 1911; reprint 1927, p. 76: The theses written out by Müntzer on the way to Prague:

Questio M Tome Munczer disputanda
Natura humana diligit sese propter semetipsam maxime, deum propter semetipsum diligere nequit
Cum divina tum naturalis lex statuit, deum propter sese diligendum esse
Quod cum non possimus, lex in causa est, ut serviliter metuamus deum
Odiise necesse est quod timetur
Lex igitur facit, ut et odio nobis sit deus
Ut odium amoris initium non est, ita nec metus servilis initium est filialis
Consectaneum est penitentie initium non esse metum servilem
Ergo Christi beneficium est iustitia
Omnis iustitia nostra est gratuita dei imputatio
Ergo et opera bona peccata esse non absimile vero
Intellectus nulli propositioni assentiri potest citra rationem aut experientiam
Nec voluntas per sese intellectum eiconibus cogere potest, ut assentiatur
Hic assensus fides est seu sapientia
Catholicum praeter articulos, quorum testis est scriptura, non est necesse alios credere

twenty-two propositions, while at the end of the document there is the enigmatic phrase: 'Emulus Martini apud dominum, distat duo semimiliaria a Praga'.

These theses have been a rock of offence to many. They were taken to embody Müntzer's own theology, until Lydia Müller drew public attention to the fact that they were in fact theses offered by Philip Melanchthon for his disputation as Bachelor of Theology, 9 September 1519. It is a pity, therefore, that M. M. Smirin should discuss them as Müntzer's own, and should conclude that, despite superficial resemblances, they have no real similarity with Lutheran theology! Annemarie Lohmann gets into difficulties also of her own making, in trying to divide Müntzer's theology into set phases of development and therefore to fit his Lutheran theology into a pre-'Storchismus' phase when he came under the spiritualist influence of the Zwickau prophets – and she falls back on the extremely dubious hypothesis of suggesting they were written on some other visit to Prague.

Conciliorum auctoritas est infra scripture auctoritatem
Ergo citra heresis crimen est, non credere caracterem transsubstantiationem etc.
Fides acquisita est opinio phantastica
Qui delinquit in uno, reus omnium
Precepta sunt diligere inimicum, non vindicare, non iurare, communio rerum
Leges naturae habitus sunt concreati anime
Natura magis affectat bene esse quam esse simpliciter
Deus est unus, in categoriis divinis omnium summa est

(Written across the outside of this paper are the words: 'Emulus Martini apud dominum, distat duo semimiliaria a Praga')
On the connexion of the theses with Melanchthon, see *Melanchthons Werke* ed. R. Stupperich, i (1951), 23–4.

There is a facsimile in Smirin, op. cit., opposite p. 116, and in Husa, op. cit.

It is possible that 'aemulus Martini' might refer to Melanchthon, who at this time might properly be described as Martin's successor since his disappearance on the Wartburg. We have the evidence of Müntzer's letter to Nicholas Hausmann (Franz, II, No. 25, p. 372) that Müntzer used 'aemulus' in the sense of 'successor', though of course 'rival' or 'imitator' are possible translations.

Husa, despite their Melanchthonian origin, takes them seriously as themes which Müntzer wished to debate, and, on the ground of them alone, conjures up a vision of Müntzer submitting them for disputation at the Charles University of Prague, and entering Prague, much as Luther entered Leipzig and Worms, as a distinguished academic guest. But there is a much simpler possible explanation, which, if it falls short of demonstration, at least shows how very precarious are these and other surmises of Husa. For if we ask how Müntzer could have got hold of these Melanchthonian opinions, the obvious source is his travelling companion M. Thome (Stübner), known to have been an ardent student of Melanchthon at Wittenberg. The reading, then, of the heading of the theses could equally well be: 'Questio M. Thome [Stübner] Müntzer disputanda'. The MS. could read thus equally well. We have a letter in which Müntzer addresses Stübner as 'erudito viro domino Marco Tome'. It is possible, therefore, that these theses were debated by Müntzer with Thome on the journey and before a group of friends, or even by themselves, and that just outside Prague Müntzer took a copy of them. All the evidence suggests that Müntzer did in fact go to Prague as a preacher, rather than as a theologian or academic.

It seems likely, then, that Müntzer found hospitality among Lutheran sympathizers, and that these provided him with Czech interpreters. It seems more than likely that his unrestrained preaching got him into trouble, and that his anticlericalism became, as usual, more and more vehement, the more opposition he roused. None the less, he had come to Prague with a purpose: it can be no accident that he had turned in this direction rather than to the great cities of south Germany, like Augsburg or Nuremberg.

At any rate, the result was his famous 'Prague Manifesto'.[1] And if 'Aemulus Martini' – 'Another Martin' – was Müntzer's thought of his own mission, then there would be no coincidence but deliberate

---

[1] Conveniently, in Franz, III, 2, pp. 491–511; but see O. H. Brandt *Thomas Müntzer: sein Leben und seine Schriften* Jena 1933, pp. 59–62 and note ad loc. See also E. Wolfgramm, 'Der Prager Anschlag des Thomas Müntzer in der Handschrift der Leipziger Universitätsbibliothek', in *Wissenschaftliche Zeitschrift der Karl-Marx Universität Leipzig* 1956/7, pp. 295–308

imitation in the fact that at least one version of the document was signed and dated, 'All Saints Day' (1521).[1] The Manifesto is extant in four versions, and the fact that these have all survived in Germany raises the question whether in fact Müntzer's demonstration ever took place, or was only planned (the complete silence of Czech sources is not perhaps much evidence either way). It looks as though the real Manifesto was the short German version, which is written on a great sheet of paper, $42\frac{1}{2} \times 33$ cm. There is also a much longer German version, which may be the original, which is dated 'St Catherine's Day'. There is a more restrained Latin version, and an apparently unfinished Czech translation. We cannot tell what Müntzer intended: whether one or all were to be nailed to any particular church (say, the Bethlehem chapel, or the cathedral). Certainly the long German version is much more like a pamphlet or a long open letter – a kind of Appeal to the Christian nobility of the Czech nation – though, unlike Luther's great prototype, it played much more strongly to the popular gallery. There can be no doubt that the Latin version was addressed to the humanists and clergy.

> I, Thomas Müntzer of Stolberg, confess before the whole Church[2] and the whole world, wherever this letter may be displayed, that I can bear witness, with Christ and all the Elect who have known me from my youth up, that I have used my utmost diligence, above all other men, that I might have or attain a higher understanding of holy invincible Christian faith. Yet all the days of my life (God knows, I lie not) I have never been able to get out of any monk or parson the true use of faith, about the profitableness of temptation (*Anfechtung*) which prepares for faith in the Spirit of the Fear of the Lord, together with the condition that each elect must have

---

[1] The suggestion that this was, in fact, in June according to the Czech calendar was made in order to tidy dates, since in the letter to Nicholas Hausmann, 15 June 1521, Müntzer says, 'Cognoscito me Bohemiam visitasse' as though he had already been in Prague. But this does not seem the only possible interpretation of the text, and in fact it does not seem that Prague did use the Slavic calendar which could put the feast on 26 May; cf. Franz, II, No. 25, p. 372, note 9.

[2] 'of the Elect', in other versions of the Manifesto.

the Sevenfold Holy Ghost. I have not learned from any Scholar the true Order of God which he has set in all creatures, not the least word, and that the Whole perfect work is the way to understand the Parts – these are never to be obtained from those who set up to be true Christians, especially from those damned parsons. It is true I have heard from them about the bare word of Scripture, which they have stolen, like thieves and murderers from the Bible, which robbery Jeremiah in Chapter 23 calls stealing the Word of God from the mouth of one's neighbour, which they themselves have never once heard from the mouth of God.

Yes, I reckon they are fine preachers, anointed by the Devil to this end. But St Paul writes to the Corinthians (2nd Epistle, chapter 3) that the hearts of men are the paper and parchment on which God writes with his finger his irrevocable Will and Eternal Wisdom, not with ink, and this writing any man can understand if his understanding has been opened, as Jeremiah and Ezekiel say, God writes his law on the third day of Sprinkling, when the understandings of men will be opened, and God has done this from the very Beginning in his Elect, in order that they may not be uncertain, but have an invincible testimony from the Holy Ghost, who gives a sufficient witness to our spirits that we are the children of God. For whoso cannot discern God's Spirit in himself, yea, who has not the assurance of this, is not a member of Christ, but of the Devil (Romans 8). Now the world (led astray through many sects) has long desired exceedingly to know the truth, so that the saying of Jeremiah has come true: the children have asked for bread, but there was nobody to break it to them. But there were many then, as there are now today, who have chucked bread at them, that is the letter of the Word, without breaking it to them. O mark this, mark it, they have not broken it up for the children. They have not explained the true Spirit of the Fear of the Lord which would have taught them they are irrevocably God's children.

So it comes about that Christians (to defend the truth) are about as competent as knaves, and dare in consequence to jabber in lordly fashion that God does not speak with men any longer, just as though he had now become dumb. And they think it is enough that it should be written down in their books, and be it never so raw, they will spit it out as a stork does with frogs into its nest. They are not like the hen who covers up her young and makes them warm, they do not share out the good nature of the Word of God (which lives none the less in all Elect men) in the heart, as a mother gives milk to her child, but they teach them Balaam-wise, so that they keep the poor letter in their mouth, but the heart is a hundred thousand miles off.

On account of such folly, it would be no wonder were God to smite us in pieces for such fool's faith. It is no wonder to me that men of all races reproach us, and none can do otherwise. 'Thus and thus, it is written'. Yes, dear masters, it is superfine work that they have set up in the fowl-house. If a simple person or an unbeliever came among us into the congregation, and we sought to overwhelm him with our silly chatter, he would say 'You are all mad or wicked, what has your Scripture to do with me?' But when we learn the true living Word of God then perhaps we will win over the unbeliever and judge plainly, when the secrets of his heart are revealed and he will humbly confess that God is in our midst.

See, St Paul also bears witness to this in 1 Cor. 14 where at the same time he says that a preacher must have a revelation, or else he cannot preach the Word. The Devil believes that the Christian faith is true. And, if this be rejected by the children of Antichrist, then they make God mad or wicked, who has said that his Word shall never pass away. But must it not have passed away if God has stopped speaking?

Mark well the Text, if you had something else in mind Heaven and earth shall pass away but my words shall not pass away. If that is just written down in a Book, and God said it once and then it disappeared into thin air – that cannot then be God's Eternal Word. Then it would be only a creaturely thing, put into our memory from the outside, which is contrary to the True Order and against the rule of holy faith as Jeremiah writes. That is why all the prophets have used this manner of speaking – 'Thus saith the Lord —', they don't say, 'Thus did the Lord say', as though it were all over, but they say now, in this present time.

This insupportable and wicked shaming of Christendom I have taken pitifully to heart through reading with all diligence the Histories of the Fathers. I find that, after the death of the pupils of the Apostles, the immaculate Virgin Church was turned to whoredom through Adultery (by reason of the Scribes who have always to sit on top) as Hegesippus writes, and after him Eusebius in the 4th

Book, the 22nd Chapter.¹ Moreover, I find in no Council of the Church that they take seriously the expounded living Order of the undeceivable Word of God, but a lot of kid's stuff. Through God's Inscrutable Will this was allowed, that the work of men might be exposed. But it will never happen, God be praised, that such parsons and Apes should come to constitute the Christian Church. Which shall rather be the Elect Friends of the Word of God who learn to prophesy as Paul teaches that they may truly know, how friendly and how heartily God loves to talk with all his Elect. In order to bring this truth to the light of day, I am ready to offer my life, if it be God's will. God will do marvellous things with his Elect, especially in this land. When the New Church begins, this nation shall be a mirror to the whole world. Therefore I appeal to Everyman, to come to the defence of God's Word. And also that I may make visibly plain among you in the Spirit of Elijah those who have taught you to sacrifice to the Idol Baal. If you will not do this, then God will let you be beaten by the Turk in the coming Year. I know truly what I am saying, that it is so. Therefore I will suffer those things which Jeremiah had to suffer. Take this to heart, dear Bohemians, I demand an account of you, not only such as Peter teaches but as God himself demands. I will give account to you also, and, if I do not in fact possess the knowledge of which I boast so openly, then am I a child of temporal and eternal death. I can give no higher pledge. Christ be with you.

Given at Prague in 1521 on All Saints' Day.

The longer German version fills out these sentiments with a long series of pejoratives against the clergy, of an extreme and vulgar kind (though not perhaps surpassing Luther's invective against the papists when he really got going).

It is the last part, which is apocalyptic, that is the real Manifesto. Here is his curious doctrine of the Fall of the Church (drawn from Hegesippus-Eusebius) in the 2nd century, and his depreciation of Church councils (the fruit of hard reading in previous years) but obviously a propaganda point in Bohemia with Hussite memories of

¹ Eusebius *Ecclesiastical History* IV, xxii (Loeb ed., p. 375): 'For this cause they called the church "virgin" for it had not yet been corrupted by vain messages, but Thebouthis, because he had not yet been made bishop, begins its corruption by the seven heresies to which he belonged, among the people.'

the Council of Constance. But here again he says nothing which Luther had not said about such councils. Then comes his assertion that the New Church is to begin in Bohemia – his appeal to Czechs to pledge themselves to defend the Word (a favourite ploy of Müntzer, as we shall see): a warning that, if his appeal is refused, the Turks will overrun Bohemia in the coming year, an affirmation of his own mission, and his readiness to die on its behalf.

In the longer German version this is more excitedly written in words which suggest Müntzer's preaching style when he really got worked up, in German.

> Oho, how ripe are the rotten apples. Oho, how soft are the Elect. The harvest time is here, and this is why God himself has put it out to harvesting. I have made my sickle sharp, for my thoughts are firmly centred in the truth, and my lips, hands, skin, body, life itself curse to unbelievers . . . in your land the new apostolic church will start, and then spread everywhere . . . whoso despises this appeal, is already given over into the hands of the Turks, after which raging fury the true person of Antichrist will rule, the very opposite of Christ who in a short time will give the kingdoms of this world to his Elect, for ever and ever.

We shall examine its theology in detail at a later stage, but here we may note how deep the conflict with Egranus had cut into Müntzer's mind – for from Egranus he gained the image of the Scribe, the Scholar who for him became more and more the object of his scorn, an image which in the last resort he was to transfer to Melanchthon and to Luther. His first complaint is that no monk or parson had ever taught him the truth about faith: the need for a first initiation into the Fear of the Lord, the importance of Temptation, the Sevenfold gift of the Holy Spirit. He then attacks the parsons for confining the gospel to the Scriptures and recurs to the, as it seemed to him, outrageous statement of Egranus, that the Spirit no longer spoke directly to Christians since the time of the Apostles, and that now we have God's voice in the Scriptures. It is this thought of God as a dumb God who does not speak which Müntzer now vehemently attacks. He himself puts forward a doctrine of Christian assurance in the Spirit, a view that God loves to talk directly to his friends. Despite the obvious emphasis on the Spirit and his direct speech with the Elect, the thoroughgoing biblicism of much of Müntzer's argument needs to be noted. This is the first long theological document we have from him, and it is soaked in Scriptural citation and allusion, and, in a most impressive way, from all levels of Old and New Testament writings.

The natural supposition would be that the shorter German version (dated 1 November) preceded the longer one (dated St Catherine's Day, 25 November) and that it is an expansion of the short Manifesto. Internal evidence suggests rather the contrary, however, and one is left with the impression that, in fact, the short version is the abridgement. In one place, for example, Müntzer abridges his argument so much as to suggest that it is Jeremiah and Ezekiel who speak of a 'sprinkling' on the third and seventh day, whereas in the shorter version it is correctly cited from Numbers. The opening paragraph or exhortation links disparate thoughts in the long version, to make one sentence in the shorter version.

At any rate, the core of these documents is the same. It is a sustained theological and religious document with the slightest possible reference to social and political conditions. It is indeed so much an exposition of Müntzer's own mystical theology that one wonders what readers could possibly have made of such a document, had it been pinned up on some church door. One can assume that into this document Müntzer had conveyed the matter of his sermons during his time in Prague, but even so it is a strange, and to the uninitiated must have seemed a thoroughly mysterious, document.

Müntzer's theological gunpowder seems to have failed to explode. Certainly, collectively or singly, the four versions of the Manifesto seem singularly ill fitted for an appeal *Urbi et Orbi*. Embedded in the shorter German version there is indeed a summary of his gospel, but, even as expanded in the longer recension, it is compressed and enigmatic. What could the average citizen of Prague, or even the average churchman, make of Müntzer's references to the 'Sevenfold Spirit', the 'Sprinkling', and the 'Parts and the Whole', even if we assume that for some months perhaps he may have been expounding these notions before his congregations. Nor is it easy to see what action Müntzer expected to follow his appeal.

We can understand that, if this was in fact the climax of an evangelical campaign, it should get him into trouble. It is little use speculating about the various Czech radical groups: they certainly existed and it is plausible that Müntzer was in contact with them. And it seems likely – Husa cites a German source – that both Müntzer and Mark Thome were soon in trouble. Stübner was stoned and barely escaped with his life (which seems to indicate popular as well as magisterial disapproval). Müntzer was put in jail.

It is likely, then, that Stübner returned alone to Germany at the end of 1521 to find his comrades in Zwickau in serious trouble. Led by Nicholas Hausmann, the town priest, the magistrates and parsons made a determined effort to uproot the radical element, among whom Storch was now the most prominent figure. They were hauled up before the magistrates and a joint appeal against them sent to John Frederick by the council and the clergy. This is dated 18 December 1521, and it must have coincided with the flight of the ringleaders, for the Prophets turned up in Wittenberg just after Christmas, among them Stübner who made a bee line for Melanchthon, engaging him in ardent theological and biblical disputation, in which he succeeded in shaking his old teacher considerably.

Husa suggests that it was during their stay in Prague that both Müntzer and Stübner became acquainted with the views of the Czech radicals against infant baptism (Lukas of Prague did write a tract about the doctrine at this very period): he suggests, therefore, that it was from Prague that there came the denunciation of infant baptism which Storch and Stübner now put forward in Wittenberg, and which may be one source of the Anabaptist doctrine. But the earlier letter of Hausmann is evidence to the contrary, for among the charges against the radicals in Zwickau is that they had 'doubted whether the faith of godparents is of any use to infants at baptism – and indeed some of them believe that men may be saved without baptism'. Repudiation of medieval belief and practice about infant baptism is, therefore, to be found in Zwickau before the return of Stübner – it sounds like doctrine well known and therefore inculcated for some time, so that it could be put forward a few days later, at the end of December 1521, in

Wittenberg by Storch, Drechsel and Stübner (only Stübner had been with Müntzer in Prague).

Unless he were still in Prague, there seems no reason why Müntzer should not have joined his friends, the 'Zwickau prophets' at Wittenberg. Whether the two men, Müntzer and Thome, quarrelled or not, Müntzer certainly kept away from them during the first months of 1522, though he knew what was afoot and seems to have ripened his acquaintance with Karlstadt. The next year is a period of which we know little about Müntzer: his second failure, at Prague, may well have cast him down in spirit, and seems to have led to a period of real hardship. In December 1521 four Benedictine monks wrote from Erfurt offering him a post to teach Latin for a stipend of '30 fl. with expenses and board',[1] but it was already a time of confusion – 'Inter nos maximum est dissidium' – with the contagious influence of the Wittenberg and Erfurt Augustinians, and it may be that when Müntzer reached Erfurt the post was no longer available or the brethren in no position to offer it. It was from Erfurt that in March 1522 he wrote to Melanchthon, in the very days when Luther had returned from the Wartburg and, in his famous series of sermons, was redressing the balance of the Wittenberg revolution under Karlstadt.

The letter is friendly and deferential on the surface, but with an acid undercurrent. Müntzer as 'Christ's nuncio' addresses 'that Christian Man, Philip Melanchthon, Professor of Sacred Scriptures' in terms that show him still a Martinian: 'Hail, Instrument of Christ, I embrace your theology with all my heart, for you have rescued many souls of the Elect from the snare of the fowler.' The letter avoids direct reference to the troubles in Wittenberg or to the Zwickau prophets. Müntzer's first criticism is his reserved approval of the marriage of the evangelical clergy (this had been defended in a writing widely believed to be from Melanchthon) – if this is mere pandering to human lust then the result would be a 'Satan's brothel worse than all the popish anointings': 'Let us use our wives as though we possessed them not!' for 'no precept is more strictly binding on Christians than – Sanctification.'

Here perhaps is the point at which Müntzer begins to leave the

[1] Franz, II, No. 29, p. 378

Martinian camp, as his doctrines of the Spirit, and his apocalyptic view of the Church and of the present time as one of final judgement, are quite contrary to the doctrines of the Wittenberg theologians. He now ominously transfers from Egranus to Melanchthon the reproach of worshipping a 'Dumb God', and of repudiating the Coming Great Church, in which the fullness of the knowledge of God will be shed abroad. He commends the Wittenberg theologians for the abrogation of the Mass, yet asserts that they have not acted altogether according to the Apostolic yardstick. He must have heard of Luther's vehement counterblast to the Karlstadt programme, with Luther's concern for the unconvinced and unconverted among his opponents who must be treated as 'little ones'. 'Our most beloved Martin acts in ignorance when he refused to offend the "little ones" – such children are a hundred years old in wickedness! But the time for concessions is past, for this is the hour when the reprobates have to be rooted out. Mark well the time! The Harvest is at the door.' There is a cryptic warning, 'Do not toady to your Princes' – a tiny cloud which would swell into a storm in coming months. Finally, there is a curious defence of purgatory – Müntzer commends the denial of Popish fantasies, but nevertheless 'Beware the error denying purgatory.' But a mystical purgatory is part of Müntzer's realized eschatology. It was a view publicized in Wittenberg early in 1522 by the publication of the *Farrago* of Wessel Gansfort. But Müntzer gives it his own idiom – 'None may enter into rest unless they experience the Seven Degrees of reason of the Seven Spirits.' In a postscript Müntzer attacks Archbishop Lang, 'for he is a Reprobate who in his immortal Pride persecuted the Servant of God'. There is therefore a running undercurrent of criticism, and a sting in the tail of the letter – 'You precious Scribes [a phrase hitherto reserved by Müntzer for Egranus and the papists], do not be obstinate. I can do no other!'

It seems that the Catholic authorities would prevent his appointment as a notorious Martinian, while the rumours of his misadventures in Prague and the turbulence of his Zwickau friends in Wittenberg prevented the Martinians from giving him practical help. Franz Günther sent him a friendly letter and a warning: 'All sorts of gossip is going on about you. . . . Let's hope you have proved the Spirit of Christ and not some other spirit' – but he did nothing.[1] To another friend Müntzer had to write denying that he had recanted his doctrines or was on the run.[2] Another friend, John Buschmann, wrote explaining the difficulties about finding him a job.[3] Karlstadt, preoccupied with his own economic problems, invited him to stay on his farm at Wörlitz, and to do a bit of digging. The letter possibly suggests that they had not yet met face to face, but it also hints at common concerns which cannot be put into letters.[4]

The letter is clear evidence that Müntzer was having a hard time, about which Karlstadt moralizes in their common jargon: 'Believe me, this is the way in which God chastises his Elect with Judgement.' There is also the revealing sentence: 'Here I teach more than any other professor about dreams and visions.'

In these months Müntzer seems to have moved between Erfurt, Nordhausen and Halle.[5] He probably kept clear of the further colloquies held between Luther, Melanchthon and the Zwickau prophets, for when Luther later asserted that he had given Müntzer's Devil a good theological punch on the nose, Müntzer vehemently denied having been in Wittenberg – 'You lie deep down in your throat!' In spiritual despondency and probably real physical poverty, Müntzer in these months proved his own doctrine of purgation through suffering, his mood perfectly portrayed in a rather poignant letter to an unknown adherent in March 1523:

> Let my suffering be an example for you. Let the tares grow where they will. They have to be, along with the wheat, for the Lord God is sharpening his scythe on me, so that later on I may be able to cut off the red poppies and the blue cornflowers.... I have had two guilders from the Lady [Abbess] the whole winter ... given in the misery of my exile ... Thomas Müntzer a dedicated messenger of God.[6]

---

[1] Franz, II, No. 30, Jan. 1522 [2] Franz, II, No. 35, 14 July 1522
[3] Franz, II, No. 36, Sept. 1522 [4] Franz, II, No. 37, 21 Dec. 1522
[5] There is some evidence to support O. Schiff's suggestion that he preached for a time in St George's church, Halle: *ARG* 23 (1926), pp. 288ff.
[6] Franz, II, No. 38, 19 March 1523. Goebke thinks that the kindly abbess may have been Maria von Stolberg in Quedlinburg.

CHAPTER FOURTEEN

THE PROPHET OF ALLSTEDT 1523-4

The pleasant country township of Allstedt had none of the bustling importance of Zwickau, but it had once been the residence of a Saxon emperor, and it was still a favourite resort of the Elector of Saxony. Close to the mining areas of Mansfeld, it was an admirable centre for Müntzer's propaganda. These remote towns, far from any military or police supervision, conjure up the setting of a 'Western' film where lynch law and rough justice prevail, and where the sheriff's is a precarious trade. Certainly the life of a mayor of Allstedt was likely to be nasty, brutish and short, and most of them had died a violent death since 1496.[1] Although Müntzer was called and nominated by the Council, the presentation and confirmation of the parish church of St John in the New Town lay with the Elector, but nobody mentioned that at this stage, and the Council probably contented itself with the reflection that their new Preacher[2] was, after all, on trial. At any rate, he soon dominated the town: the only other Preacher in the Old Town, Simon Haferitz, turned into an echo of himself. He was soon on intimate terms with the Electoral official, the castellan, Hans Zeiss, and the mayor, Nick Rückert. He was soon writing letters of counsel and exhortation to other small neighbouring towns, to his native Stolberg and to Frankenhausen. There is some point in the suggestion of Hinrichs that Müntzer made Allstedt into a counter-Wittenberg, with an alternative centre and programme of reform to Wittenberg.

Yet in these days Müntzer made his last Martinian appeal, a

---

[1] Otto Merx *Thomas Müntzer und Heinrich Pfeiffer 1523–1525* Göttingen 1889, i, 15, note 3

[2] but this time he was *parochus* – parish priest as well as preacher.

letter to Luther which in its mixture of respect and defiance recalls Luther's own last appeal to Pope Leo X. He knew how critical Luther's support or enmity must be. But he must also have known how compromised he must be in Luther's eyes. Luther's disciple and friend in Zwickau, Nicholas Hausmann, could not have failed to have told him all about Müntzer's part in its troubles. Worse, Luther had first-hand experience of Müntzer's doctrines and programme in the Zwickau prophets. The letter turns into an apologia after its complimentary beginning:

> Hail, most sincere Father ... for from the beginning I have surely known that what you have done was not for yourself alone, but the good cause of all men.

There follows a reference to Zwickau, with a vitriolic appraisal of Egranus and the famous alibi for his part in the Zwickau revolution, 'I was in the bath at the time.' Then comes the critical issue between himself and Luther, his view of the Spirit and of revelation, 'for Christ himself wills that we should judge concerning his doctrine'.

Müntzer next gives his view of Faith, which he was coming to believe was the real issue between himself and the 'Learned Scribes'.

> A man cannot know Christ's doctrines unless he has suffered the waves and billows of great waters which overwhelm the Elect ... so that a man hopes beyond hope and seeks the one will of God in the Day of Visitation, beyond all expectation. Then are his feet marvellously stayed on a rock and the Lord appears wonderfully from afar, and then he receives credible testimonies from God. For those who glory in Christ are not to be believed unless they have his Spirit.

It was foolish of Müntzer to try to argue with Luther: to preach at him was fatal. He then tries, not very happily, to dissociate himself from the Zwickau prophets – 'My very dear Patron ... you know the name and condition of Thomas – I would not go in for ecstasies and visions if God did not compel me – I do not support anything unless it has the testimony of Scripture on its side.' But even now he is willing for Luther to correct him:

> I am not so arrogant but that I will not be corrected by your superior testimony that we may walk the one way in love. ... You

object – but what about Nicholas and Marcus?... what they have said and talked about I do not know. You say the jargon nauseates you – I suppose you mean all that about the Waiting Time [*longanimitate*] and the 'Constrained Mind' [*angustia mentis*], but believe me I will say nothing unless I am able to demonstrate it with the clearest and plainest texts of Scripture, which if I neglect, I am not worthy to live... may the Lord keep you and renew your old love ... salute Philip, Karlstadt, and Justus Jonas and others... in your Church.

He signed himself more soberly than usual: 'Thomas Müntzer the parochus – of Allstedt'.[1]

It was hardly a real 'if'. Luther had heard more than enough of Müntzer and he lumped his ideas with those of the Zwickau prophets (not unjustifiably). If Müntzer's letter was his last Martinian act, the letter of Luther to Spalatin (for he seems to have ignored Müntzer's letter) on 3 August marks the slamming of Luther's mind against a former adherent.

At some time in the next week the castellan, Hans Zeiss, seems to have visited Luther, and to him the Reformer spoke words of forthright warning. Of Müntzer, Luther speaks to Spalatin with an amused contempt: 'He praises me in one breath and attacks me in the next ... and he uses an absurd jargon not to be found in Scripture – so that you wonder whether he is mad or drunk.' Luther has suggested that Müntzer should come to a private conference with theologians and considered this the test of Müntzer's sincerity. As usual, Luther's intuitions were sound enough: Müntzer's teachings were vulnerable and dangerous where Luther said they were. And yet it was not so long since Luther himself had used a theological jargon, not found in Scripture, in the doctrines of 'synteresis' and of 'resignatio ad infernum' and in an exposition of 'Anfechtung' in his exposition of the Psalms and of the Book of Jonah which comes very near to Müntzer's existential reference. As for Müntzer, hell has no fury like a prophet scorned and henceforth he would direct towards Luther, as the evil genius of all his troubles, a venom and hatred hitherto reserved for Egranus. Only two years hence, Oecolampadius would recognize his unknown

[1] Franz, II, No. 40

guest simply by the vitriolic invective which poured out at the name of Luther.

In July 1523, then, Müntzer ceased to be a Martinian. Luther now rated him high among the dangerous band of fanatics whose heady doctrines might jeopardize the whole Reformation in social anarchy. He had seen the danger of all this in Karlstadt's abortive revolution and the uproar it had caused. At this very time, Müntzer wrote a note to Karlstadt which showed a growing intimacy between them, and the fact of a correspondence dangerous enough for Karlstadt to be apprehensive lest it be intercepted.[1] During 1522, in the spring and summer, Luther had debated with the Zwickau prophets, and such friends and converts to their cause as Michael Cellarius and Gerhard Westerburg. He knew enough of Müntzer's relations with these men and must have known that he was perhaps their leading theologian. The effect of all these things on Luther, and of the still menacing political situation on his Prince, was to put the brake on all liturgical reform in Wittenberg. Luther was content to expound the principles of worship in a lucid tract, 'Von Ordnung Gottesdienstes in der Gemeinde' (1523),[2] while he further expounded the structure of evangelical communion in his 'formula missae et communionis' (1524), the latter being significantly dedicated to Nicholas Hausmann in Zwickau.

Thus the first thoroughgoing liturgical experiments in Saxony were carried out by Thomas Müntzer in Allstedt. We shall reserve detailed comment on them, but may stress the originality of his handiwork. Like another famous schismatic and liturgist, the antipope Hippolytus, Müntzer's liturgies and his translations (often very free indeed) reflect his own idiosyncratic theology, but some of his hymns are finely done. We may believe that much of the work had been done during Müntzer's 'hidden' months following his return from Prague. By July 1523 he was able to send to his 'Brothers in Stolberg' his own version of a favourite Psalm 93.[3]

---

[1] Franz, II, No. 43, 29 July   [2] *Ausgewählte Werke* iii, 104ff.

[3] Franz, II, No. 41, 18 July 1523; W. Elliger, 'Müntzers Übersetzung des 93 Psalms' in *Solange es Heute Heisst* (Festgabe für R. Hermann), Berlin 1957, pp. 56ff. Who were the 'brothers in Stolberg'? Perhaps recent converts to Müntzer's doctrines; but, in view of the fact that every version of the Prague

Müntzer's preaching would in any case have been enough to attract attention, but the effect of the new liturgy was sensational. Visitors thronged the country roads, and the curious and the converted mingled together on excursions from the neighbouring towns. Within Allstedt itself there began a build-up of foreigners so that a year hence there would be at least 2,000 outsiders in the little town. The ferment could not be hid, and the local landlord, Count Ernest of Mansfeld, repeatedly forbade his subjects to attend such heretical goings-on. This, as usual, roused Thomas's wrath, and in a sermon on 13 September he attacked Count Ernest as an heretical knave. When that princeling demanded that the Council arrest Müntzer, he convinced them that it was indeed the Count who was trying to clamp down on the Gospel, and himself wrote a fiery reproach (but did not Luther so address dignities?) threatening to make Ernest a laughing-stock before the world in an exposure which should be translated into many tongues. In words which remind us of another Angry Young Man with another Prince (John Penry and Elizabeth I of England) Müntzer claims, 'I am as much a Servant of God as you are', and he ended with the warning: 'You had better keep quiet, or the old Garment may be rent – I will deal with you a thousand times more hardly than did Luther with the Pope – signed, Thomas Müntzer, a Destroyer of the Ungodly'.[1]

Now in a fine rage, not without cause, the Count appealed to the Elector himself, demanding the arrest of Müntzer and citing the latest Imperial Mandate (drawn up in March, and available in Saxony in May) which forbade innovation, and condemned seditious preaching. The Elector wrote at once to his castellan, Zeiss, condemning such abuse of dignities, asking for more information, and raising for the first time the question who had installed Müntzer as preacher, and by what authority?[2] He suggested that the arrest of Müntzer would be an act of appeasement. But he did not press this, and he said nothing of it in a note to the aggrieved prince. The truth is that Frederick the Wise was reluctant to

---

Manifesto contains an appeal to the Elect who have known Müntzer from his youth up, there may have been a radical community already in existence.

[1] Franz, II, No. 44   [2] Hinrichs *Luther und Müntzer* p. 7

arrest a preacher: he had had his knuckles rapped enough by Luther about overstepping his own authority, and he knew that Luther himself had been opposed to arresting the Zwickau prophets. If Müntzer's screaming diatribe against Count Ernest shows him at his worst, he now, on 4 October, addressed a much more sensible letter to the Elector.[1]

The letter is respectful, and thoroughly studded with Scriptural quotations from all parts of the Bible. In language recalling the Prague Manifesto, Müntzer asserts his divine call to be 'an earnest Preacher', a trumpeter of the Lord. It is because of his obedience to the Word of God that the reproaches of the ungodly have befallen him, and he has unjustly been driven from one city and another. Now that he has been able to take the cover off the Word of God, and set it forth not only in preaching but in Psalms and spiritual songs 'for the edification' of the Church, he has been attacked by Count Ernest. Müntzer himself had at last been driven to speak publicly about this, had challenged Count Ernest to do things the proper way and to bring to Allstedt the Ordinary of the diocese, and theologians who could listen to Müntzer and, if need be, refute him. The Imperial Mandate is, therefore, on Müntzer's side since it claims to support the preaching of the Word of God. Müntzer then appeals to Romans 13, within the apocalyptic setting of Daniel, and Revelation. But he ends respectfully and signs himself soberly: 'Thomas Müntzer, a Servant of God'.

In the matter of Count Ernest, Müntzer had won a small, short-term victory, which at the end of the day was to cost him dear. But meanwhile he had a breathing space. It seems that in the next weeks he had a theological interview with Spalatin. Dr Irmgard Höss, Spalatin's modern biographer, thinks it must have been in November, when the Saxon court stopped at Allstedt for eight days, on its way to the Imperial Diet at Nuremberg. Spalatin put Eleven Questions about Faith to Müntzer (did Luther perhaps say, 'Be sure and ask him about Faith'?).

1. What is true Christian faith, and of what does it consist?
2. How is faith born?

[1] Franz, II, No. 45

3. Whence is faith to be asked and sought?
4. How can faith be obtained?
5. How may we usefully and safely teach faith?
6. How may we be sure of our faith?
7. How can and ought each man to prove his faith?
8. Who are the true faithful Christians?
9. In what temptations is faith born, sown and increased?
10. How does faith stand amid temptations and emerge as victor?
11. What is faith and how does it save?[1]

About the interview we know nothing, but Müntzer's first theological tract 'Von dem Gedichteten Glauben' ('Of False Faith')[2] has an evident relation to Spalatin's inquiries. It was finished by 2 December (and Müntzer in an appended note to Hans Zeiss speaks of it as 'my answer'). Müntzer's German Fourteen Points do not exactly correspond to Spalatin's Eleven Latin Questions, but it does cover them all. What Müntzer has skilfully done is to turn his answers into a counter-attack, a polemic against the wrong way of teaching faith which he found among the papists, the humanists (Egranus, and perhaps Spalatin?) and now the 'precious Scribes' of Wittenberg. Müntzer opens with a definition of faith which is Martinian enough, for, as Martin Schmidt has pointed out, his Lutheran inheritance is a 'Word of God' theology within which his own pattern of salvation is embedded.

> Christian Faith is a sure reliance [*eine Sicherung*], a casting oneself on the Word and Promise of Christ.

But Müntzer might have said to Spalatin that it was not the 'quid est' but the 'quae est' which was the important matter at issue between himself and the false preachers. For the false preachers speak as though faith comes easily, smoothly. Before a man can hear the Word or Promise of Christ, his ears must be purged from the sound of the cares and lusts of the flesh. Just as the field must be ploughed up to receive seed, so a Christian must first be made receptive

---
[1] Höss *Georg Spalatin* p. 265   [2] Franz, pp. 217–24

through the Cross, to attend God's Work and Word. Thus the Elect Friend of God learns to wait on God.[1]

Müntzer, without using the phrase, seems to think here in terms of Law, for he says that a man must see the whole of Holy Scripture as a two-edged sword, to kill and to make alive. An untempted man may blather about God's Word but he will be catching the Wind, for God has tried and tested his Elect from the beginning.

Müntzer illustrates this from the two patriarchal figures of Abraham and Moses. Abraham knew misery and distress and had to go into a strange land, trusting only in God. A reprobate man would have stayed shut up in himself, instead of fastening on Christ, that most derelict of men. Only through tribulation did he come to see the Day of Christ. Moses too would hardly believe the promise of Christ, even though he could see the Order which is set by law in God and in the creature. Though all the world perceives something of God, the Poor in Spirit come to him through tribulation.

So a godly Elect Man will find in the Bible that

> all the Fathers, the Patriarchs, Prophets and especially the Apostles have come with great difficulty to faith – not like our modern crackbrained easy-going swine who are scared by the hurricanes of roaring billows and the great waters of the Divine Wisdom. The Apostles too were staggered by the promises of Christ, disbelieved the Resurrection – and we think that with a feigned faith and a false mercy all we have to do is believe a natural promise and therewith to storm heaven itself. But not so, dearest Christians, let us use the Bible for the purpose for which it was intended, to kill and not to make alive, which only the Living Word can do, when the emptied soul hears it.

If here Müntzer seems to be saying that the Bible is the Law, and the Living Word the Gospel, it is perhaps within an Augustinian view of the relation between the Letter and the Spirit.

---

[1] That there is a preparation for Faith is something which is nearer to Luther than we might think: his early massive exposition of the Epistle to the Romans is really about this, the destruction of human self-righteousness, in which the soul is humbled, made ready to trust the Righteousness of Christ. Later Protestant theology would describe these things under the category of 'Repentance', and in terms of a dialectic of Law and Gospel.

When the underlying Faith is not penetrated, a man receives only the outward Word, but in the time of the thunderstorm, the shelter fails.

So men have to be brought in the highest Ignorance and Wonder, freed from the false Faith and instructed in true Faith.

A true Preacher will not preach the Word of God with honey-sweet words and flattery but with . . . proper earnestness will destroy all knavish Faith which men, through hearsay or out of the books of men, have stolen like thieves.

But this is the plight of poor Christendom which, not willing to have its false faith taken away, is worse off than the Heathens, Turks and Jews. That is why the Church is prey to sects and schisms – for the most part divisions coming through ceremonies and church traditions (to say nothing of false and true Faith).

What is needed is an earnest Preacher, another John the Baptist who shall teach the Work of God, how men may receive the Word of God, in which is showed forth the River of Blessedness, the Son of God, the meek Lamb who opened not his mouth. God feeds his own sheep with true salt in suffering. But this 'Sweet Christ' of the false preachers is the real deadly poison, through which men cease to long to be conformed to God and made conformed to Christ. It is the voice of the Stranger which says, 'Only Believe! Believe!'

There is no foundation of Faith save the Whole Christ: whoso refused the bitter Christ will find death in the honeyed Christ. But the man who will not die with Christ cannot rise again with him. The recollection of the Elect man is lifted from the earth to see the Lamb of God who takes away the sin of the world. He says, 'With my ears I have heard what the old Fathers in the Bible have received from God's handling of them, that nobody can be made one with God until he has overcome, through suffering.' Genuine Christianity is built on such a ground, when men learn to beware the leaven of the knavish Scribes with their untempted Faith.

O Elect One, read Matt. 16 and you will see that none comes to Faith in Christ unless he first become like him. Then he sees that no outward witness can give him a new nature, and so he looks not to the words of men, but to divine Revelation. He has to break through all manner of Unbelief, Despair and manifold contradictions, indeed must first suffer hell itself. The reprobate simply hugs the Scripture – he is only too ready to believe that Christ has done all his suffering for him. But he will not behold the Lamb of God who opens the Book – for he will not let go of his own soul, or become conformed to the Lamb of God. The real Poor in Spirit is the one who finds no faith in himself, only a longing for Faith. That really is Faith, small as a grain of mustard seed. In this way a man experiences the Work of God, and grows from day to day in the knowledge of God. Only so can men be taught by God and not from the creature. What all the creatures know is for him bitter gall, for it is a perverted way, from which may God guard and save all his Elect if they stray into it. Christ grant it. Amen.

Müntzer's exposition of true Faith is set against a picture of false Faith. This is the smooth preaching of formal Christians who know nothing in their own experience of the heights and depths of temptation. They simply repeat texts of Scripture and parrot-like clichés – 'Believe, Believe!' – 'Christ has atoned.' However unfair this is as a caricature of Luther and Melanchthon, it is a criticism of evangelical Protestantism which has often been needed throughout 400 years. Moreover, Müntzer's teaching cannot be accused of egocentricity or abandoned subjectivism. It is Christocentric, and constantly grounded in the Bible. Müntzer's appended note to Zeiss expands his meaning about the sufficiency of the atonement.

> Adam is the shadow, Christ the reality.
> The unbelief of the creature has to be done away by the obedience of Christ, the Word made flesh – just as our Fleshly nature in the Part must be done away through the working of Faith in Part, so has happened in the Whole Christ as Head. So Christ has atoned for the whole sin of Adam, so that the Parts should cleave to the Whole.
> For we have all to follow the footsteps of Christ and be armed with such thoughts.
> Untempted men are but neophytes, what the early Church called 'Catechumens' unfit to have the cure of souls.

Müntzer significantly adds that he has to revise his manuscripts and garnish them with Scriptural arguments if he is to meet his opponents on their own ground, 'because of those fleshly Scribes'.

We can understand, then, why nothing was done as a result of Müntzer's interview with Spalatin. What he had to say about Faith – and in the whole of 'Von dem Gedichteten Glauben' there is no mention of dreams or visions, no stress on the Holy Spirit – was neither blasphemous or heretical, or even offensive to pious ears. If Spalatin was indeed in Allstedt and if he witnessed Müntzer's liturgy, he could hardly have failed to be impressed. Among his own correspondence at this time was a letter from Luther on the need for vernacular hymns, suggesting that he, Spalatin, might try his hand at the kind of thing which Müntzer had in fact already done. We do not know if Müntzer's experiments spurred Luther in this direction, and it is indeed difficult to know how closely Luther really was in touch with Müntzer and his affairs. It seems clear that he judged Müntzer almost entirely in terms of the heady notions of the Zwickau prophets, and of Karlstadt, with the knowledge that in Müntzer there was violence thrown in. But in that age of sparse communications we must remember the difficulties of keeping in touch with things. Luther himself had more than enough to do with his own programme of writing, and of university and church reform in Wittenberg. We find him grumbling to Spalatin at the lack of letters, of information of how his own affairs were going at the Diet of Nuremberg. We need to remember how obsessed Luther had been for months, ever since the Edict of Worms, with the imminence of his own martyrdom and the danger that the other Princes would attack Frederick the Wise. When it came to trouble-makers, he had Strauss and Stein to contend with, and that which came upon him all too frequently, the case of Andrew Karlstadt, his neglect of university duties, his spate of pamphlets, his parochial revolution at Orlamünde. Müntzer, in comparison, was remote.

Though Luther always saw Müntzer's theology through the spectacles of the Zwickau prophets, his intuition was sound enough. There was a violent ferment within the soul of Müntzer which must sooner or later erupt, and between the radical and his own theology there lay a deep gulf. Luther himself chafed at the continuing scandal of an unreformed Chapter at Wittenberg, his 'Bethaven', but he could not advocate violence against it, still less mob action.¹ But Müntzer too had a local 'Bethaven'. This was the chapel at Mallerbach, where a miraculous picture of the Virgin drew pilgrims in ecstatic and financially profitable demonstrations. This not only seemed to Müntzer and his disciples intolerable, but in paying tithes to the nuns at Naundorf to whom the chapel belonged, they could claim to be entangled in keeping up the blasphemy. In March 1524 some thirty of Müntzer's closest followers met in the local cemetery and swore a solemn covenant, 'to uphold the Gospel, to pay no more tithes to Monks and Nuns, and to help expel them and drive them away'. Central to Müntzer's Liturgy was the theme of the New Covenant between God and Man: now he extended the notion into a solemn agreement between the Elect Friends of God to maintain the Gospel and to drive out the ungodly.

Drastic action followed. On 24 March, the custodians having been warned to flee, the chapel was burned, the shrine destroyed, by about nine of Müntzer's men, in the presence of Müntzer. Promptly the nuns appealed to the Elector, and his officer on the spot, Hans Zeiss, was henceforth caught between the upper millstone of his official loyalty, and the nether millstone of his allegiance to Müntzer. A letter (perhaps drafted by Thomas) was written in the name of castellan, mayor, Council and congregation – here at least was the local *Obrigkeit* and no mob action – which put the blame on the continuing menaces of the Catholic authorities. On 9 May the officials of Allstedt were summoned to Weimar, to the Chancellery of Duke John (Frederick's brother and Count of Thuringia) and bidden to produce the perpetrators under arrest within a fortnight.²

They returned on the eve of Whitsun (always a high day for the Thuringian radicals – a kind of 'full moon' for their fever) and Müntzer celebrated the occasion with a sermon in which, according

---

¹ though in these months he became convinced that they constituted an open blasphemy, not to be tolerated, and began to exercise a kind of spiritual blackmail on the Elector, bombarding him with memoranda threatening to leave Wittenberg and finally to excommunicate the Chapter and expose them to economic sanctions since the townspeople would refuse to feed them.

² Hinrichs, pp. 11ff.

to Duke John, he described the old Kurfürst as an 'old greybeard who doesn't understand the Gospel' and 'who has about as much wisdom in his head as I have in my behind': while his ecclesiastical echo, a former Carmelite, Simon Haferitz, preached a tirade against Princes:

> These hereditary nobles are no use. Choose your own rulers and repudiate the Princes of Saxony – write no longer, 'By the Grace of God, Dukes of Saxony' but rather 'By the Disgrace of God, no longer our rulers'.[1]

Playing for time, the Allstedt authorities asked for three weeks in order to find the culprits (who must have been quite well known). Zeiss wrote a letter full of self-pity to Duke John (29 May) in which he lamented his lot in a town where a high proportion of officials died by violence (he should have thought of that before). But it was plain that some action must be taken and, on 4 June, Zeiss arrested a member of the town council, Ziliax Knaute, and clapped him in the castle stocks. This touched the very nerve of Müntzer's association, which was nothing if not 'all for one, and one for all', and Müntzer now addressed a notable letter in the name of the Council and Congregations of Allstedt to Duke John (7 June).[2]

It is a clever, moderate, respectful letter. It protests the obedience of the people of Allstedt in all things lawful and honest, despite the intolerable threats of Catholic authorities.

> But it is plain and well known that, through ignorance, the poor people have worshipped the Devil at Mallerbach under the name of Mary. Now that this same Devil has been destroyed by good-hearted, godly people – why ought we to help apprehend and imprison such people, at the Devil's instigation?

The letter now respectfully reminds the Prince of his God-given office under Romans 13, but stresses not Romans 13:1 – the obedience of subjects – but rather Romans 13:3–4, the duty of rulers to use their swords to defend the gospel and punish the ungodly. 'If monks and nuns are idolatrous, how can they with equity be defended by Christian princes?' We, at any rate, will obey our rulers

---

[1] Hinrichs, pp. 13–14 [2] Franz, II, No. 50, pp. 404–6

in all that may in equity be put upon us, 'but that we should permit further worship of the Devil at Mallerbach, and sacrifice a brother to it, is something we are as little bound to as to obey a Turk.'

This letter was forwarded to the Elector Frederick, who passed it to Spalatin (it may also have got to Luther, and it is possible that Luther's phrase, 'The Devil at Allstedt', is a riposte to this letter's 'Devil at Mallerbach'). At the end of the month, the Elector replied in good Lutheran theological terms, perhaps in the words of Spalatin:

> If your teaching is of God, that which you imagine you can smother and suppress by force will be destroyed by God's grace, power and merit and without any human force, agency and suppression.[1]

We perhaps should note that, if Müntzer's actions were diametrically opposed to Luther's theology, they were not utterly remote from later actions of other Reformers. The claustrophobia of encirclement by hostile Catholics was to force Zwingli into the armed association of his Christian Civic League, while it would be a solemn moment of the Geneva Reformation, in 1536, that the Council should swear (like Müntzer's association, with uplifted hands) to defend the gospel. Another decade would see in Thuringia itself the growth of the formidable military Schmalkaldic League. At any rate in mid-June 1524 Müntzer took further measures in a dangerous situation. This was the extension of the associations of covenanted believers, pledged to come to the defence of the gospel, with weapons and armour at the hour of danger.[2]

To the 200 members now inside Allstedt were added 300 from outside the town, mainly from the miners of Mansfeld, divided into five companies, each with its registrar.[3]

---

[1] Hinrichs, p. 16. That Müntzer took this to heart, as the critical point of disagreement, is shown by his evident reference to this in his *Fürstenpredigt*: 'Dear Friends, let's have none of that twaddle about the Power of God doing it all without the help of your swords – otherwise they might as well rust in the scabbard' (Franz, p. 259).

[2] There were innumerable medieval sodalities from whom points of organization might have been taken. The emergency invasion arrangements in England in 1588 would be another parallel.

[3] The names of the leaders – Hans Reichart, Peter Behr, Peter Warmuth,

THE PROPHET OF ALLSTEDT 1523-4

Zeiss and Rückert now knew that, if they were to implement their instructions, it would be with the town and formidable neighbours against them. They decided to browbeat the Council, with the help of a few hand-picked friends. The night 13-14 June was one of panic on both sides. The town was filled with strangers; Müntzer's men panicked on rumours that horsemen were approaching the town. The alarm bells were rung by Müntzer himself, and his men rushed into the street, aided by a contingent of bloody-minded matrons with knives and pitchforks. The allies from Mansfeld appeared and at some point Müntzer seems to have addressed an open-air assembly, his head sticking out of an upper window, rather like a cuckoo from a clock. The next day Zeiss went off to Weimar to plead the hopelessness of further action, and indeed secured permission to release the hapless Ziliax Knaute. Hinrichs comments that 'the victory of Müntzer and his Bands was complete'.[1]

The truth is that Allstedt was safe in its remoteness, and in the absence of a superior military or police force. Just as Luther's and Frederick's Saxony owed very much to the preoccupation of the Emperor and the Catholic Princes with other affairs, and notably the Turkish wars, so Allstedt found it could get away with its radicalism. Luther seems to have recognized this, in a letter which he wrote to John Frederick on 18 June:[2] 'Satan in Allstedt . . . threatens us, high in his small corner.' Luther suggests that Müntzer be summoned to give account of his teaching – seeing he attacks ours so vehemently, or else let him go and see how he gets on in the territories of Duke George! Luther then gives voice to one of his deepest resentments, that this radicalism was able to exploit the very situation which his own stand for liberty had made possible:

> It is not a fine thing, to make use of our Victory under our very shadow, a victory gained without any help from them! They sit

---

Bartel Krumpe, Balthasar Stübner – have a certain ring about them, but despite the imposing words and oaths (like the early English trade unionists) they were little people, ignorant and inefficient. We shall discuss below, pp. 298–302, what social and political facts were involved.

[1] p. 28 [2] Brandt, op. cit., p. 214f.; WA,Br. 3, No. 753, p. 308, lines 76ff.

and make their cat calls on our dunghill – it is an Evil Spirit: let him go and do as I, and stand before other Princes outside this Principality and we shall see where his Spirit comes from.

This has to be said, however, from Thomas's point of view. A year before, Müntzer had challenged Count Ernest to bring the bishop and theologians to test his teaching. He could hardly be blamed, in the situation provoked by the Mallerbach crisis, for not venturing outside the circle of his allies, or for not wanting to defend himself alone against the Wittenberg team.

Thomas's view was stated plainly in a respectful letter to Duke John (13 July).[1] To his own calling the undeceivable witness of God has been given (Romans 8) and this is a call to witness to all the world, whatever the Scribes, plainly denying the spirit of Christ, may say. This is why he will not be heard by the 'Wittenbergers alone' – 'I want the Romans, Turks and heathen to be present.' It is this sense of universal testimony which gave to Müntzer a concern about printing his works, something more than the normal radical enthusiasm for seeing one's own works in print.

> If you will allow my books to go out, that is what I would like; but if not, then that I leave to God's will. But I will faithfully let you see all my writings.

Hinrichs, moreover, makes clear how much more confused the situation seemed to others in authority who did not share or understand Luther's doctrine. If the Elector Frederick, and the young John Frederick, were wholly on Luther's side, the Duke John found it not so easy to repudiate entirely the new teaching. Johann Strauss at Eisenach was in conflict with Luther about the vexed matter of tithes and interest, and was treating these things in the pulpit. Duke John's chaplain, Wolfgang Stein, had raised the whole question of the validity of Old Testament laws in relation to those of Saxony, and had helped to provoke Luther's profound but subtle exposition of the sphere and functions of civil government in his 'Von Weltlicher Obrigkeit' (1523). There seems to have been a suggestion for a summit conference of theologians, Luther, Melanchthon, Bugenhagen, Strauss, Stein, Karlstadt, Müntzer – one of the

[1] Franz, II, No. 52, p. 407

THE PROPHET OF ALLSTEDT 1523-4

most intriguing 'ifs' of Reformation history; as a firework display it would have far outshone the future Marburg Colloquy – but the idea never matured. In these weeks, Luther himself, at his Prince's request, was on a preaching tour of disaffected areas of Thuringia, but he never went beyond the Karlstadt country.

In fact, the authorities adopted a reasonable and wise stratagem. Duke John and Duke John Frederick would themselves visit Allstedt, and see the situation for themselves. They would hear Müntzer preach – what could plausibly be looked on as a trial sermon (since no Princely confirmation had ever been asked or given for Müntzer's installation in Allstedt). They would, at Frederick's request, look into the allegation that Müntzer had set up a printing press, without the kind of censorship which the Imperial Mandate required and which was in use at Wittenberg.

So it came about that on 1 July the Princes entered Allstedt and arranged for the Sermon which was preached before them by Müntzer in the Castle, in their presence and in that of Saxon officials – including Gregory Brück, Chancellor of Saxony – and presumably of castellan, mayor and council of the town.[1]

Müntzer's 'Princes' Sermon' (*Fürstenpredigt*) is, on any showing, an astonishing performance, one of the most extraordinary utterances in a century of remarkable preachments. As it has been ably edited by Hinrichs, and an entirely adequate translation of it by G. H. Williams exists, we shall give no detailed résumé of its contents.[2]

Müntzer had got what he asked for: a hearing. It was his great, last chance and he must have known it. It is his all-out effort to enlist the authorities in Saxony on behalf of his programme of anticlerical war, and for the protection of his gospel. However much his sympathies were with the common man, and if deep down he knew that in the end the Princes would not support him, he would not refuse, indeed must welcome, their protection and support. What he has to say is still within the orbit of the classic doctrine of

---
[1] Hinrichs, p. 39
[2] see Hinrichs (ed.) *Thomas Müntzer: Politische Schriften* (*Hallische Monographien* 17) Halle (Saale) 1951; G. H. Williams *Spiritual and Anabaptist Writers* pp. 47–70: for German text, see Franz, pp. 241–63

civil obedience, Romans 13, though with breath-taking audacity he takes this doctrine and turns it into a revolutionary manifesto.

The appeal to his rulers is accompanied by a virulent attack on their theological advisers: and now, for the first time, he attacks Luther with the gloves off, as 'Brother Porky-boy' and 'Brother Soft-Life'. Nor is it all polemic. In main outlines, here is the Gospel according to Thomas, the plan of salvation deriving from 15th-century 'inward religion', even something which might be a Hussite reminiscence of an older Wycliffite doctrine of 'dominion by grace': the whole set within a terrible realized eschatology. No doubt the text, as we have it now, has been edited, and fuller Scriptural references supplied; but, as always with Müntzer, these are remarkably full, and from every level of the biblical literature.

The choice of text was a gauntlet thrown at Wittenberg. No longer does Müntzer argue within the Theology of the Word. The 'Princes' Sermon' defends those revelations through dreams and visions,[1] that doctrine of assurance through the Spirit which Müntzer had, for the sake of peace, been earlier willing to play down.

The text was from Daniel 2, brilliantly conceived for Müntzer's purposes. Here is a prince, Nebuchadnezzar, worried and unable to make up his mind, made to choose between conflicting authorities: on the one hand, the false prophets who cannot explain his visions; on the other hand, the true prophet, the earnest servant of God, Daniel. And it is an apocalyptic story, a series of visions which seem to rehearse all history, culminating in an eschatological 'Now is the hour!', apt for a summons to action and decision.

All Müntzer's characteristic theology is brought into play: the theme of the Fall of the Virgin Church which he thought to find described in Eusebius, the continual betrayal of Christianity by the 'Scribes and Parsons', the sowing of Weeds among the Wheat, splendidly coloured as cornflowers and poppies, but now to be rooted up. There is one of his fullest expositions of the Fear of the Lord, and of the Coming of Faith, the Work of God in the abyss (*Abgrund*) of the Soul, the purging of the soul from creaturely lusts that it may become a dwelling place of God.

[1] Among his adherents were a visionary father and son whose dreams were carefully recorded. But this is medieval as well as radical.

We know that Müntzer had collected New Testament examples of dreams and visions.[1] Now he adds to them the ways in which God had spoken to the Patriarchs of the Old Testament in such direct revelation. 'Yes, it is a truly apostolic, Patriarchal and prophetic Spirit which attends to Visions' – nor is it enough to plead that these things happened only in the Apostolic age (an old point against Egranus, and also against Luther) – 'For if Christianity is not still apostolic, what on earth are we preaching about? What's the use of the Bible with its visions?' Then comes a terrible realized eschatology. The parsons are the vipers and the persecuting princes are eels – they are all led astray, though the poor people and peasants see further than their rulers. Romans 13 is, properly interpreted, a call to action, to cut off with the sword those who get in the way of the gospel. Did not Christ himself say: 'Take mine enemies and slay them before me'? Princes are the means which God employs to drive away the enemies of the Elect. 'For a godless man has no right to live if he gets in the way of the godly.' A catena of passages from the Old Testament and New are pressed into support of this view, that idolaters are to be destroyed with their idols. You ask why the Apostles did not act in this way, but truth is that Peter was a timid man to the end of his days. If men will heed God's revelation and obey it, mercy must be shown to them. But if they refuse then they are to be strangled without any grace, as Hezekiah, Josiah, Cyrus, Daniel and Elijah did with the prophets of Baal. 'Otherwise the Christian Church cannot be restored to her original purity.' 'The angels, who must sharpen their sickles to this work, are the earnest servants of God who are filled with the zeal of the Divine Wisdom.' Nebuchadnezzar, Müntzer concluded, fell down before Daniel, conquered by the power of truth, and he honoured God's prophet by making him one of his Officers that the judgement of God might be carried out – so must it be with you, my Lords – for the godless have no right to live save that which the Elect grant to them – 'Rejoice, true Friends of God, that the heart of God's Enemies is broken!'

It must have been a terrific occasion, in the exact sense of that

[1] G. T. Strobel *Leben, Schriften und Lehren Thomas Müntzers* Nuremberg/Altdorf 1795; Franz, III, 7: Aufzeichnungen (h), p. 538

much abused word. We have no evidence of its immediate effect. But there seems to have been no objection put in the way of Müntzer printing the sermon. Immediate events seem to show that Müntzer himself was not out of heart.

Before Müntzer could be told of the decision of the Princes, perhaps before they had made up their minds, new events intervened which gave rise to a flurry of important communications on Müntzer's part. Perhaps to encourage his Ernestine cousins, Duke George of Saxony had taken action against Müntzer's disciples and followers in Sangerhausen. Some he threw into prison, others made their way as refugees to Allstedt. Duke George then proposed to send his own officer from Sangerhausen to demand their surrender from Zeiss, and Müntzer had reason to believe that Zeiss might surrender them. At the same time a Catholic knight, Frederick von Witzleben, had attacked his own subjects, at Schönewerthe.[1]

The new crisis moved Müntzer to extreme utterance. First, he wrote to 'Those who Fear God' in Sangerhausen, telling them to stand firm – 'for there exist more than 30 Leagues of Covenanted Elect – the game is on in many lands.' To the authorities in Sangerhausen he wrote one of his warning letters: 'I know there are no more idolatrous people in this land than you – be warned by me – do not strive against the Spirit.'[2]

In contrast is the warm, fatherly letter which he wrote to those imprisoned in Sangerhausen itself. They are to expect tribulations and 'Anfechtungen' as he had always said. But they are to speak firmly to their rulers:

> A Prince, a landlord is appointed to rule over temporal goods, and his power extends no further – but our souls he shall not rule, for in this matter we must obey God rather than men. The time is at hand – a great bloodshed will come upon the hardened world on account of their unfaith . . . God will not abandon his Elect – he will execute vengeance at the right time.[3]

In three letters to Zeiss, Müntzer interprets the new crisis in terms of his 'Princes' Sermon'. The thought of handing over

[1] Hinrichs, p. 65   [2] Franz, II, Nos 53, 54   [3] Franz, II, No. 55

refugees for the gospel's sake, to their godless enemies, appals him. Rulers, he now says, are to be obeyed when they are not against the gospel – 'But now, when they act not only against the gospel, but against natural law itself, they ought to be strangled like mad dogs.'[1]

It is quite plain to him that the Catholic authorities have ceased to be Christian – 'they hold nothing at all of Christian Faith – therefore their authority is also at an end, and will in a short time be handed over to the common people.' The letter ends with an appeal to Zeiss himself and a reminder that 'whoso would be a stone in the New Church must risk his own neck or be rejected by the builders'. In a second note, Müntzer tries to avoid misunderstanding: his violent utterance was about the enemies of the gospel, but not 'godly civil servants' – that be far from me![2] Like all Müntzer's utterances in these weeks, there is an Apocalyptic stress – 'the regeneration of all things is at our door!'

The third letter deals with an important new happening. Müntzer had recently delivered another oration – a 'Covenant Sermon', the text of which has not survived and of which we know only through Müntzer's allusions and a report from Zeiss. Once again he had chosen a marvellously apt theme, 2 Kings 22–23, the story of the Covenant under Josiah, by which king, priests and people joined in new allegiance to the Word of God. This is Müntzer's new plea, his suggestion how the rulers of Saxony might implement the challenge of his 'Princes' Sermon'. They should join themselves with their people, no longer in terms of the existing feudal (and heathen) oaths, but in a new covenant to protect the gospel and to defend it against the ungodly. If they simply 'look through their fingers' at what is going on around them, they will in the end come to open shame. But – and this is important for the understanding of Müntzer's idea of his associations – we are not to suppose that anything can be done by men alone, or by putting trust in human action. They are to be a kind of umbrella, protecting their people, while the real renovation goes only by the preaching of the gospel and the

---

[1] Franz, II, No. 57; 'strangled like mad dogs' is the phrase to be used by Luther about the peasants in his own violent broadsheet a year hence.

[2] Franz, II, No. 58

action of the Elect Friends of God. The Covenant is only an emergency device (*Notwehr*) and an instrument of human reason which can work by itself.

It is difficult to piece out what followed. We know that Müntzer and a small band of Allstedt officials, leaders among his own followers, were summoned to Weimar on 1 August. According to a vivid broadsheet published some months later, Müntzer came away from his own interview 'yellow as a corpse' and to the question 'How did it go?' answered bitterly, 'How else should it go? I have to get out!'[1] Hinrichs (pressing the evidence rather hard) thinks that Duke John tried to handle things on good Lutheran principles and to treat the matter of the preacher, Müntzer, separately from the question of the seditious behaviour of the civic officers in relation to the Imperial mandates. In any case, it is likely that Müntzer was given separate treatment, and it may be that it was not until he met his comrades again in Allstedt on 3 August that he realized the extent of their betrayal. For on their part there seems to have been abject surrender. They promised to abandon all unlawful associations, and to give up their printing press. They probably threw a good deal of the blame on Müntzer.

When Müntzer found out that he had been abandoned by his followers, there was a stormy session (he wrote a bitter note about 'the Archjudas Iscariots' who had betrayed him, excepting rather notably the castellan Zeiss from any condemnation). In their presence, when things had calmed down, he dictated a letter to the Elector, which would be sent with the report of the officials.[2]

This is a respectful letter; Frederick the Wise was his last hope, able to overrule, if necessary, the actions of his Brother. But now Müntzer knew of Luther's warning Open Letter to the Rulers of Saxony ('that forsworn person with his shameful letter') – and this for Müntzer is another reason why he pleads against censorship. He may need to reply in writing against Luther, for he preaches another kind of Faith – one 'which does not agree with Luther's notions but is the same, conformed to the hearts of all the Elect on earth'. 'My appeal, therefore, is to all nations, and must be heard by them' – he must therefore be given facilities for the widest possible audience:

[1] Hinrichs, pp. 78ff.   [2] Hinrichs, pp. 91ff.; Franz, II, No. 64

THE PROPHET OF ALLSTEDT 1523-4

'That is why I avoid a hearing in a corner, to which the Scribes would constrain me.' But Müntzer does not want to avoid proper oversight and has already handed over two documents to the authorities, an exposition of Luke 1 and a tract about 'how to defend the gospel'.

The weight of growing anxiety and uncertainty seems to have told on Müntzer, as it had done on Luther in the hours following the interview with Cajetan in 1518, and with the same result. In the night of 7–8 August once again Müntzer climbed over a wall, and fled with a goldsmith from Nordhausen, leaving a note to his followers saying that he had had to go out on business – he wrote a further defence of his action a day or so later, in which he begged them to look after his wife. What provoked the flight cannot be known, though Hinrichs plausibly suggests that it was the fact that 7 August was a Sunday on which Müntzer must have intended to preach – Hinrichs suggests that his former followers had threatened to arrest him if he did.

So ended Müntzer's ascendancy in Allstedt. He had ruined his own positive work by the virulence of his anticlericalism. But it is no good trying to separate out those elements which suggest he was a Bucer *manqué* or a Calvin before his time. The apocalyptic, anticlerical ferment was not to be discarded. The defence of the gospel by force was something which Luther could at this time denounce, but a decade later most of Protestantism, in Switzerland and Germany, had capitulated to the use of diplomatic and military means. Luther's 'The Word alone shall do it' looks odd against the programme of the Schmalkaldic League. Had Müntzer confined himself to his mystical evangelical pattern, he might have had considerable success. He had a passion and a directness of speech which is in marked contrast to Andrew Karlstadt's tedious ramblings, and, as a preacher, he must have outclassed him altogether. His liturgical experiments were indeed notable and pioneering, and it is significant that, when they were put forward by John Lang of Erfurt (whose liturgy survived, a document deeply indebted to Müntzer), Luther himself approved. In Allstedt itself the liturgy was to survive the Peasants' War, and Visitations a decade later found the parson celebrating from behind the altar and a people singing Müntzer's hymns. It was a tragedy that all this suffered from the attempt to uproot everything connected with the discredited prophet.

Nor had Müntzer's influence been confined to Allstedt, for we have evidence that other towns had begun to imitate his rites and he had followers throughout the whole region. How firm was their loyalty within his Covenant technique cannot be said, but it was no doubt enough to bring many of them into the Peasants' War a year hence, and to leave many of them for the rest of their days marked by his teaching. Allstedt had been his great chance. Fate would not give him such another.

CHAPTER FIFTEEN

ALLSTEDT WRITINGS

To Müntzer's Allstedt period belong three other writings, of which some summary notice may be taken at this point. The first, the 'Protestation oder Entbietung'[1] is a further apologia for his teaching about Faith – 'Concerning the Beginning of true Christian Faith and Baptism' – and begins with the significant apostrophe: 'Hear thou, O world! I preach Christ Crucified for the New Year and thou and I with him – if it please you, receive it; if not, reject it!' Like his earlier discussion of Faith, the tract consists of numbered paragraphs, in this case twenty-one of them. It begins with a characteristic apostolic opening:

> I, Thomas Müntzer, of Stolberg in Harz, a servant of the living Son of God, through the immutable will and irrevocable mercy of God the Father, invoke and wish in the Holy Ghost for all you, the Elect of God, the Pure Fear of the Lord and that Peace to which the world is foe.

His favourite image of tares and wheat, poppies and cornflowers, evokes the eschatological judgement now at hand – and the knavery of this world is contrasted with the Elect who 'sigh and long after God's Eternal Will' over 'poor, fallen Christendom'. False and phoney Faith (paragraph 2) have made the Christian Church worse than heathendom, and this abomination in the holy place has to be recognized (paragraph 3):

> For the only comfort of the Church in its misery is that it expects that the Elect ought and shall be brought into conformity with Christ – and take account of the Work of God with all kinds of suffering and chastening.

[1] Franz, I, pp. 225-40

But others have made of Faith a trivial thing – 'Ready to write great books and shout "I believe! I believe!"' (paragraph 4). 'O thou Daughter of Zion', remember how it was in the time of the Apostles (paragraph 5) when only grown men after long instruction were received as catechumens – not our superstition which has made an outward thing of a holy sign. None of the doctors of the Church have taught true Baptism.

> I ask all you Scribes to show me where it is written in Holy Scripture that an inarticulate child was baptized by Christ or his disciples, or where it is laid down that our children should be baptized as we now practise it. Yes, since you put so much upon this head, you will not find that Mary, the Mother of God, or the disciples of Christ, were baptized with water.

In the sixth paragraph there is a short examination of John 3:5 – the meaning of baptism in Water and the Spirit against the context of other parts of the Fourth Gospel, where the Holy Spirit is linked with Faith and where Water is 'The Movement [*Bewegung*] of our Spirits into God'. By making infants into Christians (paragraph 7), we have turned Christians into children. The whole business of godparents has perverted the true baptism – followed by the ceremonies of the unchaste woman with the scarlet cloak, the Church of Rome. As a result we no longer (paragraph 8) spare a thought for the origins of Faith, in the heart. The Scribes think they use the Scripture, but in effect it makes them blind, 'but it was written for us ignorant men for the sake of that Holy Faith which is as a grain of mustard seed' (paragraph 9). The heathen, Turks and Jews also have faith of a kind, no better than this is the faith which the Scribes say we must take on authority. And even the heathen believe that there is an unchangeable God (paragraph 10) and that those who specially do good in the world are comrades with God. Even the Mohammedans in the Koran speak of Christ. The heathen (paragraph 12) with their gods and goddesses have much in common with us, and with the superstitions now practised, with our plain idolatry. And yet false scribes say that we can come easily to Faith, when in reality we have to suffer while God ploughs us up and roots out the thistles and the thorns from our hearts –

Even if you had swallowed the Bible, it avails nothing, you must still suffer the plough of God – you must be stripped of all the clothing of the creaturely by God through his Work, and if a man says 'But Christ has done all that needs to be done by himself alone', this is much, much too simple. Unless you grasp together the Head and the Members, how can you follow in his footsteps?

What we have done is simply to chalk over the Roman indulgences when we preach this honey-sweet Christ (paragraph 13). But ours must be the narrow way, Judgement not by outward things but the all-loved Will of God in his Living Word as we experience it in the very temptation of Faith. 'For I have to know whether it is God who is speaking or the Devil, and I must distinguish between them in the Ground of the Soul' (paragraph 13). To preach that Faith alone justifies and not Work, is immodest, for a man comes to Faith through God's Work (paragraph 14). The well-meaning light of Nature thinks: 'Oh, well, if that's all I have to do, just believe, it's simple' . . . and 'no doubt, you were born of Christian parents, you have never known what it is to doubt, you will stand fast in Faith. Yes, yes, I'm a good Christian man. Ah, can a man so easily be saved? Pooh-pooh, to you parsons!' Others (paragraph 16) go to the other extreme and turn to outward things, fasting and prayers, and become proud Devils. But there are others still who realize that the Word, on which true Faith depends, is not a thousand miles off, but springs out of the ground of their heart, as it comes from the Living God. With inward eyes they have waited long upon the Lord.

It is this diligent waiting upon God which makes the true, 'Beginning Christian' [paragraph 17] when a man desires Faith, but has to cry desperately to God, and when God torments him in his conscience with unbelief, despair, reproach. But when men come in such a state to the Scribes and address them: 'Dear worthy, reverend, learned Sir' – and all that kind of dirty muck, then the Scribes (who charge high fees for the smallest consultation) reply: 'Ah my good man, either believe, or go to the Devil!' And when the poor man says: 'but my unbelief consumes me, how can I believe?', then the Scribe says: 'Ah, dear friend, you must not bother about things too high for you. Just have simple Faith and put such thoughts away. It is all imagination. Go and make merry with your friends. You'll soon forget your worries.' This kind of comfort has turned earnest Christianity into an abomination. Such are the false Scribes then [paragraph 18] who grind their teeth if anybody so much as criticizes them. Christ denounced such as false prophets [paragraph 19] who make the narrow way broad, the sweet call bitter and turn light into darkness. This, then, [paragraph 20] is the shame of the Church which has come upon us through a false Baptism and false Faith. If I have erred about this I will be instructed, not in some corner, but before the whole world, and to it I pledge my body and my life. If I have offended any, let him write to me in a friendly way, and I will reply in good measure that none should wrongly judge the other, may the tender Son of God, Jesus Christ, help us to this end, who has made us brothers – and also [paragraph 21] I would that my cause be heard before men of all nations and every kind of faith. I charge you to avoid snap judgements for the mercy of God!

The Psalms counted for much with Thomas Müntzer, and into or out of two in particular, Psalms 93 and 19, he read much of his own theology. Of the first he made his own free, idiosyncratic translation, which he sent to his disciples in Stolberg.[1] On 24 May he wrote a short exposition of Psalm 19 which he sent to his friend, Christopher Meinhard, in Eisleben.[2] The writing has survived because it was published by Agricola after Müntzer's death, with a satirical running commentary, as an example of his 'devilish' theology. As a succinct summary of Müntzer's view of salvation, it is, however, oddly impressive. This Psalm teaches how a man's eyes have first to be opened, through suffering the Work of God declared through the Law. 'Whoso has not suffered the Night knoweth not the art of God [*Kunst Gottes*].' A Christian man must hear Christ preached in the heart through the Fear of God. The Works of the Hands of God[3] must first have shown him Reverence before God,

[1] Franz, II, No. 41, 18 July 1523
[2] Franz, II, No. 49, 30 May 1524; Brandt, op. cit., pp. 145, 241. Meinhard was a cousin of the Allstedt castellan, Hans Zeiss.
[3] The distinction between the Works of God and the Works of the hands of God is an Augustinian doctrine used by Luther in his first lectures on the Psalms, 1513–15. It seems to have counted for Thomas Müntzer.

or all preaching is vain. He who knows these things has the power of Judgement in all things.

This instruction from God is displayed to all, irrespective of the 'frontiers of the godless', though, in their case, for judgement. But to his Beloved, God is as a bridegroom, allowing them to be treated like Cinderellas (*verworfne Dienstmagde*) that he may save them. So Christ awakes as a bridegroom, as he did when asleep in the ship during the storm, and the Elect rejoice similarly with Jesus. So it is with a man, who is like a fish swimming against the wild current in order to climb upstream to his true home. The Elect man cannot get away from God who sends him fire in the conscience. And even if an Elect man fall into great and mighty sin, yet the fire of his conscience brings him disgust and loathing – and when such grief and loathing become habitual, then he cannot sin. 'This is what I mean by *Langweil* [Waiting] – which the loose-living swine find sticks in their nostrils!' They talk so much of Paul, jeer at the Law as an outward thing and yet they don't understand the apostle. The Law of the Lord which enlightens the eyes of the Elect makes the godless blind. These stupid Bacchantes think they have won when they point to Romans 4, but ignore Genesis 15 and Psalm 31, which Paul also quotes. 'As highly as Paul rates Faith without merit of Work, so high do I rate the need to suffer the Work of God' – 'so I agree with Paul and not with these Scribes.' They dream up a Christ who is the fulfiller of the Law, because they wish to avoid suffering his Work, which is the Cross. But the Righteousness of God so strangles us in unbelief that we come at last to recognize that our desires are sinful. If we persist in them we simply become hardened. As Paul says in 2 Timothy 3, those who do not suffer the Work of God cannot understand – for they deny the need for Contemplation (*Studierung*) and Meditation (*Betrachtung*) in God's Law, in order that the Work of God may be known.

Müntzer's last Allstedt tract, the 'Expressed Exposure of False Faith in an Untrue World',[1] is intended as an exposition of the first chapter of St Luke's Gospel. Written during the hectic pressures of the last weeks of his Allstedt ministry, it is the most formless of his writings, and may consist of older sermon material worked up into

[1] Franz, I, pp. 265-319

polemic, with perhaps a sharper apocalyptic note than any of his writings since the Prague Manifesto. It was submitted to the Censor at Allstedt, shortly before Müntzer's flight, but he took a copy with him when he left, and this, slightly revised, was printed at Nuremberg by Hans Herrgott. There it fell foul of the appointed censor, the preacher Schleupner of the Sebaldus church, and 400 out of the 500 copies were confiscated. It is a meandering document, the positive exposition interlaced with repetitive invective, so that the continual 'False Scribes', 'Thieves of Scripture', becomes wearisome (was the prophet turning into a bore?). On the other hand, the polemic against Wittenberg is widened: he attacks not only their 'False Faith' and their Dumb God, but also Luther on the Zwickau prophets – and perhaps on Karlstadt too: the view that the radicals are Pharisaic, in despising the 'poor sinners' of Wittenberg, for their championing of the Augustinian principle that the personal worth or unworthiness of the clergy does not invalidate their ministry.

Müntzer's claim that the Elect can have true judgement[1] between Elect and Reprobate is of great and seminal importance, for it underlies the whole of his apocalyptic and radical programme of revolution and anticipates Reformation Puritanism, if not the Calvinist programme. When Müntzer turns to expound, as he does more fully than is usual with him, the way in which Faith and the Spirit comes to us, through temptation, suffering and unbelief, into the abyss of the soul, he does at least make plain that he has a plan of salvation which Luther and his followers perhaps made very little effort to understand. Stripped of its pretentious jargon, it was more respectable than Luther thought.

As usual, the text is peppered with Scripture from all levels of the Bible, though perhaps Müntzer tended to dwell more and more on his own resemblance to Jeremiah and to John the Baptist. Thus, the frontispiece is bespattered with texts from Jeremiah and Ezekiel and signed 'Thomas Müntzer with the Hammer'.

The opening chapter of St Luke, with the doctrine of the Incarnation at its heart, with the prophetic visions and pronouncements of Zacharias, Elizabeth and Mary, with the premonition of the fiery

[1] 'Judgement', 'discrimination' (*urteil*) and 'distinction' (*unterschied*) are important radical terms.

ministry of judgement in John the Baptist – here is a theme as marvellously apt for Müntzer's own doctrine as was the *Fürstenpredigt*. Faith was no light, trivial thing as the false Scribes say, to Zacharias and Mary. They did not just say: 'I'll just believe and it will all come right' as the drunken world does, with a Faith worse than that of Turks, Jews or Heathen.

> Oho, it is clean contrary to nature, this Fear of the Lord which is the Beginning of Faith, by which the power of the Lord works in the abyss of the soul [*Abgrund der Seele*]. This Fear of the Lord creates Reverence [*Verwunderung*] in the Impossible Work of Faith. But if you ask the Scribes about this, they say shamelessly, 'Oh, I believe the Scriptures', or, 'Oho, but this contradicts Scripture'. The high Movement and the heartfelt anguish of the Elect, they throw to the Devil. And they make it impossible for the common man to learn Faith because of his immersion in the struggle for existence. They say 'Dear Thomas, you are raving' – according to them it is all nicely worked out: they are to read fine big books, and the Peasants must just listen to them.[1]

In a short Preface addressed to 'poor, shattered Christendom', Müntzer enunciates the principles of his own biblicism, namely, that the divine Judgements (*Urteile*) are made plain 'out of Scripture, through the Holy Ghost' – 'for all judgements by themselves contain the highest contradictions, which is why they have to be compared with one another'.[2]

It has fallen to Müntzer to expose the false deceit of the Scribes who would make Faith into a trivial thing. And he will do this, publicly before the world, refusing the challenge of his opponents to argue with them 'in a corner'. 'Our Scribes want to send the Holy Ghost to College' (*auf die hohe Schule*), they alone are to be the judges of Faith.

They have put the Lid of Shame (*Schanddeckel*) on Scripture, hiding the nature of true Faith from the world. The Son of God says

---

[1] Franz, pp. 272–5

[2] Franz, pp. 266–8. This dialectic of contraries in Scripture may have an Erasmian origin, but it was to become a feature of radical exposition of Scripture; what Müntzer hints at here becomes explicit in compilations of such contradictions in Huth, Denck and Sebastian Franck.

that Scripture gives Witness: no, say the Scribes, it gives Faith. But that is imitation, monkey Faith.

> If a man in his whole life had neither heard nor seen the Bible, he could none the less have an undeceivable Christian Faith through the teaching of the Spirit – like those who wrote the Scripture without any books.[1]

And he could surely discern that this was true Faith and not the devil's counterfeit. We Christians ought to agree with all the Elect from many races and all kinds of Faiths, for, according to Acts 10, it is possible for a man to have lived among unbelievers from his youth up, and yet to experience God's teaching without any books – and we ought so to use the Scriptures that we may give a friendly Judgement to Jew or Turk. But our Scribes demand miracles, send to the Devil anyone who disagrees with them, mock the Spirit of Christ and say 'Away with the Spirit! I will praise my own writings – look what I have done'.[2]

They insist that Scriptures give Faith, but in the end they fall back on human tradition – no better than Jews, Turks or Heathens. But the Patriarchs show us that Faith is an impossible thing with men, as we also have to experience with the coming (*Ankunft*) of Faith

> that we fleshly, earthly men shall become gods through the Incarnation of Christ, and at the same time God's scholars, taught and made godlike by himself, nay, utterly and completely transformed into him, so that our earthly life is taken into the Heavenlies.[3]

But Brother Soft-Life and Father Sit-on-the-Fence (*Leisetritt*) want to keep all their desires, their pomp, their riches and still have Faith.

Meanwhile godless, senseless Rulers rage and roar, and because man has fallen away to the creatures, he has come to fear them more than God. Yet Romans 13 shows that Princes are only Hangmen and Executioners – that is all their trade. Rather should the whole world fear the Man who has true zeal for the honour of God. The world says:

[1] Franz, p. 277   [2] Franz, p. 279   [3] Franz, p. 281

'Oh, yes, a man can preach the gospel, fear God alone, and at the same time hold stupid rulers in all honour, even though what they do is clean against equity and God's Word – ah, for conscience sake, they say men must obey the Nobs [*Junkers*]'

Nor do they heed what Matthew 13 says about the separation of the godless from the Elect. They cock a snook at the Holy Ghost and impudently say that God reveals his judgements to no man – they mutter in their beards that nobody can know who is Elect and who is Reprobate.

Yes, a fine faith that is, which will raise up a right subtle people of God – such as Plato the Philosopher speculated about in his *Republic* and Apuleius in the *Golden Ass*.[1]

It is true that the Elect man is also a sinner, but his conscience rebukes him when he perceives the Movement of the Spirit in anguish – whereas the conscience of the ungodly is not like that at all, but the more hardened in sin. The Elect man has the Holy Spirit as his schoolmaster into Faith. The common people think that parsons must know all about Faith because they read big, fine books:

'Ah they are great men with their red and brown academic hats – they surely know what is true and what is false.'

As a result the poor common man is kept from faith through being immersed in getting his living.

To put Christendom right means that the usury-seeking knaves must be put down and turned into lackeying dog's-bodies. But the common man must look for a new John, rich in grace, one who has the experience of coming to Faith through Unfaith, who will turn men to the Lamb of God. The divine way of it, true Christian Faith, comes only through the Eternal Word of the Father in the Son, explained through the Holy Ghost in suffering of heart – after which a man can rejoice in God his Saviour.[2]

God has exalted the humble and meek:

O, my dear Friends, not the Big Nobs, with their proud titles – as the church of the godless has them – poor muddleheaded common

[1] Franz, p. 290, note 150   [2] Franz, pp. 293–9

men think that those great fat thick Chubbycheeks ought to pronounce Judgement about how Christian Faith comes.¹

But what should they know of it, who spend all their days in guzzling and swilling, delicately nurtured people who never had a bad day in their lives, nor would be able to endure one for the sake of truth, who will not give up even a halfpenny of their tithes and yet set up as Judges and Defenders of the Faith. If the Church is to be renewed, there must appear a Servant of God, in the spirit of Elijah, to awaken those who with burning zeal will purge Christendom from these godless rulers.

This is why so few can talk about what this means – this Beginning, this Movement of the Spirit – shameful it seems to those who have never tasted the Patience (*Langweil*) through which the Work of God is found in the First Sprinkling (Num. 19) when the Waters of Divine Wisdom are lifted up – and yet there is no other way to Peace, Joy and Righteousness in Conscience.²

The soul trembles in darkness and the Shadow of Death until his feet are turned into the way of Peace in the extremity of un-Peace. His desires are stretched towards this Sprinkling through the in-breathing of the Holy Spirit. This is how the victory of Faith comes, which is a thousand times more inward than outward:

> You see, you literalist fellows, how desperate is your position when you say that men must simply believe Scripture without experiencing the sure Witness of the Spirit.

meanwhile nobody can get to Faith because of their usury, taxes and tithes. If we do not soon amend, we shall even lose natural reason from our adherence to our own private commodity (*Eigennutz*).

The Scribes say: 'Ah, but they are all poor sinners – if Christ does not despise us, why should these new Pharisaic spirits?' They say this to excuse their own sins. But let them say what they like, they seek their own bellies, oho, with what earnestness do they go for the red guilders.

Then they put up another lie – they say that, though a parson be good or bad, yet he may handle the mysteries of God and preach the

¹ Franz, p. 299   ² loc. cit.

True Word. But this is a grievous perversion of Scripture. Exodus 23. Psalm 49.

> But the truly resigned Man of God must be awakened out of the wilderness of his heart, which must be broken up, and fight against his sensual lusts which are harder than Adamant ... through a proved and tested life he must open up the Cross to others and cry in the wilderness of those hearts which fear God and begin to awaken to the Truth.

In a kind of marginal gloss, Müntzer adds a hermeneutic note:

> You must always consider the whole context, one word alongside the other, if you would understand aright what I say about Unbelief and its Impossibility.[1]

The Elect Friend of God finds a deep joy when his comrade, also through such a similar Coming, finds similar Faith, even though to the poisonous Black Raven this is as ridiculous as he makes out in his book of slanders.[2]

Yet this makes the true Christian Church, the separation of the godless from the Elect. Now is the time for the Tares to be shaken in the sieve:

> It is always harvest time ... soon the Gospel will come into much fuller reality [*viel hoher Wesen*] than in the time of the Apostles. Out of many lands and from strange Nations manifold Elect will arise far superior to our slothful and neglectful Christians ... many of these wild, strange heathen will be received to the shame of the False Scribes, for as I myself have heard from them, they are above measure astonished at our Faith.

There is no people under the sun which has so perverted its own laws as our present-day Christendom and especially the literalist Scribes – and those who ought to be the first to understand Christendom – which is why they are called Princes (*Fürsten*) – show the worst unbelief. They like to be called 'Most Christian this and that' ... but will not defend their subjects if they are persecuted by their neighbours for the Gospel's sake. Then they want only to be Hangmen and Executioners.

---

[1] Franz, p. 309   [2] The reference is, of course, to Luther.

I would far rather teach Heathen, Turks and Jews about the smallest Word of God and the Divine Order, about the meaning of Dominion, both our own and towards God.

For all this the Scribes deny, though I have admonished them in a friendly way, how they must learn from the Beginning of the Bible about the dominion of God and of ourselves over the creatures. They think this is all – Enthusiasm! But I say to them, if you will not learn the Bible properly you will never have understanding or judgement, and God, through heathen plagues, will put you to shame. But the Elect grow sweet and green, blooming in the Wisdom of the Cross – and every sensual Sit-on-the-Fence counts them mad.

Like those of old, then, we are affrighted when God wants to make us divine through the Incarnation of his Son, and our Faith is tried as gold in the Furnace. Yet this is the true Kingdom of David where Christ rules from his Tree – there the power of the Most High is displayed through the Impossible Work of God in our sufferings through the overshadowing of the Holy Ghost – this, then, is the sum of it, that God will give us true Christian Faith through the Incarnation of Christ and our conformity with him in suffering and in life, through the working of the Holy Ghost. This is the Holy Covenant which God swore to Abraham to give us. But this Faith is so rare that it comes only through Temptation – to which may Christ help us all, Amen.[1]

[1] Franz, p. 319

CHAPTER SIXTEEN

MÜHLHAUSEN

Much as Thomas Müntzer might resemble the shepherd in Milton's 'Lycidas' – a poem the anticlerical invective of which he would have found highly congenial – the possibilities of fresh woods and pastures new were now strictly limited. He could not venture within the orbit of Wittenberg and of Luther's influence which stretched at least as far as Mansfeld, nor put himself within the grasp of Catholic Princes – least of all, Count Ernest of Mansfeld or Duke George of Saxony. There was little safety or scope for him in the scores of tiny towns and villages, and he had probably already blotted his copy-book in Halle and Nordhausen. But there was one obvious city of refuge for him, by all accounts ripe for his intervention: the Imperial Free City of Mühlhausen, 45 miles south-west of Allstedt.[1]

Mühlhausen was a city of moderate size: 5,000–6,000 inhabitants, twice the size of contemporary Leipzig and Dresden. Its economic fortunes had been dwindling and, apart from vegetables and cloth, it was best known for the quality of its local beer (a motif which recurs in our story). Its wealth was concentrated among the inmates of the Inner city, the less privileged inhabitants residing in the Outer town, while, with the civic imperialism of all Swiss and German cities in that age, there was a penumbra of influence on the

---

[1] not to be confused with Mühlhausen in Alsace: see Merx *Thomas Müntzer und Heinrich Pfeiffer*; Manfred Bensing *Thomas Müntzer und der Thüringer Aufstand 1525* (Berlin 1966); also D. Lösche, 'Zur Lage der Bauern im Gebiet der ehemaligen freien Reichstadt Mühlhausen zur Zeit des Bauernkrieges' and G. Günther 'Der Mühlhauser Rezess vom 3 Juli 1523', in G. Brendler (ed.) *Die frühbürgerliche Revolution in Deutschland*.

surrounding countryside over some seventeen villages in which there was a considerable range of prosperity. As in other cities, there was a large number of churches and religious houses, here especially those of the order of German Knights. Here too was the old, old medieval story of the tussle of the citizens to win privileges and liberties from feudal overlords, in this part of Germany very complicated, so that Philip of Hesse, Duke George of Saxony, the archbishop of Mainz were in various ways involved in Mühlhausen, while for an Imperial city there was an ultimate appeal to the Emperor. Here, as in most other cities, there were inner social and political tensions, attempts by the under-privileged and less wealthy to gain power, or at least a fair voice in civic affairs. And though there is some irony in the way in which recent East German historians dismiss all the older histories as 'bourgeois' – ideologically perverted overnight in 1945 – there were in fact signs of a class struggle in the city. Mühlhausen was yet another Venetian oligarchy, at its core a group of patrician families who dominated the closed circle of the *senatus seniorum*, and through this controlled the city council. But this left a dangerous element of well-to-do but politically unprivileged citizens within the city while in the suburbs there was a still more restless population including moderately well-to-do burghers, but extending also to a proletariat and unemployed. Into this unstable situation there came the Reformation, a heightening of religious tensions between old Catholics and new Reformers, and an aggravation of anticlerical grievances. It needed only the advent of the new radicalism to upset the situation completely and it is no accident that a series of political crises durning 1523 had at the heart of them the fiery polemic of a radical preacher, Heinrich Pfeiffer.

Pfeiffer was a local boy made good or bad, according as you looked at it. He had friends and relatives within the city. He had been a Cistercian monk in the wealthy monastery at Eichsfeld, but had fled, to become for a time cook and butler (and no doubt a Joseph as well) in the castle of a German knight, Hans von Enzenberg. Thence he was pitchforked by officers of the archbishop of Mainz, but he left the Eichsfeld neighbourhood with a good knowledge of the locality – and especially of the kind of monasteries and castles which would once have been four-starred in Baedeker, and no doubt with quite a crop of old scores he would much like one day to pay off. He was an effective preacher in the current anticlerical and ill-mannered vogue. How long he lived quietly in Mühlhausen is not known but on the Sunday of Septuagesima 1523 he made a startling intervention. For this was 'Beer Sunday' when free drinks were handed round after Procession from Church, and Pfeiffer, in secular dress, halted the throng and preached a fiery evangelical utterance on the true wine of the gospel. An attempt of the Council to muzzle him forthwith brought disconcerting evidence of opinion favourable to the new preacher. The Council were reinforced in their misgivings by a warning from the archbishop of Mainz, and the receipt of an Imperial rescript against the Lutheran preaching, but words were not much help at this stage.

On the Wednesday in Holy Week, Pfeiffer retorted by preaching before the main church, of Our Lady, where his excited followers swore with uplifted hands to defend the gospel.[1] They then elected eight men, two from each of the Suburban Quarters, the parishes[2] outside the city unrepresented in its government, and had unwittingly stumbled on a device, the 'Eight Men', which was to persist as part of the new political struggle, the real popular counterpoise against the Establishment. At this time two other preachers, one an escaped monk, appeared in the city, and for the next two years there was at least one Lutheran preacher who kept in touch with Wittenberg and acted as a clerical counterpoise to the radical ferment. It did not lower the temperature.

In May 1523 there was a fierce demonstration before the Town Hall, and the opposition demanded that the Eight Men be recognized in the town constitution, while a long list of grievances ranged from the old rallying cry that the Gospel go free to the very practical demand that tithes and interest should cease. Of fifty-four Articles, the Council accepted thirty-nine, but dared not yield to the critical demand that the *senatus seniorum* be abolished, and played for time.

---

[1] This is such a Müntzerian gesture that one wonders whether the chronicler has not read it back into 1523. But it seems supported by facts.

[2] The difficult word 'Gemeinde' can mean a community, or a congregation, or the inhabitants of a parish.

On 3 July there was another uproar, when armoured bands gesticulated with weapons about the streets. The citizens of Mühlhausen were always prone to find political occasions thirsty affairs, and as the long day wore on, tempers were softened by the good beer, so that it all fizzled out in an amiable plundering expedition on religious houses. In the next days the Council had to accept a series of compromises with what the Marxists call the *kleinbürgerliche* elements. But they were strong enough to demand the expulsion of Pfeiffer as unruly and his friends were not strong enough to defend him. He had to go.

He was back at the end of the year, and the ferment was renewed. The matriarchal element in the Radical reformation awaits its historian, and here, as in St Gall on another occasion, a brawl of matrons attacked the parson of St Kilian's, chivvying him along the streets with bloodthirsty screeches. That the Council showed itself timid at this time may be, as some historians have suggested, because they were afraid that the Princes might seize the excuse of unrest to intervene and to renew old suzerainties. For a month or two there was quiet, but it was a time of general unrest in the land and in the spring anticlerical agitation and iconoclastic rioting broke out. Runaway monks, who had nothing to lose by any kind of verbal extravagance, made their appearance, and played upon old hatreds and new cupidities. Such was the situation when Thomas Müntzer arrived – a fiery, if perhaps disconcerting, ally for Pfeiffer, whose own views may have been embittered in a more radical direction by his exile. Luther wrote warning letters to friends, and the Council sought to make inquiries as to whether Müntzer had left Allstedt with the goodwill(!) of his prince. Müntzer himself wrote to his friends at Allstedt, asking them to help his wife financially and to send 'the Mass and Vesper books'.[1] He also wrote to his 'famulus' Ambrosius Emmen, a faithful lad about whom we should like to know more, who was no doubt used to coping with disastrous emergencies, bidding him to follow his master to Mühlhausen and to bring with him his dad, and the Müntzer pig-

---

[1] Franz, II, No. 67: 'the people are well disposed to receiving them' (pp. 435–6).

let[1] – but not apparently Mrs and baby Müntzer. But even this was premature.

Three weeks later the situation blew up. On 20 September in all the churches and religious houses altars were despoiled, reliquaries broken, and relics scattered. It was proclaimed that tithes and rents to parish clergy and to the religious would cease at once. Now anticlericalism and politics were blended. A wedding led to a drunken brawl between Mayor Rodemann and an opposition citizen: the insurgent was arrested, but the arrival of the Eight Men reversed the situation, and in the small hours, the Mayor and a few companions escaped to Salza, where the *Amtmann*, Sittich von Berlepsch, was as uncompromisingly against the radical reformers as his master Duke George – whom he supplied with a running commentary on Mühlhausen affairs. The citizens were all shocked, and the radicals infuriated, to learn that the Mayor had decamped with the town banner, the mace, seals and keys, and apparently upon the town mare.[2]

Now the rebels drew up a series of eleven articles, perhaps drafted by Pfeiffer and Müntzer – No. 8 of which accused the diehards of having for twenty years opposed the common weal (*Gemeinnutz*), and there was a demand, of which more would be heard, for a permanent and new council. But if Müntzer had helped to prepare this crisis, it looks as though it was Zwickau over again, and that political events swept him along, and into premature action. For there were strong moderate elements in the Council – even though the Town Syndicus, Dr von Otthera, was on Müntzer's side. Moreover, the rebels had made a fatal mistake in fermenting opposition within the town and suburbs and neglecting to consult or soften the peasants and farmers in the villages, who sent 200 men to stiffen the Council. Then, from outside, came at least advice – as the cities of Erfurt, Goslar and Nordhausen sent delegates for a conference at Volkerode (26 September).[3] That Philip of Hesse and

---

[1] Franz, II, No. 68, 3 September

[2] Merx, op. cit., p. 77; this horse was the 16th-century counterpart of the modern Civic Rolls-Royce

[3] as neighbouring cities intervened in a similar crisis in Basle in 1529; see pp. 38ff. above.

Duke George were also interested may have consolidated moderates and extremists in common fear of renewed feudalism. Müntzer and Pfeiffer were expelled and left, probably about 27 September.

They made their way to Nuremberg, possibly via Bibra where Müntzer may have given the manuscript of his 'Ausgedrückte Entblössung' to his disciple, the book-agent Hans Huth. In October they were in Nuremberg, and it is very likely that Müntzer stayed with Hans Denck, the gifted schoolmaster of St Sebaldus.[1]

Müntzer had written a curious letter to his friends in Mühlhausen[2], in which he urged them to put down in writing, and get into print, the happenings in Mühlhausen in the last days, that the whole world might know and understand the justice of their cause and the scandal caused by the ungodly. It seems that Heinrich Pfeiffer did this very thing, for on behalf of the Council Andrew Osiander (at this time more Lutheran than Luther) examined two writings by Pfeiffer,[3] 'the first, in which he seeks to show how the Mühlhausen uprising came about', the second about the 'Law and Jewish judgement' which is to be exercised upon false prophets. And although we have to read between the lines, and Osiander's report often seems to be handling the teaching of Hans Denck rather than Pfeiffer, and replying to it in the most rigid Lutheran language, it does seem that this second tract, which has not survived, contains a discussion of Müntzer's principles at this time, about the validity of the Law, and the propriety of using force against the ungodly – i.e. rulers who opposed the gospel, and false prophets like the Lutherans. It looks, too, as though Pfeiffer had been making himself a nuisance: his pamphlets were confiscated and on 29 October he was ordered to take himself off and spend his money elsewhere![4]

Müntzer, on the other hand, seems to have kept quiet. He refused to preach. All he wanted was to get writings published. There was his 'Ausgedrückte Entblössung', the exposition of Luke 1 which was now in a longer and more finished form than the draft

---

[1] G. Bäring, 'Hans Denck und Thomas Müntzer in Nürnberg, 1524', *ARG* 50 (2), 1959, pp. 145ff.

[2] Franz, II, No. 70

[3] W. Möller *Andreas Osiander* (Elberfeld 1870), pp. 63ff.

[4] Bäring, op. cit., p. 153

which he had submitted to the Saxon censors before leaving Allstedt. But this, though printed, was confiscated. He had brought with him another writing, still more controversial, a reply to Luther's attack on himself in the 'Open Letter concerning the rebellious spirit'; this new, short, vitriolic tract was entitled 'A Highly Justified Apology against the Spiritless, Soft-living Lump of Flesh at Wittenberg' – the 'Hochverursachte Schutzrede'.[1] He found a printer in Hieronymus Höltzel, and the work was ready by the middle of December, when it was immediately confiscated. About this time Müntzer left for the south and made his way to Denck's old tutor, Johannes Oecolampadius, at Basle.

As a piece of invective, Müntzer's last tract surpasses anything even by Martin Luther or by Thomas Murner.[2] But it contains some interesting anecdotes – the glimpse of Luther sniffing a bunch of carnations during the Leipzig disputation, 1519 – and the extremely interesting suggestion that if Luther had recanted or compromised at the Diet of Worms in 1521 the knights or the Princes would have disposed of him. Nor, despite the bitter invective, is it a worthless tract, though obviously hurriedly produced – in Allstedt, Mühlhausen and perhaps finished off in Nuremberg.

We can understand Luther writing to the Elector Frederick in anger that Müntzer should be able to propagate dangerous error in his little corner of Thuringia, cashing in, that is, on the very liberty which Luther himself had purchased for Saxony, and which Luther's Prince had extended to its inhabitants. But there was a vast difference between the Müntzer invulnerable of May 1524, and the Müntzer on the run, of October, after the failure of his *Fürstenpredigt*, the betrayal of his disciples, and a personal situation as desperate as it had ever been, more distressing, indeed, than it had been for him in 1522, since he now had a wife and child and no hope at all of a fixed income – how different from that of Luther and his comfortable position as Professor and Preacher in Wittenberg, and

[1] Franz, I, 9, pp. 321–43
[2] We shall not quote at length from it, since a useful translation by Hans J. Hillerbrand appeared in *MQR* Jan. 1964, pp. 20–37: 'Thomas Muentzer's Last Tract against Martin Luther'. The notes in that article need to be checked with Franz.

as inmate of a monastery building completely at his own disposal. No wonder that Müntzer retorts savagely about the so-called liberty which he enjoys – 'liberty of a sheep to be hunted by wolves' – or that he thinks of what has happened to his work in Allstedt with immeasurable bitterness, or that he is almost beside himself at the way in which his efforts to speak have been forcibly muzzled. Whether Müntzer's own thought had become more radical, or whether the failure of his *Fürstenpredigt* led him to be more explicit, he now puts forward what sound like Taborite or Wycliffite notions – that not only is Romans 13 to be understood in the apocalyptic context of Daniel and Revelation, but that the sword is now to be taken from the godless rulers, who are to be stripped of their dignities and titles. It is not just crude humour, therefore, that makes Müntzer begin his tract by ascribing to Christ the honorific titles with which Luther began his Open Letter to Frederick the Wise, as, a year later, he would address the two Counts of Mansfeld, Ernest and Albert, as 'Brother'.

Müntzer in this tract addresses a theological argument, not always very clear, about the validity of the Law and the place of punishment in the Christian religion, and accuses Luther not only of misunderstanding this, but of using Scripture to cover the injustice of the ungodly. He refers back to his *Fürstenpredigt* but adds a new corollary:

> I stated clearly that the entire congregation [*Gemeinde*] is in possession of the sword, and that key which is to unloose. Quoting Daniel 7, Revelation 6, Romans 8, and 1 Kings 8, I said that Princes are not masters, but servants of the sword. They should not behave as they please but do justice [*Recht*]. Therefore according to ancient and honourable custom [*altem gutem Brauch*] the People must be present when someone is to be tried and judged according to the law of God (Numbers 15). Why? So that if the magistrate judges wrongly, the Christians present will repudiate it and not tolerate it, for God demands an account of innocent blood (Ps. [79]). . . .
>
> All evildoers by reason of the First Transgression of all Christendom must be justified by law as Paul says [Rom. 2:12] so that the earnestness of the Father may take godless Christians out of the way, who oppose the healthful teaching of Christ, so that the righteous may have time and space to learn the Will of God: for it

would not be at all possible for a single Christian to give himself to contemplation[1] under such tyranny, if it was open for anybody, even the godless, to punish sins by the law, and that so the innocent should let themselves be molested, and the godless tyrants should be able to make use of this against the godly saying, 'I must make a martyr of you: you must not resist me, for Christ also suffered' (Matthew 5). This would be a great perversion, according to which the greater the persecutor, the better the Christian.[2]

[1] of the law; see p. 292 below
[2] With the help of the notes in Franz we have given a translation of Müntzerian freedom, trying to bring out the sense of a difficult but important sentence: see Franz, p. 330; Hillerbrand, p. 29.

CHAPTER SEVENTEEN

THE PEASANTS' WAR

But now history itself twisted the dialectic of Luther and Müntzer's argument, which had all along been coloured by a social and political unrest first observed by Luther on his journeys to and from Worms in 1521, but which events now showed to have deep roots and to be far more widespread as, one after another, savage and desperate insurrections broke out from Alsace to the Tirol, and from the Black Forest into Franconia, Hesse and Thuringia.[1] These sporadic, often unconnected, revolutionary enterprises are loosely called the Peasants' War. They were no new thing: the peasant war-cry of the *Bundschuh* was old indeed, and there had been intermittent insurrections for almost a century.[2] They varied very much according to the political and social circumstances of time and place. In some cases, it was revolt against Imperial and Austrian rule, as in the area of the Hegau and Klettgau and Waldshut; in others, as in Salzburg and Mainz, against the authority of Prince bishops. Yet underlying all was a common burden of oppression and discontent, in a world of change where the causes of change were little understood and where the upper classes were always better able to fend for themselves than the underdogs.

There was, on the one hand, the desperate conservatism which tried to put the clock back to the good old days which never were,

---

[1] Günther Franz *Der deutsche Bauernkrieg* (Darmstadt 1956); Smirin *Die Volksreformation des Thomas Münzer* part ii; Bensing *Thomas Müntzer und der Thüringer Aufstand* parts iii–vi; Engels *The Peasant War in Germany*

[2] There were serious risings in Württemberg and Alsace in 1493, 1503 and 1514.

the appeal to ancient German custom and law, a concern not so much for abstractions – justice, liberty and the like – as for liberties, and for rights of hunting, shooting, fishing, game and forest rights filched or slowly disappearing. But there was also a new element. There was the subtle influence of Luther and the Reformation, a sharpened anticlericalism which vented economic grievance against the Church and against the religious corporations which were often the most rigid and conservative of landlords. Where there is appeal to abstractions and where a few lettered parsons become articulate on behalf of the rebellion, there is an appeal to 'Divine Justice' (*Göttliche Recht*) which might owe something to the teaching of Ulrich Zwingli, and sometimes to ancient Catholic doctrine. Not for nothing did the south German rebels, with their watchwords of 'Christian Brotherhood' and 'Christian Revolution', plead that such Reformers as Luther, Melanchthon and Strauss be appointed as mediators. There were very few systematic programmes[1] and not many leaders. For the most part rebels roamed the countryside in armed mobs, living off the land, attracted by violence and loot – the modern race riots in America have some similarities and affinities, as explosions of violence.

Now and again a colourful and gifted leader appeared: the soldier Hans Müller von Bulgenbach rode like some Italian *condottiere* in a carriage with damask curtains, his men bearing a black and gold standard; or the men of Ulm with their white and blue banners bearing the words 'Only the Justice of God'; or the red banners of the Swabians under their own craftsman prophet Ulrich the Smith. For nine months, the vast countryside boiled and bubbled as first one, then another peasant rising worked up to a climax, subsided and disappeared. For the peasants could not stay in the field indefinitely and most of them had no stomach for far adventures. They were sadly lacking in military equipment or leadership, and never survived a pitched battle. On the other hand, it was very difficult for the authorities to deal with them, in lands like the Black Forest or Thuringia, or the Rhineland, where the territory was split between innumerable local authorities and where, save in the case of the

---

[1] In south Germany there was the mysterious *Artickelbrief*, and the famous 12 Articles.

Swabian league, there was nothing like a standing army. No wonder that many of the authorities played for time, that some of the local gentry went over to the rebel side, like the famous Götz von Berlichingen, and Florian Gayer.

Thus for a time a swelling flood of peasantry were able to terrorize whole countrysides. Monasteries and nunneries were easiest game, but castles too. And it was one of the counts of Luther against them that they conscripted innocent bystanders into their savage ploys, with ruthless measures against those who refused to co-operate. There were a few Princes – Frederick the Wise was one – who recognized how much justice there was in the peasant demands. But there were others whose object was to get the peasants to disperse on any terms, and then to put into effect sanctions so savage that such revolution could never occur again. No wonder that, as time went on and one after another rebellion fizzled out, the more radical elements became more and more violent and uncompromising, more and more suspicious of all professed treaties, and all appeals for parley. The Weinsberg massacre, when fourteen of the nobility were executed, hardened opinion on both sides. Here and there intimidated gentry were put on display, like the two counts of Loewenstein who had to march along dressed as peasants and carrying beggars' staves, or the ci-devant Duke Ulrich of Württemberg, ready to fish for his lost kingdom in any troubled waters, who walked about with a peasant 'crew cut', just in case![1]

All this would have happened, and the grand course of events transpired, had there been no Thomas Müntzer and had he never said or written a word. It is a great pity that there have been so many religious and ideological vested interests to play up or play down his importance in the Peasants' War, and above all in Thuringia. It was the argument of Bullinger and Melanchthon that Müntzer was the great incendiary, and they used his fate to denigrate the whole radical and Anabaptist movement. The Marxists who are inclined

---

[1] In Thuringia, the most interesting of these gentry is Count Günther von Schwarzburg, who seems to have been accepted by Müntzer as a comrade and ally, and who could describe himself as a 'vorsteher christlicher gemein', i.e. overseer or *episkopos*! – see Franz, II, No. 87 (12 May 1525), p. 467

to emphasize Müntzer's revolutionary importance, and who perhaps exaggerate his social and political doctrines at the expense of his theology, find themselves in some embarrassment, since for them it is in the end the logic of historical determinism which counts, and not personality, and in the end no set of ideas, least of all theological ideas, can be determinative in historical change. On the other hand, the point of view which sees Müntzer as a beautiful and ineffectual archangel or arch-devil a little damaged, of moving and fiery eloquence, but little practical effect, seems to need checking by a recital of events. On the whole we shall try to keep to description of events and words, noting how many features of the Thuringian rebellion can be paralleled elsewhere.

We know that Müntzer spent several weeks in Switzerland and in the extreme south-west of Germany. He certainly visited Oecolampadius.[1] He may even have visited Conrad Grebel and the Swiss Brethren, if the letter of Grebel and the first Anabaptists ever reached him.[2] He was more probably in contact with two radical preachers, Hugwald and the more formidable character, Balthasar Hubmaier.[3] We know from Müntzer's own confession under torture that

> in the Klettgau and Hegau near Basle, he drew up some articles about 'How to get the upper hand according to the gospel', and made further articles out of them . . . he did not cause the insurrection in those parts, but it already existed. Oecolampadius and Hugowaldus showed him where to go and preach: and he had there preached that unbelieving rulers were also godless, and that there must be a judgement upon this.

This is extremely interesting, for it chimes with what we hear from other sources. The Catholic prosecutor, John Faber, discovered among the papers of Balthasar Hubmaier, at the time of Hubmaier's execution in 1528, a manuscript draft which he describes as 'How to gain control of Towns, Markets and Villages', which recalls Müntzer's phrase, 'how to get the upper hand' (*wie man herrschen sol*). From what we can learn through Faber's description,

---

[1] see p. 24 above   [2] see p. 139n. above, and pp. 322, 345 below
[3] Fast *Heinrich Bullinger und die Täufer*; Bergsten *Balthasar Hubmaier*; and refs. ad loc.

this writing is full of Müntzer's ideas; and what Müntzer's confession goes on to say about godless rulers exactly corresponds with Müntzer's teaching in these very months.[1] How much at this time Müntzer personally influenced Hubmaier, and how much he affected his ideas, must be very doubtful and Torsten Bergsten's sober reserve deserves to be imitated. The leader of the south German Peasants was a Mühlhausen[2] man, but we cannot know how much Müntzer contributed or how much he learned from what he must surely have seen at first hand of the plans and leadership of the Black Forest rebels. No doubt he had a hard time of it in these months, in what would eventually be a round trip of over 1,000 kilometres. In December he had written a pathetic letter to his friend, Christopher Meinhard of Eisleben, begging 'anything you can spare'.[3] But at the end of the year, Pfeiffer had returned to Mühlhausen, where events had taken a favourable turn. Müntzer betook himself thither, after spending a few days in jail at Fulda, whether because he was arrested as a stranger and vagabond, or because he was recognized as who he was, does not appear. At any rate he reappeared in Mühlhausen in the latter end of February 1525, to find the revolutionary party dominant, and was himself soon provided with official lodgement as parish priest of the church of Our Lady.

[1] see Smirin, op. cit., pp. 376ff.; Bergsten, op. cit., pp. 295ff. Bergsten would date this MS. many months later, in 1525; but he cannot deny the presence of Müntzer's ideas and influence, and I think there is some basis of Müntzer in the document, and therefore in the mysterious *Artickelbrief* of the peasants in this south German area – which might correspond to the 'other articles' referred to in Müntzer's confession.
[2] If this does not mean Mühlhausen in Alsace, it is interesting!
[3] Franz, II, No. 71, p. 450

CHAPTER EIGHTEEN

FRANKENHAUSEN

Müntzer returned to Mühlhausen convinced that the time was ripe for the maturing of his felonious little plans, and he expected the moving ferment of revolt soon to reach Thuringia. But he had first to consolidate his position in Mühlhausen itself. During his absence the balance of forces had tilted in the radical direction. This was in part because of the threatened intervention of the two feudal powers, the Landgrave Philip of Hesse and Duke George, the one Protestant, the other Catholic, both sabre-rattling in the background and demanding that the *émigré* councillors still at Salza be reinstated. Then the town council became itself involved in the secularizing of church property, for the German knights were expelled and their property confiscated, while Müntzer himself took up quarters in the empty building. Into the town there came numbers of refugees, who swelled the radical ranks. Although there seems no evidence at all of any military skill among the peasant leaders, Müntzer did what he could to prepare the Mühlhausen men and succeeded in getting the town militia out for military exercises in March, under the leadership of five *Landsknechte*. All went well until Müntzer interrupted the war game with a typical harangue: calling on those present to raise their finger and swear an oath that they would defend the Gospel, and on those who would not do so to leave the field. The captain of militia, Eberhard von Budingen, unlike Müntzer did not do his military reading in the Book of Judges, and preferred old-fashioned notions that wars are won by the one who 'gits thar fustest with the mostest'. At any rate, he rounded on Müntzer, saying that every man Jack of them wanted to defend the Gospel, that since Müntzer had come to town they had sworn basketfuls of oaths, and that if he wanted to preach, his place was in church and not on the field of war. For once Müntzer had the worse of a verbal exchange and, chagrined, left the field. However, what he had failed to do with the intoxication of his own verbosity, the town council did for him, for it provided the tired and licentious soldiery with a barrel of beer for each platoon. By early morning the troops of Mühlhausen were ready to fight anybody anywhere, and got rid of their bellicosity by raiding a convent on the bridge, scaring away the nuns and running off with all movable goods.

More important was the political revolution now carried through, under the leadership of Pfeiffer and Dr von Otthera, with a new election and new leaders, the new council of sixteen having only two members of the former one, henceforth to rule as a permanent council (*Ewiges Rat*). This was the situation when at the end of April, and perhaps before Müntzer was ready, the Peasants' War flooded through the Pass at Fulda, and Thuringia began to seethe.

From the beginning, things were ominous for the Thuringian rebels. In a land with so many and such scattered and intermingled jurisdictions, the rebels might scare the small gentry into making terms or joining their ranks, but they could have no long-term objective, there was no one with whom they could finally treat, and in these days the one dignitary most sympathetic and just, Frederick the Wise, lay dying, believing that it might be the divine will that the peasants would win. The result was that each locality tended to fight its own war. The extreme example of this was the town of Erfurt which succeeded in the end in diverting rebel grievance and enthusiasm against the overlordship of the archbishop of Mainz and to the destruction of all signs of his authority in the city. On the other hand, there was little co-ordination between the Princes, for a strong religious barrier divided the two Counts, Ernest and Albert of Mansfeld, in the critical area where the miners lived. And Duke George, though he breathed fire and slaughter and threats of retribution, found it very difficult to get moving in any military strength. To this there was one exception, Philip of Hesse, who had shown himself capable of swift and ruthless action, and who at the beginning of May defeated the southern rebels and cut the Pass at Fulda. Peasant armies rising in the Werra land were pressed back on Eisenach. But here again, though Eisenach had enjoyed the fairly radical preaching of Strauss for long enough, and though some of Müntzer's most tough and intimate disciples lived in the town, the moderate elements made a *coup*, and arrested and executed rebel ringleaders – about which Müntzer could only write a shocked and threatening letter of protest, to no effect.[1]

It is very difficult to see how far Müntzer himself was able to direct events. Always a *prima donna*, he found himself at odds with his colleague Heinrich Pfeiffer – a rift which did not help, if it did not greatly affect the ultimate issue. We know that a year and a half before, Müntzer had been in touch with disciples over scores of little towns and villages, and that he had many disciples among the miners, some hundreds of whom were enrolled in his Covenantal bands. We do not know whether, when it came to the test, many of them thought again. Nor do we know how he got in touch with his friends. Without means of modern propaganda, it seems that in that age rumours spread wildly and fast, though sometimes news itself travelled more quickly than we might suppose. But there was in Thuringia nothing at all resembling the knitted leadership and intelligence service which had marked the English Peasant War in 1381.

As we might expect, Müntzer's most dramatic and powerful appeal was written to his old disciples at Allstedt in the famous manifesto which is quoted in all the history books.[2]

> The pure fear of God be with you, brothers. What are you still sleeping for, why have you not recognized the will of God – do you think he has abandoned you, is that it? Ah, how often have I told you that God can only reveal himself in this way, in your apparent abandonment [*gelassen*]. If not, the offering of your broken and contrite hearts must be in vain. And you must then come into another kind of suffering. I tell you again, if you won't suffer for God, then you will be Devil's martyrs. So take care, cheer up, do your duty, and stop pandering to those fantastic perverts, those knaves. Get going, and fight the battle of the Lord!

[1] Franz, II, No. 84 (9 May)   [2] Franz, II, No. 75 (*c.* 26–27 April), p. 454

It is high time, keep the brethren together so that they do not mock the divine witness, or they will be all destroyed. The whole of Germany, France and the Roman lands are awake – the Master will start his game, and the knaves are for it! At Fulda in Easter week four collegiate churches were destroyed, the peasants in Klettgau and Hegau are up, three thousand strong, and the longer it goes on the more they are. . . . So now rataplan! rataplan! rataplan![1] [*dran, dran, dran*] – it is time to hunt the knaves down like dogs – rataplan! rataplan! rataplan! – have no mercy even though Esau gives you good words – Gen. 33. Do not look at the misery of the godless. They will beg you, will whine and cry like children. But you are to have no mercy, as God commanded through Moses – Deut. 7 – and has also revealed to us. Get going in the villages and towns, and especially with the miners and the other good fellows. We must sleep no more. . . . And see, as I write, here is a piece of news which has just come in – from Salza – how the good people there have taken Duke George's officer from his castle . . . the peasants of Eichsfeld have turned enemies to their lords (*Junkers*) and in brief will have none of their favour. Here's an example for you! rataplan! rataplan! time's up! Balthasar and Bartel Krump, Valtin and Bischoff,[2] you lead the dance out on to the floor! . . . Rataplan! rataplan! rataplan! Let not your sword grow cold, let it not be blunted. Smite, cling, clang, on the anvil of Nimrod, and cast the tower to the ground. . . . rataplan! rataplan! rataplan! while it is still day – God goes ahead of you, follow, follow – be not fearful, for God is with you, and you shall not be put off by the numbers against you, for it is not your battle but the Lord's. So go to it through God who will strengthen you in the right faith, without any fear of man. . . .

Thomas Müntzer, a servant of God against the godless.

Curiously, Mühlhausen itself was kept out of the maelstrom. The first point of consolidation for the peasants was Langensalza, where the odious Sittich von Berlepsch was entrapped and for a

---

[1] with due acknowledgement to Bouncer in *Cox and Box*

[2] The evocation of names, almost rhythmically, recalls the famous description by John Gower (*Confessio Amantis*) of how the Kentish men were rallied by name in 1381:

> *Watte vocat, cui Thomme venit, neque Symme retardat*
> *Betteque, Gibbe simul, Hykke venire jubent.*

time held prisoner by a force of peasants, to which a strong Mühlhausen contingent was attached under Pfeiffer. Strong threats from Duke George which might at last be implemented seem to have caused the victorious peasants and the conscripted town officials hurriedly to leave the town and engage on a plundering and intimidating expedition to other towns including the Catholic stronghold of Weissensee. A sudden stroke by local gentry led the inhabitants of Sangerhausen, an old Müntzerian nest, to send Müntzer a desperate appeal.[1] At this time too – the end of April – there began a fateful concentration of peasants on the town of Frankenhausen, the geographical position of which seemed to show strategic advantage and was in the heart of the Müntzer country.

It was now that real dissidence appeared in the Mühlhausen ranks, what Thomas later bitterly described as a fatal 'self-interest' (*Eigennutz*). There could be no greater proof of the military innocence of the peasant leaders than that in these critical four or five days, while the forces of the Princes were widely separated and indeed scattered and when a number of local gentry had come almost enthusiastically over to the Peasant side, the Mühlhausen leaders should be away on plundering expeditions. Pfeiffer was perhaps largely responsible for this folly, for he overruled Müntzer by insisting that now was the time to plunder the rich monasteries and castles of the Eichsfeld – 'just a piece of cake!' he assured them. Müntzer's alternative plan was a march on Ernest of Mansfeld's formidable castle, recently rebuilt, at Heldrungen. At first sight, this might seem equally *eigennutzlich*, for Ernest was his most bitter enemy ever since he had forbidden his subjects to attend Müntzer's liturgy. To him in the next days Müntzer would address a most violent ultimatum beginning 'Brother Ernest', and asking him,

> Tell me, you miserable, shabby bag of worms, who made you a ruler? . . . God has commanded you to be cast down from your seat. . . . We must have your answer by tonight.[2]

But there may have been more to it than personal revenge. At least Heldrungen was a military strongpoint. At this time it was touch and go whether the whole power of the miners might not be thrown

[1] 6 May   [2] 12 May 1525: Franz, II, No. 88

into the war – and here the territories of Counts Ernest and Albert of Mansfeld were critical. So the peasants went off, and on 9 May returned jubilant to Mühlhausen with immense booty. Müntzer himself had his share of the loot, but there was no venality in him; and as he sat alone in his large hall, he must have stared bitterly at more riches than he had ever had, put together in one heap – surely with some premonition of imminent disaster. In the next days, the tension grew, and when it became evident that the concentration of peasant strength would be at Frankenhausen, Pfeiffer decided to stay behind. Müntzer wrote a letter to the Council at Mühlhausen who might be presumed now to be wholly composed of his friends, begging them to take action against Judas – but not naming Pfeiffer. He himself led the numerous, but now not too powerful, contingent from Mühlhausen, with nine guns from the town arsenal.

Yet Müntzer was not without his success. Miles away, the streets of little Allstedt were empty – they at least had loyally obeyed their leader, hurrying after their Pied Piper, to their doom. It has been a great argument among the Marxists, who badly need the miners in the story, since on the whole peasants fit awkwardly into an interpretation of history which makes sense mostly in an industrial revolution. Manfred Bensing, whose careful and in many ways excellent study is the fullest and most up-to-date monograph on Müntzer and the Thuringian rising, does not really solve the problem why the miners never came in force – though he pinpoints the crisis, when the rebels of Frankenhausen were to have joined those of Sangerhausen on 10–11 May and the whole of the mining community was expected to rise. But he has to admit the strength of moderate elements in the Mansfeld area, that too many of the miners were involved in the capitalism of the mine owners, that Ernest and Albert of Mansfeld were vigorous, and that, at great personal risk, Luther himself was preaching in the area between Stolberg and Mansfeld, – writing to his friend John Rühel that he would await death, 'if it is to come, and my new lords, the murderers and robbers'. It is in any case an unwarranted exaggeration to say that Luther had 'lost the support of the common people' at this time. Luther himself had to watch the long foretold results of a creed of terrorism and violence. It is in this context that we must understand his hysterical broadsheet, which in its way is as brutal as Müntzer's manifesto, 'Against the murdering hordes of peasants', which he wrote at a time when it seemed that the rebels might gain the day, but which read very differently a week later when, after the complete peasant collapse, it was published during the bloodbath of the Junkers.

Anyway, Frankenhausen was to be the place of decision. None of the historians, not even Manfred Bensing with his careful maps, makes military sense of what happened. The peasants did not shut themselves up in Frankenhausen itself, though one would have thought its walls the best protection against cavalry and artillery, their own vulnerabilities. They took their stand instead on the summit of the mountain adjoining the town, and perhaps ranged their few small cannon across the river between the town and the hill. On 13 May Philip of Hesse and Henry of Brunswick had left Salza with 1,400 cavalry and 1,500 foot. There was a skirmish outside Frankenhausen in which the peasants got the upper hand, and as a result were more confident than they had any right to be. Philip protected his flanks and rear in the proper manner and on the night of the 14th sat down before the town and encampment. The peasants seem to have been at least 6,000 strong. At their centre was the Mühlhausen contingent with its great silk banner bearing the emblem of a rainbow and the watchword of the south German Peasants, 'The Word of the Lord endureth for ever'. They felt themselves strong enough at this moment for an act of savage judgement. They had for some time had three notable prisoners: Matern von Gehofen, Georg Büchner, and the parson, Stefan Hartenstein, all protégés of Ernest of Mansfeld. Now they were made to stand in a ring of peasants, for any who would to impeach them: a scene of rough justice, against a background of torches and camp fire, such as might happen in any war at a drumhead court martial, or in a modern Western film. For Müntzer it was much more. It was Deuteronomy 7 in action, his theory of authority, of the judgement and justice of the Christian congregation against the ungodly. One by one, peasants from their district gave vote and voice, and judgement was given – by the sword. It was a senseless act of butchery which sealed the fates of all the executioners. And indeed a few hours later, the rebels had other thoughts. For next day it became apparent that their strategic strongpoint had become a trap. There had been a Wellington–Blücher-like conjunction. Duke George had at last arrived with an army – no doubt in better trim than old Blücher with his rhubarb and 'Ich stinke etwas . . .', but no less certainly assuring victory. Now the peasants found their retreat cut off, and cannon ranged across the woodland through which they might have hoped to escape. No wonder that they were ready to talk. They sent the obviously scared message: 'We confess Jesus Christ. We are not here to harm anybody but to maintain divine justice. We are not here to shed blood.' It was too late, and the Princes sent a cold ultimatum promising some vague lenience if Thomas Müntzer and his leaders were surrendered.

Hans Huth, the wandering book-agent, was in the camp and he confirms later gossip that on the day before the battle, 14 May, and on the morning of the 15th, Müntzer preached encouragement to his troops – fanatically, still with the wild theme of Gideon and David, and the invulnerability of the tiny few on whose side fought the justice of God. 'Don't be afraid of their bullets, I'll catch them in my coat' seems like rough banter. And if the stars in their courses were not evidently on his side, at least the heavens showed a sign. For with the unlikelihood with which life constantly outwits fiction, it seems there was seen a rainbow in the sky – the very image of their Peasant banner.[1] But by now it was high noon, and the last of Duke George's cannon was in its place. It is plausible that as the peasants kneeled to sing Müntzer's *Veni, Creator Spiritus*, the guns roared and the attack began. Like every other set-piece fight in the Peasants' War, it was over in minutes, and soon became a bloody rout which gave the title 'Blood Alley' to the hillside for centuries to come.[2]

Müntzer was no Zwingli: he fled. He was found hiding in the

---

[1] For the interesting suggestion that this was not a rainbow but a complete halo round the sun, which was reported as seen in several parts of Germany, see Bensing, op. cit., p. 225, note 53

[2] The numbers engaged seem to have been about 6,000 peasants, and 8,000 for the Princes; the latter being much better furnished with artillery, muskets and, above all, cavalry.

city, in bed and feigning illness. He might just have got away with it, but those engaged in the house-to-house search discovered his letters, and his identity was revealed. There was no hope for him. At the bridge at Heldrungen his old enemy, Count Ernest, was waiting for him, perhaps with an evil grin, rather like Mephistopheles at the end of *Doctor Faustus*. In his castle Müntzer was tortured until, white and broken, he could hardly gasp his *Credo*.

His interrogation followed the usual pattern, what was called 'friendly interrogation', and then questioning under torture. Because the sacrament of the altar was a high matter of heresy, his first admissions were

> that he would not have the blessed sacrament outwardly reverenced but only in spirit – and that he had administered the sacrament to the sick, and himself partaken, after eating at midday and also in the evening.[1]

We have quoted his admissions about his activity in south Germany, to which must be added his confession that he had preached there that unbelieving rulers were ungodly and that there must be a judgement on them.

> He says that the castles are a burden and overfull of servants and other impositions on their subjects.
>
> He says that princes should ride with eight horses, a count with four, and a nobleman with two, but no more.

Under torture he had been pressed, in the usual way, to give names of his accomplices, and the authorities evidently wanted stuff about Heinrich Pfeiffer. Whether from agony or final bravado, he admitted his intentions regarding Count Ernest:

> He says that if he had taken the castle of Heldrungen he would have beheaded Count Ernest. . . .

About the three camp executions he admitted that

> he had pronounced the verdict on Matern von Gehofen and the other servants of Count Ernest on behalf of the congregation, and had agreed with it – and did it out of fear.

[1] Franz, p. 544

He gave a list of his chief friends, and the leaders of his Covenant at Allstedt:

> It was their policy and they would have established it, had they been able – 'Omnia sunt communia' and to each according to his need and opportunity. And any prince or lord who would not agree, after admonition, should be beheaded or hanged.

There was an interesting admission about what we called Mühlhausen imperialism.

> If all had gone well, as his associates well knew, the land for ten miles round Mühlhausen would have been taken over and [?the land belonging to Philip of] Hesse – and the other princes and lords treated as already indicated.

His admissions under torture are recognizably his own and, apart from names of his associates, do not amount to very much. Much more wooden, and obviously dictated, are the words of a recantation, issued by the Princes, in which he forswore his views about political authority and acknowledged that he had preached sedition. He also confessed many 'opinions, fancies and errors against the Blessed Sacrament and against the order of Holy Church – and that he wills to hold all that the Church teaches'. The final words, 'he asks that his farewell letter, lately written, may be sent to Mühlhausen and his possessions to his wife and child' sound authentic and may be the price of this recantation. It is possible: there is something to be said for the view that Müntzer was the last medieval heretic rather than the first radical Reformer. But far more poignant, dignified and significant is that last letter to the men of Mühlhausen which he wrote in the Castle of Heldrungen on 17 May.

He begs his friends to look after his wife, and to see she gets his few possessions. He pleads with the men of Mühlhausen to take the dread lesson of Frankenhausen to heart, and at all costs to avoid further bloodshed and any action which might provoke the vengeance of the Princes. He blames the whole disaster on self-interest (*Eigennutz*). The letter is characteristic, if subdued, and the constraint is from his own conscience – he is anxious, as he says, to be rid of the burden of innocent blood. But this is not quite all. Müntzer bids his friends read between the lines and take a longer view. God's Work can only be understood when it is complete, 'which is not to be judged by outward appearance, but judged by the truth'. Appeal to ordeal by battle was common in the 16th century – Cappel was another case in point – but perhaps Luther, Melanchthon and Bullinger too easily assumed that this had decided once for all who was the false and who the true prophet.

After the letters which Müntzer wrote from Heldrungen on 17 May we hear no more from him. But he was kept, strictly guarded, while the Princes concentrated on Mühlhausen where they captured Pfeiffer and the radical remnant, trying to escape. To make the public example as awful as possible, Müntzer and Pfeiffer were beheaded outside Mühlhausen on 27 May. There is a bit of gossip that he laughed in the face of his executioner. If so, it must have been, like Christian's smile in the face of Apollyon, 'the dreadfullest sight you ever saw'.

Without capitulating to Marxist dialectic, or a régime which in the 20th century would exploit Thomas Müntzer's memory to support the view that theirs is the true, Christian revolution – views which none the less are not to be dismissed out of hand – recognizing the evident element of tragic fanaticism, and the theological weaknesses of Müntzer's great argument, at least this is true, that in him we come nearer than in any other Reformer to contact with the smothered undercurrent of medieval pain and injustice. Now voices were cut off and silent, in the time of savage reprisal. They would not be heard again for a long time but they would one day return, angry, one-sided, anticlerical and anti-Christian, to knock at the gates of a Christian world; and to them a Christian Church, by reason of its own failures of nerve, of justice and of compassion, cannot return an unqualified No.

Carl Hinrichs, in his monograph *Luther und Müntzer*, has lucidly disentangled the differing views of the two men on authority and government, on the duty of obedience and the right of resistance, centring in the interpretation of Romans 13. But at least Müntzer poses the question whether in fact Romans 13 and the classical doctrine of civil obedience could fit the dynamism of history. Luther himself admitted that there is movement and tension between the Two Kingdoms, as God wars against Satan. But Müntzer raises the question which later Protestants, from the days of the Huguenots to those of Dietrich Bonhoeffer, were to press, having rejected Luther's passive doctrine: whether, in fact, there may not have to be drastic Christian action against tyranny, not least against a tyranny bolstered up by the religious guarantees of an obtuse Establishment.

Neither Luther nor Müntzer make much of compassion, forgiveness, and mercy in political ethics. If for Luther love is the author of both his kinds of righteousness, it is about punishment and judgement that he talks in political and public terms. That is a far cry, of course, from Müntzer's talk about 'that crap about mercy' – who for all his speech about the suffering Christ had so little to say about pity: his is the apocalyptic vision of the hard 16th and 17th centuries; the day had not yet come for William Blake.

His 'Theology of the Cross' was set in the minor key. He knew nothing of the holy worldliness of Luther. There may be truth in the gossip that, when the news was brought him that a man-child had been born to him, he straightened his face and showed no joy, as a sign of his own *Gelassenheit*. Because he represents a rebellion against reformation itself, he has much in common with Kierkegaard, and many of his most striking sayings can be paralleled in the Danish prophet, whose 'Knight of Faith' and 'Knight of Infinite Resignation' is a good definition of Müntzer's *Gelassenheit*. His reaction against Christendom, against an addled and introverted Christian society, led him to stress the extent to which God's purposes and God's people were to be found among Turks and heathen – in remarkable anticipation of some of the things which Dietrich Bonhoeffer framed in his view of 'mankind come of age'. We hope we have shown that his mind was rich and fertile and his theology unexpectedly coherent, in his own way touching things which the traditions of the Reformed Church and of the Free Churches in England were one day to adumbrate and for lack of which, maybe, Lutheran Christianity, rich and strong as it has always been, has been one-sided and impoverished.

FRANKENHAUSEN

Was he a physical coward, a clerical Duke of Plaza Toro?[1] Günther Franz, whose writings about Müntzer are always perceptive and who has done such immense service to Müntzer studies, thinks he was a coward. He ran away from city to city, with perhaps more than evangelical alacrity. There is the plausible story that he stood, yellow with fear, outside the room in Weimar, in August 1524. He was found hiding in bed after Frankenhausen. Was he, like a good many visionaries, an escapist – shattered when he found in real life the issue of his wild threats, and finally broken with disillusionment? Was there in him a streak of brutal cruelty which would none the less be compatible with cowardice? Or may we trust the tribute of the Landgrave Philip that he died bravely? Like Mr Fearing, was he well at the last? No doubt a case might be made out for paranoia, with a touch of genius, but driven in hypersensitiveness to wild threatenings, from a persecution complex – or is the good Mühlhausen beer, perhaps, a more earthy explanation, and the clue to the extravagance of his manifestoes that he was shouting in his cups? Nobody will ever know.

After his death, and in the aftermath of the Peasants' War, his name became a dirty byword, and all his followers, not least those who joined the ranks of the Anabaptists, had every reason to play down their association with him, and to abandon a programme of violence for one of apocalyptic supernaturalism (much as, on another plane, Bullinger abandoned Zwingli's military policies). Dr James Stayer has recently reminded us that there were some hawks as well as many doves among the first Anabaptists, men like Krug and Hans Schott.[2] One of Müntzer's most faithful disciples, Hans Römer, plotted to kill those inhabitants of Erfurt on Christmas Day

---

[1] In enterprise of martial kind,
  When there was any fighting,
 He led his regiment from behind –
  He found it less exciting.
 But when away his regiment ran,
  His place was at the fore, O –
      —W. S. Gilbert

[2] J. M. Stayer, 'Terrorism, the Peasants' War and the Wiedertäufer', *ARG* 1965 (2), 227–8. There is evidence of a few bloody-minded groups among the Anabaptists in the region of St Gall.

1527, who should refuse baptism, because they had strangled 'his father, Thomas Müntzer'. Among other of Müntzer's marshals was Melchior Rinck, of some creative theological ability.[1] There can be no doubt that Hans Huth, who was present at Frankenhausen, as we might say, representing the Press, was more deeply influenced by Müntzer than he admitted to his interrogators in Augsburg, and the influence of Müntzer's ideas are to be found in the writings of such radicals as Haug von Juchsen, Leonard Schiemer and the ex-priest Hans Schlaffer. No doubt the Swiss Brethren (and Karlstadt!) are the true Founding Fathers of pacific Anabaptism, but a number of historians, Mecenseffy, Zschäbitz, Hillerbrand, seem to me to have rightly shown the influence of Müntzer and his teaching on the radicals of south Germany. He is one of the first in a succession of apocalyptic Anabaptist writers, and the least crackpot of them all. Nor ought we to hide or play down a real streak of violence and wildness among the radicals, with a pretty continuous pedigree of incidents in Switzerland, south Germany, Strasbourg and Amsterdam, which make the catastrophe at Münster intelligible.

Earnest and deluded, brilliant yet unbalanced, we can at this distance realize more positive qualities in him than his enemies could even begin to understand. There was, in the end, no dialogue, no confrontation of Luther and Müntzer in the modern ecumenical sense, and modern scholarship is only beginning to construct one, for Müntzer studies have quite a way yet to go.

Today in East Germany, and in Müntzer's Zwickau, there is inscribed on the wall of the Town Hall, in huge blue-lettered facsimile, the words with which once their Preacher, Thomas Müntzer, signed the receipt for his none too generous stipend: 'Thomas Müntzer qui pro veritate militat in mundo'. Perhaps he would have liked that to be the epitaph of one of the most fascinating and tragic of God's delinquent children.

[1] There is a useful appendix about Müntzer's associates in Bensing, op. cit., pp. 253ff. On Melchior Rinck, see G. H. Williams in *Kirche, Mystik und das Natürliche bei Luther* (Göttingen 1967), p. 201, note 12, and references there; also *MQR* 35 (1961), pp. 197–217

CHAPTER NINETEEN

THE GOSPEL ACCORDING TO THOMAS MÜNTZER

1. Ingredients

About Müntzer's theological and philosophical training, we have no evidence. What we know of trends at Leipzig and Frankfort on the Oder is inconclusive, since in most German universities the various schools were represented, even though from time to time, under some eminent divine, one school – Thomist, Scotist, Ockhamist – might predominate.[1] On slight comparison with Staupitz and Karlstadt, we might hazard a guess that Müntzer too may have been trained in the *via antiqua*, though what sound like Thomist echoes in his writings generally turn out to be Augustine.

As a secular priest, he had been less exposed to a scholastic teaching entrenched most deeply in the religious orders, and it is perhaps significant that humanism had been early established in Leipzig. But here is something wider and more diffused than literary humanism, a thought-world loosed from scholasticism, the world of Valla and the Florentine Academy, of Cusa and Gerson, of Tauler and Erasmus, with the new biblical tools and the zeal for the old Fathers.

Müntzer was of scholarly temper, and books and reading counted for much with him. The early years of tiresome chores and minor appointments gave him room for avid study.[2] In the last years of his life he must have had less and less time to read, and in the final

---

[1] K. Aland, 'Die Theologische Fakultät Wittenbergs und ihre Stellung im Gesamtzusammenhang der Leucorea während des 16. Jahrhunderts' in *Kirchengeschichtliche Entwürfe* p. 302

[2] Franz, II, No. 7 (1 Jan. 1520), to Franz Günther: 'copiosum tempus studio meo superesse gaudeo.'

months, when he was on the run, can have read little beyond his Bible. Yet in his very last letter he could remember his wife and his books, proper scholarly priorities.[1]

The evidence supports the view that he was a devouring reader, with many interests. Like John Wesley, he dabbled in medicine, and his friends sought his advice from his knowledge of primitive physic and herbals.[2] He was interested in science, or perhaps in the no-man's-land between science and alchemy,[3] and may have had the fashionable humanist interest in geography.[4]

As a young Martinian, he had to be abreast of controversy, and not least of that in which Luther and Karlstadt were involved with the theologians of the religious orders. In 1520, as assistant to Günther, and then in Zwickau in his own right, Müntzer was especially involved in polemic against the Franciscans. There is a long book-list in his papers which includes most of the important tracts published 1518–19, and though it would be precarious to judge the mind of a modern parson from a Blackwell's catalogue found among his posthumous effects, and though the possession of all these writings would demand a high proportion even of a bachelor income, it is very possible that he did indeed own, or read, most of them.

If this collection of seventy-five pamphlets were really his, they are an interesting collection.[5] There are humanist writings, Valla on 'Free Will', orations on the humanist programme by Celtis, Mosellanus and Melanchthon: the defence of Reuchlin, and Erasmus' attack on the new Barbarians, with his more positive 'Exhortation to the study of Scripture', and Aesop's Fables (which also delighted Luther). There follow the polemic of the day, almost the whole of the Eck–Karlstadt controversy, and the writings of Alveldus against Luther with his replies. Then, Luther's own sermons and manifestoes 1518–20, including his edition of the *Theologia*

---

[1] Franz, II, No. 94: to the citizens of Mühlhausen

[2] Franz, II, Nos 1 (30 Aug. 1516), 32

[3] Franz, II, No. 24; with interesting quotations (?) scribbled on the back of a letter, as: 'Si mundus esset perpetuus, terra impleret totam machinam mundi, ut videmus clarissime in resolutione' (Franz, p. 534).

[4] Extracts in Dresden MSS. [5] Franz, pp. 556–60

THE GOSPEL ACCORDING TO THOMAS MÜNTZER

Germanica, and writings of Gregory Nazianzen and John Cassian.

These stresses – humanism, Luther, biblical humanism and the old Fathers – are confirmed by direct evidence. We know that Müntzer read and re-read the works of St Augustine[1] and Tertullian, and he seems also to have read some writings of St Basil.[2] Some day a liturgical scholar will elucidate the hard reading which must have gone into his liturgical experiments. More striking is another book-list which suggests that he may have read Plato's *Parmenides* on 'The One and Many' and other important writings of Plato, including the *Symposium* and the *Republic*.[3]

From allusions, we gather that Müntzer had read the *Golden Ass* of Apuleius,[4] and the Koran.[5] It is probable that he had read the *Theologia Naturalis* of Raymond of Sabunde, and there are passages which seem to echo the theology of Nicholas of Cusa.

Like Luther, about the same time and perhaps for something of the same reason, Müntzer read church history and canon law in the months after the Leipzig Disputation (1519), at which he had been present, and where the problem of church authority had been acutely raised by John Eck. We have an exchange of letters between Müntzer and Achatius Glov, a Leipzig bookseller. On his side, Glov seems to have been a kindly bookman, of that sort who so orders his shop that those who stand may read. He was aware of the tension in a young scholar's mind between the books he wants and those he can afford. In the manner of the day he let Müntzer have a Concordance of Canon Law on approval (though how one browses in a Concordance is a mystery) and offered the usual discounts. At any rate, Müntzer, though probably unable to afford the nine-volume Erasmian edition of Jerome, and an expensive edition of Augustine's Letters and Sermons, made two fateful purchases, the *Chronography* of Eusebius and Hegesippus – works in which he thought to find his own idiosyncratic version of the Fall of the Primitive Church in the sub-apostolic age.[6]

We have used the term 'Martinian' to indicate, even to underline, the debt of Müntzer to Luther, and, as in the case of Zwingli,

[1] Franz, II, No. 7 (1520): probably the Amerbach edition, Basle 1506
[2] Dresden MSS. [3] ibid. [4] Franz, p. 290 [5] Franz, p. 232
[6] Franz, II, Nos 8, 9

Vadianus, Bucer, this initial indebtedness to Luther remained a permanent sediment in his thought. Above all, and like Luther's, as Martin Schmidt has perceptively remarked, Müntzer's is a 'Word of God' theology.¹ But it is surely confessional bias alone which can see Müntzer simply as a Lutheran deviationist, taking from Luther his categories of thought and vocabulary.² It would be interesting to have a list of the works of Luther which Müntzer had read, the writings about indulgences (about which Müntzer himself had been consulted before the indulgence controversy broke out) assuredly, the early expositions of justification by faith – sermons on good works, and on double and triple righteousness, and the manifestoes, the 'Babylonish Captivity' and the 'Liberty of a Christian Man'. Later he read, and violently disagreed with, 'Of Civil Authority'. He could not know that whole rich world, open to the modern scholar, of Luther's courses of biblical lectures, in which the 'theology of the Cross' with its doctrine of *Anfechtung*, so near to Müntzer's own, was powerfully expounded. Probably he had read Melanchthon's *Loci Communes*.

It is when we come to the influence on Müntzer of mystical and apocalyptic writings that the differences between Luther and Müntzer most clearly emerge. We have already noted that conflation between the modern devotion and Rhineland mysticism which is part of the background of the age, and which influenced a number of south German Reformers and humanists. This was something by no means confined to the religious orders, but seeped over, much as the modern devotion had done, into a penumbra of lay influence, of which the 'Friends of God' were the concentration.³ Here too the importance of printing. It has been suggested that at the beginning of the 15th century there had been a revived interest in the works of such writers as Hildegard of Bingen and Raymond of Sabunde. Now, two generations later, printing made them newly accessible.

---

[1] M. Schmidt *Das Selbstbewusstsein Thomas Müntzers und sein Verhältnis zu Luther* (Theologia Viatorum 1954)

[2] see the extraordinary statement of Gerdes (*Luthers Streit mit den Schwärmern* p. 94): 'Müntzer hat fast all seiner Schlagworte und Thesen bis ins einzelne von Luther übernommen.'

[3] see p. 327 below

The heady possibilities of reprinted sedatives and stimulants of this kind have never yet been explored in relation to the 16th century. We need somebody to do for the 'Friends of God' in the late 15th century what Landeen has done for the infiltration into Germany of the 'modern devotion'.

For this lay spirituality we might prefer an 18th-century phrase and speak of 'inward religion', to describe an experiential and affective piety, or religion of the heart. The word 'mystic' is one of the most nebulous of the Christian vocabulary and, in the case of Müntzer, had best be defined in terms of the books he read and the ideas he employed. Like Karlstadt, he was a secular priest and, unlike Luther and the members of religious orders, had not been so exposed to the classic tradition of mysticism from Dionysius the Areopagite to Bernard and the Victorines. But it is perhaps worth noting that his early employments were in nunneries, and that it was to these congregations of devout women that the utterances of the German mystical writers had been addressed, and in their houses the literature was preserved. It is in a teasing letter from a nun, Sister Ursula, that we hear of his acquaintance with Tauler and with Suso.[1]

Tauler,[2] significant for Luther, was for Müntzer of catastrophic importance. Strobel tells us that Müntzer carried round with him Tauler's sermons, bound in a double volume. In them Müntzer found that pattern of sanctification which supplied the lack of such description in what he knew of Luther.[3] Here is the picture of a soul growing to conformity with Christ, knowing the 'bitter Christ' of the Cross, and sharing his tribulations, as he is weaned from

---

[1] Franz, II, No. 11 (1520): 'der Taullerus noch pruder Sewss'

[2] Among many essays, see K. Grünewald *Studien zu Johannes Taulers Frömmigkeit* (Leipzig 1930); I. Weilner *Johannes Taulers Bekehrungsweg* (Regensburg 1961)

[3] The relation of Luther to Tauler is not fully explored. Bernd Moeller ('Tauler and Luther' in *La mystique Rhénane* Paris 1963) plausibly suggests that Luther was 'impressed' rather than 'influenced'. But from Luther's early marginal notes (1509) on Tauler's Sermons to the later Table Talk there is a positive and permanent debt; cf. Otto Scheel *Dokumente zu Luthers Entwicklung* 2nd ed., Tübingen 1929, Nos 21 (p. 12), 56 (p. 24), 59 (p. 25), 60 (p. 26), 719 (p. 283), 753 (p. 296), 786 (p. 315).

creaturely desires, and attains that complete renunciation which is called 'Gelassenheit'. There is the recurring image, which haunted Müntzer, of the soul as a field, full of weeds until it is ploughed by God, and where the good seed finally grows, an image used by a modern poet to describe a modern mystical experience:

> *That I should plough, and as I ploughed*
> *My Saviour Christ would sing aloud,*
> *And as I drove the clods apart*
> *Christ would be ploughing in my heart,*
> *Through rest-harrow and bitter roots,*
> *Through all my bad life's rotten fruits.*[1]

Important and influential in Catholic and Protestant circles then and later is the pseudo-Tauler (accepted as genuine in the 16th century) *The Book of the Poor in Spirit*. It is a work which Tridentine orthodoxy considered as more extreme and heretical than Tauler's sermons. I think there are definite traces of it in Müntzer, and not least in its stress on the Work of God.[2]

From Suso, Müntzer may have learned to include the sufferings of Christians with Christ under the all-embracing concept of the Divine Wisdom. It seems certain that he knew the *Theologia Germanica* (1518), but I suspect that he came to it when his main outlines were drawn, and that on him it had not the impact which it made on Hans Denck and Andrew Karlstadt.[3] It is not safe to adventure either the generalization that Karlstadt got his mysticism from Müntzer, or the reverse.[4] But doubtless Müntzer read Karlstadt's

---

[1] John Masefield, 'The Everlasting Mercy'

[2] *The Book of the Poor in Spirit* by a Friend of God, ed. C. F. Kelley (London 1954). In the 18th century it was read, along with the *Theologia Germanica*, by the Manchester High Churchman, John Byrom, and by John Wesley. For interesting parallel influence in the 16th century on the Irish Capuchin, Fr Nugent, see F. X. Martin *Friar Nugent* (Rome/London 1962), pp. 45-6, 68. The thought of Müntzer as an Irish Capuchin *manqué* is intriguing.

[3] There are no whole fragments of the *Theologia Germanica* embedded in Müntzer's writings, as there are in Karlstadt's.

[4] Karlstadt had written about 'Gelassenheit' as early as 1520. We must also reckon with the influence on him of the visit of the Zwickau prophets, who spent months in the Wittenberg area after their dramatic intervention at Christmas 1521.

THE GOSPEL ACCORDING TO THOMAS MÜNTZER

writings, and discussed them with his friend, for they were correspondents and allies at least until 1524. Then the social ferment and Müntzer's programme of violence revealed the difference between them which had been under the surface all along. For the passive words 'Müssigkeit', 'Studierung', 'Langweiligkeit', 'Gelassenheit', which are overtones for Karlstadt, are undertones in Müntzer's more dynamic pattern.

Indeed the relation between Müntzer and Karlstadt is not unlike that between Brer Rabbit and Brer Terrapin in *Uncle Remus* (which Müntzer, who quotes Aesop's Fables, would, like Luther, have loved) – Karlstadt's piety being like that of Brer Terrapin's existence which he described as 'lounjun' roun' en suffer'n' '. But the main difference between them is that Müntzer's mysticism is blended with apocalyptic. Of this the perfect emblem is his constant description of the Christians as 'Elect Friends of God'. 'Friends of God' had for a century and a half denominated mystical pietism: but 'Elect' is the dynamic phrase which was to set a militant Protestantism on the march for the next two centuries.

And here two volumes which Müntzer knew very well are of significance. The first is the Commentary on Jeremiah, ascribed to the Calabrian seer of the 12th century, Joachim da Fiore, but in reality the work of a Spiritual Franciscan of the 14th. In this the famous Eternal Gospel of Joachim, with its division of history into the past ages of the Father and the Son, and its proclamation of an imminent age of the Spirit, was adjusted to a German situation and the advent of the new age pegged down in the reign of the Emperors Henry I and Frederick I – an Armageddon which might be called 'Operation Barbarossa'!

About this Müntzer's avowal is of interest:

> They ascribe this teaching to the Abbot Joachim and call it 'The Eternal Gospel' in great ridicule. And with me the Witness of Abbot Joachim has counted for much. I have only read him on Jeremiah. But my teaching is from a far higher authority – I get it not from him, but from the God who speaks to me, as I will show with all the writings of the Bible, at the proper time.[1]

[1] Franz, II, No. 46, p. 398

The second volume which, according to Strobel,[1] Müntzer caused to be bound together with his Tauler – a hefty tome to carry round – was the remarkable anthology of mystical and prophetic writings which Le Fèvre edited and published in Paris in 1513: the *Liber trium virorum et trium spiritualium virginum*. Two of the men, Robert d'Uzès and Huguetinus, are innocuous, but the third is none other than the Shepherd of Hermas, who now enters the modern world, in all his apocalyptic glory, and bearing with him a sheaf of images about the Church, revelation vouchsafed to a common man which could not have failed to interest Müntzer. The ladies are an interesting group. Mechtild of Hackeborn is one of the band of Thuringian mystics, inmate of Thuringian nunneries, devoted to the theme of the sacred humanity of Christ. Elizabeth of Schönau is a visionary: one of her visions, concerning St Ursula and her 11,000 martyr virgins, succeeded in elevating what had been originally a misprint (for '11') in a MS. into a mass murder, and a medieval best-seller.

But the most important selection in the volume is from the writings of a really great prophetess, St Hildegard of Bingen: one of the most remarkable women in history, abbess, seer, thaumaturge, poetess, dramatist, naturalist, geologist, administrator, adviser to half the crowned and mitred heads of Christendom. This sanctified female dragon is represented by her Two Ways (*Scivias*) in which her lovely meditation on the Divine Light within the soul is geared to an astringent appraisal of the defects of a feudal age which she dismissed as 'effeminate'![2]

It is often assumed that Müntzer was influenced by Hussite writings. But he knew no Czech[3] and there is no reference to any Hussite Latin literature. Such influence is possible. His doctrine of the godless ruler smells like a faint whiff of the Wycliffite doctrine of dominion by grace, and his programme of eschatological war

---

[1] *Leben, Schriften und Lehren Thomas Müntzers* p. 7

[2] Migne *P.L.* cxcvii; C. J. Singer, 'The Scientific Views and Visions of Saint Hildegard 1098–1180' in *Studies in the History and Method of Science* (Oxford 1917); H. Liebeschütz *Das allegorische Weltbild der heiligen Hildegard von Bingen* (Leipzig/Berlin 1930). Her visions have been ascribed to migraine!

[3] In Prague he preached through an interpreter (Franz, II, No. 28, p. 377).

against the godless has obvious affinities with Taborite radicalism. It was not just geographical propinquity which made him launch his manifesto in Prague.[1] Certainly Zwickau was notoriously open to Bohemian influence. It is sometimes asserted that the lay Zwickau prophet, Nicholas Storch, was the medium of such infiltration, but the evidence of Storch's own beliefs is far vaguer than is often suggested.[2]

To speak of a phase in Müntzer's career when he was dominated by 'Storchismus' (A. Lohmann) seems to reverse the probable relationship between the two men. We know that Müntzer referred deferentially to Storch from the pulpit as an example of a layman more skilled in Scripture than the professional clergy. Storch refused his invitation to go to Prague at the time of his Manifesto,[3] and when Müntzer returned, he kept well away from his former friends, and could plausibly disavow his adherence to their doctrines, in his last letter to Luther.[4]

Mysticism, apocalyptic, heresy. Add charcoal to saltpetre and nitre, and three inert materials make gunpowder. So it was with the Müntzer explosion.

More influential on Müntzer's mind than all these writers was Holy Scripture. He may have had little Hebrew[5] and less Greek, but he had an excellent command of Latin and some of his Latin sermon notes have survived (one of the common requirements of

---

[1] His stress on the awakening of the child at the age of 6–7 may have a link with the Bohemian custom of communicating children.

[2] The most important document, in which Nicholas Hausmann reported from Zwickau to Frederick the Wise about a gang of radicals who had been arrested and questioned (after Müntzer had gone), does not mention Storch by name and speaks vaguely of 'Picard' notions. The only full exposition of Storch's teaching (Brandt, op. cit., pp. 53ff.) is very late (1597) and obviously garbled. Wappler asserts notions of Hussite origin, but the only explicit evidence he gives is the statement of the Zwickau chronicler that Storch 'hoc scisma ex Boemia advexerat' (*Thomas Müntzer in Zwickau* p. 30, note 115).

[3] Franz, II, No. 22, p. 370: 'Miror Nicolaum nihil scripsisse nec reversum.'

[4] Franz, II, No. 40, p. 391

[5] see p. 309 below. He has an interesting word list, of his own compilation, of Hebrew words – it suggests, as do his translations of the Psalms, a considerable facility in Hebrew; Franz, p. 539f.

preachership holders was that they should preach in Latin on feast days). His translations of the Psalms are grounded on the Vulgate, though he made use of Luther's Bible. Müntzer's mind is saturated in Scripture, and his claim to appeal to the 'whole' Bible (which may be linked with his Whole–Parts dialectic) is borne out by the astonishing range of his citations.

The opening chapters of Genesis are of great importance for him as expounding the Ordering of Creation, and the terms of man's dominion over the creatures, as well as for the orthodox doctrine of Sin and the Fall.[1] From these chapters he drew inferences to challenge the orthodox doctrine of civil obedience from Augustine to Luther. For Müntzer (as for Luther at the time of his lectures on Hebrews, 1517–18) the figures of the Patriarchs are of special significance as witnesses to the existential character of faith, the incredibility of the divine promises until proved through tribulation.

> The Elect man will find that all the Fathers, the Patriarchs, the prophets, and especially the apostles, have come to faith only through great difficulty, not like those crack-brained easy-going swine at Wittenberg who are scared by the hurricane of roaring waters and the great floods of wisdom.[2]

It is in the historical books of the Old Testament that he found his parallels and precedents for violent war against the godless, and he could rattle off with embarrassing facility the long list of war crimes committed by the servants of God, from Gideon to Elijah. It is a pity that he did not concentrate equally hard on the recommendations to mercy of the New Testament, but it is not fair to accuse him only of an Old Testament legalism, and his stress on the divine covenant shows that, like Luther, he found promise as well as Law in the Old Testament.

The Psalms were of the very texture of his soul, and not least the dualism, godly–ungodly, and the persecution complex of the servants of God. But two Psalms, 19 and 93, were for him an epitome of his gospel, and of many of them he made fine, if daringly free, translations. The theme of the divine Wisdom was important for him, and Job and Wisdom and Ecclesiasticus he had studied well.

[1] Franz, pp. 315, 327   [2] Franz, p. 220

THE GOSPEL ACCORDING TO THOMAS MÜNTZER

For that age he is unusually well read in the prophets and we have some notes which he made on passages from Amos.[1]

Isaiah he often cites (Isaiah 11 was a key chapter) and Ezekiel. But in his last years it is Jeremiah who counts, and the misunderstood, ill-treated prophet became an identity figure for Müntzer himself. Daniel was the theme of his most forceful sermon, and Michelangelo's Daniel would do for an emblem of Müntzer himself. Müntzer is equally at home in all parts of the New Testament. If he be the author of that 'Gospel of All Creatures' current among his followers, then his appeal to the teaching of Jesus in the Synoptic Gospels is fresh and startling. But he loves also to expound the Fourth Gospel. It would be wrong to speak of the influence of mystical literature on his mind and not to stress the importance for him of the Pauline teaching about dying and rising again with Christ, and filling what is lacking in the sufferings of Christ. He often quotes Colossians with its emphasis on the reconciliation of the Creation. We have some notes which he made on dreams and visions in the Acts of the Apostles, and he quotes most of the other New Testament writings, the Apocalypse less frequently than we might expect but, perhaps significantly, often chapter 5.

He peppers his polemical tracts with citations and flings whole fistfuls at his adversaries. Thus in a letter to Frederick the Wise,[2] and in a dozen lines, he quotes Ps. 68, Matt. 23, Jer. 20, Ps. 1, Jer. 1, Ezek. 13, Matt. 5, Matt. 10, Acts 26, 1 Cor. 1, Eph. 5, 1 Cor. 14, enough for a day's Bible study and none of it irrelevant. Sometimes, it is true, Müntzer can be woodenly medieval, as when Numbers 19, on the 'sprinkling on the third day', is used to attest the awakening of the soul at the age of 7. But these citations are far more alive and apposite in general than the chips and snippets of many of his contemporaries. Sometimes, too, he is plain perverse, as in that deadly use of the words of the parable, 'Take mine enemies and slay them before me', which is less a misquotation of Scripture than a misconception of the mind of Christ.

But above all, he used Scripture with the flair of an outstanding preacher. On any showing, his Sermon before the Princes is an event of magnitude, one of the most remarkable sermons of the

[1] Dresden MSS. [2] Franz, II, No. 45, p. 395f.

261

century. And granted Müntzer's (false) premisses, how apposite was this story of a bewildered ruler, torn between the advice of false prophets and Daniel, the servant of God! We may suspect that the lost sermon, delivered during the next days, on the Covenant between rulers and people in the days of Josiah, was at least as powerful. And if his exposition of Luke 1, the 'Ausgedrückte Entblössung', is an amplification of sermons, which it surely is, could a chapter be found in the whole Bible more full of themes, prophets, visions, the Spirit, divine songs, the overturning of the mighty – more apt and congenial to Müntzer's mind, more fit for his purpose? It is a demerit of the Troeltschean typology that in labelling Müntzer as a 'Spiritualist' it blurs the fact that he knew his Bible better, and that it meant more to him than to most of the so-called 'biblicists' of the Reformation.

2. Content

Those who would assess the importance of a Zwingli or a Müntzer must make allowance for battle, murder and sudden death. Cut off in their prime (Müntzer was in his middle thirties when he died), their works seem dwarfs indeed beside the serried folio volumes of the giant Lutheran Weimarana. Of Müntzer we possess only a few tracts, his liturgies, some scores of letters and a few odd papers. Most of these writings are occasional, and to a high degree polemical. It would be easy to over-systematize and over-press the evidence. The only satisfactory method is to read and re-read Müntzer's own writings until the undertones and overtones appear. The fatal method seems to be to rake Müntzer's works in terms of some preconceived ideological pattern, or with the categories of Lutheran orthodoxy.[1]

Thus, to assume that Justification is for Müntzer, as for Luther, a fundamental over-arching category is something for which evidence fails, and makes Müntzer into a harbinger of Andreas Osiander with the view that we are saved by an inherent righteous-

---

[1] cf. the weakness of the Marxist studies and also of such otherwise valuable essays as those of T. Nipperdey, 'Theologie und Revolution bei Thomas Müntzer' *ARG* 55 1964, pp. 145ff. and of E. W. Gritsch, 'Thomas Muentzer and the origins of Protestant spiritualism' *MQR* 37 1963, pp. 172ff.

There is no reliable portrait of Thomas Muntzer, but Michelangelo's Daniel would have done very well

ness. This is to put Müntzer into an ideological straitjacket not his own and which ignores the lively and subtle intuitions of his doctrine of salvation. The references to 'Rechtfertigung' and 'Gerechtigkeit' in his works are infrequent and out of all proportion to his incessant use of his key words – from Word, Spirit, Faith, to Judgement (*Urteil*). But does he, in fact, assume such a doctrine, to which he need not make frequent specific allusion? It is true that Müntzer had been consulted about indulgences and that he attacked the Franciscans on positive theological and not only anticlerical grounds, in alliance with other younger Martinians. But there is no evidence that for him 'Justitia Dei' – the quality of the divine righteousness – was the crucial question which it was for Luther. Indeed, it sometimes seems as though Müntzer's breakthrough would have been in an opposite direction. For while Luther began with a view of the divine nature as one of holy, demanding, punishing justice and came to see that within this justice was mercy and pity, it seems as though the later Müntzer, at any rate, was driven more and more to stress the 'earnestness' of the divine punishment as against what he conceived to be the easy sentimentalism of the new evangel. And it has to be said that throughout his writings Müntzer, for all his frequent subjectivism, is almost silent about the forgiveness of sins and the joy and peace which comes with the divine pardon.

We must not exaggerate. He speaks often of conscience. The sinner has to be aware of his lusts 'and of the sting of conscience – and to keep his conscience alive'.[1] Or he cries out, 'My conscience destroys all my moisture and strength . . . God torments me in my conscience . . .'[2] Although the Elect may commit great sins, 'none the less the fire of his conscience drives him to loathe and abominate sin'.[3] By the light of natural reason, no man can make a true judgement (*Urteil*) in his conscience without God's Revelation.[4] The Elect is a sinner, as his conscience shows him.[5] It is the 'Name of God' which brings a man 'joy, peace and righteousness, in his conscience'.[6] For all this, it cannot be said of Müntzer, as of Luther by Karl Holl, that his is a religion of conscience.

[1] Franz, II, No. 57, p. 419   [2] Franz, p. 237   [3] Franz, II, No. 49, p. 403
[4] Franz, p. 250   [5] Franz, p. 291   [6] Franz, p. 301

There is a fragment of a Latin sermon by Müntzer[1] on the Unjust Steward which is thoroughly Martinian on the subject of salvation by faith, and on the sufficiency of the righteousness of Christ. The sinner knows he is in judgement, but when he cries unto the Lord, 'Who shall deliver me?' – 'by this cry the unjust is justified. Then his sins are remembered no more.' 'And by this confession of faith, which believes with the heart unto righteousness, he is so sanctified as to merit to sit with the apostles on the seat of judgement.'

> For man is a servant, in that he was created exactly for this end, that he might sanctify the name of the Lord in all the works in which he is exercised that with a real, and not a feigned, faith he should acknowledge God and his own weakness by crying out 'Lord, I am an unprofitable servant', 'in all my works, help thou mine unbelief, for without thee I cannot please thee.' Even if a man could fulfil the whole law, he could not trust in his own works ... for he would only have the righteousness which is by the law and would deserve eternal death.

That is why, of all the servants of God, 'one servant is offered' – as Phil. 2. For the one signifies all, 'for he alone was righteous [*qui solus justus est*] who alone was well-pleasing in the Father's sight'[2] and in this other, all are offered for sale (*alii omnes venundantur*). 'What is "offered for sale"? – that they should renounce themselves and learn their misery and not trust in their works.' The sermon ends with the great Augustinian prayer: 'Give what thou commandest: may what thou willest be accomplished [*Da quod jubes, et fiet quod vis*].'

That Christ alone is our righteousness is asserted in Müntzer's explanation of the Liturgy at the *Agnus Dei*. 'For Christ died for our sins and rose again because he willed to justify us, which he alone does, and which we passively receive [*wir müssen sie erleiden*]'. There is a further fragment in the Müntzer papers, expounding 1 Cor. 7:17

---

[1] Dresden MSS. 75a, b, 74b; Franz, III, 4 (d), p. 523f.

[2] cf. Charles Wesley's hymn, 'Behold the Servant of the Lord', with its striking lines:

> Thy work, O Lord, is all complete,
> And pleasing in Thy Father's sight;
> Thou only hast done all things right.

(which may even be a gobbet transcribed from Luther), which treats of the relation of faith and works in a thoroughly Lutheran way.[1]

Although, as we shall see, Müntzer's stress is on the solidarity of Christians in Christ, and their conformity to the sufferings of their Head, which he accentuated against the new evangelical clichés, 'Only believe . . .', and 'Christ has done all . . .', he too firmly believes that salvation is from God alone through Christ alone. The Lamb of God who takes away the sin of the world is at the heart of Müntzer's theology, as at the centre of his liturgy.

3. *Word and Spirit*

In a famous letter, Erasmus speaks of the evangelical slogans going the rounds in 1524, the words 'Gospel, Word, Faith, Christ, Spirit'. These are important words, too, for Thomas Müntzer. And though a count of words suggests that Müntzer uses the word 'Spirit' more often than 'Word', more often perhaps than any other conception next to 'Faith', and though there is enough truth in Luther's contemptuous 'Geist hin! Geist her!' to denote the radical obsession, so that a good case can be made out for putting 'Spirit' first, or of speaking at least of 'Spirit and Word', yet we shall treat first of Word and Spirit in that order, because we accept Martin Schmidt's judgement that in the end Müntzer's is a 'Word of God' theology, and because when we treat Word and Spirit in that order, we can best understand Müntzer's view of Scripture.

For Müntzer the Word of God is alive, speaking directly to men, and in his early controversy with Egranus he accused his adversary of believing a 'dumb God', as he later warned Melanchthon also of believing that God no longer speaks directly to men. 'I get my teaching', he wrote to Zeiss, 'from the God who addresses me.'[2]

[1] There is one passage in Müntzer ('Protestation', chap. 14) which seems to attack salvation by Faith: 'If a man preaches "Faith must justify and not work" that is an immodest speech. For Nature is not regarded here, and that a man must come to Faith through God's Work.' But here it is not good works but the Work of God which is in question, that is, a divine action through Nature, which Müntzer, on the basis of Tauler and others, sees as a preliminary to faith, but none the less a divine action parallel to Luther's office of the Law.

[2] Franz, II, No. 46, p. 398

The Elect Friends of God also learn to prophesy as Paul teaches that they can really experience how friendly, yes, how heartily and willingly God talks with his Elect.[1]

For Luther the Word is the Incarnate Word, and the creative Word, but Müntzer draws also on the doctrine of the uncreated Logos, a notion which passed into the mystical tradition from Justin and the Fathers. Not that Müntzer identifies this Word with human reason or understanding, but it gives him his lively sense that God may speak directly to men, far outside the bounds of Christendom.

> I preach such a Christian faith ... which is of the same stamp in all the hearts of the Elect upon earth, and if a man were born a Turk he might have the beginning of the same faith.[2]

But it is here, in the Ground of the Soul, that the Living Word speaks.

> The Good Word of God lives in all Elect men, in their hearts.[3]
> Scripture cannot make men live, as does the living Word which an empty soul hears.[4]
> The Christian judges not by external things, but according to the most lovable will of God which he studies in his Living Word.[5]
> Paul speaks (Romans 10) of the inward Word which is to be heard in the ground of the soul, through the Revelation of God.[6]
> They know that the Word of God, on which faith depends, is not a hundred thousand miles off, but they see it as it bubbles out of the ground of the heart, and perceive that it comes from the Living God.[7]

This living Word is also the eternal and incarnate Word. 'The eternal Word was made man.'[8] As Jesus was slandered at Nazareth, 'How often has the eternal Word moved in the Elect in our Nazareth called Christendom, that is in the flowering Elect, who bloom sweet and green in the Wisdom of the Cross.'[9]

---

[1] Franz, p. 494   [2] Franz, pp. 430-1   [3] Franz, p. 492
[4] Franz, p. 220   [5] Franz, p. 235
[6] Franz, p. 251. Müntzer does not much use the phrase 'Inner Word', so important for Hans Denck; see also Franz, p. 252
[7] Franz, p. 237   [8] Franz, p. 46   [9] Franz, pp. 316-17

THE GOSPEL ACCORDING TO THOMAS MÜNTZER

There is for Müntzer a close connexion between the Word of God and the Work and Will of God. The idea of a divine energy in action, the Work of God in creation and in the human soul, seems partly rooted in Augustine and his distinction between the Work of God and the Work of the Hands of God, and it is probably reinforced for Müntzer by the pseudo-Tauler *Book of the Poor in Spirit*, one part of which is devoted to the theme of the Divine Work.[1]

The theme of the Work of God is closely linked with that of the Divine Will.[2] 'The Will of God is the Whole over all the parts . . . but the Work of God flows from the Whole and all the parts.'[3] In his liturgy the people respond: 'God teach you from day to day to perceive all his Will and Work for our good.'[4] 'Whoso has not the Spirit of Christ, is not God's child. How can he know about the Work of God if he has not suffered it?'[5] The Christian 'must expect God's Work and Word'.[6] John the Baptist spoke to the hearts of men 'that they might learn the ways of the Work of God'.[7] 'Thus a man must see how he is to suffer the Work of God, and receive it from day to day in the knowledge of God.'[8] 'The Elect ought and must be conformed to Christ, and with manifold suffering and discipline heed God's work.'[9] 'The false Scribes . . . say that because many people do not know the Work of God, they can come to Christian faith the easy way if they only think upon what Christ said'.[10] The believer 'has waited a long time, with his inward eye, on the Lord and on his hands, that is, on the divine work'.[11] 'You have to put off all the clothes that you have put on from the creatures, and let God throw them off through his Work'.[12]

4. Spirit

The Spirit is for Müntzer not so much one of the notes as the key-signature at the side of the music, determining the mood in which the whole is written. That is why it figures in his opening

---

[1] 'What is God's Work? It is simply a revelation of God in the soul when God shows Himself to the soul. God acts, and He Himself is the work that He performs' (*Book of the Poor in Spirit* p. 119).
[2] Franz, pp. 210, 253 [3] Franz, p. 418 [4] Franz, p. 166
[5] Franz, p. 209 [6] Franz, p. 218 [7] Franz, p. 221 [8] Franz, p. 224
[9] Franz, p. 227 [10] Franz, p. 233 [11] Franz, p. 237 [12] Franz, p. 234

salutations. 'The Spirit of Wisdom and the Knowledge of God's Methods, be with you, dear brother!' 'The Spirit of the Strength and Fear of God be with you, you poor people!' Compared with some other apocalyptically-minded radicals, Bader, Hofmann, Bockelson, indeed compared with some of Luther's claims about his own achievements (by the grace of God!), Müntzer is reserved about claims for his own prophetic mission, preferring to speak of himself as the Servant of God, however arrogant may seem some of the parallels which he draws between himself and Elijah, John the Baptist and Daniel. His one apparent claim to direct inspiration, his translations from Latin into German, is soberly expressed. For he gives Scriptural citation for the view that 'all the Elect may be taught of God' –

> Therefore I have sought to improve things according to our German Method and examination and have under the irrevocable orders of the Holy Ghost translated the Psalms, more according to the meaning than the Words.[1]

It is the Spirit which makes true Baptism. The Living Water of which St John speaks (John 7) is the Holy Ghost – for the 'waters are the Movement of our spirit into that of God'.[2] It is the Spirit which is essential to the Eucharist.[3]

> For he could have no rest before the driving of the Holy Ghost, who will give him no peace in order to direct him to the highest Good.[4]

> It is the Holy Ghost who teaches us faith with the spirit of the Fear of God.[5]

> It is the Spirit who brings understanding of the Scripture.

> There has to be exposition of the Holy Scriptures in the teaching of the Spirit of Christ through the comparing together of all the mysteries and judgement of God.[6]

The Scribes turn the Holy Scriptures to poison for the Holy Spirit.[7]

---

[1] Franz, p. 162   [2] Franz, p. 228
[3] Franz, p. 544: 'He will not let the Blessed Sacrament be outwardly adored otherwise than in the Spirit.'
[4] Franz, p. 301   [5] Franz, p. 274   [6] Franz, p. 268   [7] Franz, p. 306

THE GOSPEL ACCORDING TO THOMAS MÜNTZER

Animal man does not heed what God speaks in the soul, but he has to be shown it through the Holy Ghost by earnest contemplation of the plain, pure understanding of the Law (Ps. 19).[1]

It is the Holy Spirit who

> declares faith in the spirit of the Fear of the Lord, together with the fact that each Elect man must have the Holy Ghost sevenfold.[2]

It is the Holy Spirit who begins the divine Work with the Sprinkling (Num. 19:19).

> All a man's desires stretch out towards the first sprinkling through the inbreathed sighing of the Holy Ghost.[3]

Among Müntzer's marginal jottings is a list of dreams and visions in the Acts of the Apostles, and though he does not believe indiscriminately in this mode of revelation, it is a very sore point of his that Wittenberg rejects these things altogether.

> But the good apostles were up-to-date with their visions as is clearly shown in Acts. Yes, it is a real, apostolic, patriarchal and prophetic Spirit to expect visions.[4]

But on the whole Müntzer speaks of the Spirit with perfect propriety, seeing him at work at every stage in salvation.

> When the listener has first heard Christ preached in his heart through the spirit of the Fear of God, then a true preacher can give him sufficient witness. The Work of the Hands of God must have first shown him Reverence for God, otherwise all preaching and writing is vain.[5]

None the less, Müntzer is sensitive to the charge of his opponents that he and his friends are obsessed with the Spirit.

> They make a mocking bird out of the Spirit of Christ, and are so clever that they are bold to cry and write 'Spirit here – Spirit there. I praise my own writings. I have done this and that'.[6]

> They ridicule the Spirit of God and yet believe nothing ... and scold the genuine Spirit as an erring Spirit and Satan.[7]

---

[1] Franz, p. 251   [2] Franz, p. 491   [3] Franz, p. 301   [4] Franz, p. 254
[5] Franz, p. 402   [6] Franz, p. 279. Luther is intended.   [7] Franz, p. 325

They want to put the Witness of the Spirit of Jesus through college [*auf die hohe Schul bringen*].¹

Dreams are recounted in Holy Scripture in order that the Devil may not 'destroy the anointing of the Holy Ghost with its sweetness'.²

A case could be made out that Müntzer is the first Methodist on the ground of his evident stress on the doctrine of assurance. Here Romans 8 is the key passage, as it appears in the Prague Manifesto:

> The Elect have an invincible witness from the Holy Ghost, for he gives satisfying [*genugsam*] witness to our spirit that we are the children of God.³

> Nobody can be blessed unless the Holy Ghost assure him of his blessedness as it is written. Romans 8, ...⁴

> He who lacks the invincible witness of the Spirit, does not belong to you, O Christ. You have the invincible witness.⁵

We have seen that for Karlstadt the sevenfold gifts of the Holy Spirit have special significance, and have suggested that this might be part of the theology, and certainly of the jargon, of the Zwickau prophets and their circle. In his Prague Manifesto Müntzer complained that no parsons or monks have understood this teaching.

There are many references to Isaiah 11:2 as of special significance in this connexion:

> The Spirit of the Lord shall rest upon him, the spirit of wisdom and understanding, the spirit of counsel and might, the spirit of knowledge and of the fear of the Lord.

It is a text which was expounded at some length in Tauler's second Sermon at Pentecost.⁶ But though Müntzer may have known this sermon, he himself seems to set it in a thoroughly apocalyptic context. Among these radicals, it seems certain that Isaiah 11:2 was joined with Revelation 5:1–7, with that Book of the Seven Seals which only the Lamb of God, with the help of the Seven Spirits of God, can open.

We know that Hans Huth, Müntzer's publisher and disciple,

---

¹ Franz, p. 270   ² Franz, p. 253   ³ Franz, p. 492   ⁴ Franz, p. 244
⁵ Franz, p. 323
⁶ Johannes Tauler *Predigten* (Freiburg 1961), pp. 197ff.: Pfingsten II

carried round with him a mysterious 'Book of Seven Seals and Judgements'. I think there is, theologically at least, a link between this and the book published by Sebastian Franck in 1539,[1] which is also about Seven Seals and, like Huth's only certain tract, includes a collection of apparent antitheses in Holy Scripture. It may be that the Preface to Franck's work reflects a much earlier teaching about seven seals and seven spirits of God. It is true that Hans Huth and his friends thought in sevens – a notebook found on him at his arrest has a page full of sevens – as a kind of mnemonic preaching device. It is also true that the Seven Judgements were primarily eschatological. But there may also have been, as late medieval exegesis made easy, a tropological interpretation referring these texts also to the work of God within the soul. At any rate Franck gives a pattern of seven good and seven evil spirits, and there are hints in Müntzer that he and his friends worked with such a pattern.[2] Thus, as the Spirit opens each Seal, a gift of the Spirit takes its place. Here is an interesting doctrine of the Spirit in sanctification. Before we dismiss it as eccentric (as are the references to Numbers 19, and the 'sprinkling on the third day' – which also seems to belong to a wider radical circle than just Müntzer) we might notice that the ancient prayer for Whitsunday which asks for a 'right judgement in all things' comes close to this thought of divine wisdom and the radical special use of 'Urteil'.[3]

There is explicit reference to Isaiah 11:2 in many rites for Confirmation (and especially in the Book of Common Prayer). Perhaps instead of arguing whether Müntzer was an Anabaptist, more attention might be turned to him as a Confirmationist! At the

---

[1] *Das verbüthschiert mit siben Sigeln verschlossen Buch*: I am grateful to the University of Yale for a photostat of this rare work.

[2]
Seven Spirits of God	Seven Spirits of Evil
Wisdom (*Weisheit*)	Human wisdom
Understanding (*Verstand*)	Human understanding
Counsel (*Rat*)	Human counsel
Might (*Stärke*)	Human might
Knowledge (*Kunst*)	Human godlessness
Fear of the Lord (*Furcht Gottes*)	Fear of man (*Menschenfurcht*)

[3] which is not, I think, simply settling an argument with a text, but the authentic discrimination which a man gains from the Scripture 'in the Spirit'.

Reformation, those who stressed the importance of Confirmation, and notably Erasmus and Martin Bucer, did so following the late medieval notion of that Sacrament as the strengthening of the Christian warrior, and added to it the need for Christian instruction and the personal appropriation by the candidate of his Baptismal vows and what was then promised on his behalf. Modern discussion about Confirmation has returned to the Church of the 2nd century and has much discussed its place in a twofold rhythm of Baptism–Confirmation, a Christian Initiation in which the sealing with the Spirit continues the divine work begun in Baptism. Now, though Müntzer does not write about Confirmation at all, it is arguable that he does outline such a regenerating work of the Holy Spirit as needs to be included within the pattern of our salvation. Indeed, somewhere here is the non-sacramental doctrine which, through radical Protestantism and Puritanism and Pietism, was to become a main emphasis in evangelical Christianity: the doctrine of conversion, and of the sanctifying work of the Holy Spirit in heart, life and doctrine. It is perhaps not accidental that in the hymnology of the Methodists, who in their first age had no thought of erecting any sacramental rite in the place of Anglican Confirmation, there is a rich doctrine of the work of the Holy Spirit at this point. Some of the finest verses of Charles Wesley could be used to underline what Müntzer and his friends have said.[1]

5. Holy Scripture

Müntzer thinks in chiaroscuro. Deep and important for him are the shadows and the lights, more important it may be than the colours. Hence the contrast which he found in the Bible, but particularly in the Psalms, between the pious and the ungodly. Hence the antinomy between the teaching of himself and his friends and that of the Scribes – first Egranus, then the Papists, and finally, and in his eyes worst of all, the Scribes of Wittenberg. He has also a dialectic of opposites which may owe something to Nicholas of

---

[1] There are thus cogent theological reasons (though not in favour with modern liturgists, obsessed with the 2nd century) for keeping Isaiah 11:2 in any Confirmation rite, in line with an authentic theological insight of the Reformation.

Cusa. These things affect his hermeneutic, and the rather subtle dialectic of his use of Scripture.

His opponents outrage him by putting the Scripture against his appeal to the living Word. But they are false Scribes who have, in his favourite image, stolen the Scriptures (Jer. 23:30).

> They think it is enough that it is all written in books and they can spit it out like the stork with the frogs she spits to her young ones in the nest.[1]

They have put Scripture under a knavish cover, which must now be removed. Müntzer believes that this deception of God's people can be traced back to the Fall of the Church in the sub-apostolic age, but that the new Scribes, like the Papists, are the perpetuators of this deception. Against them stands Müntzer's primary insistence on the Living Word:

> If a man had neither seen nor heard the Bible all his life, yet through the teaching of the Spirit he could have an undeceivable Christian faith, like all those who without books wrote the Holy Scripture.[2] Even if you had swallowed the Bible whole, it is of no avail, you must suffer the sharp ploughshare, or you have no faith.[3]

Further, the Scripture without the Spirit is dead and is an affair of the outward letter, which counts for nothing where salvation is concerned. Here Müntzer's hermeneutic would seem to rest on the doctrine of Augustine's *On the Spirit and the Letter*, on which his friend Karlstadt lectured in 1518, and part of which he published.

In considering what Müntzer says of the interpretation of Scripture, we have to keep two things in mind. First, the false Scribes who lack true, proved and tempted faith, for whom the Scripture is dead, so that they can only pick out easy and sentimental promises here and there, and who ignore the 'whole' witness of Scripture. Second, the inert character of Scripture itself without the Spirit. But when the Spirit is present, when the Scriptures are read and diligently compared by the Elect with their proved and true Faith, then Scripture does indeed become important as Witness.[4]

---

[1] Franz, pp. 492, 322   [2] Franz, p. 277   [3] Franz, p. 234
[4] Franz, p. 276: The Son of God has said, Scripture gives Witness: then the Scribes say, It gives Faith.'

Here there are two important paragraphs in 'Von dem gedichteten Glauben':

> What a man hears or sees, that which shows him Christ, he receives as a wonderful Witness through which to hunt down, kill and crush his unbelief. So much so that he sees the whole of Holy Scripture as a two-edged Sword, for all that is contained in it is to this end, that it should always kill us rather than make us live.[1]

Like the apostles who were slow to believe the Resurrection, we help ourselves with a false faith and a dreamed-up Mercy of God, and would storm heaven with a natural promise.

> Ah no, beloved Christian people, let us use the Holy Bible for that for which it was created, to kill (as we said above) and not to make alive as does the Living Word which an empty soul hears.[2]

But in the Spirit the Bible becomes important, for Müntzer goes on to say:

> Let us not pick out a bit here and a bit there, but in the teaching of the Spirit and not of the Flesh let us put such things together which is to expect out of all places of the Scripture that it should comfort and terrify. Where knavish Faith is not shown up, a man gets only the outward word, but in a thunderstorm the fool gets lost.[3]

Müntzer recurs to this theme in his 'Ausgedrückte Entblössung', in his assertion that in our time truth can only be shown 'with the exposition of the Holy Scripture in the teaching of the Spirit of Christ, through the comparison of all the Mysteries and Judgement of God'. When you ask the Scribes, with their stolen Scriptures, 'how they came to faith, about which they too continually prattle

---

[1] Franz, p. 218: compare Müntzer's 'That which shows us Christ' (*das Christum weiset*) with Luther's 'What treats of Christ' (*was Christum treibt*).

[2] Franz, p. 220; also p. 235

[3] It will be noticed that in the Spirit the Bible is not simply law, but it also brings comfort. Müntzer's appeal to the existential test of faith is exactly parallel to Luther's attack on 'fides humana' which fails in the moment of temptation: *WA* 57: Die Vorlesung über den Hebräerbrief, p. 233, line 3: 'Tunc nec ratio nec consilium nec fides superat, . . .'; Hirsch Rückert *Luthers Vorlesung über den Hebräerbrief* (1929), p. 269

... they say, "See, I believe the Scripture." ... or "Oho, this contradicts Scripture!" Thus the common man is beguiled, for he is too preoccupied with earning a living to be able to read the Scriptures for himself. The Scribes are to read the fine books and the Peasants are to listen to them, for faith comes through such hearing. Yes, dear Thomas, you have bees in your bonnet!' There follows the passage already quoted to the effect that a man may have Faith through the Living Word, though he had never heard or seen the Bible.

Yet, as we have seen, as Witness the Bible is of great importance to Müntzer, who draws upon the Scriptures at every point and in every argument. When he attacks the traditional view of Baptism, it is to ask all the Literal Scholars to 'show me where in Holy Scripture there is a single instance of infant baptism, ... or indeed that the Mother of God or the disciples were baptized'.[1] His last outrageous tract against Luther argues with him about the interpretation of the opening Books of the Bible, and the implications of the Genesis teaching about man's dominion.

It is entirely and laudably consistent that, in his liturgical reforms, Müntzer, like Thomas Cranmer in England, should be concerned that the whole Bible be read, and not truncated snippets. For this reason, whole Psalms are to be sung, and

> we always read a whole chapter instead of the Epistle and Gospel, so that the patchwork method may be thrown aside and the holy scripture of the Bible be made common to the People.[2]

6. *The Plan of Salvation*

For Luther, the whole of the way to salvation is comprehended within justification. The Christian man lives in each moment of his existence in another righteousness than his own, the perfect righteousness of Christ, and as he so lives, 'always right with God, always penitent, always a sinner', the Holy Spirit is at work in his soul, driving out sin, and bringing into existence ever new patterns of virtue and obedience. But Luther does not draw a map – he will not draw a pattern of our sanctification, a Plan of Salvation, as later

[1] Franz, p. 228 [2] Franz, p. 209

Protestantism, and especially Puritanism, loved to do. Or perhaps his is not so much a map as an ocean chart, or like one of the maps used in the Western desert during World War II, which simply explained, 'Here the going is good . . . or bad.'

But Müntzer has a plan and a pattern of salvation. It is twofold. A doctrine of Christian Initiation – of the advent of Faith, and a doctrine of our conformity with Christ. Müntzer himself was sensitive against Luther's charge that he used an unscriptural mystical jargon.[1] We know that a common mystical jargon circulated among Müntzer, Karlstadt and the Zwickau prophets. Perhaps one day some scholar will turn up a mystical writing in which their whole pattern is explicitly discussed. It might even be that this was a kind of evangelical language which was current as oral tradition among associations of 'Friends of God', or those heretical conventicles very loosely labelled in Germany 'Waldensian' or 'Hussite', as in England 'Lollard'.[2]

Behind Müntzer's pattern there is no doubt an echo of the classical mystical division: purgation, illumination and union; but these are not words he much uses, not even the word 'Entgrobung' – purgation. A great deal of Müntzer's polemic is concerned with Christian initiation, with the Advent or coming of true faith.

7. *The Fear of the Lord*

'The Fear of the Lord is the Beginning of Wisdom', this is the clue to Müntzer's doctrine of Christian beginnings and it is one

---

[1] Franz, II, No. 40 (9 July 1523), to Luther: 'You object that my jargon nauseates you – I suppose, "longanimitate, angustia mentis, talento" etc. Dear father, I know that the apostle has set me a rule to avoid profane novelties of expression and knowledge falsely so called. Believe me that I shall say nothing which I cannot demonstrate with the clearest and plainest text.'

[2] Agricola in 1525 gives a list of such terms as 'Verwunderung', 'Entgrobung', 'Studierung', 'Langweil', 'Besprengung', 'den Creaturen entrissen sein', 'kein Bilde haben', 'ausgestrackte Lust zur Gerechtigkeit Gottes', 'die strackte Gerechtigkeit Gottes'. Luther (*Table Talk* 1532) gives as Marcus Stübner's words: 'Gröbigkeit', 'Weiligkeit', 'Langweiligkeit'. But both these testimonies are late, and may read back into the 1521 Wittenberg appearance of the Zwickau prophets some of Müntzer's words; cf. Wappler *Thomas Müntzer in Zwickau* p. 45, note 189.

which he treats with seriousness. The references to it are manifold and at every level in his writings.[1]

This fear of the Lord corresponds a little to Luther's doctrine of the Law, which brings a man to the point of despair, and so to Faith. But it is developed in Müntzer with a startling 'natural theology'. For any man (without any Bible or preacher to guide him) may be brought by God's Spirit to consider the Works of the Hands of God in creation, and come through meditation on these things to a state of Reverence (*Verwunderung*). In one of his plainest descriptions, to the educated layman Christopher Meinhard, he expounds Psalm 19 as follows:

> There it is told you through the Holy Spirit how you must learn through suffering the Work of God declared in the Law so that your eyes may be opened for the first time. You must lay one word alongside another ... for a man must walk every moment in mortification of the flesh, but especially so that our name stinks in the mind of the godless, and then a tried [*versuchten*] man may preach the name of God, but the hearer must first have heard Christ preached in his heart through the Spirit of the Fear of the Lord, and then a true preacher can give him sufficient witness. But the Work of the Hands of God must have first shown him Reverence [*Verwunderung*] before God, otherwise all preaching and writing is vain.[2]

---

[1] Franz, pp. 163, 226, 246, 249, 253, 259, 267, 272, 287, 292, 309, 319, 327, 394, 395, 416, 423, 430, 454, 457, 492

[2] Franz, II, No. 49. H. J. Goertz (*Innere und Aeussere Ordnung* p. 41, note 2) accuses me, among others, of having misunderstood the meaning of 'the Work of the Hands of God' in Müntzer's exposition of Psalm 19, and suggests that in this place 'the Work of the Hands of God' means simply 'men'. I admit that in Müntzer there is no natural theology, or much thought of 'nature' in a 19th-century sense, but I am sure that Müntzer is thinking of 'the creatures' here as elsewhere. I think this can be sustained by an examination of all the references to this theme in Augustine's exposition of the Psalms, which Müntzer had read. Luther, whom Müntzer had probably not read, in this connexion is nearer to the exposition which Goertz suggests, but even in his case we need to remember how both Augustine and Luther ring the changes on a Christological, tropological and allegorical reference. But I agree with many of Goertz's conclusions as to the importance of the mystical writings for him, and that these are more important even than apocalyptic

This surely has links with the 'Gospel of All Creatures', important to Müntzer's disciples, and which must have originated with him, with its startling appeal to the Jesus of the Gospels and his teaching in the parables, a view theologically linked with the *Theologia Naturalis* of Raymond of Sabunde. Men are to contemplate the Works of God in creation and through the Spirit they are brought into Fear and Reverence of the Lord. For this Müntzer uses the word 'Betrachtung'.

> You must hold one Word always against the other and direct the meditation [*Betrachtung*] of your heart there.[1]
>
> A man has to be shown through the Holy Ghost an earnest contemplation [*Betrachtung*] of the plain pure understanding of the Law [Psalm 19].[2]

This earnest contemplation extends in the second place to the Law of God, expounded in the beginning of the Bible.

> Christ began with Moses and declared the Law from beginning to end.... I from the Beginning of the Bible and the Order of the first Distinction strive after the purity of the Divine Law [Psalm 19] through all judgements, declaring the fulfilment of the spirit of the Fear of the Lord.[3]

The Beginning is, therefore, the Fear of the Lord in which the soul, through the Holy Spirit, is brought to wonder, awe, reverence (*Verwunderung*).

> People must be brought to the highest degree of Unknowing[4] and 'Verwunderung', otherwise they can never be released from their false faith.[5]

(op. cit., p. 148) – only I think 'mysticism' is expounded too rigidly and with too much reference to Eckhart, whom Müntzer could have known only through the inclusion of three of his sermons in works ascribed to Tauler.

[1] Franz, p. 402   [2] Franz, p. 251

[3] Franz, pp. 326–7. It will be seen that Psalm 19 is as important for Müntzer's understanding of the Beginning, as is Psalm 93 for the End of our salvation.

[4] One of the echoes of Cusa?   [5] Franz, p. 220

THE GOSPEL ACCORDING TO THOMAS MÜNTZER

You Scribes say 'We know that the Scripture is right.' And it is true that Scripture is right – to kill, and not to make alive, for which it is not left on the earth. But it is written for us unknowing men, that the holy faith of a mustard seed may come as sourly to a man as though there were no Scripture at all, for the sake of mighty 'Verwunderung'.[1]

The Work of the Hands of God must have demonstrated the first Reverence [*Verwunderung*] for God.[2]

You ask – how does the Word come in the heart? I answer it comes from God above down into here, in a high Wonderment [*Verwunderung*] which I will leave to another time. And this Wonderment, whether it be the Word of God or no, begins when a child is 6 or 7 years old, as is prefigured in Numbers 19.[3]

In this gospel [St Luke's] there is to be noted from beginning to end the overshadowing of the Holy Ghost which teaches us Faith with the pure Fear of God, which brings forth such high Wonderment in the impossible Work of Faith.[4]

In short, a man must crush to pieces his stolen false Christian faith through high suffering in his heart and painful tribulation and through ceaseless Wonderment.[5]

---

[1] Franz, p. 231 [2] Franz, p. 402

[3] Franz, p. 251. It would be interesting to compare Müntzer's 'Wonderment' etc. with modern writing about the 'numinous'. It was one of the most telling points in Luther's 'Against the Heavenly Prophets' (*WA* 18, p. 137; *LW* xl, 147) that they dodge the question 'How does faith come?' (cf. also Höss *Georg Spalatin* p. 265). 'For when you ask them how one comes by this lofty Spirit, they don't point to the outward gospel, but go up into cloud-cuckoo-land and say, "Ah, you must have the experience of waiting [*Langweil*]" . . . they teach that you may sail up into the sky, ever so high, and ride upon the wind, only they can't tell you how or when or what it is, but only that you shall have the same experience . . .' (cf. E. G. Rupp, 'Word and Spirit in the First Years of the Reformation' *ARG* **49** 1958, p. 24n.). But Müntzer might have replied with Myers's St Paul:

> How should I tell or how can ye receive it,
> How, till He bringeth you where I have been?

He would certainly have echoed Myers:

> Whoso has felt the Spirit of the Highest
> Cannot confound nor doubt Him nor deny.

[4] Franz, pp. 273–4 [5] Franz, p. 298

8. *The Beginning*

Though the Fear of the Lord, contemplation of the Law, and Wonderment are strictly speaking the Beginning, Müntzer also uses the expression to cover the whole of Christian initiation to the coming, through temptation and tribulation, of true Faith.[1]

9. *The Movement*[2]

But now this apparently rather passive phase is ended with the dynamic movement of the Spirit, in the waters which test the soul, and which Müntzer, like Luther, describes as 'Anfechtung' (Temptation – but a stronger word than the normal 'Versuchung').

> Doubt is the Water, the Movement to good and evil. Who swims on the water without a saviour is between death and life. But the hope which he reaches through the work of faith establishes a man in the best things.[3]

In John 7, the

> Waters are the Movement [*Bewegung*] of our spirit into that of God.[4]

> A man is sure of his divine origin [*Ursprung*][5] in the wild tempestuous seas of the Movement when he is in travail in it, and he must behave as a fish which swims against the water ... in order to come home to the place of his breeding and origin.[6]

If a man is to be sure that he has received Faith, then

> God must take away his fleshly desires, and when the Movement [*Bewegung*] comes into the heart, he will kill all the sensual desires of the flesh.[7]

---

[1] Franz, pp. 164, 219, 237, 249, 271, 281, 300, 325, 394, etc. 'Anfang', 'Ankunft' are the usual expressions – and perhaps the translation 'Advent' would link these expressions with his liturgy and his opening office for Advent.

[2] 'Bewegung'   [3] Franz, p. 418   [4] Franz, p. 228

[5] An interesting allusive word of Müntzer, obviously important but never developed in his extant writings; cf. also Franz, p. 291

[6] Franz, p. 403   [7] Franz, p. 251

THE GOSPEL ACCORDING TO THOMAS MÜNTZER

> Then must the deep Movement [*Bewegung*] of Holy Christian Faith rouse the wild waves and the raging billows.[1]

The false scribes

> simply want to assuage the high Movement and tribulation of the Elect.[2]

His conscience shows the Elect that he is a sinner

> if only he perceives his Movement in tribulation.[3]
> Every man has to turn inward into himself and there mark by his Movement that he himself is a holy temple.[4]
> Ah, my dear brethren, how shall such people show Judgement, who deny us all Movement of Faith?[5]
> But in fact very few men know about the Beginning Movement of the Spirit.[6]
> ... when the waters of divine wisdom begin to rise. Then the sad sinner knows that God is starting incredible things in him. Then he is first shocked at the Name of God which is opened to him from the first Movement of the divine Work.[7]

In one place, Müntzer turns almost immediately from the thought of a divine movement in the conscience, which turns man against sin, to the thought of contemporary society:

> I must tell you a man must take great account of the New Movement of this present world.[8]

But generally this is a word about the work of God in the soul:

> If our singing in German and reading it in church is to be called 'un-Christian', what shall we say when we are to expound our 'Movement' to Faith?[9]

All the Reformers repudiated a mere *fides historica*, what Tyndale called a 'story book Faith', but none more vehemently or powerfully

---

[1] Franz, p. 269. Not a fantastic image; or at least it inspired Charles Wesley's:
> While the nearer waters roll,
> While the tempest still is high.

[2] Franz, p. 275   [3] Franz, p. 291   [4] Franz, p. 292   [5] Franz, p. 299
[6] Franz, p. 300   [7] Franz, p. 301   [8] Franz, p. 419   [9] Franz, p. 214

than Luther himself. It is true that Müntzer could not know the passages in Luther's early (unpublished) lectures in which his 'theology of the Cross' adumbrates this very theme, or Luther's private correspondence, or such sermons as his exposition of Jonah. But it is a flagrant example of historical misunderstanding, and proof that there was no real dialogue or confrontation between the two men. One other point has to be made. It was not Luther, but the little Luthers, who gave rise to some of the worst discords of the Reformation (and the little Zwinglis and the little Calvins) and it may very easily be that there were Martinians who seemed to preach this easy kind of faith, and to overstress the objectivities of preaching and sacraments. We have to remember that the only person close to Luther with whom Müntzer had the chance to explain his convictions was Spalatin.

10. Anfechtung

Here the dynamic thought of Movement links with the theme of temptation, 'Anfechtung', and the image of storms and water serves both.

> Before a man can be sure of salvation, there come so many streams of waters and great storms and tumults of waters that he almost loses the will to live, for the great billows of this wild sea destroy many just at the point when they think they have won through. But a man must not run away from these waves, but break through them in a masterful way like a skilful sailor, for the Lord gives nobody his holy witness unless in his Wonderment [*Verwunderung*] he has first worked his way through.[1]
>
> God knows, [says Müntzer in his Prague Manifesto] I never knew a Monk or Parson who could understand the true use of Faith, and the usefulness of *Anfechtung*, which declares Faith in the spirit of the Fear of the Lord.[2]
>
> My appeal is to all Nations of men, who have undergone

---

[1] Franz, pp. 21-2; cf. also Müntzer's letter to Luther (Franz, II, No. 40, 9 July 1523, p. 390) with its similar image of a tempest and a drowning man – well calculated to put Luther off! – even though Luther's sermons on Jonah powerfully expound this very theme of 'Anfechtung'.

[2] Franz, p. 491

invincible *Anfechtung*, found despair in their heart, and through this have been reminded.¹

The well-living, lusty swine are shocked at the storm wind of roaring waves and before all the Waters of Wisdom.²

It is *Anfechtung* which makes all the difference between true and false faith. The false faith of the Scribes, old and new, is something untempted, untried, which they have got out of books, and which can be easily acquired – 'Simply believe!'³ There is no doubt that Müntzer here recovers for Faith its existential dimension. The wonder is that he should so grievously misunderstand Luther at this very point.

Having passed through the storms of temptation, the soul at last escapes,

> hopes beyond hope and seeks the one (Divine) will in the day of visitation, long after his expectation. Then his feet are based on rock and God appears miraculously from afar.⁴

Like a drowning man, the believer comes gasping to the shore and there he rests. This drastic, dynamic, catastrophic set of experiences through which God himself dynamically works, now is exchanged for a seemingly more passive phase, which Müntzer calls 'Langweil' – the time of patience and expectation, in which the soul receives the gifts of the Holy Ghost.⁵

11. *Langweil*

Then a man becomes for the first time an enemy to his creaturely desires, with *Langweil*.⁶

Very few men know how to talk about the Beginning, the Movement of the Spirit. They have never tasted the *Langweil* through which alone the Work of God may be found.⁷

Though the Elect may sin deeply, yet the fire of their conscience drives them to nauseate and abominate sin, and when they give

---

¹ Franz, p. 431
² Franz, p. 220. Müntzer also uses the images of silver and gold tried in the fire. Or he speaks simply of suffering and tribulation (Franz, p. 278).
³ Franz, pp. 220, 227, 233, 423, 431, 492
⁴ Franz, II, No. 40, p. 390: to Luther!
⁵ Franz, pp. 300, 403, 419 ⁶ Franz, p. 419 ⁷ Franz, pp. 300–1

themselves to sorrow for and hatred of sin, then they cannot sin, and this I call 'Langweil', which sticks up the nostrils of those worldly swine.[1]

12. Wohnung Gottes

As 'Anfechtung' is an over-all word for the initial movement of the soul to faith, so this second part of salvation is a growth of renunciation, towards the complete commitment to God which is *Gelassenheit*.[2]

Here *Langweil* ends in the indwelling of God in the human soul, as in a House or Temple. It is a favourite image of the German mystics, but for Müntzer is focused in his own daringly free and introverted translation of Psalm 92 (Vulgate: AV 93): 'Domum tuam decet sanctitudo, Domine, in longitudinem dierum' as 'Do siht der mensch, das er ein wonung Gottis sey in der lanckweil seyner tage'.[3]

> Then the heart of a man is so strangely captive with the true Spirit of Christ, the possessor of his soul, that it has a foretaste of eternal life, before his heart is prepared through the torment of hell for the length of eternal day.[4]
>
> So it is above all needful to esteem most highly the most lordly Word of Christ to show all men from the beginning of this life who will have his memorial, essence and Word in the soul of man. Not as in an animal, but in his Temple which he has so dearly purchased with his precious blood.[5]
>
> Then a man is first assured that he is the dwelling place of God and of the Holy Spirit through all his length of days.[6]
>
> Observe how Zacharias went into the Temple... This is what Ps. 5 expounds: ... it means that every man should enter into himself and accordingly note by his Movement how he himself is a holy Temple.[7]

---

[1] Franz, p. 403. I do not think we can read 'perfectionism' into this one phrase.

[2] Franz, pp. 21, 305–8, 454

[3] see Franz, p. 115; also W. Elliger, 'Müntzers Übersetzung des 93 Psalms' already cited, p. 188n. above; Franz, p. 252

[4] Franz, p. 22   [5] Franz, p. 211   [6] Franz, p. 252

[7] Brandt, op. cit., p. 175; Franz, p. 292

13. Conformity to Christ

We shall not devote a separate section to 'Faith' in Thomas Müntzer, because he himself made it the theme of one of his most important writings.[1] For Luther, faith covers the whole dimension of the Christian life, from the beginning to the end. For Müntzer there is special emphasis on its place in Christian Initiation – the arrival of true Faith through temptation and tribulation. And yet no doubt for Müntzer too faith has an eschatological quality and undergirds the whole of the relation of the Elect with God. Certainly it is a notion which recurs at every stage of his descriptions of the Christian life.

It is already apparent that here is something which deserves to be treated more seriously than as a meaningless mumbo-jumbo of pretentious jargon.[2] Moreover, this is much more than a mystical pattern of emotional states of the soul, which might indeed lead to a dangerous antinomian quietism. For the content of this is ethical, though its background is the austere puritanism of the Tauler tradition. It is set within a pattern of our conformity with Christ, the language of which goes back through St Irenaeus to the New Testament.

> Thus we experience the Arrival of Faith, and we earthly men shall become gods, through the Incarnation of Christ, and with him also become God's scholars, taught and made divine by himself, yes, indeed, utterly and wholly transformed into him so that our earthly life is caught up into Heaven (Phil. 3).[3]
>
> The thorns and thistles are the worldly desires (Mark 4) and crush all the Working of the Word which God speaks in the soul. ... For a man will not crucify his life with all its cares and desires

---

[1] 'Von dem gedichteten Glauben'; see pp. 191–5 above. The definition, 'Christian Faith is a sure reliance [*Sicherung*] on the Word and Promise of Christ', is interesting. Franz, p. 218. So is the frequent reference to Faith as a mustard seed – Franz, pp. 224, 231, 272 – and of faith as tried and preserved as gold in fire – Franz, pp. 258, 317.

[2] It will not do to dismiss it as religious gobbledegook in the manner of Böhme, Swedenborg or modern Anthroposophy.

[3] Franz, p. 281; see also the interesting sermon fragment (Dresden MSS., 44a), and Franz, p. 317

as Paul teaches... and so the field of the Word of God stays full of thistles and thorns and great shrubs which must give room before this Work of God... and yet it is in this way that the gentle goodness of the field appears and at last the good fruit.[1]

Hence, Müntzer's recurring image of the soul as a wheat field, as in the poignant letter to a disciple, which he wrote at the time of poverty and ebbing fortune, after his return from Prague:

> I beg you not to be vexed at my expulsion, for in such *Anfechtung* is the soul's abyss cleared and more and more enlightened to know that the invincible witness of the Holy Spirit may be created... So let my suffering be an image for you. Let the tares blossom as they will – the living God is sharpening his sickle in me, that one day I may be ready to cut off the red poppies and the blue cornflowers.[2]

When Nebuchadnezzar forgot the warning of God:

> This was no doubt caused by his fleshly desires, which he directed towards lust and creaturely things.[3]
>
> John deserves praise, not by the merit of his works, but on account of his earnestness, which gives birth to a bold soberness which reaches out to the Estrangement [*Entfremdung*] of lusts, where the powers of the soul are laid bare, that the foundation [*or* abyss! *Abgrund*] of the Spirit may appear through all his powers, so that the Holy Ghost may address him.[4]
>
> Adam was warned by God of ruin to come, that he should not by creaturely lusts be given to manifold desires, but delight in God alone, as it is written: 'Thou shalt delight in God alone'.[5]

Thus Müntzer views salvation as the pilgrimage of the Elect Friend of God from a life dominated by selfish and creaturely desires

---

[1] Franz, p. 252 [2] Franz, II, No. 38, March 1523; pp. 243, 317

[3] Franz, p. 253. The question whether this is a Pauline or a Platonic view of 'flesh' hardly arises, since this usage is that of Tauler and the *Theologia Germanica*.

[4] Franz, pp. 306–7

[5] Franz, p. 334. The reference to the soul being split into many desires (*vermannigfältigt*) is in Tauler and pseudo-Tauler, with the notion of the One and the Many, deep in mystical thought, and perhaps linked for Müntzer with his notion of the Parts and the Whole.

to conformity with Christ. It fills in the map, as in the 18th century Pietism and Methodism were to do, with their own technical terms and categories. But there are respects in which Müntzer's pattern is more wholesome than theirs (as, in others, his is less satisfactory than theirs). He is free from that atomism which from the time of William Perkins has marred evangelical Protestantism. Fundamental for Müntzer is the phrase 'Christ – in Head and Members': the great 'Totus Christus' of Augustine, to which Pope Paul VI movingly referred in his opening address to the second Vatican Council. The whole Bible, says Müntzer, and indeed the whole creation too, teach nothing else but the suffering Christ – in Head and Members.[1] Suffering is indeed for Müntzer a mark of Christian existence, and, if he seems to exaggerate, he joins hands across the centuries with Kierkegaard, in similar protest against the holy worldliness, the bourgeois mediocrity, of the new Protestant Establishment.

> A Man cannot come to the first true Christian recollection without suffering, for the heart has to be torn away from the cleaving to this world, by tribulation and heartache.[2]
>
> No man can be filled with divine and eternal Goods unless by long discipline he has been emptied for this purpose through his suffering and Cross, that he may be filled with the Measure of Faith and with the highest treasures of Christian Wisdom.[3]
>
> The disobedience of the creature must be done away through the obedience of the Word who became Flesh in nature as our fleshly nature in Part must be taken away in Part by the effect of Faith, as happened to the Whole in Christ the Head. Therefore Christ did penitence for the whole Ruin of Adam, in order that the Parts should keep to the Whole as the holy command of God clearly says. 'I complete what is lacking in Christ's afflictions': for his Body the Church suffers. Paul could not suffer for the Church alone as a Member that waits on his Office. We all must follow in the footsteps of Christ, armed with such cogitations.[4]

---

[1] 'The whole of Holy Scripture is about nothing else – as are all the creatures – than the crucified Son of God' (Franz, p. 324). The other safeguard against individualism is his liturgy; see p. 315 below.

[2] Franz, p. 419   [3] Franz, p. 298

[4] Franz, II, No. 46, pp. 397–8. On Müntzer's doctrine of Whole and Parts, see pp. 329f. below

> For the one hope of the Church in her misery is to expect just this – that the Elect should and must be conformed to Christ and regard God's Work with manifold suffering and discipline.[1]

This is, therefore, not mere outward imitation of Christ, under the sign of the Law, but a comradeship in solidarity of the whole Church with its Head in the fellowship of his sufferings. This leads, of course, to an immense stress on 'Christ in us', which, we shall see, is reinforced in his liturgical writings. But it is arguable that this insistence on the active presence of Christ with his people, and of the dynamic working among men of the Holy Trinity, was a healthy and salutary one. Nor can it be justly said (for the case could be made even more forcibly against St Paul) that this leads to a 'Christ myth' abandoning the Jesus of History (Bultmann!) and so to an incipient anti-Trinitarianism.[2]

> Christ is declared in us through the witness of the Holy Ghost – as he is preached by the Prophets, born, died and risen, who, with his Father and the same Holy Ghost, ever rules and makes us his scholars. Amen.[3]

In the Liturgy, the *Sanctus* is sung that men may know

> how the Father without intermission reveals his Son in us, and the Holy Ghost declares none other than the crucified in us through heartfelt suffering.[4]
>
> I, Thomas Müntzer ... a servant of the Living Son of God through the unchangeable Will and irrevocable Mercy of God the

---

[1] Franz, p. 227

[2] So E. W. Gritsch, *MQR* **37**, pp. 192–3: 'It took only one logical step to "de-historicize" the revelation in Jesus of Nazareth and make the identification of Christ with the Holy Spirit. Müntzer accomplished this in his description of the drama of man's suffering and salvation. To this extent Müntzer was moving also towards a theological Anti-Trinitarianism.' This seems to me to be refutable by abundant evidence.

[3] Franz, p. 162

[4] Franz, pp. 210–11. 'In us' is, of course, the whole heart of the Liturgy, its point and purpose, as the collects abundantly testify that what Christ did once for all 'for us' is to be recapitulated 'in us'. Paul, Irenaeus and the whole liturgical tradition of East and West are on Müntzer's side.

THE GOSPEL ACCORDING TO THOMAS MÜNTZER

Father, beg and wish in the Holy Ghost to all you Elect Friends of God...[1]

A man must learn the Christian Faith ... through the mighty eternal Word of the Father in the Son with explanation by the Holy Ghost.[2]

The sum of this chapter [Luke 1] is about the strengthening of the spirit in Faith, which is none other than that the Most High God, our dear Lord, will give us the most excellent Christian Faith by means of the Incarnation of Christ, that we may be conformed to him in his suffering and Life through the overshadowing of the Holy Ghost.[3]

The imitation of Christ is no outward thing, what Müntzer calls 'monkey imitation'. But it is not simply mystical, for it is linked firmly with the Incarnation. It is sometimes more daring to be orthodox than unorthodox, and it is not simply that Müntzer is relapsing into doctrinal conservatism from which bolder radicals were to break free.

Christ took upon himself flesh and blood in order that through his divine understanding we should be rid of our rational, sensual, animal understanding – John 10 – the Word of God must make us into gods when our understanding is made captive in the service of Faith. The same must uproot our animal, fleshly desires so that we hunger after the best of all food, which is to do the Will of God.[4]

Nobody can believe in Christ without first being like him ... for he sees that no outward Witness can make an essential difference in him ...

With Peter he cries:

I know that Christ is the Son of the Living God! – for the Unbelief, hid in my flesh and blood, is quite overcome in part through the desire that the Mustard Seed and good Leaven devour and press,

---

[1] Franz, pp. 225–6. So far from being anti-Trinitarian, Müntzer delights to stress the threefold action of the whole Godhead in our salvation – like Charles Wesley.

[2] Franz, p. 298

[3] Franz, p. 318

[4] Dresden MSS. 44a. The fragment is interesting because the argument moves at once into a meditation on the Eucharist.

and break through in all Unbelief. A man must have experienced Despair and all high opposites. He must first have suffered hell. ... The godless man takes the Scripture willingly, above measure. That another suffers for him, on this he builds his strong faith. But when it comes to seeing the Lamb who opens the Book, then he will not leave his own soul, will not be made like the Lamb.[1]

Even if we except the 'Gospel of All Creatures', there are many examples of Müntzer's appeal to the teachings of Jesus in all four gospels, and to the events of his earthly life, and his acceptance of the 'once for all'-ness of the Cross, as witness his frequent stress, in writings and liturgy, on Christ as 'the Lamb who takes away the sin of the world'.[2]

In fact, Müntzer again and again sets the work of our redemption within the work of the one Holy Trinity. In the fine fragment of a meditation in his MS. he begins:

> The whole incarnation of Christ must be understood in supreme degree, if it is to be fruitfully enjoyed. Otherwise the precious mysteries of God become a monkey's imitation. For Christ the true Son of God became man for this one reason, that the Holy Ghost might be declared in the hearts of the Elect.[3]

Here, as in Tauler, is the contrast between the 'sweet' and 'bitter' Christ:

> That a sweet Christ is preached to a sensual world is the greatest poison which from the beginning has been given to the flock of Christ . . . so that he never will, and will not even desire to be conformed to Christ. . . . we must have the whole Christ and not half. . . . Who will not have the bitter Christ will feed himself dead on the honey.[4]

Müntzer's insistence on Christian solidarity and on the conformity of the Body with its Head in suffering affects his whole doctrine of the Church. Here there is a polarity of thought between 'Christ-

---

[1] Franz, p. 224
[2] Franz, pp. 219, 221, 223, 297, 318
[3] Dresden MSS. 44a
[4] Franz, p. 222; cf. John Wesley's attack on those who only preach comfortable words.

enheit',[1] historical Christianity, and the 'Elect' or 'Elect Friends of God'.[2]

Christendom is for Müntzer always 'poor, fallen Christendom' and he expounds the notion that the perversion of the Church took place in the sub-apostolic age.

> I have read with diligence all the old histories of the Fathers... and I find that, after the death of the scholars of the Apostles, the immaculate virgin Church was made into a whore through the spiritual adultery of the scholars who always want to rule, as Hegesippus, and after him Eusebius, writes in Book 4 in Chapter 22. Moreover, I have found in no Church Council any serious reckoning with the untroubled Word of God, but only a lot of kid's stuff.[3]

This highly idiosyncratic doctrine Müntzer makes the starting-point of his liturgical experiments.[4] For this is the condition in which the Church was 'when our Fathers received the Faith'. None the less those who converted Germany were 'pious, good-hearted Fathers', who sang Latin for the sake of unity. In his defensive Second Preface Müntzer explains, against his own radical critics, why he has made a liturgy at all, and that it is to help 'fallen Christendom' to see how it is that the papal knaves have stolen the Scriptures, and also to recover the intention of the good Early Fathers who used the reading of the Bible and Christian songs for the edification of Faith.[5]

Here then, despite the notion of a Fallen Church, in which most of the Reformers believed, though they might pinpoint the change in different centuries, there is no fiercely sectarian dichotomy, nor

---

[1] Many references in Franz, pp. 161, 163, 223, 226, 228, 242, 243, 270, 300, 321, 322, 473, 548

[2] Innumerable references in Franz; for 'Elect': pp. 21, 124, 161, 163, 166, 208, 209, 218, 220, 223, 226, 227, 229, 242, 253, 255, 259, 262, 271, 273, 276, 278, 283, 285, 286, 289, 290, 291, 298, 309, 316, 322, 327, 421, 423, 491, 492, 494; for 'Friends of God', less numerous, but numerous enough: pp. 21, 163, 166, 218, 226, 242, 247, 263, 269, 309, 328, 494

[3] Franz, p. 494 (Prague Manifesto); also in the *Fürstenpredigt*, trans. G. H. Williams *Spiritual and Anabaptist Writers* p. 51. A judgement not unlike that of Luther.

[4] Franz, p. 161   [5] Franz, p. 163

any of that tension between the 'True' and 'False' Church which marks later Protestant ecclesiology. But it is when we come to consider his programme for the Elect that we are driven to his more dynamic dualism between the Elect and the Reprobate – and the judgement and discrimination between them which Müntzer believes to be part of the prerogatives of Faith and of the Spirit.[1]

> They speak out of their beards ... that none may know who is Elect and who is damned. ... They want to erect a subtle People of God as Plato the philosopher speculates on in his *Republic* and Apuleius in *The Golden Ass*.

14. Creation and the Law of Nature

Modern theological controversies about Natural Theology, and the literature of debate about it from Bishop Butler to Karl Barth, have a mesmerizing effect on all who discuss the 'Natural Theology' of the 16th century. In the case of Luther, it is better simply to discuss his Theology of the Natural Order, the complex way in which he speaks of Natural Law, and his often beautifully expressed hints about his view of the Word in relation to Creation.

With Müntzer the case is a little different, for it is evident that for him Creation and the created order, and God's ordinances within it, have a much more explicit and important meaning, and are, so to speak, geared into his Plan of Salvation. Like Luther, he had been trained to be aware of natural law, written in the hearts of men everywhere, and on occasion he can appeal directly to it.

In his angry letter to his stepfather, he accuses him of cheating him 'of my natural rights, as though I were a bastard, yes, as though I were a heathen'.[2] And in the crisis of July 1524, Müntzer says about the rulers, meaning especially the Catholic princes who were attacking his own followers, 'When they go so far as to act not only against Faith, but against natural law, then they must be killed like dogs.'[3]

---

[1] Franz, p. 290   [2] Franz, II, No. 14

[3] Franz, II, No. 57, p. 417. The *Bund* or 'Covenant' made with his followers at Allstedt is significantly described as a 'Notwehr' emergency action based on Natural Law.

At first sight, the width of Müntzer's appeal to men of all nations, beyond the bounds of Christendom, and his affirmation that a heathen may have the beginnings of Faith, together with his emphasis on the Living Word, might suggest that his doctrine of the Living Word is based on natural reason as the light which lightens every man. A close examination shows, however, that for Müntzer salvation is the action of the transcendent God, intervening upon the blinded reason, upon a fallen human nature, twisted and bent in terms of the fleshly, the creaturely and the animal.

15. *Natural Reason*

It is true that, according to Müntzer, Abraham wandered in far countries 'according to the Light of Nature', but it was only through great tribulation that he came to see the day of Christ. 'If the Light of Nature was so thoroughly extinguished in Abraham, what must not we experience?' While Moses was led by 'the false light of nature through the Law' he would not believe the Promises of God. Moses might have taken God for a devil, had he not seen through the cunning of the creatures and the one-ness of God in the Order which is planted in God and the creature.[1]

> If our natural understanding is to be brought into captivity by faith, it must come to the last degree of Judgement as Rom. 1. ... For the more Nature grasps after God, the further is it estranged from the working of the Holy Ghost ... Yes, if a man were thoroughly versed in the curiosity of the Light of Nature, he would no doubt not seek such help from stolen Scriptures – as the Scribes do with a gobbet here and there – but he would soon discover the working of the divine Word bubbling from his heart. He would not need to drag foul water into the clear spring as our present Scribes do who mix up Nature and grace without any distinction, and hinder the entrance of the Word which comes from the ground of the soul.[2]

Man owes his dominion over what the hymn calls 'the humbler

---

[1] Franz, p. 219

[2] Franz, pp. 250–1. The implication seems to be that, faulty as the light of nature may be, it is better than the dead letter of stolen and irrelevant Scripture.

creation' to the Divine Ordering to which the opening chapters of the Bible bear witness.

> I tell you, dearly beloved Brethren, and may not be silent, I would rather teach Heathen, Turks or Jews with the very tiniest Word of God and his Order, about dominion over ourselves and to God – for the Scribal cleversticks deny this down to the ground ... will neither hear nor look when I have warned them in a friendly way to learn from the beginning of the Bible about God and our dominion over the creatures.[1]
>
> Thus the godless Wittenberg lump of flesh treats me, when from the Beginning of the Bible and the Order of the first Distinction of the same, I strive after the purity of the Divine Law [Ps. 19].[2]

In his Prague Manifesto Müntzer says that he had never heard from any scholar about 'The Order of God which is laid down in all creatures, including the tiniest little Word and the Whole as the only way in which to know the Parts'.[3] This seems for Müntzer something other than the mystical hierarchy of creation from Dionysius the Areopagite, and it may owe something to Nicholas of Cusa, but perhaps most to his reading of Plato's *Parmenides*.[4]

With this seems to be linked some lines (a quotation copied out?) scribbled on the back of a letter in 1521:

> All knowledge of the Creatures is to be related to the Whole, which is excellent, and it is of the Works of his Hands, which is as laudable as the knowledge of God (himself?) when it is understood in relation to the Whole. But when it is directed to God, knowledge of things is excellent.[5]

---

[1] Franz, p. 314   [2] Franz, pp. 326–7

[3] Franz, p. 491. One is tempted to read 'Würmlein' for 'Wörtlein', but there is no evidence.

[4] *Parmenides* is on one of Müntzer's classical book-lists.

[5] For the letter, see Franz, II, No. 24, p. 371; for the inscription on the back of the letter, see p. 534: 'In toto exordienda est omnis scientia creaturarum, que est optima, nam est de operibus manuum suarum, que eque laudabilis est sicut scientia dei, cum in toto intelligatur. Sed cum in deum regeritur, optime est rerum scientia.' The attempt by M. M. Smirin (op. cit.) to interpret this sociologically is unhappy.

> Our fleshly nature which is in Part must in Part also be taken away by the Work of God, as happened in the Whole Christ as Head. That is why Christ did penance for the whole sin of Adam, that the Parts should hold to the Whole.[1]

What is interesting here is that a doctrine of creation, drawing on *Parmenides*, should be given a Christological setting, should appeal to 1 Corinthians 13, and to the Epistle to the Colossians, and so bind together (as does Colossians) the thought of Christ in creation and in redemption, thus unifying doctrines of natural and supernatural, nature and grace. Müntzer explains to Zeiss:

> The Will of God is the Whole over the Parts. To know the Art and Judgement of God is to know the declaration of the same Will as Paul writes to the Colossians in [chapter] 1 and Ps. 118. But the Work of God flows from the Whole and from all the Parts.[2]

Müntzer has previously suggested that a man is assured of faith 'in the Parts' by the contemplation of creation; he now further suggests that there is another assurance to be found in the ground of the human heart.[3]

16. Baptism

Nobody who reads Müntzer can fail to see how drastic and important for him is the symbol of water; but it is a symbol for him of tribulation, *Anfechtung*, judgement – as in many parts of the Bible. This underlies part of the insistence, in Hans Huth and others of the radicals, on baptism as suffering.

When we come to the Sacrament, the evidence is a little confused. In his 'Protestation' which is sub-titled: 'To the Beginning of true Christian Faith and Baptism', he refers to the fact that in the early Church only grown people were received as catechumens – there was no superstition which put more stress on the outward sign than the inner essence.

> In fact, in none of the books of the Doctors of the Church can you find an account of true baptism. I challenge you Scribes of the Letter to show me in the Bible any instance of an inarticulate child

---

[1] Franz, II, No. 46, p. 397   [2] Franz, p. 418   [3] Franz, p. 252

being baptized, or ordained to be baptized by Christ or his disciples as our children are nowadays baptized. Yes, while you are at it – you will not find that Mary, the Mother of God, or the disciples of Jesus Christ, were baptized with water.[1]

This has sometimes been taken to mean that the sacrament was irrelevant for Müntzer, but this does not seem to be the case. There is a fragment in his writings about an order for Baptism:[2]

> First, all the Scriptures about Baptism are to be publicly read – as in the early Church the Eve of Easter was so used. Then let us put away all abuse . . . would it not be a good idea to have baptism twice a year with such public meditation, and for it to be given to children so that they have a fresh remembrance all their lives of what they had received? That would frighten them off sin? . . . I know that no Godfather takes real care to do what he has promised for his Godchild . . . what proof is there of Godfathers in Scripture?

It is also to be observed that there is provision made for baptism of infants in his Liturgy. But this does not mean that Müntzer only believed in adult baptism. He seems to have wanted to abolish the customary superstitions and to abandon infant baptism, but to have allowed baptism for children from the age of 6 or 7. He believes – his own stresses on youthful knowledge suggest something personal in the insistence – that 'this Wonderment . . . begins when a child is 6 or 7, as is prefigured in Numbers 19'.[3]

17. Eucharist

Nobody who disbelieved in sacraments could have gone to the trouble to which Müntzer put himself in composing his German Mass. Perhaps because the Sacrament of the Altar was almost always a point of interrogation of heretics in the later Middle Ages, some of the articles in Müntzer's confession deal with this subject. It is said that he forbade adoration of the Sacrament 'other than in

---

[1] Franz, p. 228 [2] Franz, pp. 526–7

[3] Franz, p. 251. The Prague Manifesto refers to this 'Sprinkling on the Third Day' (Franz, p. 492). Since it seems that Karlstadt also uses the expression, this bizarre use of Scripture may have been a common reference in radical circles and not originating with Müntzer.

the Spirit'; that he had communicated the sick after midday when he had eaten (i.e. not fasting) and at night when there was convenience and opportunity. Then he had taken bread and wine and consecrated it.[1] At his alleged recantation, he admitted to 'many opinions, dreams and errors concerning the Blessed Sacrament of the Holy Body of Christ'.

If we may judge from his liturgy, he had a high doctrine of the Eucharist, and it might almost be suggested that, as with Thomas Bilney, Robert Barnes and the first Cambridge Reformers, this was a matter which at this early date he did not question.

There is, however, the interesting and unfortunately undated sermon fragment, already quoted, which reads like a meditation on the Eucharist. It proceeds from the theme of our salvation, the work of the whole Trinity, to the Incarnation with its implications for our conformity with Christ, and his taking on him our whole human nature, 'that we might hunger for the very best food, which is to do the will of God'. Thus our natural reason must be smitten to the ground through tribulation. Then Müntzer suddenly applies this to the Last Supper and to the sadness of the disciples with their 'Is it I?' Then in answer he gave them to eat and drink – and what a grim, bitter food it was he held before them. That was the victory for God's eternal will. Christ's will was made plain afterwards in the garden, when his human will fought its battle.[2] So Christ was like a corn of wheat falling to the ground. 'And gave to us an image of how we should receive – and so all that is done [in the Eucharist?] is done through the fruitful proclamation of the death of his dear Son'. 'He who is not made one with the Passover Lamb is a sheep of death' . . . 'He cannot receive the mystery of his death, in the Sacrament'. To an untried and unexperienced man it is as when one throws a bit of bread to a dog. The animal receives nothing. For the disciples, Christ 'after the flesh' was a hindrance, and they must put him from their eyes – John 16 – and must be sorrowful above measure, otherwise the Holy Ghost could not come to them. So says Paul, 2 Corinthians 5, where he proclaims the death of Christ,

[1] Franz, p. 544
[2] So far from being unorthodox in his Christology, Müntzer is thoroughly Chalcedonian in this passage.

'but now we know him no longer after the flesh'. Christ has worked a renewal of his flesh which unexperienced men reject from the Sacrament and say,

> He is so high, thick, broad and long as he was on the Cross when he hung there. Even if it were so, what use would Christ be to us in this way, about which he has left us no special witness in Holy Scripture.[1]

This is an interesting extract. Not least in its association of the Eucharist with temptation and suffering on the part of the disciples – as a genuine participation in Christ's own tribulation and surrender of his will. Here it is not a question (as the Reformers were to discuss it vehemently and long, 1525–35) of the 'manducatio impiorum' – how and whether the heathen received the Body of Christ – but of the Sacrament as received by True or False Faith. But the argument 'What use would a Real Natural Presence be, and where is the Scriptural evidence?', with the implication that Christ had 'eine Verneuerung gethan an seynen fleysch', and so made a new kind of Body – these surely anticipate the arguments of Zwingli and Oecolampadius. They may indeed be independent of, and prior to, those of Karlstadt. They are obviously firmly linked to Müntzer's own theology and are not simply late medieval anti-sacramentalism as we find it in the English Lollards and Continental heretics.

18. *Müntzer's Social and Political Theology*

The evidence so far assembled should be sufficient to support the view that he was 'altogether a Preacher, wholly a Theologian'. It is surely evident that this oddly impressive pattern is one of theology and of spirituality, grounded in Christian theology in its classic form, in the Bible and the Fathers and the Creeds, but applying them in terms of the 'inward religion' and apocalyptic writing of the later Middle Ages. It is altogether forced, therefore, to try to read a sociological ideology into all this, as the Marxists, and as some theologians in East Germany, have done.[2] But this much has

[1] Dresden MSS. 44.2

[2] This is true of an otherwise extremely valuable article by Hanna Köditz, 'Zur Ideologie der Täuferbewegung in Mühlhausen in Thüringen', in *Die frühbürgerliche Revolution in Deutschland* pp. 184ff.

to be said on their behalf – that Müntzer's theology is far from being evangelical piety in the 19th-century way, a spirituality cut off from an active programme. Just as we find a radical like Ulrich Stadtler (1537) defining *Gelassenheit* in communist terms – 'It is true *Gelassenheit* to yield and dispose oneself with goods and chattels in the service of the saints'[1] – so Müntzer's doctrine of renunciation and suffering runs on into his views of society, and mingles with his apocalyptic eschatology. But he knows what he is doing – and he knows, for example, when he is acting in terms of revealed theology and when in terms of Natural Law. Thus, for example, the word 'Bund' (Covenant) is important for him, and it is tempting to see in his use of it a premonition of its importance for the Anabaptists and for the later 'Covenant Theology'. But he uses the term because it is important in the Bible, in the Old Testament (and the New Testament appropriation of Jeremiah 31 does not escape him), and he knows that this is an important conception in the Eucharist, since it emerges at the sacred point of institution during the Last Supper. It is natural, therefore, for him to think of his liturgy as expounding the divine Mysteries and the divine Covenant.

It is tempting to go further and to suppose that his associations – organized bands, with their registrars and exact terms of conditions, and oaths – are intended as Covenanted Bands of the Elect.

But here, for once, Müntzer would have been on Luther's side when he said 'Dear Friends, Christians are not so many that they can get together in mobs'. Müntzer does not suppose that an outward political association can be composed only of the saints, or that the true renewal of the gospel can be accomplished by force. Very important in this regard is a passage from his letter to the castellan, Zeiss (22 July 1524):

> The Members [*Bundgenossen*] must not think that they will be freed through this . . . for it is most necessary and above measure to consider that nobody should put his trust in this Covenant [*Bund*] for he is cursed who puts his trust in man . . . Jer. 17[:5]. It is only intended as a threat to the godless, that they should restrain their violence until the Elect stand up to them with their

[1] G. H. Williams *Spiritual and Anabaptist Writers* p. 284

exploration of God's Art and Wisdom as Witness. When the godly make a covenanted association, although there are bad people within, they will not accomplish their will, for the loyal freedom of the good will give them less room to do ill than otherwise, so that the whole company [*Haufe*] may not be blamed.

There follows the critical sentence:

> The Covenanted Band is nothing but an Emergency Device [*Notwehr*] which is to be denied to no one, according to the natural judgement of all rational men.[1]

What would have happened had the authorities been prepared to protect and sponsor Müntzer is a vain speculation. But it seems quite clear he would have worked with them (or used them). It is noticeable that even in Zwickau he did not disdain all the help he could get from the members of the City Council, and that at Allstedt he found chief allies in the burgomaster and in the Electoral castellan. It was the enmity first of Ernest of Mansfeld and then of Duke George which provoked his first bitter attack on authority, and his letters to Frederick the Wise are, on the whole, and for Müntzer, circumspect.

But after the Mallerbach incident, he refused to accept the Lutheran ideology which insisted that tyranny must fall of its own inner weakness, and without force of arms, and Luther's arguments in 'Of Earthly Authority' simply disgusted him, not least because Luther seemed to put the office of the Sword in the hands of the Christian magistrate not because he was a Christian but on grounds which applied equally to any heathen. By this time he had already come to interpret Romans 13 dynamically. In his 'Sermon before the Princes' this becomes quite clear. Romans 13 is interpreted as a revolutionary manifesto and the Princes are exhorted to use their God-given weapon to wipe out the godless, who get in the way of the Elect. The same is true of his proposal, following his Covenant Sermon, that the Princes should 'turn the oaths and feudal responsibilities of heathendom into a faithful covenant of the

---

[1] This letter deals with the Covenant proposed after his Covenant Sermon (July 1524). It could be argued that the covenanted bands at Allstedt were closed groups of the Elect, but I do not think so.

THE GOSPEL ACCORDING TO THOMAS MÜNTZER

divine will . . . it must be a sober covenant in which the common man is joined with godly officials solely for the sake of the Gospel'.[1] We know that Müntzer tried to get some such public Covenant from the local militia, and failed.

The Peasants' War would have happened had there been no Thomas Müntzer, and it can be argued that, even in Thuringia, he had little influence on the course of events. Had he not been there, they would still have rebelled under other leaders and still have come inevitably to military disaster. None the less, the Peasants' War was, as we say, 'right up Müntzer's street'. It fitted admirably within his ideology. He had been prepared to work with the authorities. They had repudiated him. From now on, his levelling tendencies get the upper hand. No doubt, like other peasant armies, they were not above conscripting the local gentry where possible, but Müntzer's thoughts of the coming age now take a more drastic turn. His writings show little sympathy or compassion with the condition of the common man (though there is some, and it is not to be played down).

But he does seem to have contemplated a new equalitarianism, a kind of application in reverse of medieval sumptuary laws:

> He says that princes should ride with eight horses, a count with four, and a nobleman with two, but no more.[2]
>
> He made this insurrection that all Christendom should be equal and that Princes and Lords who would not stand by the Gospel should be expelled and killed.[3]

It was the principle of the Covenanted Association at Allstedt, which they wished to establish:

> 'Omnia sunt communia' – and to each according to his need and opportunity. And any prince or lord who would not agree, after admonition, should be beheaded or hanged.[4]

There is nothing improbable about all this, and it is notable that the communist programme is expounded in terms of the Book of Acts,

[1] Franz, II, No. 59, p. 422
[2] Franz, p. 545. This first is 'under friendly interrogation', the succeeding confessions are 'under torture'.
[3] Franz, p. 548 [4] Franz, loc. cit.

and so of primitive Christianity. On the other hand, we have evidence that Müntzer had studied Plato, and read the *Republic*. Nowadays, it is a serious point among Reformation students that John Calvin had read Plato to good effect, and with as much evidence we had better take Müntzer's Platonism seriously, especially as we have other evidence of his capacity to combine a Platonic idea with a New Testament doctrine (e.g. his 'One and Many'). E. W. Kohls has drawn attention to the importance, in 16th-century political theory and among reformers like Bucer, of the conception of 'Gemeinnutz'.[1] It is no accident that the phrase recurs in Müntzer's manifestoes and letters to Mühlhausen during the peasant campaign and in his very last letter. For him it is used dialectically in contrast to the disastrous venality, self-interest of 'Eigennutz', which another prophetic voice of the age, William Shakespeare, also saw to be a deep defect of his generation.[2]

Thus Müntzer's 'Communism' is part of his apocalyptic programme and, though it is not to be minimized, it is unhistorical to try to read back into the 16th century a pure ideologist basing his ideas on a theory of society. In so far as he had such a theory, it was based on a thoroughly medieval view of natural law, and was subordinated to his interpretation of the Christian Gospel. That there is something in the claim to see in him the 'first Communist', even the first Nazi, is due to the fact that he was a revolutionary, by temperament an agitator, and that he was forced by circumstances, many of them his own fault, into an itinerant existence.

19. Müntzer and his Mission

It is part of Müntzer's apocalyptic view to be conscious of his own prophetic vocation. But there is nothing of the crackpot megalomania of a Bader or a Bockelson, or even a Hofmann. It is worth remembering, too, that quite a collection can be made (Denifle and Grisar did this very thing) of utterances of Luther about his own

[1] E. W. Kohls *Die Schule bei Martin Bucer* (1963), Exkursus II
[2] An English 16th-century word for 'Eigennutz' is 'commodity', about which Shakespeare has a tremendous indictment in *King John*. But it is also attacked by the preacher, Hugh Latimer, one of the 'Commonwealth' (*Respublica – Gemeinnutz*) men of Edward VI's England.

vocation and capabilities. But even in the last weeks of his career when Müntzer's hysteria reaches alarming proportions, he speaks in the biblical phrases and calls himself only 'the Servant of God' (but sometimes in the history of the Church the most arrogant of titles!). Not unnaturally, it is in the Prague Manifesto, at a time when he felt his death to be an imminent possibility (against a parallel with Luther at the time of the Diet of Worms) that this claim becomes most explicit, and most fully expressed in the longer German version:

> The time of harvest is come, and God himself has hired me for the harvest. I have sharpened my sickle, for my thoughts are strong for the truth and my lips, hands, skin, soul, body and life are set against the unbelievers. . . . I will be ready for the people to put questions to me in the pulpit and will satisfy them. If I cannot show such mastery of science, then am I a child of temporal and eternal death.[1]

Hence, too, the hint that what is needed today is an earnest Preacher who will be another John the Baptist and another Elijah (who will deal with the godless as Elijah dealt with the prophets of Baal). Hence the ferocity of some of his prefaces and signatures: 'the Destroyer of the Ungodly'; 'Thomas Müntzer, the Man with the Hammer'; 'a Servant of God against the Godless'; 'Thomas Müntzer with the Sword of Gideon'.

There is a polarity and coherence about Müntzer's theology which is astonishing when we consider the circumstances of his restless, always changing life. Behind much that is allusive, hinted at, taken for granted, in his handful of tracts, there is a view of salvation, grounded no doubt in the 'inward religion' of the 15th century of which he is an heir, but to which he himself gave an overall unity, blending a biblical piety, a mystical plan of sanctification, with an apocalyptic messianism. He is the first great rebel against the new gospel – and this provokes him into the kind of one-sidedness of a John Henry Newman in reaction against a similar

---

[1] Franz, p. 504 (Prague Manifesto). An illuminating and perceptive discussion of Müntzer's messianism will be found in N. Cohn *The Pursuit of the Millennium* (London 1957), pp. 251ff.

too-comfortable Evangelicalism in the 19th century. And his reaction, when it came, was often savage – as when, in his final polemic, he who had five years before been an ardent student of Augustine could taunt Luther about 'your dirty humility which you filched out of Augustine – to deny man's will its freedom'. The similarities between Müntzer and Kierkegaard, often remarkable, are because the latter too was in reaction against a Lutheran Establishment. Müntzer's fierce dissatisfaction with the formal, over-clericalized religion of his day, the abuses of which were shared, he felt, by the new and reformed piety of Luther and his friends, led him to look for salvation beyond the bounds of what was generally regarded as Christendom; and his prophetic premonition of a new age, when the Word of God would come home to men from strange lands and strange people, has curious affinities with radical theology in our own time. Those who have thought of his violent activism as more like Mohammedanism, or the feudal, fighting Christianity of the age of the Crusades, are maybe as percipient as those who at the other extreme would dress him up in the garb of 20th-century revolution. At least his theology was born, like his faith, from his life in a revolutionary setting. Not reading or speculating, but living, dying and being damned, made him a theologian. 'Depend upon it, Sir,' said Dr Johnson, 'when a man knows he is to be hanged in a fortnight, it concentrates his mind wonderfully.' If that is true especially of Müntzer's last letter, on the eve of his execution, it has some bearing on all his short ministry, which was always on the edge of things, always a frontier existence.

CHAPTER TWENTY

THOMAS MÜNTZER'S LITURGICAL EXPERIMENTS[1]

No account of Thomas Müntzer's theology should ignore his liturgical achievement. All he has to say about inward religion, of the Advent of Faith, of the growth of the soul to conformity with Christ; his insistence on Christian solidarity, 'Christ, Head and Members'; his covenanted cells of the Elect, the apocalyptic messianism concerning their and his vocation on the edge of a new age: all these are set within a frame of corporate worship. To his liturgical experiments Müntzer must have devoted much time and great energy, as well as ingenuity, sensitivity and skill. Not only was he among the creative pioneers, but his stresses, as we shall see, were strikingly modern, and not least in his emphasis on worship as the common action of the whole People of God.

Müntzer was not prodded towards liturgical things by Karlstadt, Strauss or Luther, for we have interesting evidence of his interest in these things in the years 1516-17, when he was confessor to the nuns at the convent of Frohse. Here the patron saint was

[1] The best handbook, with excellent short essays and with the music, is O. J. Mehl *Thomas Müntzers Deutsche Messen und Kirchenämter mit Singnoten und liturgischen Abhandlungen* (Grimmen 1937). The most up-to-date is that in Franz, pp. 25-206. Other useful works are: Emil Sehling *Die evangelischen Kirchenordnungen des XVI. Jahrhunderts* I Abt.: Sachsen und Thüringen (1902), pp. 470-507; Julius Smend *Die Evangelischen Deutschen Messen bis zu Luthers Deutscher Messe* (reprint) Nieuwkoop 1967, pp. 94ff.; K. Schulz, 'Müntzers liturgische Bestrebungen' *ZKG* 10, pp. 369-401. O. J. Mehl delivered a fine lecture on 'Thomas Müntzer als Liturgiker' at the Lutherakademie, Goslar, in 1954, which I have read in manuscript. There is also a useful short article by him, 'Luther als Liturgiker', in *TLZ* 76 (1951).

St Cyriacus,[1] and we have in Müntzer's own hand the drafts for two offices for the saint, which could be used on high days and for processions, and the beginning of a Mass.[2] Each of these consists of three Nocturns with Antiphons, Responsories and Versicles, and there is a much abbreviated Sequence. A similar text has been found in the Breviary of John of Hildesheim (1480) and the Book of Hours of Bishop John of Lübeck. Müntzer's initial sentence 'Ne errore decipia', which Lohmann fantastically took to suggest Müntzer's loss of faith, is probably an ejaculatory prayer.

The next piece of evidence is of a negative character. Among the Erasmians it was the fashion to decry the sad state into which the recital of the Psalms had fallen, and Karlstadt had devoted one of his innumerable sets of theses to the demerits of the Gregorian chants. In his letter of 1 January 1520 to the fellow Martinian, Franz Günther, Müntzer refers caustically and in this vein to 'Jewish songs'.[3] It may be that tiresome and boring repetition had eaten into his soul also. For although, as we shall see, the Psalms meant a great deal to him, and not least in public worship, it is the one striking difference between his experiments and those of Thomas Cranmer, that Cranmer restored to divine service the regular recitation of the whole Psalter, which ticks away like the second-hand, while the whole Bible is read more slowly, like the hour-hand of a clock.

If we compare Müntzer's rationale of worship with the famous Preface of Thomas Cranmer (1549) – with its own debt to the reforms of Cardinal Quiñones – we find a striking agreement on liturgical principles and the main lines along which reform is needed. Both stress the corruption of the primitive simplicity by the intrusion of 'uncertein stories, Legēds, Respondes, Verses, vaine repeticions, Commemoracions, and Synodalles', and both lament that much of the Bible was unread. Both insist on the Pauline principle,

---

[1] St Cyriacus, a Roman deacon, was martyred in the Diocletian persecution A.D. 303. He was one of the fourteen 'Auxiliary Saints'.

[2] Franz, pp. 481–90; see also Annemarie Lohmann, op. cit., pp. 4–5; Mehl, op. cit.

[3] Franz, II, No. 7, p. 353: 'verum illo solor me non iudaicarum cantionum observationumve'.

to 'haue suche language spoken to the people in the churche, as they mighte understande, and haue profite by hearyng the same'. The national Reformation in England, and the tendency to liturgical uniformity in the Church of Rome after the Council of Trent, have obliterated the memory of the immense variety, bordering on anarchy, of the liturgies of the later Middle Ages. It was one of the merits of the German Reformation that it retained something of this diversity and flexibility.

It is generally conceded that it was an achievement of creative genius when Thomas Cranmer turned the Latin choir offices of the medieval Church into the two vernacular services of Mattins and Evensong.[1] Thomas Müntzer anticipated these great doings by more than twenty years.[2] His German Service Book ('Deutzsch kirchē ampt') consists of vernacular congregational services of Mattins-Lauds, and Vespers.[3]

Cranmer's is the more radical abbreviation – but it is arguable that only in such a drastic simplification could a genuinely congregational service be achieved, able to endure for centuries. Müntzer's is at once more conservative and more intricate – fan tracery against Cranmer's perpendicular. He retains the devotional nimbus surrounding the Psalms and Lessons – Antiphons, Responds,

---

[1] There had been vernacular offices of Morning and Evening Prayer in some of the devotional Primers. On Cranmer's work, see, above all, *Cranmer's Liturgical Projects* ed. J. Wickham Legg, London 1915 (Henry Bradshaw Society Publications 50)

[2] It is a nice speculation whether Cranmer could have heard of Müntzer's work. We know that Cranmer had a lively interest in these things during his stay in Nuremberg (1531) and that he was in close correspondence with his kinsman by marriage, Osiander, who knew all about Thomas Müntzer.

[3] 'appointed to lift the knavish Cover under which the Light of the world has been concealed, which now shines again with these Hymns and Godly Psalms, to the edifying and increase of Christendom, according to God's unchangeable will, and to the overthrow of all the pomp and pride of the ungodly' (Franz, p. 30). There is a picture of an owl on the cover, surrounded by six other birds, and though this appears to be a common printing device (cf. Franz, p. 25) on the text, 'All birds hate me', the owl is a well-known symbol for wisdom (as in the paintings of Hieronymus Bosch), while prominent among the birds is a large raven (Müntzer's favourite abusive image for Luther), so that this device may have symbolic undertones.

Versicles – much beauty here, and not least the poignancy of repetition. Yet a choir seems indispensable to Müntzer's services, which are fully choral. Unlike Cranmer who admitted he was no singing man, Müntzer cared about music – though it is uncertain, as with Luther, how much he himself composed, and to what extent he drew upon expert assistance. But his musical settings are rich and intricate: unlike Luther and Cranmer who, in the modern way, planned for one note to each syllable of text, Müntzer rejoiced in the more intricate melismatic music which weaves itself around the words in elegant patterns especially at the end of a sentence, and in using the Gregorian modes. We need also to remember that unlike Zwingli, Luther and Cranmer, Müntzer did not survive his first experiments long enough to revise them.

Müntzer had studied liturgical history and for him, as for the early Church, it is Easter which is the norm, and an Easter office which he first prepared. He has five sets of offices, covering the great seasons of the Christian Year – Advent, Christmas, the Passion ('Ammacht'), Easter, Pentecost. For these he provides a double service of Mattins–Lauds, and Vespers.

Both Mehl and Friedrich Wiechert, who contributes to Mehl's work, have shown in their researches that Müntzer must have been familiar with many missals and breviaries. But for the Service Book his chief source was the Breviary of Halberstadt: *Breviarium Halberstadiense ad Sanctam Mariam Ecclesiam*.[1]

Although he abandoned the lesser Hours, and the second and third groups of Psalms known as Nocturns, he still had great range and flexibility of choice, as the following table of his Advent Mattins reveals:

Müntzer's Mattins, Advent	Halberstadt Breviary
Invitatory	Dominica prima Adventus
Antiphon 1	Ant. in I Noct. Dom. 1 Adv.
Psalm 25	Dom. ad Primam
Antiphon 2	Ant. in II Noct. Dom. 1 Adv.
Psalm 80	In Feria V ad Matutinum

[1] Mehl, op. cit., pp. 68ff. He may also have drawn upon another Halberstadt Breviary *secundum Ecclesiae Majoris*.

THOMAS MÜNTZER'S LITURGICAL EXPERIMENTS

Antiphon 3	Ant. in III Noct. Dom. 1 Adv.
Psalm 44	In Feria III ad Matutinum
Versicle	Ad Vesperas tempore Adventus
Responsory 1	Resp. III in I Noct. Dom. 1 Adv.
Vers. to Responsory	Ant. ad Ben. Dom. 4 Adv. Vers. ad Resp. III Sabbato post Dom. 3 Adv.
Responsory 2	Resp. III in III Noct. Dom. 2 Adv.
Vers. to Responsory	Vers. to Resp. III in III Noct. Dom. 2 Adv.
Responsory 3	Resp. II in I Noct. in Vigil. Nat. Chr.
Versicle	5 Vers. ad eod. Respons.

Apart from the Lessons, one of which follows each Responsory, the staple of the service is provided by song, by the Psalms and ancient Hymns of the Church. Müntzer used Luther's translations of the Psalms where he could and took from him his rendering of the Benedictus and the Magnificat and the three Psalms – 51, 67 and 110 – which Luther had already published. For the rest, Müntzer made his own version, as he said, 'in German', 'in the immovable mystery of the Holy Ghost' and 'more according to the sense than the words'. He usually follows the Vulgate but can on occasion go direct to the Hebrew. The LXX he seems not to have known.

We have already noted Müntzer's daringly free version of Psalm 93, where the Vulgate (Ps. 92): 'Domum tuam decet sanctitudo, Domine: in longitudinem dierum' becomes the highly Müntzerian: 'Do siht der mensch das er ein wonung Gottis sey in der lanckweil seyner tage'.[1] And though this perhaps deserves Elliger's severe criticism we might also think of Müntzer's use of the Psalms in these services as more like the Paraphrases of 17th-century English and Scottish devotion than as an exact translation.[2]

[1] see p. 284 above

[2] Is it much more free than the famous final verse of Ps. 23 in the hymn: 'And so through all the length of days . . .'? *The Cambridge Hymnal* prints an extra verse to the same Psalm, attributed to Isaac Watts (!), which responds to no words in Scripture but is remarkably apt:

> There would I find a settled rest,
> Where others go and come;

We need to remember also the complex interpretation of Scripture in the early 16th century which made feasible a sudden tropological (subjective, inward) reference of verses which were obscure, but where there were no modern critical tools of elucidation. Thus, in his office for the Passion, Müntzer uses the traditional Psalm 140 to point up the pride of the ungodly, and the tribulation of *Anfechtung*, which joins Christ with his disciples.

> Ach Herr, lass die gotlosen nit lenger bezemen
> das ire missetat vorhindert die gantze welt . . .
>
> O Got, gib yn die anfechtung des glaubens,
> vorsuche sie . . .
>
> Der unversuchte mensch, so er von Got vil
> schwatzen, wirt in seynem untergang nichts
> gutes erfinden . . .
>
> Die ausserwelten such stragks den namen Gottes

Similar are the nuances which Müntzer brings into his version of the *Te Deum* where 'the Holy Church throughout all the world' becomes 'all the godfearing Elect confess thee'; 'Make them to be numbered with thy saints' and the following verses become 'Give to thy Friends that they may share thy praise' – 'Lord, save thine Elect people, and teach them to do thine Eternal Will. O Lord, keep thine Elect for ever.' Or, as in Psalm 63:3, he will freely adapt a phrase:

> Es wer uns besser das wir nicht geboren weren,
> dann dass wir dein unwandelbar barmherzigkeit
> nit erkenten mit deinem Namen.[1]

In his Service Book Müntzer includes a dozen traditional hymns

---

> No more a stranger or a guest,
> But like a child at home.
>   – *The Cambridge Hymnal* (1967), p. 151

[1] 'Better for us had we never been born, than that we should not know thine unchangeable mercy and acknowledge thy name.'

THOMAS MÜNTZER'S LITURGICAL EXPERIMENTS

of the Church, in versions which are probably of his own devising and some of which are striking and fine.[1]

Here, side by side, are versions by Müntzer and Luther of the famous Christmas hymn of Sedulius (5th cent.): 'A solis ortus cardine'. It is perhaps not quite typical, in that Müntzer's own images and words obtrude more than is his wont, but in this case his subjectivism also shows to some advantage:

Thomas Müntzer	*Martin Luther*
Last uns von hertzen singen. All Last loben mit frölichem schall, Vom auffgang byss zum nydergang Ist christ geburt worden bekant.	Christum wir sollen loben schon, Der reinen Magd Marien Sohn, So weit die liebe Sonne leucht Und an aller Welt Ende reicht.
Sey uns wilkommen, o kindlein zart, Wilche lieb zwang dich also hart, Ein schöpfer *aller creatur*, Scheint schlimmer dann ein schlechter bawer.	Der selig Schöpfer aller Ding Zog an eins Knechtes Leib gering, Dass er das Fleisch durch Fleisch erwürb Und sein Geschöpf nicht alls verdürb.
Zeych an in *unsers hertzen grundt*, Das uns der heylant werde kundt, Das wir mit dir so new geborn, Dein werck befinden unverlorn.	Die göttlich Gnad von Himmel gross Sich in die keusche Mutter goss, Ein Maidlin trug ein heimlich Pfand Das der Natur war unbekannt.

[1] They are:
- Advent – Veni, Redemptor gentium
- Conditor alme siderum
- Christmas – Hostis Herodes impie
- A solis ortus cardine
- Passion – Rex Christe, factor omnium
- Vexilla Regis prodeunt
- Easter – Ad coenam Agni providi
- Vita sanctorum
- Pentecost – Jesu, nostra redemptio
- Veni, Creator Spiritus

Des hymels thaw vons vatters thron	Das züchtig Haus des Herzen zart
Schwingt sich wol in die junckfraw schon,	Gar bald ein Tempel Gottes ward.
Des wirt die zarte gnaden vol,	Die kein Mann rühret noch erkannt,
Ins hertzen grundt do allzumal.	Von Gotts Wort sie man schwanger fand.
Eya Gots mutter, deine frucht,	Die edle Mutter hat geborn,
Die uns benympt fraw Even sucht,	Den Gabriel verheiss zuvorn,
Wie Gabriel verkündigt hat,	Den Sankt Johanns mit Springen zeigt
Und Johannes der prophet sagt.	Da er noch lag in Mutter Leib.
Got leyt hye in dem krippeleyn,	Er lag im Heu mit Armut gross
Gewunden in die tüchelein,	Die Kripen hart ihn nicht verdross
Geseuget so gar kümmerlich,	Es ward eine kleine Milch sein Speiss
Der do hirschet im hymelreich.	Der nie kein Vöglin hungern liess.
Frawet euch, ir engel, solcher ding,	Des Himmels Chör sich freuen drob
Ir hyrten und ir frembdeling,	Und die Engel singen Gott lob
Gebt Gott im höchsten preyss und sieg,	Den armen Hirten wird vermeldt
Den menschen auff der erden frid.	Der Hirt und Schöpfer aller Welt.
Des dancken wir dir, vater Got,	Lob, Ehr und Dank sei dir gesagt,
Dir son, dir geyst ein ewiges guth,	Christ, geborn von der reinen Magd,
Wilch uns *vorgötet durch* seyn Wort,	Mit Vater und dem heilgen Geist,
Yetzt *vormenschet* durch seyn geburt.	Von nun an bis in Ewigkeit.

No doubt Luther has written a much finer hymn, but Müntzer's second verse, with the line 'Scheint schlimmer dann ein schlechter

THOMAS MÜNTZER'S LITURGICAL EXPERIMENTS

bawer', is as striking as, if less tender than, Luther's notable sixth verse.

Like Thomas Cranmer, Müntzer translates and composes only as a last resort, as in this striking prayer:

> O Herr, sei gnadig deiner armen, elenden Kirchen
> und erhöre ihr Gebet, der du lebest und
> regierst in ewigkeit.

But the most striking proof of his sensitivity to tradition is his return to primitive usage, by including a processional at the end of his Easter office – beginning (and how apt for Müntzer's theology) with the splendid 'Vidi Aquam' – Ezekiel 47:1: the vision of the flood of healing waters issuing from the Temple in Jerusalem; this is followed by the triumphal song 'Cum Rex Gloriae Christus' (taken from Augustine's Sermon 137 on the Harrowing of Hell) where Müntzer's vigorous German recounts how Christ freed 'his Elect people held captive in death' who greet him: 'twice welcome, thou whom we have so long desired, whom in the darkness we have so long awaited', while this stern, majestic chant leads into the joyful climax of 'Salve, Festa Dies.'

Not less striking than his Service Book was Müntzer's 'Deutsch Euangelisch Messze' – 'German Evangelical Mass' – which he published in 1524.[1]

This, again, is in five Rites, covering the main seasons of the Christian Year. There is throughout an insistence on the participation of the whole congregation, which is evident in the Preparation, for which Müntzer uses the traditional Psalm 43 – though the reference to the ungodly in verse 1 no doubt received due emphasis. The priest (who celebrated, as we learn from other sources, from behind the holy table) is to make his confession 'with a clear voice before all the people' and is to ask of them: 'I beg of you, Elect Friends of God who surround me, that you will pray for me with

---

[1] 'Sometime done into Latin by the Popish priests and treated as a sacrifice, to the hurt of Christian faith – and now set forth in these dangerous times, for the uncovering of all idolatrous abominations through such misuse of the Mass, so long continued.' Text and music in Franz, pp. 157ff.; Mehl, op. cit.; Sehling, op. cit., etc.

heart, soul and strength that the Mystery of the Divine Covenant may be opened through my speech and your hearing.' To which the people reply: 'God be gracious to you, teaching you from day to day all his Will and Work, to profitable action or receiving [*Tun und Lassen*].' Included in the printed order, but apparently also printed separately, was a preface addressed to 'all the Elect of God'. We know that Catholic rulers, among them Duke Ernest of Mansfeld, had forbidden their subjects to attend these innovations, and it is evident that Müntzer had to face criticism nearer home, from among his own radical friends 'as though I wanted to set up the old Popish practices again'.

Müntzer's object had been rather to serve common Christian men and rescue these things from their abuse – so that the common man could see how these things had been perverted and poisoned in their misuse, and that by having these things in German they might have the word of God, and a true understanding of the Bible according to the meaning of the good Fathers. But Müntzer stresses also the tentative and experimental character of what he has done, leaving it to others to abridge or lengthen according to need and opportunity. 'In these services a man may perceive the working of the Holy Ghost, how a man should hold himself towards God, and how the advent of true Christian faith comes to a man. This will give those over-nice parsons something to do – are they to laze about and preach once a Sunday and live like a lord the rest of the week? No jolly fear! They talk about feeding milk to Christian babes – but they feed them dragon's milk. But a true priest has simply to follow Christ as Paul followed him.'

If Müntzer's Mattins and Vespers drew heavy fire from his critics, the effect of his German Mass must have been even more disconcerting upon his radical friends. Some further explanation was called for, and this Müntzer published in 1524 as an 'Order and Account of the German Services recently established at Allstedt through the Servants of God'. Though it seems to have been written quickly it is a liturgical manifesto of some ability and can stand comparison with Cranmer's celebrated Preface. We reproduce a large part of it, as Müntzer's own rationale of his liturgical work, and as evidence of his awareness of liturgical history.

THOMAS MÜNTZER'S LITURGICAL EXPERIMENTS

An order and an account of the German Rite newly established at Alstet through the servants of God. 1523.

To perform in public the divine office is given to a servant of God, not that he may keep it under his hat, but for the establishment and edification of the whole congregation, which is to be fed by the faithful steward, who gives to each his measure of wheat in due season. And this is not to be hidden under a knavish covering, but nothing is to be kept away or secret from the whole of Christendom and even the whole world, which those are wont to do who take away the key of the knowledge of God as the eternal living God has said through Isaiah 22 [:22].

Accordingly we take our entrance [Introit] into the Mystery of God from the Psalter, which is the key of David upon the shoulder of Christ, and to make everything plain, so that men may see clearly without patchwork, we sing the whole Psalm,[1] as happened in the beginning of Christianity through the good successors of the holy apostles. And as right at the beginning there has been a common confession, then afterwards when the Introit has been sung, the 'Kyrie-eleison' is added in order that the Friends of God may grasp his eternal mercy and praise his name to the utmost.[2] After comes the 'Gloria in excelsis', in which we give thanks that we are called through God's Son to eternal life, and to the highest good things of God, and so to come to our first origin [*Ursprung*]. To this end the people are comforted with the Salutation of Boaz, which he addressed to his mowers – as we sing to the ripe wheat of the sons of God, 'The Lord be with you!' Whereupon the whole Church wishes the servant of God a pure spirit (as Saint Paul teaches his pupil Timothy, saying) 'And with thy spirit', so that the poor, needy congregation may not have a godless man as a preacher. For he who has not the spirit of God is no child of God: how then can he know about the Work of God, if he has not experienced it? If he knows it not, how shall he tell it? For a blind man in such ignorance leads the blind. Therefore we go on to pray in all prayers for the whole gathering of the great Christian Church – against the deeply ingrained sins which hinder the most worthy name of God from shining in the whole world.

---

[1] In the printed 'German Mass' only part of Psalm 43 was sung.

[2] Unlike the Roman use, and Luther, Müntzer reduces the ninefold Kyrie to four.

Then the people are reminded through the holy scriptures and the letters of the worthy apostles, how each Elect man must give room for the working of God in him, before God the Father speaks through the Gospel in his dear Son. Then the gradual and alleluia are sung in order that a man may be put in good heart to cleave firmly to the Word of God. For from such hymns taken from the psalms he sees how Almighty God has dealt with his Elect, how he draws them to him, beyond their thanks, teaching them with fatherly chastening, his lovingkindness. Before the Prose or Sequence we sing Psalm 51, in the mode which is called 'Peregrinus'.[1]

Note also, that we always read a whole chapter instead of the epistle and gospel,[2] to get rid of all patchwork piety, and so that the holy scriptures of the Bible may be opened to the whole people [*dem volck gemein*], so that all superstitious ceremonies and customs may fall away through the constant listening to the Word of God, and this all the time with gentle and mild breaking off of those said ceremonies, so that all arrogance may be mitigated, and the people with accustomed song, performed in their own language, may be like children fed with milk, and yet with no concession to their bad ways. Although our opponents find this to be scandalous, yet such an improvement of divine office is more powerful to still the adversaries. That is why in the Mystery of God we sing the epistle and gospel in our own tongue, that the Apostle Paul may read his own letter publicly before the whole congregation. And Christ our Saviour has commanded that the gospel be preached to each creature, uncomplicated and undisguised, either with Latin or any other addition, but as each may come to hear and understand it in his own language, without prejudice.

In the third place, after the Gospel we sing on Sundays or on festivals, the agreement on the chief articles of faith brought together in the Creed, in which the gross errors of the Churches are met, that false Christians may not imagine that such things are denied them, after the Mystery of God has been rehearsed and put forth before the whole world.

Fourth comes the Sermon: for this is so appointed that the singing may be explained, which is in the service. For David says,

[1] Another improvement on the original 'German Mass'. This mode appears to have been Müntzer's favourite.
[2] another change

'Thy Word gives understanding to the simple'. After the sermon we sing: 'Now ask we of the Holy Ghost' – so that the preacher has a chance to get his breath back, and that the people may praise the Word of God which they have heard. We hold no Offertory in the Mystery of God.

Fifth, we sing the Preface through which Christendom is reminded that they should recognize the Firstborn of all Creation, in the fullness and knowledge of the divine will and the way of God which he himself has with all his Elect.

Sixth, we sing the Sanctus in which it is explained how a man must be disposed who is to handle the sacraments without harm. Namely: he shall and must know that God is in him – that he has not to puzzle or dream him out as though he were thousands of miles away, but as heaven and earth are full, full of God and as the Father ever bears his Son in us without any intermission, so the Holy Ghost declares none other than the Crucified in us through the tribulation of the heart. And so we have no excuse not to acknowledge our blindness, when God sets us in the highest honour through shame, or in the health of the spirit through bodily weakness, for thus he comes in his Name when he comes through our dishonour and disparagement apart from anything we have done or known.

Seventh. In order that we may patiently bear such high, mighty temptation we take the fashion in which Jesus Christ the Son of God has commanded his Church to keep, to bring home to his followers through all tribulation in order that our souls may be hungry to taste the food of life. So it is needful that we should most majestically hold the majestic word of Christ – to loose men from the grip of this life by the memorial, essence and word of him who wills to be in the souls of men, not as in a cow, but as in his temple which he has purchased with his most precious blood.

Eighth. The Words of consecration were also publicly recited in the first beginnings of the Church, and were done away only through a deceit, which arose from certain shepherds on the field. Now, in order to avoid superstition, which has come through misuse of the Mystery of God in the Church, we sing the words of consecration publicly. For Christ, the Son of God did not speak the word to one only, or in secret, but to all as the gospel text clearly says. He says several times: 'Take and eat...' 'Drink ye all of this...' And so in this way the consecration is something which happens through the whole congregation gathered together. That is the answer to our opponents who attack us on insufficient grounds, and who say that we teach that horse thieves in the field can say mass. From which sentiment any good hearted man can plainly see what they think of the Son of God, as though he were a painted mannikin or an image as a man conjures a devil with words.

So these people lead one to think that Christ the Son of God may be conjured with words hither and thither where the impudence of man may determine. No, not at all. Christ only fills the hungry in spirit and he leaves the godless empty. What should Christ do in the sacrament with men if he find no hungry and empty soul? Therefore must he be perverted with the perverted and good with the good. What is the use of a sign if it denies the essence? Now there are always many good people in the whole congregation, and on account of the faith of such men, he comes truly therein to feed their souls.

Ninth. We sing the form of Consecration of the Supper in the Preface tone according to the following words: 'The day before when Jesus would suffer, he took bread in his holy, worthy hands and lifted his eyes to heaven to thee, God, his almighty Father and thanked thee and brake and gave to his disciples saying "Take and eat all of this". Elevando manu he said "This is my body which is given for you". Vertens se minister, accipiens calicem coram vulgo dicit. Likewise, after supper he took the cup in his holy worthy hands and said thanks to thee and gave to his disciples, saying "This cup is my blood of the new and eternal covenant, a mystery of faith, which is shed for you and for many for the forgiveness of sins." Rursus vertens se ad altarem dicit. "As often as you do this, do it in remembrance of me etc." '[1]

Tenth. Soon after the elevation we sing in the same tone, 'Therefore let us all pray as Jesus Christ, the true Son of God has taught us, saying, Our Father . . .' Then we keep silence, to get our breath a little, during which time the priest divides the sacrament on behalf of the communicants and says 'Through all eternity' – and the common people answer 'Amen'. The Priest says again: 'The Peace of the Lord abide with you' and the people

[1] Unlike Luther, Müntzer follows the Canon of the Mass and includes the sign of the cross at the Consecration, for which he uses the traditional word 'Termung'.

answer 'And with thy spirit'. Soon after, in order that the death and resurrection of Christ may be meditated in the mystery of God, all the people sing three times the witness of John the Baptist to Christ, 'O Lamb of God, who takest away the sin of the world'. Added are words from Luke 17[:13]: 'Have mercy upon us' and finally, 'Give us thy peace.' . . . To such faith we give the most worthy sacrament to the people at the Agnus Dei and without the hypocritical popish confession. For they are all commonly exhorted in all sermons how each man must consider his previous life, and understand how much his desires have earned him a cross. Man sins, God lays penance on him, and it belongs to man to do it. No man can have a good, pure and peaceful conscience towards God unless he confesses perfectly. That is why the third agnus dei concludes with 'Grant us thy peace' and 'Lord, lettest thou thy servant depart according to thy word in peace.' For only such longsuffering men are worthy of the saviour of life.

Eleventh. The holy Sacrament is given under both kinds, despite all that can be said by the merchants in this or that market place, or this or that part. For if we do not perceive the sacrament, the holy sign, how shall we perceive the essence which the sign means? Accordingly after communion we say, 'Thanks be to God' over the people, and 'Blessed be the Lord'.

Finally, let no man marvel that we at Allstedt hold a German Mass, which at some more convenient time may be better defended with all the underlying reasons. But we are not the only ones to use another fashion than Rome, as those at Milan in Lombardy have a different way of saying Mass from Rome. Every diocese has its special ceremonies and uses. Why, then, should not we use our opportunities? For we at Allstedt are Germans and not foreigners and need to eat our way through the babble that we might know what to believe. That is only possible when we do it through the right Word of God. The Croats are Romans and hold mass and all offices in their own language. The Armenians keep their language and are a great people, displaying the sacrament in the paten to their people. The Bohemians hold mass in their own tongue in differing customs. The Mozarabs – and the Russians have many other customs and are no devils on that account. Why, in the very lands where Christian faith began, there are no fewer than 14 sects which have all different customs from ours. Ah, what blind ignorant men are we, who imagine that all we have to do is to be

Christian in outward custom, and quarrel about it as though we were frantic animals. May not a servant of the Word of God have power to teach his parishioners in such a way that they may be edified with psalms and hymns from the Bible as Saint Paul says with plain words in Eph. 5. 'You shall', he says, 'be filled with the Holy Ghost and speak to one another with psalms and hymns and spiritual songs, singing and making melody to the Lord and always saying thanks before all men.' The same he teaches in 1 Cor. 14. Is it therefore un-Christian to sing and read German in the church – and if so, what shall we then say when we have to set forth our Movement to Faith?

The translations of the Evangelical Mass provided little scope for Müntzer's idiosyncratic theology, except in the collects, where the prayer for Christmas underlines Müntzer's campaign against the ungodly.

> O almechtiger Gott, vorley das die new gepurt deynes eynigen sones im fleysch volfuret, uns erlöse vom enthichristischen regiment der gotlosen, das wyr durch unser sunde vordinet haben, . . .

Comparatively innocuous at a season which remembers Herod – but perhaps sung with more than usual fervour in the context of Müntzer's fiery preachments against 'the anti-Christian rule of the Godless'. Less controversial, but very Müntzerian, is the opening of another Christmas collect:

> O güttiger Gott, eröffne uns den abgrundt unser selen, das wir die unsterblickeit unsers gemütes mügen vornemen durch die new gepurt deynes sones in der krafft seynes fleyschs und thewren bluts, der mit dir lebet, . . .

On the other hand, Müntzer makes no effort to introduce his own special doctrines into the service for Pentecost, for which his collect reads:

> O barmhertziger Gott, der du gelert hast die hertzen deyner getrewen durch die erleuchtung des heyligen geystes, vorley uns im selben geyst die gerechtigkeyt zcu betrachten und besinnen, das wir stets uns seynes trostes mügen frewen . . .

His final collect for Pentecost is simple and lovely:

O Herr, vorley uns die gnad des heyligen geysts, auff das der thaw deyner güthe unsern grundt des hertzens in seyner besprengung fruchtbar mache . . .

There follow at the end of the 'Account' some details about the way in which Baptism is celebrated 'when a child is baptized among us'; Psalm 68 (AV 69) is read in German, with its reference to the waters of tribulation, and the third chapter of Matthew with the account of the Baptism of Christ. Salt is given, in the traditional way, as a symbol of wisdom and the child is addressed: 'Come to Christianity, that God may find you as ripe wheat.' The Creed is said and the pomps of the devil renounced. The child is anointed and at the request of the godparents baptism is administered in the name of the Trinity. A new white robe is put on the child, and a candle is lit.[1]

At weddings, Müntzer uses Psalm 127 (AV 128) in German and reads John 2. The sacrament is taken to the sick with reading from Luke 12, creed and Lord's Prayer and the administration 'with a loud voice'. The dead are buried with the Benedictus in German, without Vigils and with the mourners singing 'In the midst of life...' and the priest sings the Epistle, 'I would not have you ignorant...' and John 5 [:24–29] as the Gospel.

Müntzer ends his account with the characteristic: 'And if any child can teach us a better way of doing things, we will gladly receive it.'

It was only to be expected that among the casualties of the battle of Frankenhausen should be Müntzer's liturgical work, and his Psalms and Hymns. But in fact, they survived in strange ways. Some of the hymns survived as 'Anonymous' or were tacked on to other authors. Most striking of all were the ways in which Müntzer's liturgies were taken into the Service Books of Erfurt 1525–7.[2] This was not done in ignorance, for John Lang at Erfurt was almost the last of the Reformers to keep in friendly touch with Müntzer and with Luther. Lang sent to Luther an account of what he

[1] In connexion with Müntzer's views on baptism, see pp. 295f. above
[2] Mehl, op. cit., p. 47; Smend, op. cit., pp. 118ff. At Erfurt offices were added for the Holy Trinity, for Ascension, and, somewhat mysteriously, 'for the Promises of God'.

proposed to do, and received the extraordinary reply from Luther (28 October 1525): 'Vehementer nobis placet sollicitudo vestra pro formandis ceremoniis, neque forma a vobis descripta ingrata est.'[1] It is plausible to suppose that Lang only sent a general description of what he proposed to do, otherwise we have the situation of Martin Luther praising Müntzer's liturgies after having openly derided them.

Less pleasing are the activities of the Visitors, Justus Jonas and Bugenhagen, when they drew up regulations for Allstedt in 1533. They found many of Müntzer's usages and abstinences still prevalent: celebration in a plain surplice from behind the Table; no candles; the bells not rung for the Sermon, but only for the whole Service. But least defensible, though understandable enough, was the abolition of Müntzer's Psalms and Hymns; 'for although some bits of them were taken from Holy Scripture [!] yet these are un-Christianly introduced, and have inconvenient Latin notes – and we have other perfectly good German hymns available ... and so we will have conformity [*Gleichförmigkeit*] in Saxony.' It is perhaps ironical that the Visitors should have picked on Müntzer's great Christological word 'Conformity',[2] to impose a rigid party line.

We have spoken of Müntzer's Catholic and Lutheran critics. How obtuse his radical friends were to this side of his religion, is most plainly evidenced by the famous letter which Conrad Grebel and the other Swiss Brethren addressed to Müntzer in September 1524. From being a humanist of very highfalutin artificiality, Grebel had become a conservative evangelical of the most wooden biblicism, and his denunciation of Müntzer's liturgical experiments is a classic example of the inability of fundamentalists to understand the Scriptures.

> We understand and have seen that thou hast translated the Mass into German and hast introduced new German hymns. That cannot be for the good, since we find nothing taught in the New Testament about singing, no example of it. Paul scolds the

[1] *WA, Br.* 3, No. 934, p. 591
[2] Bugenhagen had to complain of Müntzer's usages on 28 April 1539 (Smend, op. cit., p. 117, n. 1), and as late as 14 April 1543 there were reports of this from Wolfenbüttel.

learned among the Corinthians more than he praises them, because they mumbled in meeting as if they sang. . . . Since singing in Latin grew up without divine instruction and apostolic example and custom, without producing good or edifying, it will still less edify in German and will create a faith of outward appearance only. Paul very clearly forbids singing in Eph. 5:19 and Col. 3:16 since he says and teaches that they are to speak to one another and teach one another with psalms and spiritual songs, and if anyone would sing, he should sing and give thanks in his heart. . . . do thou drop singing and the Mass and act in all things only according to the Word, . . .[1]

Pacifism apart, there really seems no good reason why modern Baptists should be so eager to disavow Thomas Müntzer in favour of the sectarian pietism of Conrad Grebel and his friends.

Like Thomas Cranmer's, Müntzer's liturgical work is conservatively creative. He was a pioneer, and his orders of service are like some complicated Gothic decorations in some contemporary German church. Apart from his use of the Psalms, and a turn of phrase here and there, his orders are singularly free from subjectivity. We miss altogether the growing weight of edifying and informatory material such as, a few decades later, were to unbalance the liturgies of Martin Bucer or John a Lasco. There is, as Smend points out, none of the pietism of Urbanus Rhegius and the new Lutheran rites, and Müntzer's might seem cold in comparison. But we have to look at Müntzer's work as a whole, to balance these things against his fiery preaching, his messianist programme, and his many-sided conception of religion and of the growth of the soul. It all adds up to something theologically and religiously rather impressive and it emphasizes that the story of Thomas Müntzer is indeed a tragedy. We do no good service to Martin Luther, to Lutheranism, or to anybody else, if we undervalue Müntzer's gifts or achievements.

[1] G. H. Williams *Spiritual and Anabaptist Writers* pp. 75–77

CHAPTER TWENTY-ONE

THOMAS MÜNTZER, HANS HUTH AND THE 'GOSPEL OF ALL CREATURES'[1]

1. *Thomas Müntzer's Theology of Nature*

Theological labels have a limited utility value, but they become dangerous when rigidly applied, when the evidence is blurred or over-simplified, or when their nominalist significance is forgotten. The warnings should be remembered when discussing the Reformation radicals, a historical field where typology has been carried to extravagant lengths. Thus, if we had to choose, in terms of the typology of Troeltsch, whether to label Thomas Müntzer a 'Spiritualist' or a 'Biblicist' we must no doubt opt for the former designation. It calls attention to what differentiates him from Martin Luther: to his stress on the immediate, unmediated work of the Holy Spirit in the human heart, to his insistence on visions and dreams as vehicles of revelation, and to his conviction of his own prophetic calling.

The distinction is mischievous if it leads us to underrate the importance of the Bible for Thomas Müntzer or the extent of his biblical knowledge. This was remarkable. His writings, and not only his sermons but his correspondence, were as heavily peppered with Scriptural citations as a modern reference Bible. He appeals frequently to the 'whole Bible', and his quotations are drawn from all levels of the Scriptural testimony. His use of the word 'Schriftgelehrter' (Scribe) is in polarity to the use by his opponents of the word 'Schwärmer' (fanatic), but his all-out opposition to the Scribes

[1] reprinted, with permission, from the *Bulletin of the John Rylands Library*, Manchester vol. 43, No. 2: March 1961

of Wittenberg – and the word covers not only Luther and Melanchthon but such opponents as Egranus and Urbanus Rhegius – for their obsession with the letter, and with a 'false faith', must not obscure the importance for him of the appeal to the 'whole Scripture'. And the typological label becomes pernicious if it leads us to overlook other important features of his thought and not least that third dimension which with some hesitation we may designate his 'theology of nature'.

We know Thomas Müntzer to have been a voracious reader, a scholar in whose life books really counted,[1] and that he contrived to keep abreast of the latest tools: the new printed editions of the Fathers, and of medieval writers, of the humanist programmes, and of the intricate polemic in which Erasmus, Luther and Karlstadt were involved. Some of this new printed material was exotic and explosive, and scholarship has not yet properly appraised the dangerous potentialities of much of the literature which was printed and reprinted in the first years of the 16th century. Our information about Müntzer's reading is haphazard. A casual sentence in a letter, for example, tells us that the pseudo-Joachitic commentary on Jeremiah counted for much with him.[2] A line in a rather skittish letter from the nun, Ursula,[3] tells us (though this we might have guessed) of his familiarity with Suso and Tauler.

Reference has been made to the volume of mystical and prophetic writings edited by Le Fèvre, and published in 1513 as *Liber trium virorum et trium spiritualium virginum*.[4] Here was stress on prophetic vocation, and on revelation through dreams and visions, and an often vehement and apocalyptic criticism of the contemporary Church. A reasonable tradition has it that Müntzer had his copy bound together with Tauler's sermons and that the bulky double volume was for him a vade-mecum.[5]

There are many elements, perhaps never co-ordinated, in his thought: medieval apocalyptic, radical Hussitism, the teaching of

[1] Franz, V, 2, 3: pp. 554–60   [2] Franz, II, No. 46, p. 398
[3] Franz, II, No. 11, p. 356
[4] H. Etienne, Paris 1513; see p. 258 above, and A. Renaudet *Préréforme et Humanisme* pp. 601f., 635f.
[5] see p. 255 above

'GOSPEL OF ALL CREATURES'

Luther and Melanchthon and Karlstadt, 1517–22. But even more important was the influence of German mysticism as in the 15th century it became conflated with the *devotio moderna*. That the little *Theologia Germanica*, which Luther edited and republished, has left less trace on him than on Karlstadt and Hans Denck is perhaps because in his case the mystical influence had been earlier formed. In Müntzer's case, the influence of Tauler was paramount. Here he found his insistence on conformity with Christ and on following, in suffering, his footsteps; on the need for renunciation, resignation and waiting on God ('Gelassenheit', 'Langweil'); on the need for the soul to be purged from lusts and creaturely desires and seek the one will of God. Much of this was fairly widespread 15th-century piety, and left its mark on such diverse thinkers as Gerson, Staupitz and Oecolampadius.

Within this mystical tradition was a good deal of speculation about the relation of man to the creatures, and of man to the universe, and of both to God (in Eckhart, but remarkable also in St Hildegard of Bingen) but in the 15th century it found a new development in the thought of Italian humanists and in Nicholas of Cusa. A focus for this was the Parisian humanist Le Fèvre. We cannot know if Müntzer was acquainted with two writers who much intrigued the Le Fèvre circle, Raymond Lull and Raymond of Sabunde. If he did know, and make use of, the bold speculations of the latter Raymond's *Theologia Naturalis* he transmuted them into his own theological idiom. Raymond's doctrine of the creatures is set in the major, Müntzer's in the minor key. In Raymond there is a remarkable paean on the joy (*gaudium*) of the creatures which recalls the first fine Franciscan raptures, whereas in Müntzer it is the soured apocalyptic of the pseudo-Joachitic writings of the Spiritual Franciscans of a later day; and the thought, so striking in Raymond, of the analogy between the service of the creatures to man and that of man in relation to God is something which Müntzer can only think of in terms of suffering.[1] For Raymond, as for most Catholic patterns of salvation, 'Love of God' is the key; we might say that

[1] see p. 288 above, and Renaudet, op. cit., pp. 485, 520, 521. Both Le Fèvre and Beatus Rhenanus possessed copies of Raymond's *Theologia Naturalis*; it was often reprinted, e.g., Deventer 1484, Strasbourg 1496, Paris 1509.

for Luther it is 'Faith in God': but with Müntzer it is perhaps 'The Fear of the Lord' and, with even more propriety than in the case of Luther, his might be called a 'Theology of the Cross'. If we speak of Thomas Müntzer's 'Natural Theology' we must not modernize it, as though he were a potential Gifford Lecturer, or as though he were interested in theistic proofs or in the relation of philosophy to theology. What concerns him is preaching and polemic; and what he has to say about the evidence in the universe and in the heart of man, about the power and glory of God, never gets far from the Bible and from Christology. What is written in the universe and in the mind of man is 'the suffering Christ – in Head and Members'.

Of this theology of nature there are hints and allusions in Müntzer's writings, and nowhere a direct and full exposition. His writings were occasional and few, as compared with the scores of pamphlets from Karlstadt, and the hundreds from Luther. But there are two strands which we may distinguish. First, there is a stress on the existence of faith outside Christendom, among Jews, Turks and unbelievers. His references to them are surprisingly frequent. He had read the Koran (from Cusa onwards a theme of the age) and had disputed with Jews. Acts 10, the story of the vision of Cornelius, with its emphasis on works, was too good a polemic weapon against Wittenberg to miss (as John Wesley used it against the Calvinists later). There is also the well-known preaching technique of playing up the godliness of the outsider in order to rebuke those within the household of faith. But there is more here than apologetic or polemic.

> I preach such a Christian faith as does not agree with that of Luther, but which is in conformity with the hearts of the elect in all the world. And even though he were born a Turk, a man might yet have the Beginning of this same faith, that is, the moving [*Bewegung*] of the Holy Ghost, as it is written of Cornelius, Acts 10.

Thus he defends his refusal to meet Luther and Melanchthon in open disputation:

> If I am to be given a hearing before Christendom, then those ought to be informed, bidden, invited from all nations of men who have suffered invincible temptation [*Anfechtung*], found despair in

'GOSPEL OF ALL CREATURES'

their hearts and through the same been all the time brought to remembrance [*durch dieselben allenthalben erinnert weren*]. Those are the people I will admit to be my judges.[1]

In an apocalyptic passage, he prophesies:

> The Gospel will come into a much higher reality [*viel höher ins Wesen*] than in the time of the Apostles. Out of many lands and from many strange nations there will come the Elect who will be far superior to us slothful and neglectful Christians. . . . See how aforetime from among the heathen were chosen fellows with the Jews. . . . and so many of these strange, wild heathen will put the false scribes to shame.[2]

The second characteristic of Müntzer's theology of nature is his thought of the relation of the creatures to the Creator, of the parts of the Universe to the whole, of the One and the many. We may begin with the enigmatic sentence which may well be a quotation, that he scribbled on the back of a letter in 1521.

> All knowledge of the creatures is to be referred to the Whole, and this is best, for it is knowledge of the works of his hands, which is as praiseworthy as the knowledge of God, when it is understood in terms of the Whole.[3]

There is a similar reference in the Prague Manifesto (1521):

> I have learned from no scholar . . . how the Whole is the only way in which to understand the parts.[4]

In the longer German version, which Müntzer worked over at the end of November 1521, this is expanded with interesting Scriptural references to 1 Cor. 13, Luke 6, Eph. 4, and Acts 2, 15, 17.[5]

---

[1] to the Elector Frederick, 3 August 1524 (Franz, II, No. 64, pp. 430–1)

[2] Franz, pp. 311–12. Müntzer seems constantly aware of this wider audience. In a letter to Count Ernest of Mansfeld he threatens to have his letter translated 'into many languages . . . and hold you up to ridicule before Turks, heathens and Jews' (Franz, II, No. 44, 22 September 1523, p. 394). The citizens of Prague are told that if they reject his ultimatum they will be 'beaten by the Turks in the next years' (Franz, p. 494).

[3] see pp. 294f. above   [4] Franz, p. 491   [5] Franz, p. 496

The same thought is expressed in a letter to Hans Zeiss, in 1524: 'The will of God is the whole over all the parts.'[1] This thought is allied with the theme of a divine Order (*Ordnung*) implanted in the creatures, recognized by men as the law is written in their hearts.[2] Thus he declares in the Prague Manifesto:

> I have learned from no scholar of that Order [*Ordnung*] which is implanted in every creature down to the very smallest word.[3]

It seems that Müntzer had been derided when he had put this doctrine before the Scribes (?Urbanus Rhegius).

> I would sooner talk with the Heathen, Turks and Jews about the very smallest of all the words of God and about his Order [*Ordnung*] and reflect on possessions, ours and towards God . . . they would not receive it when I gave them a brotherly admonition about the ownership of God and of ourselves over the creatures. It is all fanaticism to them. So I say, if you will not learn the truth about the beginning of the Bible, you will understand neither God nor the creatures.[4]

In his last vehement polemic against Luther, Müntzer defends the view that Christ – with all his members – is the fulfiller of the law.

> Christ began at the beginning, as did Moses, and he declared the Law from the beginning until the end. That is why he says 'I am the light of the World'. His preaching is true and moreover so fashioned as a Whole that he took account of human reason also among the godless . . . now I too, through the beginning of the Bible and the Order [*Ordnung*] of the first distinction, strive after the purity of the divine law, and declare the fulfilment of the spirit

---

[1] Franz, II, No. 57 (22 July 1524), p. 418; cf. No. 46, p. 398. Some such doctrine seems to be part of the Thomism of Karlstadt, whose 'De intentionibus' (1507) includes: 'Totum perfecte et distincte non scimus, nisi partes scientes. Et tamen partes non sunt per se in consideratione scientiae de toto, sed per totum.'

[2] see p. 292 above

[3] Franz, p. 491; see also the important letter to Jeori (Franz, II, No. 61, p. 425): 'widder an Got anzeygt, auffenbart durch dye ordenung yn sich und yn alle creaturn gesatzt'.

[4] Franz, p. 314

'GOSPEL OF ALL CREATURES'

of the fear of God ... thus the Elect have all known from the beginning in their unbelief through the use of the Law (Rom. 2 and 7). I set Christ with all his members as a fulfiller of the Law (Ps. 19) for the will and work of God must be perfected through contemplation of the Law.[1]

This 'natural theology' is biblical and Christological, and a key sentence is Müntzer's,

> Holy Scripture shows nothing else – as all the creatures bear witness – than the crucified Son of God.[2]

There is, then, a revelation of God, in the created universe, and among the heathen. From this man can derive what Müntzer calls 'The Beginnings' (*Ankunft*) of Faith, which will lead them through the 'Movement' (*Bewegung*) of the Spirit, through 'Temptation' (*Anfechtung*) to the real and genuine Faith. There is finally an important testimony to the fact that this was no mere speculative doctrine for him, but part of the plan of salvation which he expounded to his peasant hearers. In 1525 Urbanus Rhegius in a tract against Karlstadt declared:

> It is now two years since your comrade Thomas Müntzer wanted to put away the Bible, imagining he could teach the peasants faith out of natural things.[3]

2. *The Authorship of the Homily 'Of the Mystery of Baptism'*

Lydia Müller published in 1938 a collection of early Anabaptist writings.[4] It included a tract entitled 'Of the Mystery of Baptism, Of the Sign and of the Essence, a beginning of a right and truly Christian life'.[5] It exists only in manuscript versions, one of which,

---

[1] Franz, pp. 326–7; cf. Franz, II, No. 49, pp. 402–3
[2] Franz, p. 324
[3] 'Widder den newen irsall T. Müntzers und D. Andreas Karlstadt' (1525), folio B iii
[4] L. Müller *Glaubenszeugnisse oberdeutscher Taufgesinnter* Leipzig 1938 (Quellen zur Geschichte der Täufer, III)
[5] Müller, op. cit., pp. 12ff.: 'Von dem geheimnis der tauf, baide des zaichens und des wesens, ein anfang eines rechten warhaftigen christlichen lebens.' A complete translation will be found in the Appendix, pp. 379–99.

in a shortened form, is contained in the recently re-discovered *Kunstbuch* in Bern.[1]

The authorship is attributed to Hans Huth, though this is not directly claimed in the text. But there is evidence in the Anabaptist trials that this tract, or something like it, was in use among Huth's disciples, and that he used it as a basis for his preaching and teaching.[2]

Huth[3] himself is a striking figure, the leader of the south German Anabaptists, able to hold his own against such eminent and learned radicals as Denck and Hubmaier. He was a layman, literate, but not academically learned.[4] He was a Thuringian, from Haina, and lived

---

[1] Codex 464: Anabaptistarum opuscula germanice. For a description of this manuscript, see H. Fast *ARG* **47** (1956), pp. 212ff. The title of the tract in the *Kunstbuch* is 'The beginning of a right and truly Christian life'. There are many minor variants between the *Kunstbuch* text and that published by Lydia Müller.

[2] Testimonies of Peutelhans (1527) given in L. Müller *Der Kommunismus der mährischen Wiedertäufer* (Leipzig 1927) p. 55, n. 1; Ambrosius Spittelmayer, Q.G.T., V, Bayern II, ed. Schornbaum (1951), p. 56; Martin Weischenfelder, in P. Wappler *Die Täuferbewegung in Thüringen von 1526-1584* (Jena 1913), pp. 236-43; see also Urbanus Rhegius *Zwen wunderseltzam sendbrieff, zweyer Widertauffer, an ire Rotten gen Augspurg gesandt. Verantwurtung aller irrthum diser obgenantē brieff* (1528), folio ii. The second *Sendbrief* may be a letter of Hans Huth and deserves attention. It is not the same as the letter of Huth to which Rhegius devoted a separate tract and which is printed in L. Müller *Glaubenszeugnisse* p. 12.

[3] *Mennonite Encyclopaedia* ii, 846 (not always accurate); W. Neuser *Hans Huth* (Berlin 1913). I am indebted to Dr W. Neuser for the loan of the manuscript of his Dissertation, which was never fully published and never completed. The important documents concerning Huth's trial are in the Stadtarchiv in Augsburg, where I inspected them. They were printed by C. Meyer in his important article, 'Zur Geschichte der Wiedertäufer in Oberschwaben' *Zeitschrift des historischen Vereins für Schwaben und Neuburg* (1874), pp. 207-53. The documents belonging to Huth are described in a further article in the same journal (1900), pp. 38ff. by F. Roth. See also articles by H. Klassen in *MQR* (July and October 1959).

[4] He is described by the Nuremberg authorities as 'ain vast gelerter, geschickter gesell' (26 March 1527: Wappler *Die Täuferbewegung* p. 245). Urbanus Rhegius ('Ein sendbrieff Hans Huth' 1528) says that he had been a student. He himself said that he had heard Luther and Melanchthon at Wittenberg. It is unlikely that he knew Latin.

'GOSPEL OF ALL CREATURES'

for many years in the town of Bibra. There he had been a sexton and a wine seller, before turning to the roving occupations of bookbinder and bookseller. The travelling workman, and especially bookseller, has a special importance in England and on the Continent as a carrier of Reformation germs, and Huth's wide itinerancy gave him an interested clientèle in dozens of towns and villages in south Germany and Austria among whom he was to found cells of Anabaptist principles. Like other radicals in 1524 he was an opponent of infant baptism; he himself was not baptized until 1526, at the hands of Denck, after which he became an outstanding leader and the central figure, perhaps the chief organizer, of the Augsburg Anabaptists and of the missionary apostolate which went out from that city. He also figured in the famous debates which took place in Nicolsburg in Moravia, where his apocalyptic prophecies were a point of opposition between himself and Hubmaier. He was arrested in Augsburg in the autumn of 1527 and underwent repeated interrogations in prison, sometimes under torture. He died as a result of burns, perhaps incurred during an attempt to escape, in December of that year. There is no doubt of the magnetic effect of this Anabaptist Pied Piper, at whose words men left goods, honour, fortune, wife, like the Anabaptists of Erlangen, whose story is a real-life anticipation of the opening scene of Bunyan's *Pilgrim's Progress*.[1] He became a legendary figure, said to possess a mysterious book of prophecies and a drinking potion, one draught from which bound men to him and his doctrines.

That he was a deep and original thinker is less certain. The contents of his notebook are evidence of biblical study, with an insistence on apocalyptic and on numerology (the number 7 seems to have more than a mnemonic value for him). He taught a doctrine of the 'seven seals' or 'judgements',[2] and among other preaching

---

[1] This very remarkable story deserves to be told at length; the documents were printed by Berbig, 'Die Wiedertäufer in . . . Königsberg i. Fr., 1527–8', *Deutsche Zeitschrift für Kirchenrecht* **13** (1908), 291ff.; Wappler *Die Täuferbewegung* pp. 231, 234; Q.G.T., V, Bayern II *Dokumente* 6, 115, 116, 199

[2] The statement by L. Müller that the homily 'Of the Mystery of Baptism' is the 'Book with the seven seals' which Huth used, rests on a misunderstanding by W. Neuser of a document in F. Roth's article (p. 40), where Huth

heads are the sentences: 'the destruction of the godless', and 'the believers desire vengeance over the godless'. For the rest his only printed work is 'A Christian Instruction, how the Holy Scriptures should be judged and compared'.[1] After a short introduction the work consists in the main of sentences from Scripture which appear to contradict one another. This was a theme in the air at this time, having been sharply raised by Erasmus, and it seems likely that Huth is dependent on a similar compilation of Denck,[2] or perhaps (since there are a few citations different in both) from a third document used by both.

Thus, apart from the short *Sendbrief*[3] in which Huth pleads with those acquainted with the eschatological mysteries not to offend the brethren who have not heard or understood about them, the main source of our knowledge of Huth's thought, and certainly the main evidence for its depth and originality comes from the Homily, 'Of the Mystery of Baptism'. Of the originality of this tract there can be no doubt at all. It is a remarkable exposition of Mark 16:15 which stands out among the radical literature of this early period, and to which I can parallel only that other *tour de force*, the *Fürstenpredigt* which Thomas Müntzer delivered before the rulers of Saxony.[4] It contains the only full-length exposition of the radical 'Gospel of all creatures', and also a doctrine of faith and of justification, and an interpretation of baptism in terms of suffering which clearly sets out the difference between radical and Wittenberg theology. One is bound to ask whether it fits what we know of Huth's background, and his other writings.

It is at this point that we run foul of an old controversy, recently

---

has simply a series of texts about the seven seals of the Apocalypse. There is no trace of this kind of thing in the homily 'Of the Mystery of Baptism'. From other references to the 'Book of the seven seals' it seems to have consisted of a description of the doctrine of Faith, the two sacraments and the four last things.

[1] 'Ein christlicher underricht, wie gottliche geschrift vergleicht und geurtailt solle werden' (Müller *Glaubenszeugnisse* pp. 28ff.)

[2] 'Wer die warheit warlich lieb hat' (1526) in W. Fellmann (ed.) *Dencks Schriften* ii, 67ff.

[3] printed in L. Müller *Glaubenszeugnisse* p. 12   [4] see pp. 201–4 above

revived, of the relation of Hans Huth to Thomas Müntzer; for there have been those who would play down altogether the debt of the Anabaptists to the peasant leader.[1]

It was understandable and proper for Mennonite scholars to expose an ancient calumny which from the time of Melanchthon and Bullinger sought to discredit the Anabaptists by fathering the movement on Thomas Müntzer. None the less, the evidence continues to suggest a real link between him and the south German Anabaptists, first in the influence of his writings, and second in that apocalyptic ferment which begins with Müntzer, persists in Huth, Römer, Bader, and others and continues until the disaster at Münster in 1536. The battle of Frankenhausen discredited Müntzer and ended his 'realized eschatology'. But what of the thousands of followers of him and other radical peasant leaders? A few of the more doughty among them, like Hans Römer, were bold enough to confess ten years later that Müntzer was their 'spiritual father'.[2] The recently published Strasbourg documents show that as early as 1527 the Strasbourg leaders, Bucer and Capito, recognized that Müntzer had disciples who became Anabaptists.[3]

The battle of Frankenhausen did not immediately end the apocalyptic hopes among Müntzer's followers. The ferment which was at its height at Easter 1525 lasted at least until Whitsun (Pentecost remained a focus for Huth's hopes for some time), and Huth seems to have preached the overthrow of the godless in a sermon at Bibra on 31 May,[4] though the collapse of a peasant resistance

---

[1] see articles by H. S. Bender *Theol. Z.* (1952); R. Friedmann, 'Thomas Müntzer's relation to Anabaptism', *MQR* (April 1957). The latter is an unhappy example of the lengths to which prejudice can go. Essays by Mecenseffy, Bäring and Zschäbitz have shown how very one-sided this attempt has been.

[2] cf. Hans Römer's charges against Erfurt that they had slain his 'Father': 'seinen vater Thomassen Munzern erwurget' (Wappler *Die Täuferbewegung* p. 363)

[3] Q.G.T., VII, Elsass I, ed. Rott (1960) *Dok.* 86 (Warnungsschrift der Strassburger Prädikanten: 2 July 1527), p. 105: 'Etlich teüffer des Müntzers jünger'

[4] C. Meyer, 'Zur Geschichte der Wiedertäufer in Oberschwaben', pp. 249, 251; G. Zschäbitz *Zur mitteldeutschen Wiedertäuferbewegung* pp. 49–76

led him to substitute a vaguer apocalyptic in the following months, stressing the supernatural inauguration of the new age.

This oratorical vehemence does not tally with Huth's statement under interrogation that he did not understand Müntzer's teaching.[1] But by then he had the most pressing reasons for not emphasizing any association. He had to admit that Müntzer, on the run, had stayed in his house at Bibra 'for a night and a day' and had entrusted to him a manuscript, 'given him a book to print, on the first chapter of Luke', as he was a bookseller by trade.[2]

Moreover, he had turned up on the eve of the battle at the rebel camp where, according to his own account, he was arrested by the peasants and released at the orders of Müntzer. There he remained, and heard Müntzer preach several times. His excuse that he hoped to sell books among them sounds a little disingenuous and prompts the thought that perhaps, like David of old, in the naughtiness of his heart he was come that he might see the battle. He has left some vivid details of proceedings in the rebel camp.[3]

And here a dilemma emerges for those who would discount the association between Hans Huth and Thomas Müntzer. If the rela-

[1] Meyer, op. cit., p. 243

[2] loc. cit. It is not clear whether this was on Müntzer's flight from Allstedt to Mühlhausen in August 1524, or on that from Mühlhausen to Nuremberg later in the year (in any case not, as the *Mennonite Encyclopaedia* ii, 847 seems to suggest, after Frankhausen). The book seems to have been the 'Ausgedrückte Entblössung', which bears the imprint 'Mühlhausen'; this would tally with Huth's statement. But Brandt says that it was really printed in Nuremberg, where most of the edition was confiscated. If so, why should Müntzer give it to Huth when he himself was on his way to that city, where, as he tells us, he spent his time in getting his writings printed? See Brandt, op. cit., pp. 243ff.; Franz, II, No. 71, p. 449. H. Bäring, 'Hans Denck und Thomas Müntzer', in *ARG* 50 (2) 1959, assumes that it was *en route* to Nuremberg, and that Pfeiffer was with Müntzer. There is no word of this in the document.

[3] There is an enigmatic sentence in a letter of Müntzer to the Allstedt citizens, written from Mühlhausen at the end of April: 'My publisher [*Drucker* = printer] is arriving in a few days' time' (Franz, II, No. 75, p. 455). The reference is vague, might refer to Hans Römer, and cannot be pressed: but on his own showing, it could fit Huth. The Anabaptist depositions in Franconia show that he was by no means reluctant to talk to them about his experience at Frankenhausen, and of what he had seen and heard.

'GOSPEL OF ALL CREATURES'

tionship were as casual as Huth stated, then we must give up the attribution of the homily 'Of the Mystery of Baptism' to him, and its use as a major source for Huth's thought. For its relation to the vocabulary and teaching of Müntzer is so close that it cannot be explained in terms of a common background of radical jargon and mystical doctrine. Either this tract was written by Huth, who in that case emerges as one who was thoroughly soaked in Müntzer's doctrines, or this writing is by Thomas Müntzer himself, trimmed, edited and even interpolated perhaps, but bearing the imprint of Müntzer's originality upon it. For, as we shall see, it is not that Müntzer's doctrines, which are fully expounded elsewhere, are echoed in summary hints in this tract, though this is true to a certain extent, but that allusions and half-developed doctrines in Müntzer's writings are here worked out in a logical and extended form.

The possibility that we might have here a lost treatise of Müntzer himself was first suggested by Lydia Müller.[1] She rejected the idea on the ground that the author was apparently ignorant of Greek and Latin. She obviously grounded this judgement on the exegesis of the text of the Homily (Mark 16:15) which is interpreted 'Go ye into all the world and preach the Gospel of every creature'. Here the dative 'aller kreatur' is treated as if it were the genitive singular with which it is identical, an interpretation impossible in the Greek or Latin. None the less it is a possible interpretation, though equally forced, of the Latin of Colossians 1:23: 'Quod praedicatum est in universa creatura', the text to which the Homily immediately appeals, and on which, together with Romans 1:20, the 'gospel of all creatures' really relies. This exegesis is accepted by Hans Schlaffer, a disciple of Huth who also expounds this gospel and who was a former Catholic priest and presumably knew enough Latin to know that such an exegesis would not be permissible from the Latin of Mark 16:15. Might not the author of the Homily have found Mark 16:15 an irresistibly apt opportunity to expound in one text his natural theology, his teaching about faith and his conception of Baptism?

---

[1] *Der Kommunismus der mährischen Wiedertäufer* p. 74, note 1: 'His name is unknown. He knew neither Greek nor Latin – otherwise one would almost imagine an unknown writing of Müntzer himself before one.'

Moreover, if 'aller kreatur' is only possible in the German, there are other quotations where the Latin may be preferred to the German. Thus if we do not press his use of 'Gleichnis', where the Vulgate has 'parabolis' and Luther 'Sprüche', on the ground that 'Gleichnis' is a common usage in early German Bibles, the use of 'Urteil' for 'judgements' (Vg 'judicia') is rarer (ML 'Rechte', Zw 'Ordnungen').[1]

That there are expressions in the tract which come from Müntzer has been pointed out by Mecenseffy and Bäring, as well as by Lydia Müller.[2] They are more numerous, however, than anybody has yet indicated, and extend from technical vocabulary into the wider field of theological doctrine. Thus if we do not press the word 'Scribe' (*Schriftgelehrter*) as a radical commonplace, there is the expression 'Brother Soft-Living' (*Bruder Sanftleben*) which Müntzer applies specifically to Luther. There is the constant denunciation of the parsons as carnal, covetous and precious (*wöhllüstigen, geizigen, zarte*); they behave with Scriptures like apes (*wie die Affen*); use Scripture as a cloak (*Deckel, Schanddeckel*) and lead astray and pervert the poor common man; they teach a false (*ertichten, erdichten, gedichteten*) Faith; they tell simple folk 'Only believe', and pretend that there are mysteries too high for them; they deride those who disagree with them as fanatics, treating them in fact as the Scribes once treated Christ; they erect a new and worse kind of knavery than Popery; they suggest that Christ has made sufficient atonement for sin and they apply to Christ alone, what is true of Christ, Head and Members. The whole polemical preamble of the tract abounds in such exact Müntzerian phraseology, and there is no single idea in this opening part of the homily which cannot be paralleled in his writings.

There is a common Taulerian and mystical vocabulary: 'Gelassenheit', 'Langenweil': the 'friends of God' (Tauler, Suso, but here as in Müntzer, 'Elect friends of God'); there is reference to the Beginning ('Ankunft'), the Movement ('Bewegung') and to 'An-

[1] I am indebted to Dr F. W. Ratcliffe of Manchester University Library for expert judgement at this point. (N.B. Vg = Vulgate; ML = Luther's Bible; Zw = the Zürich, Zwinglian Bible)

[2] Mecenseffy *ARG* 47 (2) 1956, pp. 257-8; Bäring *ARG* 50 (2) 1959, pp. 155ff.

'GOSPEL OF ALL CREATURES'

fechtung'. Common to both is the imagery in this connexion of water, storms and waves, and a reference to the sign of Jonah. Then there are turns of expression which are characteristic of Müntzer's exuberant and hyperbolical style. He is wont to appeal, as does the homily, to the 'whole world' and to 'the whole Scripture' and to say that this or that existed 'from the beginning'. Both say 'the world is full, full ('voll, voll'[1])' and both use the cry 'Oho!' and like the word 'allerhöchst'. Important for both are biblical citations such as 'The clean fear of the Lord' (Ps. 19), the 'Fear of the Lord is the Beginning of wisdom' (Ecclus. 1:14) and 'these last dangerous times' (2 Tim. 3:1). The subtitle of the tract, 'Of a Beginning of a right and truly Christian life' is thoroughly Müntzer.[2] There is a long list of technical words; they include, as theological phrases common to the tract and to Müntzer: 'Geheimnis' (mystery); 'Urteil' (judgement – scores of times in Müntzer and a key word in the tract, as also for Huth); 'Ordnung' (order, ordinance); 'Bund' (Covenant); 'Bewegung' (Movement, esp. of the Holy Spirit); the Work of God ('Werk Gottes'); the Method of God ('Kunst', from Lat. *scientia*?); the witness ('Zeugnis') as distinct from the essence ('Wesen') of baptism; anxiety about bodily welfare ('Sorge um Nährung'); the poor common man; real or genuine ('recht, rechtgeschaffen') faith, as against false and feigned ('ertichten, gedichteten'); faith proved by fire; the earnest ('ernst') righteousness; conscience ('gewissen'); both speak of the Church in terms of 'Christenheit' and 'people of God'. There is one major word in the tract which I have only found in Müntzer once, the word 'Verwilligung' which occurs in passages relating to the rite of baptism. But the analogy of the Pauline epistles, a literature comparable in size with the Müntzer corpus, suggests that it would be possible for one expression to appear in only one writing.[3]

---

[1] so Müntzer's *Fürstenpredigt* (Franz, p. 243): 'er wirt [die welt] . . . voll, voll machen'; cf. also his 'Ordnung und Berechnung' (Franz, p. 210): 'wie himel und erden vol, vol Gottis seint'. The Bern *Kunstbuch* version of the homily has only one 'vol' but the other manuscripts having the harder reading are to be preferred.

[2] e.g., the subtitle to his 'Protestation oder Entbietung' (1524): 'zum anfang von dem rechten christenglawben und der tawffe' (Franz, p. 225).

[3] It occurs in Huth's short *Sendbrief* (L. Müller *Glaubenszeugnisse* p. 12n.), but

As we have already hinted, this common vocabulary comes from identical doctrine. Both stress the antithesis between the real faith which comes through temptation, and the false, glib faith of the Scribes who can only point to their preaching and to the letter of the Bible. Both insist that there is a revelation through the creatures, which precedes the coming of faith. Both use the parable of the Sower, and use more than once the analogy of a field, which must be ploughed, then cleared of thorns, thistles and stones, which are creaturely lusts, before the seed of the Word can be implanted by God. Both stress the 'Movement' of the Holy Ghost through the waves and billows of temptation; and the theme that baptism is in essence this purging by tribulation is described in terms which are used by Müntzer to describe temptation and the coming of faith. Both the tract and Müntzer treat the essence of baptism (as distinct from the sign) as being suffering and tribulation. Both insist that there has to be a complete purging of the heart from bodily and creaturely lusts, and that for this the soul must passively wait on God. Both stress the importance of the solidarity of Christians with Christ, their Head, and that atonement is made by Christ as Head and Members and not alone as Head. Of critical importance to the argument of the tract, as the bond between its natural theology of the creatures and its Christology, is the expression: 'the whole of Scripture, and all creatures, show nothing else save the suffering Christ in all his members' – to which there is the striking counterpart in Müntzer's 'Hochverursachte Schutzrede': 'the holy scriptures say nothing else, as also all the creatures show, than the crucified Son of God . . . the suffering Son of God'.[1]

---

it is not in question that Huth knew the Homily. On the other hand 'Verwilligung' appears not less than six times in the Tract and seems to be a technical or at least jargon expression about the rite of Baptism. I regard this as the strongest point in favour of Huth's authorship.

[1] 'die ganz schrift und all creatur nichts anders anzaigen den den leiden Christum in allen seinen glidmassen.' Franz, p. 324: 'Die gantze heylige schrifft saget nit anderst (wie auch alle creaturen aussweysen) dan vom gecreützigten sone Gottes . . . den leydenden son Gotes'. That Müntzer means also Christ in Head and Members here can be easily demonstrated from his other writings and correspondence (Franz, II, Nos 47, 49, pp. 398, 400; No. 38, p. 388).

'GOSPEL OF ALL CREATURES'

Moreover, there is one Scriptural allusion in the tract which is only intelligible in the light of Müntzer's own version. It occurs in the last section, about baptism (this section is missing from the Bern *Kunstbuch* but style and vocabulary establish it as part of the original manuscript). It describes how God uses the waters of tribulation to flush the soul from creaturely lusts and proceeds:

> Da wirt der mensch in der langen weil seiner zeit, in der erduldung Gottes hand ein fertig und beraiter stuel und wonung Gottes.

> There a man becomes, in the length and waiting time [there is a play on both senses of the word] of his days a ready and prepared seat in the patience of God's hand and a dwelling place of God.

The use of the mystical jargon 'Langeweil' at this point seems obscure until we turn to the version of Psalm 93 which Müntzer introduced into his 'Deutzsch kirchē ampt' at Allstedt (a version he also commended in a letter to the Stolberg brethren in 1523). A central section of the Psalm, which describes how the floods lift up their voice, is characteristically described by Müntzer in terms of the 'flood of sin', but the remarkable verses are 2 and 5. In verse 2 the Latin has

> parata sedes tua ex tunc : a saeculo tu es.

Müntzer has

> Darumb das du ein unwandelbar got bist
> Hast du den auserwelten gemacht zu deinem stule.

In verse 5 the Latin has

> Domum tuam decet sanctitudo, Domine, in longitudinem dierum.

Müntzer has

> Do siht der mensch, das er ein wonung Gottis
> sey in der lanckweil seyner tage.

[Luther follows the Latin, but his rendering of verse 5, 'Heiligkeit ist die Zierde deines Hauses, O Herr, ewiglich', is completely different from Müntzer's.] Dr Ratcliffe has found no reading similar to Müntzer's in any pre-Reformation Bible.

Dr W. Elliger,[1] in his interesting examination of Müntzer's version of this Psalm, has shown how perfectly it illustrates his free use of Scripture. It is, of course, possible that Hans Huth knew this version of Müntzer, for it had been published in the Allstedt liturgy, but I am bound to say that this allusive, almost casual, use of it in the Homily suggests the greater likelihood that this is Müntzer quoting his own version of a favourite Psalm.

The wealth of scriptural allusion in the Homily is itself very like Müntzer. We know, however, that Anabaptist leaders, like Pilgram Marbeck, attained a remarkable depth of biblical learning, and Hans Huth may have been similarly skilled. But we have to ask a further important question. Is there evidence in the Homily of theological and academic learning such as we know that Müntzer possessed but which we cannot predicate of Huth? I suggest there are at least three places where such learning is apparent. There are references to the creatures as reaching their 'end', and to man as attaining the 'end' of his perfection.[2] This sounds very much like Aristotelian doctrine, as filtered through 15th-century mystical and philosophical speculation.

More important is the following very striking passage:

> For the whole *world with all creatures is a Book, in which a man sees in work, all the things which are read in the written book.* For all the elect from the beginning of the world to Moses have studied in the *Book of all creatures*, and have understood it by their reason, as it is written by nature through the Spirit of God written in the heart, because the whole Law is expressed in terms of the *works of the creatures*.

The second half of this paragraph is closely paralleled in Thomas Müntzer, as we have quoted him above, from his 'Hochverursachte Schutzrede'. But the first paragraph is surely a reminiscence of the *Theologia Naturalis*, or *Liber Creaturarum* of Raymond of Sabunde?[3]

---

[1] see p. 188n. above

[2] It should be said that Hans Huth in his printed 'christlicher underricht' has a reference to the 'highest good'.

[3] Raymond of Sabunde (d. 1436) was a Spanish Franciscan who became Professor at Toulouse. His *Theologia naturalis* is a highly original work which hardly ever quotes directly from Scripture, Fathers or Schoolmen. He has

'GOSPEL OF ALL CREATURES'

This remarkable book, which was often reprinted and much read in humanist circles in the early 16th century, had a still more remarkable preface. Indeed, the preface so exalted natural theology and the evidence to be found in the study of the creatures that it was put on the Index in 1595 and omitted from later editions. In this preface, and also in the body of the work,[1] Raymond teaches that God has given two Books to men, the Book of Nature (or the Book of creatures), and the written Book of Holy Scripture.

The Book of the Creatures is written in terms of the Works of God (*facta*); that of the Scripture, of his words (*verba*).[2] In the preface Raymond extols the Book of the Creatures because, unlike Scripture, it is not subject to mistakes and glosses. Moreover – and this is an important link with the Reformation radical disparagement of clerical learning – 'The Book of the Creatures is necessary and fit for every man' – for, whereas the Scriptures need learning, the science of the creatures is 'accessible alike to laymen and to clerks and can be had in less than a month and without trouble'.

The imagery of two books, one of the creatures and the other of Holy Scripture, is common to the Homily and to Raymond. John Keble would have found Raymond of Sabunde and Thomas Müntzer rather exuberant travelling companions, but he would one day express the same thought:

---

been described as an Ockhamist, but there is in him a good deal of Thomist Aristotelianism, and some affinities with Raymond Lull; see C. C. J. Webb *Studies in the History of Natural Theology* (Oxford 1915), pp. 292ff.; A. Renaudet *Préréforme et humanisme* pp. 485, 520, 521; I. S. Reval *La Théologie naturelle de Raymond Sébon* (Lisbon 1955). Part of the work (as turned into a dialogue form) circulated as the 'Viola Animae' of Petrus Dorlandus. Montaigne translated Raymond's work and gave it a new lease of fame in France.

[1] We have used the 1502 (Strasbourg) and the 1852 (Sulzbach) editions and the reprint of the latter (Stuttgart 1966); see tit. ccxi: 'Liber creaturarum debet primo sciri antequam homo veniat ad librum sacrae Scripturae, ... Et ideo liber creaturarum est porta, via, janua, introductorium et lumen quoddam ad librum sacrae Scripturae' (p. 311); tit. ccxii: 'omnia, quae probantur per librum creaturarum, sint scripta in libro sacrae Scripturae' (p. 314).

[2] tit. ccx

> *There is a book who runs may read,*
> *Which heavenly truth imparts,*
> *And all the lore its scholars need*
> *Pure eyes and Christian hearts.*
>
> *The works of God above, below,*
> *Within us and around,*
> *Are pages in that book, to show*
> *How God himself is found.*
>
> *Two worlds are ours: 'tis only sin*
> *Forbids us to descry*
> *The mystic heaven and earth within,*
> *Plain as the sea and sky.*

If John Keble could light on the same imagery, why not Hans Huth? But there are other indications in the Homily, of Raymond's arguments. Of major importance in Raymond is the analogy between the obedience of the creatures to man, and of man's obedience to God. This is an important part too of the argument of the Homily, in the section concerning the 'Gospel of all creatures', though transmuted into the theme of suffering and sacrifice (even though the argument here of both Raymond and the Homily derives ultimately from the Book of Genesis). Thus the Homily says

> that it will always hold true for man, that he is to be in relation to God as such [animal] sacrifice is in relation to man.
>
> All animals are subordinate to man: if a man needs one, he must first dress, cook and roast it . . . if God would use and enjoy us we have first to be justified by him and cleansed within and without.
>
> So men can perceive the invisible being and eternal power of God in the creatures and see how God deals with men, and prepares them for the 'end' of their perfection . . . that is why all creatures are subject to man, that men may rule over them.
>
> So men recognize in their own works which they exercise over and in all creatures, the will of God towards them.[1]

---

[1] see also in Raymond, tit. xcix: 'Sic ergo creaturae ligantur cum homine, quia sunt propter hominem, et exinde homo ligatur cum Deo per talem obligationem' (p. 127); tit. cxvii: 'Vero duo sunt servitia: primum est servitium creaturarum ad hominem; secundum est servitium hominis ad Deum, (p. 158) . . . Creaturae enim serviunt homini, ut sit et duret et permaneat in esse; et

I do not contend that the Homily quotes Raymond, but that it seems to be the work of one who had read him, mastered and adapted his arguments. If this is so, then we must conclude, I think, that we have here a work of Thomas Müntzer.

I do not say that this is a demonstrative case, but that it is a strong one.[1] I think that the doctrine of Baptism in terms of suffering, linked with a doctrine of faith and justification which is thoroughly Müntzerian, is entirely compatible with what we know of Müntzer's teaching,[2] down to and including the denunciation of infant baptism.

At the risk of prolonging what may seem to some a subjective argument, we may suggest two points when Müntzer might have passed on the manuscript. The first would be in 1524 when he gave Huth another manuscript to print. The second, more likely, would be on the eve of Frankenhausen.

There is one other consideration which may be mentioned. Conrad Grebel and his friends (signing themselves 'seven young Müntzers against Luther') wrote to Müntzer a letter and postscript in the summer of 1524. In it Grebel requested Müntzer and Karlstadt to write some further treatise on the doctrine of Baptism. Grebel said, 'In the matter of Baptism thy book pleases me well, and we desire to be further instructed by thee . . . if thou and Karlstadt will not write against infant baptism sufficiently . . . I will try my hand.' From the fact that this document turned up in the St Gall archives, where it presumably came to Vadianus on Grebel's death, Dr Bender concludes that Müntzer never received it. And though

---

ipse homo debet servire Deo, ut ei bene sit et optime (p. 159).' tit. ccx: 'Scientia creaturarum est scientia de factis et operibus Dei, et illa jam dicta est. Sed nunc restat tractare de verbis Dei, et videre . . . si est aliquis liber, in quo sunt verba Dei scripta (p. 306).'

[1] Points in favour of Huth would be the use of 'Verwilligung' and the rather banal reiteration of 'darum', 'derhalben', 'alhie' which suggests an untutored style (? or one who thought in Latin – *etiam, quemadmodum,* etc.). I am not excluding an element of editing of such a manuscript.

[2] as against H. Klassen *MQR* (1959), who does not appear to me to do justice to Müntzer's theology, and leans too heavily on Karl Holl. He also tones down Huth's apocalyptic.

he shies away too eagerly from the possibility of contact between Grebel and Müntzer, and misreads what Grebel says about there being no copy of the letter,[1] he is probably right. But we do know that at the same time Grebel and his friends wrote in similar terms to Karlstadt, and that Karlstadt seems in fact to have done as they requested, for in October 1524 his son-in-law Gerhard Westerburg was in Basle arranging with Felix Mantz (one of the signatories of the letter) for the publication of Karlstadt's tract on Baptism, a writing which was confiscated. In these weeks Müntzer came himself to Basle and thereafter spent weeks, perhaps months, in the area of the Klettgau in south Germany. There were thus many possibilities of his having news of the Swiss Brethren and hearing that they wanted literature about Baptism. May he not have done so, and have turned one of his powerful sermons[2] into an exposition of his major doctrines, his natural theology, his view of faith in relation to temptation and to justification, and his doctrine of Baptism as related to his theology of the Cross?

One thing is sure: such a homily by Müntzer would be dangerous property after Frankenhausen. But I can imagine that a radical like Huth would regard it as too valuable to lose, that he might circulate the manuscript, use it as the basis of preaching, perhaps trimming it here and there, but not attempting to print it, not directly acknowledging it as a writing of his own. Much of this may be hypothetical, but it is surely not unreasonable. In any case, all that is contended for here is that either this writing is by Thomas Müntzer or else it is the writing of one so closely connected with him that we must label it 'School of Müntzer', as we might name a picture 'School of Breughel'.

3. The 'Gospel of All Creatures'

After a greeting and long preamble, the main part of the Homily

[1] Grebel appears to be referring to his letter to Luther, not to the letter to Müntzer at this point in his manuscript. I am grateful to the St Gall archives for a photostat of the originals.

[2] It is a pity that his writings are not in the main polemically occasioned. There is testimony that he was a fine and powerful preacher on the less eccentric themes of the Gospel.

'GOSPEL OF ALL CREATURES'

follows, an exposition of Mark 16:15, with its three parts, 'the gospel of all creatures', faith, and baptism.

Insisting that a right understanding of God's mysteries and judgements depends on keeping his 'Order', the writer stresses the importance of the 'Order' of the three parts of the text: first must come the 'Gospel of all creatures', then faith, and then baptism, in its outward sign and in its essence, which is 'to follow in the footsteps of Christ in the school of all tribulation'. The section begins with the insistence that

> By the gospel of Every Creature nothing less is displayed than Christ and he alone crucified, but not simply Christ as Head, but the whole Christ with all his members . . . the whole Christ must suffer in all his members and not as our scribes teach . . . that Christ the Head has borne everything and accomplished all.[1]

But by this 'Gospel of every creature' you are not to understand[2]

> that the Gospel is to be preached to all creatures, to dogs and cats, cows and calves, leaves and grass, but as Paul says, the gospel which is preached to you, 'in all creatures'.[3]

But this gospel is hidden from the carnal preachers and is now almost unknown. But this is how Christ himself preached.

> He always showed the common man the Kingdom of heaven and the power of the Father by means of a parable, by means of the works of the hands of man, in all those daily works with which men are occupied.

Unlike the senseless scribes, he did not direct men to books, but he

---

[1] This is a recurring theme in Thomas Müntzer; see references in his writings in Franz, p. 224; p. 234: 'wenn man sagt, Cristus hats alleine alles aussgericht, ist vil, vil zu kurtz. Wenn du das heubt mit den glidern nicht verfassest, wie mochtestu dann seinen fussstapfen nachfolgen?' cf. pp. 318f.; also p. 327: 'Ich setze Christum mit allen seinen gelidern zum erfüller des gesetzes'; see also the important letter of 11 December 1523 to Christoph Meinhard (Franz, II, No. 47).

[2] The statement that the 'Order' (*Ordnung*) must be put together with all its parts recalls Müntzer's doctrine of the Whole in relation to the parts.

[3] The immediate appeal to Col. 1:23 is to be noted; a citation of Rom. 1:20 follows.

showed them the gospel in their work, the peasant through his field, seed, thistle, thorns, and rocks.

> As the peasant does with his field before he sows seed in it, so does God also with us before he plants his word in us, that it may grow and bear fruit.

So it is in the Bible.[1]

> He teaches the gardener from his trees, the fisherman from his catch, the builder from his house, the goldsmith by the testing of his gold, the housewives from their dough, the vinedresser by his vineyard, vine and shoots, the tailor by the patching on an old garment, the merchant by his pearls, the reaper by the harvest, the woodcutter by the axe laid to the tree, the shepherd by his sheep, the potter by his pottery, the steward and the bailiff by their accounts, the pregnant woman by her childbearing, the thresher by his winnowing fan, the butcher by his slaughtering. Paul illustrates the body of Christ in and through a human body. So Christ always preached the Kingdom of God by the creatures and in parables.'

This is an astonishing and surely highly original appeal to the teaching of Jesus, something even more radical than the Erasmian 'philosophy of Christ'. It seems almost startlingly 19th-century in its appeal to the Jesus of History, though its realism is more that of Breughel and Bosch than of Rossetti and Holman Hunt, and the argument turns at once in a medieval way from parable to allegory. These parables and analogies are to teach men that

> all creatures have to suffer at the hand of men, and so come through pain to that end for which they were created, and . . . no man can come to be saved other than by suffering and through tribulation . . . so the whole of Scripture and the creatures teach nothing else but – the suffering Christ in all his members.

The next section shows how the ceremonial and sacrificial law of Moses agrees with the natural law of the heathen. Thus the laws of Moses are not to be understood literally (*Rede*) but in terms of spiritual meaning (*Kraft*). Thus God commands the Jews to avoid

[1] Numerous citations are given.

'GOSPEL OF ALL CREATURES'

eating unclean animals, that Christian men may learn to avoid the company of the ungodly. Again the analogy between the creatures and God is used:

> All animals are subordinate to man; if a man needs one for himself he must first prepare, cook and roast it and the animal has to suffer according to his will. If God would use us, we have first to be justified by him and cleansed within and without, inwardly from desire and lust and outwardly from all improper behaviour and misuse of the creatures.

Again the author turns to allegory.

> The carpenter does not build houses from whole trees, but first cuts them down and then fashions them according to his will, and makes a house out of them. We should learn from this how God treats us, as a man builds his house, before he dwells in it, which house (Paul says) we are.

Again, as

> on a tree a branch sticks out, now in one direction, now in another, so it is with the desires of men, one branch stretches out towards possessions, another towards wife and children, a third towards money, a fourth towards fields and meadows, to temporal pomp, to luxury and honour.
>
> So every work which we accomplish with the creatures should be as the Scriptures to us, which we diligently mark. For the whole world with all the creatures is a book in which a man may see in the work, all those things which are read in the written book. For all the elect from the beginning of the world to Moses have studied in this book of all creatures, and have understood it by their reason, as it is written by nature through the spirit of God written in the heart, for the whole law is described in terms of creaturely works.

Similarly the heathen also are concerned with the creatures. The law commands that animals be killed before being eaten: thus do the heathen also: the law commands that lamp trimmers be put with the lamps: this is the heathen practice!

> And so the law is described and shown forth in all the creatures and we read it daily in our work. In this book we are occupied daily, and the whole world is full, yes, full of the will of God so

illustrated, of which our own hearts bear witness if we keep them from the coarsening of worldly lusts, and so men can understand the invisible being and eternal power of God in the works of the creatures, and see how God deals with men and prepares them for the end of their perfection, and this can only take place under the cross of suffering, according to his will.

Not only is this direct appeal to the preaching of Jesus and to the manner in which his parables spoke to the condition of the common man highly original and perceptive, but it had obvious immediate polemical value for the radicals. The appeal to books, and chief among them the Bible, by the Scribes was utterly different from the methods of the Lord, who, it is plausibly argued, only used the appeal to Scripture itself when confuting the Scribes on their own ground. This 'Gospel of all creatures' could by-pass the Church machine, not only of Rome, but of Wittenberg, for here was a simple gospel which was not bound to the preaching and scholarship of the Lutheran preachers. Thus this 'Gospel of all creatures', as expounded in the Homily, corresponds exactly to the complaint of Urbanus Rhegius in 1525 that two years previously Thomas Müntzer had sought to discredit the Bible by saying that he would teach the common man directly from the study of natural things.

The later sections of the Homily are not our main concern, but there is one section which was also part of the radical polemic, the retort (? first made by Karlstadt) to the Lutheran insistence on abiding in one's vocation, a doctrine which hit hard at the itinerancy of the Anabaptists.

> And so nowadays . . . everybody says, 'Each man must abide in his calling'. If that is so, why did not Peter remain a fisherman, Matthew a publican, why did Christ tell the rich young ruler to sell all and give to the poor? If it is right for our preachers to possess so much, then the rich young ruler was right, too, to keep his possessions. O Zacchaeus, why did you give up your property so easily – according to your preachers you would have done better to stick to it, and still have been a good Christian. Oho, comrades, how do you like that? – can't you smell arrant knavery here?

That the 'Gospel of all creatures' was taught by Huth himself is to be admitted. There are, we have already suggested, clear traces of

'GOSPEL OF ALL CREATURES'

such teaching among the examinations of his disciples.[1] It is explicitly set forth in his 'Ein christlicher underricht, wie göttliche geschrift vergleicht und geurtailt solle werden'.[2] But this document seems far less reminiscent of Müntzer, and what Huth has to say about it here seems not more original than what is said by other members of this circle. Leonard Schiemer's[3] exposition of the Creed uses the analogy of the suffering creatures, 'the means whereby all creatures come to the use of man, that is suffering, and the creature holds itself passive before man and suffers for faith's sake'. The ex-priest Hans Schlaffer[4] recurs to this theme as of major importance. In his 'Kurzer Underricht zum Anfang Eines Recht Christlichen Lebens' he speaks of three witnesses, of the creature, the Scriptures, and Christ. His first witness, the creature, is described in language which shows knowledge of the text of our Homily, and he cites the text 'aller creatur'. Schlaffer sometimes quotes the examples from the Homily, sometimes extends them 'as a hen, a fish, or some other beast' has to be 'plucked, washed, cleaned and so to suffer, so it is with men and God when he prepares us for justification'. He gives a further exposition of the gospel of all creatures in his 'Kurzer bericht und leer eines recht christlichen lebens'[5] and again in his 'Bekandtnuss und verantwortung'.[6] But Schlaffer adds no new ideas, and applies the analogy, creatures–man, man–God, in a rather wooden way, which contrasts with the liveliness of our Homily. Much more original and striking is the writing of Jörg Haug von Juchsen, 'Ein christliche Ordnung eines wahrhaftigen Christen zu verantworten die Ankunft seines Glaubens' (1524?).[7] He was elected preacher at Bibra by the peasants and asked Huth to preach to them in the days following the battle of Frankenhausen,

---

[1] see p. 332 above; also Q.G.T., V, Bayern II *Dok.* 16, also p. 56

[2] L. Müller *Glaubenszeugnisse* pp. 28ff.

[3] Schiemer was an ex-Franciscan who was converted by Huth's teaching; he was beheaded and burned at Rottenburg on the Inn, in January 1528.

[4] see L. Müller, op. cit., pp. 84ff. Schlaffer had been a priest in Austria, and joined Huth's party at Nicolsburg in 1527. He was executed by the sword at Schwaz in 1528.

[5] Müller, op. cit., pp. 94ff.

[6] ibid., pp. 110ff.

[7] ibid., pp. 2ff.; *Mennonite Encyclopaedia* iii, 679

1525. His teaching probably stands in a more direct relation to Müntzer than Schiemer and Schlaffer whose chief debt was to Huth, and he expounds in this tract a doctrine of the seven spirits of wisdom which we know to have been one of Müntzer's doctrines. Jörg Haug sees the timidity of wild beasts and the violence of beasts of prey as examples of the fear of the Lord, and he expounds the original order of creation, Adam's dominion over the creatures, and the results of the fall in a way which must be very like the teaching which Müntzer himself gave. It is to be noted that there is a fairly high theological content to this tract of Haug, who speaks of man's goal of perfection, and of the highest good, and uses the Taulerian vocabulary about suffering, and about conformity with Christ. The study of these writings raises interesting questions. Is there behind all this the teaching of one man, Thomas Müntzer? We have real evidence that this might be so, and that during his ministries at Allstedt and Mühlhausen he may well have given some fairly coherent theological teaching not expounded in his polemically occasioned writings but given from the pulpit of which he was a master. Or is it not so simple? Are we to think more in terms of ideas gained through books – of little groups of radically minded laymen discussing what had been gleaned from Tauler's sermons and from Müntzer and Karlstadt? Are we to think that in the years, perhaps months, preceding the emergence of the Anabaptists there were groups of radicals, much as in Switzerland the 'spiritualists' 'preceded the formation of the Swiss Brethren'. At any rate there is evident in these writings a fairly coherent pattern of theology, with its obvious debt to the modern devotion as conflated in Germany with Taulerian mysticism, so that one has to reckon with epigrams of the learned which have become, or are becoming, the evangelical clichés, the jargon of the unlearned. One can only list the intriguing possibilities.

The 'Gospel of all creatures' persisted for some time among Anabaptist circles, certainly long enough to intrigue Pilgram Marbeck. But there were perhaps reasons why it should prove of only transitory importance. Obviously it had an immediate polemical value in its contradiction of the Scribes of Wittenberg, Zürich and Strasbourg, with their appeal through the Bible and the Preaching of the Word, to a learned, teaching Church. But its startling simple gospel, which claimed to speak directly to the simple people, was not really the method of Jesus of Nazareth. We need not blame them for their inability to create parables comparable with those of their sublime Master: or for their failure to perceive the difference between a parable and an allegory. But they did in fact fall into an allegorizing which was thoroughly medieval, and the superficiality with which one analogy is spiritualized time after time recalls the 'Emblems' of the English Puritans. More important, by making the 'Gospel of all creatures' a preliminary to real faith, a teaching which men were encouraged to draw for themselves from their own vocation and the natural world, they came very near to re-erecting the very 'false faith' against which they were protesting, a mental and theological technique (the Homily seems uneasy at some points about this – when it asks readers not to despise such 'written judgements').

One thing might have extended its survival value: the immense stress of our Homily on suffering, only too relevant to the condition of a martyr church. When Felix Mantz's execution order was read out in Zürich, with its sentence of drowning, he cried out, 'Ah, that is real Baptism', and one ponders the folly of the Swiss Protestant authorities for a form of punishment which must recall the 'red baptism' of the early Church. But the teaching of the Homily is of a pre-martyrdom vintage, and we may conclude that on the whole the teaching of this Homily stood too near to the world of late medieval mysticism and devotion to have enduring value for a movement which despite many real links with the past was so swift to develop its own authentic ethos, its own disciplinary frame, its own picture of Primitive Christianity.

Part IV

A Sixteenth-century Dr Johnson and his Boswell

The Reformer as Layman

CHAPTER TWENTY-TWO

VADIANUS AND JOHANNES KESSLER OF ST GALL

The statue which St Gall has erected to Vadianus[1] is one of the sights of the pleasant, cultured modern city. He stands Bible in hand, sword sheathed at his side, his other hand stretched out as in some great argument. With whom? Surely, one feels, with the great Abbey which he faces along the street. But if so, is it not an argument which the Reformers lost? On that dire day in February 1529, Vadianus himself presided – while the images were destroyed, and Mass abolished. But the modern visitor, on Easter or some other high day, will find an overflowing congregation kneeling at Mass, and by an irony of history the modern baroque church has more *putti*, more graven images to the square yard than almost any church in Europe.

Or is it not so simple? May not a renovated Catholicism, where Mass may be said without error, and images portrayed without superstition, itself be reckoned a fruit of the Reformation? Is there not something in the St Gall story which dwarfs even the Reformation, of which Vadianus himself was more than a little aware.

For the great Abbey fascinated him, even when it repelled. As a schoolboy he learned to sing there, and without exaggerating choirboys' bump of reverence, we may guess that he must have often

[1] Joachim von Watt 1484–1551. There is a pleasant mystique about Vadianus studies, from the classic study by Werner Näf *Vadian und seine Stadt St. Gallen* 2 vols, St Gall 1944, 1957. Notable monographs include Bernhard Milt *Vadian als Arzt* (Vadian-Studien 6), St Gall 1959; Conradin Bonorand *Vadians Weg vom Humanismus zur Reformation und seine Vorträge über die Apostelgeschichte (1523)* (Vadian-Studien 7), St Gall 1962; also C. Bonorand, 'Stand und Probleme der Vadian-Forschung', *Zwingliana* (1954–8), pp. 586ff.

357

been awed as the lovely music echoed in the dim vaults of the Münster. As a young don he rummaged among the manuscripts of the famous library, itself a monument to earlier spirituality and love of learning. On that day of destruction in 1529 it was Vadianus who carried off the precious records, not to burn them, but that he and his friends might continue the succession of its chroniclers. The story of St Gall became for him a main clue for the interpretation of Christian history, on which in his last years he would ponder, watching the slow decline from the apostolic quest of evangelical perfection to a complacent acceptance of worldly commodity. None the less, the memories lingered. Eight hundred years before, an Irish monk, from that bright island in a dark sea which was Celtic monasticism in the Dark Ages, had made a Livingstonian adventure into Darkest Europe and cleared room in the forest for holy oblation.

But there was little romanticism and a good deal that was very earthy about the marriage between the Abbey of St Gall and the town which grew up round its borders, between the great Prince Abbots with their numerous dependents – the 'God's House People' – and the citizens who more and more coveted freedom as their prosperity grew and the linen trade stretched long fingers along the the roads to France and Italy, Poland and Germany. It is the familiar medieval story of a growing town, snatching rights and liberties from temporal and spiritual overlords, playing off one against another. In St Gall by the end of the 15th century there was an intricate tangle of competing jurisdictions. The town had vested interests in the Münster; the Abbey in the parish church of St Laurence. A sale of property in the town must pass through the hands of the Abbot, but he himself could not pass from the Abbey to his other possessions without crossing an area where the town had jurisdiction. As its relation to the Emperor became more remote, there came the new domination of the Swiss Confederacy, especially of Appenzell and Zürich. Vadianus was a child in 1489–91, when there was political crisis, when a rash attempt to overthrow completely the authority of the Abbot led to military intervention from the four neighbouring cantons, to the imposition of a crippling fine, the end of St Gall's hope to become a self-sufficient *Stadt-Staat* – and

An eighteenth-century view of St Gall

The modern town of St Gall, with the cathedral and
the parish church of St Laurence

the ignominious acceptance of a resident officer from the 'protecting' cantons. The attempt of the mayor Varnbüler to stage a comeback by a desperate appeal to distant Bern failed and he had to go into exile. But the plot had been hatched within yards of the Vadianus home, and we may suppose that he grew up to know how delicate was the political balance between the small city and its powerful neighbours, soon to be still more delicately poised between the permutations and combinations of reform and counter-reformation.[1]

The von Watt family was well known and long-established in St Gall and had important business connexions with the linen trade. If Leonard, Joachim's father, could not afford to live in the most fashionable part of town, he was a respected citizen, a Councillor (*Ratsherr*), member of the Inner Council of the oligarchy which ruled the little republic. Wealth on the scale of a Peutinger or Pirckheimer he never knew; yet Joachim grew to moderate affluence, seems always to have had all the books he needed, and escaped the economic pressures which drove many to a clerical career.

His schooling in St Gall seems to have been unremarkable. But when he went, as a burly youth of 17, to the university of Vienna, he was the first of the family to enter the academic world. He was not the first student to find the new freedom unsettling, and a friend of the family, the merchant Kobler, was asked by worried parents to give their too bright offspring a good talking to. Their feelings were again ruffled, however, when with the whole-heartedness of youth Joachim now seemed to be working too hard; he had flung himself into the new learning of humanism and wrote home that he would henceforth abandon the family name and style himself humanistically Vadianus – an announcement which thoroughly upset Father Leonard and Uncle Hugh who would rather that their Joachim should figure in the local *What's Watt* than in a remote academic *Who's Who*.[2] Medieval universities were always susceptible to changes in political temperature and Vienna was no exception. In 1481 the number of matriculants dropped to five. Then, after artificial respiration had been vigorously administered

---

[1] Näf, i, 59ff.
[2] *Johannes Kesslers Sabbata mit kleineren Schriften und Briefen* ed. E. Egli and R. Schoch, St Gall 1902: 'Vita Vadiani', p. 602

by the Emperor Maximilian, things had improved and the intake in the year 1500 – Joachim went up in 1501 – had risen to 326.

Here as in many other universities there was a conflict between the schoolmen and the humanists. It was a weakness of the struggle that in fact both traditions derived from a classical tradition of learning in which rhetoric predominated. This was particularly unfortunate in Vienna where the imposing place given to the nascent sciences was hindered by the mummifying wrappings of literary humanism. Thus, in the field of medicine, the humanist preference for classical over medieval texts was actually a retrogressive influence.

Of great moment for Vienna was the advent of the famous German scholar and polymath, Konrad Celtis.[1] He did not try to work the university machine from within, but set up alongside it a School of Poetry and Mathematics, which combined some of the ideals of the Florentine Academy with the interests of the humanist sodalities of the Rhine and the Danube. In a few years he gathered notable colleagues and pupils, and we may believe that Vadianus was among them though he was not a member of the new college.[2]

After Celtis, who died in the year when Vadianus proceeded M.A. (1508), the outstanding figure was Cuspinianus, Professor of Poetry,[3] Laureate of the Empire, historian, Doctor of Medicine, Rector of the university, but who turned more and more to the career of a diplomat. This wealthy scholar with his rich library and his great house was on the grand scale – beyond that of Vadianus, and with this teacher, eleven years his senior, Vadianus never became intimate. From another, Angelo Cospus, he may have become acquainted with the revival of the sacred languages, though he never had much Greek. With the Italian theologian, John Camers, he could have had little theological sympathy, and their common interest, geography, divided at the point where Camers blindly accepted authority, while Vadianus was all for empirical observation.

[1] see L. W. Spitz *The Religious Renaissance of the German Humanists* ch. v, 'Celtis – The Arch-Humanist'

[2] Näf, i, 129; see Bonorand *Vadians Weg* ch. 1, for the clerical as well as humanist background of Vienna during Vadianus' university career

[3] Näf, i, 169ff. There is a fine portrait of him by Lukas Cranach.

VADIANUS AND JOHANNES KESSLER OF ST GALL

More attractive and more lasting was his friendship with his contemporary Collimitius.[1] He too was a Doctor of Medicine and a Rector of the university, but his main interest was in mathematics and astronomy, so that his medical knowledge was highly theoretical. Like Chaucer's Doctour of Phisyk,

> *he was grounded in astronomye.*
> *He kepte his pacient a full greet del*
> *In houres, by his magik naturel.*
> *Wel coude he fortunen the ascendent*
> *Of his images for his pacient.*

Vadianus shared his friend's interest in cosmology, dabbled too in astronomical calculations, which he would brush up after thirty years in the agreeable fuss over Halley's Comet.

The circle of Viennese humanism was small. Despite its imposing syllabus – with its wide range of lectures in poetry, history, mathematics, geography, astronomy, medicine, music – the teaching concentrated on a few dull texts. And as the staff lectured on them, edited them, published them, and then lectured on them again, dedicating their efforts to their brighter pupils, they could hardly avoid treading on one another's toes; and so the German Cuspinianus became involved in waspish battle with the Italian Camers about their rival editions of the Roman History of L. Florus, dragging their pupils John Marius and Vadianus into a silly academic rumpus of the kind which justifies Knox's parody that

> *Dons delight to bark and bite,*
> *For 'tis their nature to.*

Vadianus followed his seniors up the academic ladder. In turn he too taught, edited and published texts for his pupils. He too became Professor of Poetry, University Orator; he too was crowned a Laureate of the Empire (that year laurel leaves were in short supply, so he had to make do with box). He too became Doctor of Medicine, Rector of the university. By 1518 there were no more academic worlds for him to conquer in Vienna.

[1] Näf, i, 176ff.

Yet Vadianus was not a type. There is about him an independence which marks him out from his contemporaries. He went to Padua and indulged at first hand the fashionable Italian enthusiasm for poetry. He himself wrote and published poems, notably 'The Cockfight' ('Gallus Pugnans'), a satire which attracted some attention. His *De Poetica* was a less popular work, rather like a modern Inaugural Lecture, in which he tried to relate the science of words to the wider realms of natural knowledge. He made and published some notable orations.

Rhetoric alone, however, did not touch the springs of his mind. On a visit home in 1509 he had fished out of the great Abbey library a wonderful find: Walafrid Strabo's *Hortulus*, which, with its combination of poetry and botanic lore, made him an admirable text on which to lecture and which he successfully published. His interest in historical studies was a later development; but at this time it was geography which enthralled him, and in this field he achieved real eminence, showing a taste for first-hand observation which ranks him among the pioneers of modern geographical science. His great achievement was his edition of the three books of Pomponius Mela. His colleague, John Camers, had inevitably also published an edition, but he had concentrated on the text and showed a typically scholastic deference to authority. Vadianus would have none of this and he roundly rejected Aristotle and Pliny when they ran counter to proven observation.

He loved to travel and was a keen observer of the countryside. In 1507 he toured the coast between Venice and Trieste and spent some time investigating the marvels of the underground river Timavus. His *scholia* to his edition of Pomponius Mela were an astonishing medley of learning and observation. This was specially true of the enlarged edition of 1522.

Then he had a modern way of dragging pupils with him on expeditions, and he took Conrad Grebel and Oswald Myconius to the top of Mount Pilatus, perhaps the first time that the mountain was scaled for scientific purposes.[1] But the trip illustrates the limitations of scientific humanism, for Vadianus wanted most of all to test the legend that at the summit there was a magic lake whose

[1] Näf, i, 272

waters boiled and bubbled when anything was cast into it by human hand. With a Jules Verne-like polarity he also explored the centre of the earth, going down into two Polish salt mines, leaving his scared research assistant Agricola – 'caput vertiginosum' was the excuse – outside, but himself subordinating his inner qualms to keen observations of his own physical reaction, examining the structure of the rocks, and probing with questions the miners about the organization of the mining industry.[1] His *scholia* show that he had devoted a good deal of thought to what we might call the rationale of geographical study and its relation to cosmology.

In 1514 he began medical studies and took his doctorate three years later, so that these studies were pursued in addition to his own miscellaneous teaching programme. In turning to medicine he may have been influenced by his old school teacher, Johannes Schürpf, one of whose sons would become his pupil. More probably he was following the academic fashion in Vienna, where, if one did not study law, medicine was not so much a vocation as the highway for a layman to acquire a doctor's degree. The discipline was appallingly literary and theoretical, so that, while regular syllogistic disputations were indispensable, there were no practical tests and a woeful minimum of clinical experience was demanded. Small wonder that when the plague struck Vienna the entire medical faculty, with the exception of Martin Stainpeis, hastily stampeded elsewhere. There was about this Viennese polymathy a peril of dilettantism and it may have been responsible for the one real failure in Vadianus' career.

By 1518, then, he had arrived. He had published. He had held all the offices of honour in the university. He had a circle of devoted pupils including some very bright young men indeed – Andreas Eck from St Gall, Conrad Grebel, and his own younger brother Melchior (this last to die tragically young). He had a widening circle of correspondents so that some 4,000 letters to him have survived. He was in touch with eminent musicians like Hofhaimer of Salzburg and wrote the scripts for some musical works.

Then, abruptly, he abandoned his university posts and went off home, to spend the remainder of his days in the small town of

[1] Näf, ii, 66ff.

St Gall (not above 4,500 inhabitants). It disconcerted his friends, but it was a providential decision. Vienna had little more to offer. He had reached his academic ceiling. It would always be nice to have seen the view from the academic summit, but it was perhaps not as exciting as ambitious young men are wont to believe. Now the way was to open to increasing fruitfulness and satisfaction.

In September 1518 the Council of St Gall appointed Vadianus as Town Physician with a stipend of 50 florins. Vadianus evidently took it much as Erasmus took his pensions, as a retainer for scholarly services – as his letter to the Freiburg statesman, Peter Falck, clearly shows. Certainly his movements in the next year and a half show no serious preoccupation with his medical responsibilities. He was away for many months, travelling with Grebel to Zürich and making a long journey through Poland and then back to Vienna, on his faithful humanist horse, Mutz, renamed Mucius. Grebel persuaded him that he needed a wife, and that his sister might do. So he married Martha Grebel. It was between his betrothal and his marriage, when he was away from home, that the plague struck St Gall with unparalleled ferocity, carrying off a third of the inhabitants, over 1,700 in a few months. All this while Vadianus, Town Physician, stayed away.[1]

A good enough case can be made out. What good could he have done had he returned, with an entirely academic training which could hardly cope with common colds, let alone this cruel and baffling horror? The only probable effect would have been to add his name to the list of victims. It is a fact that many contemporary physicians added 'non-attendance in time of plague' to their terms of contract. It was the parsons who were expected to stay at all costs, as they stayed and died with their flocks in St Gall that year; but they had something they could do – bury the dead, offer ghostly comfort to the dying, cheer those overshadowed by the cruel penumbra of fear and the dread of the brutal measures, so vividly imagined a century later by Defoe, with which plague-stricken towns sought to isolate the demon in their midst. What could be done medically could be done as well by an apothecary, and in July 1519 Matthias Oswald was appointed as a kind of medi-

[1] Näf, ii, 75ff.; Milt *Vadianus als Arzt* pp. 50ff.

cal vicar. None the less there was murmuring in some quarters by citizens unimpressed by the news that their doctor had married a wife and therefore could not come. Nor did it help that he had written a manual for them, 'How to deal with the Plague', still less that this do-it-yourself handbook was held up in the press, appearing only when the dark waters were subsiding. There is something a little cold-blooded about a letter from Father Leonard at this time in which names of neighbours who have died give pride of place to a long and moving description of the death of old Mucius – the faithful horse.[1]

That Vadianus had a conscience about it is shown by the fact that he wrote, and submitted to a spiritual adviser, a memorandum on the duty of a Christian in time of plague, in which perhaps he protests too much and the arguments come out a little too pat on his side. But the best proof that he knew there had been a failure of nerve came later, in his own courage in later epidemics, in 1530 and 1541. In 1541 he organized a large-scale evacuation to Marbach, and packed off his wife and his daughter Dorothy. He himself stayed, and in one of his finest letters wrote: 'I am not scared . . . I stick to the job . . . though I can neither eat or drink, and joy has withered.' And if even here we feel it is the Burgomaster rather than the Town Physician speaking, he was by then an honoured father of his people, knowing them by name, not needing to send to inquire for whom the bell tolled.

The next years show Vadianus growingly preoccupied with the cause of the Reformation. His theological studies begin now with the biblical humanism of Erasmus. Though the two men met only once in an interview which kindled no warmth on either side, Vadianus is an Erasmian. He accepted the new critical methods of Valla, Reuchlin and Erasmus. The Erasmus New Testament, with its critical apparatus, was of moment for him. This turned him to the direct study of the New Testament, to the philosophy of Christ in the Gospels, to the pattern of Primitive Christianity and to the study of the Old Fathers in the new printed editions, such as that of Tertullian by Beatus Rhenanus in 1521. Then came the influence of Wittenberg, of Luther and Melanchthon. He had been in contact

[1] *Vadianische Briefsammlung* ii, No. 139 (wrongly dated)

with Zwingli since 1511, but not until 1523 did their correspondence become regular and intimate.

In these years when Zwingli had published little, a flood of writing was available from Luther, and like many another European scholar, Vadianus' attention was held, and his reading conditioned, by every crisis of the growing Church struggle in 1517–21. Luther's arguments, above all about the authority of Scripture, made great appeal. Vadianus became the centre of a small 'Academy' which included the clergy, Benedict Burgauer, Wolfgang Wetter, and the schoolmaster Dominicus Zili. For their benefit he copied out many scriptural passages about the papal primacy and its history, and followed this with important quotations from Erasmus and Melanchthon. He also penned a discussion of the creeds, *Brevis indicatura symbolorum*, which had been initiated by a discussion in the group of the Descent into Hell, a favourite theme of 16th-century theological discussion groups.[1]

There was nothing unusual in a layman tackling such a theological theme. Pirckheimer wrote about purgatory, and the two Peutingers, man and wife, could debate whether St Paul was married. Vadianus followed Valla and dismissed the view that the Apostles' Creed was what Coleridge once called a 'picnic contribution' of the twelve apostles in turn. But he quotes Luther with approval, upholds the supreme authority of Scripture, and there is some indication that he has moved theologically beyond the Erasmian position. That view is confirmed by his next and major theological achievement, lectures on the Acts of the Apostles which he gave, no doubt in Latin, to the learned group, and the MS. of which, *Collectanea in Acta Apostolorum*, has survived.[2]

It was an admirable choice. Like himself, St Luke was 'medicus evangelicus', and a study of the Acts would bring home to his own mind and that of his audience the contrast between primitive and contemporary Christianity ('fateor me non videre aliam magis

[1] cf. Joachim Vadian *Brevis Indicatura Symbolorum* (Vadian-Studien 4), ed. Bonorand, text and translation by Konrad Müller, St Gall 1954

[2] Näf, ii, 151ff.; Bonorand *Vadians Weg* gives an important analysis with extracts, pp. 111ff. Our observations derive from first-hand inspection of the never published MS. (No. 59: Stadtbibliothek St Gallen).

commodam rationem reformandae ecclesiae ... quam ut ad apostolorum exemplum ... omnes consilium nostrum accommodemus': MS. fol. 112). It offered in addition pleasant scope for Vadianus' historical and geographical learning. He took great pains with the MS. and it is neatly written, with texts marked out in red. It begins with a quotation from Bede to the effect that the Holy Spirit protected St Luke from error, and it ends by submitting the commentary to the supreme judgement of Holy Scripture. Vadianus went about the business in a scholarly way, making good use of previous commentaries, notably of Jerome and Bede. There is also evident a humanist debt to Valla, to Budaeus and above all to Erasmus. It is perhaps a scholarly and academic rather than a theological commentary. Then at Acts 12 he paused and for several weeks gave a great geographical excursus which he illustrated with maps. Those of us who suffered in our adolescence with a surfeit of St Paul's missionary journeys – with maps – will find a certain sombre interest, if little joy, in the thought that probably Vadianus was the first to teach in this way in modern times. At any rate the geographical excursus was important enough to be published separately at a later date. The theological comments are not profound and often range from the banal to the obscure. I do not find it easy to say how far he has stepped beyond Erasmus, though he is certainly Augustinian and perhaps Lutheran in his view of grace and predestination and the relation of saving faith and Christian liberty.

I do not think there is any real connexion between these extramural lectures by Vadianus before a small learned audience and the popular Reformation which developed in the city later that year. Meanwhile great events were taking place in Zürich which were to set the pace and pattern for the Reformation in the Swiss cities. Vadianus may not have attended the first Zürich Disputation in the Grossmünster in April 1523; but he not only attended the second, in October 1523, which dealt with images and with the Mass, but was elected one of the three Presidents of the debate. It fell to him to make the closing speech in which, speaking with deference of the authority of the magistrates of Zürich, he echoed Zwingli's (and his brother-in-law Conrad Grebel's!) assertion that the sole supreme judge must be the Word of God. In St Gall his authority was growing and he became a *Ratsherr* on the death of his father in 1521. In the next months it was of great importance that he was within the town council, able to defend and expound events, and to keep the magistracy in some sort of step with public opinion. He himself was no demagogue, and perhaps lacked the common touch which might have made him the leader of a popular movement. He had perhaps a too scholarly knack of seeing many sides to a question, and perhaps, despite his great gifts, not too much imagination?

At any rate, what Vadianus could not give, another son of the little town supplied. On 9 December 1523 a student, bedraggled and shabby, returned to the town, a kind of academic prodigal son to Vadianus as Elder Brother. For Johannes Kessler[1] had little to show for his study at a foreign university, and had come down without taking a degree. But then, that university was Wittenberg, and he had come back with his head and his notebooks stuffed with first-hand and exciting notions from the lectures of Luther, Melanchthon and Karlstadt. So much so that when, quietly and contentedly, he tried to settle down at the trade of saddler, his fellow citizens would have none of it. Some days later, he was taken to lunch by some of them, who suggested that he might lead some sort of Bible class for the citizens. And Kessler could not deny that he had a splendidly apt set of notes from Melanchthon on John. The little gathering was an immediate success and had to adjourn to a larger room, and then to a still larger hall. Soon a rumour of these happenings reached the Diet of the Confederacy, who charged a member of the Council to visit Kessler and suggest that he stopped.

Was this Council member Vadianus? If so, then the encounter, never described, is as important as the famous meeting of Dr Johnson and James Boswell in the back parlour of Mr Davies. For, wherever and however they met, there was something of their relationship which was similar, of sage and disciple. Kessler was to become the biographer of Vadianus and his literary heir, and though their economic roles were reversed and poor Kessler was no Laird of Auchinleck, he was, in his naïve admiration and his sublime innocence of his own immortal powers, another Boswell. For Johannes Kessler is one of the world's great story-tellers, and there is more

[1] 1502-74

life in a paragraph by him than in all the thousand pages of the Vadianus MSS. He is an inspired gossip, a sanctified Pepys, with a gift for making thumb-nail sketches of people and events, and with the instincts and imagination of a true historian.

His marvellous *Sabbata*[1] is far above the average contemporary chronicle, of which there were not a few. He wrote it for and dedicated it to his two little sons, in words which illustrate that priesthood of a Christian parent which joined the best medieval with the best new Reformation doctrine:

> To my dear sons David and John and all my successors I, John Kessler, wish grace, peace and true knowledge of the right faith. . . . I felt myself in duty bound as your father, bishop, teacher and Obrigkeit not only to nourish your bodies but your soul, and to write down and hand over to you some account of what happened in my lifetime in the city of St Gall.[2]

The title 'Sabbaths' is explained because he wrote only on Sundays and holidays

> to forestall your reproof . . . for I have never neglected my handiwork or any other labour to write this book, but only used the times and hours of holidays . . . in those evening hours when other people take their ease and go to sleep.[3]

And the failed B.A.(Wittenberg) had perhaps got the root of learning in him when he wrote:

> Many people spend their leisure in idling . . . but he who loves books is well situated in a corner, by himself, yet open towards heaven, and he speaks with God and God with him. O sweet and friendly conversation! He looks across the whole earth and sees the wonders of the Lord. Himself in quiet and safety, he crosses the great oceans, learns the ways of folks in many strange lands, their customs and their way of life. He treats with Kings and Emperors, takes part unharmed in their great conferences – and in their wars, defeats and victories – and so in a tiny space of time and without going any distance he can overlook a thousand years; he can think back as far as Adam the first man – is not that a

---

[1] An English anthology is much to be desired.
[2] *Sabbata* p. 3   [3] ibid., p. 13

marvellous moment of time! – and can go on to see all the marvellous things which God has wrought. It is impossible to tell the wonderful things which can befall a student. . . .[1]

He has a talent for particularity, can tell you the house where the Bible readings began, show you the mark in the floor where the broken images were burned. There was no chronicler of the time who could speak more charitably and truthfully about the Anabaptists – and the fanatic fringe well represented in St Gall; while, like Vadianus himself, he has a lively sense of the colour and beauty of much of the old religion, and a sense of hurt at wanton destruction. He had therefore a gift and a flair which led his fellow citizens to drag him out again and again to be their helper. And he never grumbled, never gave himself airs, kept lowly modesty.

In St Gall there was no parson of eminence, for Benedict Burgauer perhaps deserved Grebel's acid comment: 'pastor nebulonem' – Johnny head-in-the-clouds! Burgauer seems always to be a step behind events, puzzling about purgatory when the people were excited about baptism, arguing about the Real Presence when the city was in imminent likelihood of becoming the first City of Refuge for the Anabaptists. It was therefore owing to Vadianus that in the disturbed years 1524–31 St Gall did not meet with irreparable disaster, thanks to a moderation which, as Zwingli said of him, 'required neither spur nor bridle'. In February 1524 the Council, following the strategy of other cities, passed a decree ordering that preaching be according to the Gospel. But they did more: the enactment was not left to become a dead letter, but a committee of four was appointed to judge of preaching in case of controversy, and Vadianus was a standing member of the committee, originally half but finally wholly lay in composition. He was becoming known as champion of Reform and at the Diet of Zug there was a hubbub when he rose to speak. Indeed so menacing were his adversaries on that occasion that he had to withdraw through the streets ever more quickly until at last with a companion he arrived muddy and dishevelled and weary at the house of the friendly Abbot of Cappel.

Vadianus did not direct the popular movement. Here the

[1] ibid., p. 14

initiative came from the guilds and from the Bible classes. Kessler had stopped for a while, but a crisis was provoked when an unfrocked monk from Chur, Ulmann, succeeded him, and took charge of immensely popular gatherings which had again to move to ever larger premises. The authorities wisely did not interfere, but simply asked Kessler to resume Bible readings, accompanied by Dominicus Zili in the parish church of St Laurence. But there were comings and goings between the two groups, and when Kessler began to expound the 6th chapter of Romans he was loudly interrupted by Laurence Hochrütiner, newly out of gaol in Zürich, where he had been imprisoned for breaking images. Now began the debate about infant baptism which had begun in Zürich with Conrad Grebel and his friends.

Grebel himself, from being a classical humanist of rather nauseating artificiality – his letter to Vadianus on the death of his father has the word 'dolet' nearly 70 times! – and one of the more rumbustious students of Glareanus, whose academic gang brawled from university to university, now became an uncompromising biblicist, a Founding Father of the Swiss Brethren and one who did his best to convert Vadianus to his own views. In the early months of 1525 the Anabaptists became a mass movement and Grebel visited St Gall, where at Easter he baptized some hundreds in the river Sitter. At this time the whole town was in a ferment. On that same day Vadianus was called out to deal with a female mob of 60 housewives who menaced the nuns of St Leonard – headed by a nasty and very pious virago named Frau Mutter Wiborata Mörli, who uttered blood-curdling threats about what ought to happen to the magistracy. It says much for Vadianus that he was able to talk her round and restore order and good humour. By now the Council was alarmed indeed – it was the full spate of the Peasants' War – and it seemed as if St Gall might go right over to the radicals and indeed become a city of refuge for the Anabaptist Reformation. On 12 May 1525 the Council asked for memoranda from both sides, one from Vadianus, the other from the Anabaptists, while armed guards were standing to, and cannons primed. At this juncture Zwingli's tract against the Anabaptists arrived, dedicated to the citizens of St Gall. Dominic Zili announced that he would read it aloud in St

Laurence's, but when he did, it was found that the Anabaptists were there in force and they began to interrupt with 'Tell us what the Word of God says, not what Zwingli says . . .!', though in the event they clamoured to have a letter from Grebel read aloud.

It was a turning point. On 5 June the Council made up its mind. It acted with firmness but also with a leniency and moderation which won back many from the extremist ranks. Anabaptist practices would not be permitted within the city and any who were rebaptized were liable to heavy fine, but – astonishing concession! – they might hold their Bible readings at the same hour as the official ones. Thus the onus of separation was passed to the radicals, who became more and more an underground movement with a more than average share of wild men and women, of which the terrible Schugger fratricide, when one brother beheaded another at the alleged behest of the Holy Spirit, was the culminating scandal and deterrent.

At the end of 1525 Vadianus became Burgomaster, and for the rest of his life alternated between the three civic offices: Burgomaster, ex-Burgomaster, and Imperial Officer or Reichsvogt. But not for another year was the town settled enough to proceed to public reformation. Then at the end of 1526 came the reforming edicts, for the removal of images, the abolition of the Mass, the institution of evangelical communion in both kinds (Vadianus was the first to receive in this way, in St Laurence's at Easter 1527).

The Abbey, that great emblem of the past, was another proposition. Vadianus knew how intricate were the issues involved in its secularization – what political cross-currents would be set up throughout the Confederacy. To lay hands on the Abbey in the name of the town would not be a religious act alone but a political *coup* – another round in an ancient struggle which had cost so dear in 1491. And St Gall could not consider this in isolation. The Baden disputation of 1526 had already hardened and strengthened the recovering opposition of the Catholic cantons. The reformers had also drawn closer together and in the great Bern disputation of 1528 Vadianus was a President of debate and an eminent figure. Now Zürich had begun to build up the Christian civic league and into it St Gall must be inevitably drawn.

VADIANUS AND JOHANNES KESSLER OF ST GALL

The crisis for the Abbey came on 23 February 1529, when Vadianus and other civic officers entered the precincts and presented an ultimatum, ignoring the protests of the Dean and Chapter and their appeal to the protection of the surrounding cantons. The Council intended to remove the images, but rumours had gone through the town and Vadianus and the leaders were roughly brushed aside by a great and excited mob who exercised for hours their destructive propensities in the name of their holy religion. How they turned the great nave into a battlefield is one of the great stories of Kessler, who wondered that no lives were lost but only sticks and stones broken that day, and looked on sadly as forty cartloads of imperishable beauty were turned to rubble and taken to the market place.[1]

The formal secularization of the Abbey which followed was a complex financial, legal and political affair in which St Gall was not allowed a free hand. The town was free of the Prince Abbot, but had now to accept the presence of officials from Zürich – which seemed to many a bit of power politics. The truth is that most of the great cities of that age had a strong vein of civic imperialism, and in a crisis tended to play for their own hand. None the less Zwingli and Vadianus were on good terms, and when a Synod was held at St Gall in 1530, Zwingli took advantage of the absence of Vadianus – he had gone to arbitrate in a dispute between Bern and the Count of Savoy – to say, 'And now, in his absence let me say something about your Vadianus – in all Switzerland there is not his like.' But St Gall was not able to dictate the pace of events and was drawn into the desperate policies which culminated for Zürich in the disaster of Cappel in October 1531. St Gall lost a score of men (out of a banner of fifty) in a secondary skirmish a few days later – among them Andrew Eck. When Vadianus read the casualty list and saw that among those dead were twenty-four chaplains he shook his head and frowned, and took it to be a sign from heaven that 'ministers of the Word should teach peace and ensue it, not war!' He took part in the long peace negotiations and when the harsh peace terms were read out from the Catholic side, he collapsed, stunned and crying, 'Oh, the dear, godly people of St Gall!'[2]

[1] Näf, ii, 292; *Sabbata* pp. 209ff.   [2] Näf, ii, 340

But he soon recovered, and was able to resume his constant travels for political and religious consultation, journeys arduous but also leisurely enough for him to alight and pick a bunch of violets in an uncommonly early spring and bring them home safely from the Rheintal for his Martha. And in fact the years of crisis were over, and St Gall was able to benefit from the more peaceful policies at Zürich of Henry Bullinger. One breach remained open, the unhealed ulcer of the Reformation – the eucharistic controversy; and as bitter disputation swelled between the Swiss and the Germans, Vadianus was more and more attracted by the eirenical policy of Martin Bucer. He had never lost his admiration for Luther, and when Bucer pulled off the Wittenberg Concord in 1536 Vadianus felt that the views of the Swiss to be set forth at the Basle Synod, might not be unreconcilable either. So he wrote *Six Books of Aphorisms* and sent a copy with a covering letter to Luther – all in vain. It is interesting that he also sent a copy to Archbishop Thomas Cranmer in England, who perhaps read them a little hastily and took what was intended as an eirenicon to be a statement of the extreme Swiss point of view. Vadianus was also interested in Christological problems and became engaged in not very fruitful controversy with that virtuoso among theologically minded laymen, Caspar Schwenckfeld.[1]

Because in that age theology was news, he had no difficulty in getting his theology published, and he was not perhaps a very good theologian. But his historical studies, which remained in MS., are of real interest.[2] He resumed them in 1533 and kept at them on and off for the rest of his life. If he had led the attack on the great Abbey, he had capitulated to its fascination – and if he robbed it of archives it was to brood for years upon their content. He read up the geographical and historical background so that he has dissertations on the history of St Gall and of Lake Constance, and an historical account of the Roman emperors and the Frankish kings. He wrote two Chronicles of the Abbey and handed some of his material to Stumpf for his well-known Chronicle. But he never lost sight of the wider perspective, and composed an intriguing examination (1544)

[1] Näf, ii, 422–62
[2] Vadiana MSS. Nos 43, 45: Stadtbibliothek St Gallen; Näf, ii, 377ff.

of the four ages of Christian history, an interpretation of the story as a decline and fall from primitive Christianity. In the next years he wrote a dissertation on the history of monasticism, drawing lessons for the reformers, and for the whole Church. It is strange that he found the ideal monk to be – Erasmus! But then for him Erasmus is the combination of contemplation and of learning, the very genius of St Gall.[1] These thousands of pages, often hurriedly but never carelessly written, witness to the alertness of his mind and interests. He went on learning all his days, a scholar to the very end.

Amid so many occupations, medicine must always have been something of a sideline. But he had long ceased to be merely an academic, for he took an interest in his patients and was but little concerned about fees. Eminent friends consulted him for free advice about their divers diseases and he sent good advice. A little memorandum on the stone, from which he himself suffered, is full of common sense and shows that he put a stress on diet and on baths. Like Chaucer's doctor,

> *He knew the cause of everich maladye,*
> *Were it of hoot or cold, or moiste, or drye,*
> *And where engendred, and of what humour;*
> *He was a verrey parfit practisour.*
> *The cause y-knowe, and of his harm the rote,*
> *Anon he yaf the seke man his bote.*

And anon, on the other hand, he was not so successful. There are two vivid letters from a nun, written in an ecstasy of fear that she had contracted leprosy – with all her fear of death and of solitary confinement; and his reply reflects his kindness and common sense as he assures her that the symptoms she describes may be something trivial. And there is the letter, which should be in any 16th-century anthology, about his little grandchild Sabine and her fever – how a worried grandfather noted all the symptoms: the headaches, flushed face, sickness. Then the crisis, and a great sweat and a sleep, and the little girl awoke to eat some raspberries and, from the privileged position which she knew she now enjoyed, began to order the whole household about.[2] But when the great Paracelsus

[1] Näf, ii, 408 [2] Milt *Vadian als Arzt* pp. 78, 110, 107

was summoned to St Gall to treat Christopher Studer, a former burgomaster, we wonder if it was with Vadianus' approval and connivance – or whether he suspected him as a famous charlatan?

His evangelical convictions had rather strengthened than weakened his interest in the world of nature, and in his later years his earlier belief in the unity of truth found coherence in a simple faith. This comes out in Kessler's wonderful story of how Vadianus greeted Halley's Comet in 1531. As of old, he organized an expedition; and with a few friends, Andreas Eck, Kessler, and his bosom friend John Rütiner, they climbed half-way up the Berneck. The professor, long emeritus, got out his old astronomical tables and proved to his own satisfaction that it was indeed a comet, and not a planet, that they were going to see. Then he suggested they climbed to the top. But Andreas Eck voiced the sentiments of the younger men when he cried, 'Oh, doctor! that is not for you. You are a heavy man and the going will be hard. And those fine leather breeches will be ruined by the dew.' To which Vadianus gave the Johnsonian reply: 'Sir, I am coming. For such company I would give not only my breeches, but my legs!' So they sat down under a velvet sky at the summit, lightened by the brilliance of the heavens in the still, clear air. And Vadianus began to speak – of the wonders of the sky, of the machinery of the heavens, pointing with stubby fingers, singling out the constellations by name, until there burst from his lips, 'Ah, how dearly I long to see the wonderful Creator of all this!' Then he turned his gaze to the earth and told them of how he had brought his fellow geographer and reformer, Sebastian Münster, to this very spot, and of the earlier centuries, how the Romans had been here long ago, leaving their memory in the local names. They went into the little half-way house – Vadianus on a bench near the window – and then at last! the star, which proved to be, not after all the comet, but Venus, morning star.

Amid the dawn chorus of the birds they picked their way down again, and once more he motioned them to sit. And now they stared down at their own beloved little St Gall – its roofs and towers and steeples shining in the morning light; and he spoke to them of the great Abbey and its long story, of the town, and of the love-hate struggle between them, and of the families and notables and people of other days. Could there be a finer picture of true humanism than this microcosm and macrocosm joined in one, in reverence before the Creator who stretches out the heavens as a curtain and who has set the solitary in families! Here is something which looks back to the Psalmists and forward to Ray and Newton and Teilhard de Chardin. It may be small-scale greatness, but it is authentic and fine.

'Consul vigilantissimus', said his obituary; and the lapidary phrase has the root of the matter. If St Gall, so exposed and so more vulnerable than almost any city of the Reformation, survived in freedom through critical years, it owed more to Vadianus than to anybody else. A city which could only raise a banner of fifty understood better perhaps than its more powerful neighbours that it is the Word of God which guards the Church, and God who guards a city. Swarthy, bull-necked, massively built, in age his grizzled hair framing his bald head, he had a genuine dignity. He was perhaps a little heavy in manner, but he had humour and kindliness and was never pompous, and had qualities of modesty and friendliness at which Kessler never ceased to marvel. It was an age of great laymen: lay humanists even, Conrad Peutinger, Willibald Pirckheimer, Sir Thomas More; of lay reformers like Sir John Cheke or Lord Burghley: or Caspar Schwenckfeld and Pilgram Marbeck. Vadianus did not go on the great embassies, to Bruges or Augsburg or Ratisbon; but he exercised his vocation in the place where God had called him, and that which came upon him daily, the care of his dear, godly people of St Gall.

His health deteriorated swiftly in the spring of 1551 and soon, with the certainty of his profession, he knew that nothing could be done. He arranged for his fine library and for his manuscripts to be given to the town. He handed to John Kessler the book which had sustained him in all dark and dangerous hours, his New Testament. He confessed plainly his faith in Christ and grasped firmly his friends' hands before going on his greatest journey, to contemplate with his own eyes his 'wonderful Creator'.

We left Kessler teaching the Bible, but during the years 1525-7 he had gone back quietly to his trade. He had married in 1525 and soon had children to provide for. But St Gall was a small city, with few citizens of intellectual equipment, and he was not allowed to stay a craftsman. In 1537 to his astonishment he was made master of the School of St Gall, and he made a very good one, attracting scholars from other towns and other lands, though he sent his own boys elsewhere. Then in 1542 he was invited to become town preacher and, though sermons were not his gift and he must have been what the 17th century called a 'painful preacher' in an all-round sense, he did what he was told. In the next years he became preacher of St Laurence and chief pastor of St Gall. Finally in 1571 he became first Secretary and then Superintendent and evangelical Bishop of the region of St Gall. His wife died in 1573 after a remarkably happy married life, and when John Kessler followed a few months later in 1574, he also was honoured as a pillar of the Church and a father of his people.

The two men, Vadianus and Kessler, are entirely dissimilar. Both illustrate the difficulty of defining 'Layman', then or now. Both were in their ways ecclesiastical persons. Yet Vadianus somehow is the emblem of the godly magistrate, the leading layman – while Kessler, dodge it how he might, was essentially a minister of the Word. He had the gifts of teaching and of the cure of souls. Compared with Vadianus (and it is a comparison he would never have dreamed of making) he was a man of two talents but by zeal and diligence they became ten. The style is the man, and the style of the great *Sabbata* is that of a faithful, humble Christian. Vadianus and Kessler take their place in the long witness of St Gall to the light of divine wisdom.

'You are here to kneel
'Where prayer has been valid.'

APPENDIX

'OF THE MYSTERY OF BAPTISM'[1]

Of the Mystery of Baptism, both of its Sign and of its Essence, a Beginning of a Right and True Christian Life; John 5 [:39:] 'Search the Scriptures; for you think you have life in them; and they it is who bear witness of me.'

The pure fear of God as the Beginning of divine Wisdom, I wish to all brothers and sisters in the Lord, the pure genuine Christendom, the people [*gmein*] of God, the only spouse and bride of Christ, united in the bond of charity through the Moving of the Holy Ghost, and to all those who with contrite hearts and broken spirit yearn after the earnest righteousness of the crucified Son of God, and to all those who seek to be fed by it, I wish grace and peace in the Holy Ghost, Amen.

Whereas the last and most dangerous age of this world is now come upon us, so we see and recognize with seeing eyes, how all those things which from the beginning have been foretold and preached by the prophets, patriarchs, and apostles as to happen, are now at work afresh and will be restored, as Peter prophesied to us beforehand in the Acts of the Apostles, concerning which the whole world (God have mercy on us!) has not the very slightest power of discrimination [*urtl*] and especially those who teach other men and have less understanding of such things than apes, even though they would be masters of the Scriptures and teachers, and yet it is seven

---

[1] A translation of the radical tract ascribed to Hans Huth, and published in L. Müller *Glaubenszeugnisse oberdeutscher Taufgesinnter* (1938), pp. 13ff. Part of it was also contained in the *Kunstbuch* recently rediscovered in Bern (Codex 464) and I have collated it with this, and with the manuscript in Budapest. The variants are not of major importance.

times sealed to them and they will not and may not let it be opened to them through the Work of God, to which they are enemies, as Paul says. That is why all they teach and read has a perverted Order and a false Judgement, and is in the highest degree concealed and hidden, and because of this the common man is led astray and deceived and brought to all manner of dangerous and baleful harm, which nobody will believe, although it has been told and preached to them.

No worldly, carnal-minded Scribe can or may know the Judgements of the Lord, for as they are perverted, so are they perverted in all things, and lead both rich and poor astray with their ornate words. So be it, whoso will be misled, will always be misled. Therefore I warn all godly men, who bear a desire and love of righteousness, diligently to guard themselves from all grasping, carnal-minded, ambitious and hypocritical Scribes, who preach for money: they do not mind you, but their bellies, for in them is to be seen no other kind of life than is seen in other worldly men, and whosoever relies on them will be deceived. For all the teaching you get from them is nothing but 'Believe!' and goes no further. For they do not say by what means a man shall come to it, which is why the world draws back in horror before them. For where the Order of the divine Mystery is not kept, there is sheer error, and it may not stand. That we see in everything. Therefore, my dearly beloved brethren in the Lord, you must learn the Judgements of God about his own commandments and word, and be instructed by God in these things, otherwise you will be deceived along with the rest of the world. For they do not know a single Judgement, still less what Judgement is. So they say we are not to know the Judgements of God for they are incomprehensible to us.

This they prove against themselves from St Paul, and forget what he says in 1 Corinthians [2] and also Solomon [Wisdom 9] and also how David diligently besought the Lord that he would teach him his Judgements.[1] This God called them with solemn commandment to learn, keep and accomplish. And if we are to keep and do the same, then we must also know them. How cruelly they now deceive the whole world under the cloak of holy Scripture with their

[1] Vg: 'judicia'; ML: 'Rechte'; Zw: 'Gebote'

'OF THE MYSTERY OF BAPTISM'

false and feigned faith, from which not a jot of improvement comes. This let each judge for himself, and watch them and he will see that when two or three of them preach on one text, no one expounding agrees with another.

And so, my dearly beloved brethren in the Lord, choose you the Judgements of God, and learn aright the witness of the holy Scriptures to the truth, and pay no heed to the cries of these hireling preachers, but give heed rather to the poor, despised by the world, who will be railed at as fanatics and devils, after the example of Christ and the apostles. Hear them. For no man may come to the truth, unless he follow in the footsteps of Christ and his elect in the school of all tribulation, or have at least in some small part pledged himself[1] to follow the will of God in the justifying [*rechtfertigung*] of the Cross of Christ.

For none may learn the mystery of divine Wisdom in the dens or thieves' kitchens [*mördergrueben*][2] of all manner of knavery as they imagine in Wittenberg or at Paris. Neither is it to be learned from the courts of princes, or from fat benefices. For the wisdom of God does not dwell where Brother Soft Raiment[3] is. Our new gospellers, the dear Scribes, have put down the pope, the monks and the parsons from their seats. And now when they have succeeded in this, they go a whoring afresh with the Babylonish drab, in all manner of lust, pomp, honours, ambition, envy and hatred, to the detriment of the whole world, and set up, God have mercy on us, a worse popery than before against the common man, will not listen and cannot suffer themselves to be convicted by the Scriptures, for they would not be found out to be ignorant or unlearned, and so all those who do not believe as they do must be the most arrant knaves, devils, false prophets and fanatics, as also happened to Christ.

So be it, let us leave them to cool their spirits with their gods and

---

[1] 'verwilligt'

[2] lit. 'murderpits', from ML: Jer. 7:11; Matt. 21:13; Mark 11:17; Luke 19:46; cf. also Karlstadt, 'Von abtuhung', p. 4: *MQR* (1960), p. 28

[3] lit. 'Soft Life'. This phrase, applied by Müntzer to Luther ('Sanftleben') may have a more general reference here, and I have used the phrase 'Soft Raiment', with its suggestion of the contrast between John the Baptist and those who dwell in palaces, because of its Scriptural association.

great ones, whose ears they tickle, as long as God consents, for they have still a little time before every man will see them publicly come to a shameful end. And so I, moved by Christian love and brotherly fidelity, will declare the Judgements, which are needful for the beginning of the Christian life, as much as God gives me grace thereto, to deliver as a witness to all those brothers and sisters in the Lord, who from their hearts hunger and thirst after righteousness and not at all after the will of worldly, carnal-minded men, for such Judgements are to these incomprehensible, too subtle, perverted, heretical, despicable and damnable.

So I admonish all brothers and sisters who have a love and desire for the truth, that when at the beginning such written Judgements shall have been read to you, you will not despise them, where you cannot understand them, for it seems impossible to everybody, on account of the improper way in which he is misled and deceived by the new Scribes (and to their own understanding too) by which the world is deceived. And so at the very beginning if we would come to a right understanding of such Judgements, we must become as little children and fools, for it is a high and impossible thing for a carnal man to grasp the Judgements of God in the truth, where they are not put together and composed with all the parts[1] in a proper Order.

And so at the beginning, and first of all we will treat the Judgement of Baptism, a beginning of the Christian life, and diligently see and mark how Christ instituted it, ordained it and how it has been kept by the apostles with proof from the divine witness of Holy Scripture and not according to the good pleasure of human wisdom as it has hitherto been put out by those who boast of their gospel. May God please to have mercy on all men, and especially the poor, so help us the Cross of Christ, Amen.

If we would reach a right understanding and Judgement about Baptism, we must not deal with it according to our own good pleasure, leaving aside the form and devising of Christ and his apostles, for God has forbidden us to do as we think fit, but what he commands we are to do and keep, and not turn aside either to the

[1] On the significance for Müntzer of the relation of parts and whole, see pp. 294f. above.

right or to the left. If, then, that proper Order of Baptism is to be kept which was ordained by Christ and kept by the apostles, we must with all diligence and earnestness mark the commandment of Christ well when he institutes an Order and gives us a rule or guide with which a true foundation of Christian faith may be laid. Whoso has ears to hear, let him hear. Let whoso will, be offended.

First Christ says, 'Go ye into all the world and preach the Gospel [*aller creaturen*]'. Then he says, 'whoso believes', and thirdly, 'and is baptized, shall be saved.' This Order must be preserved, if a true Christendom is to be set up, and though the whole world should be broken in pieces about it. Where it is not preserved, there is no Christian people of God, but of the devil, and the dregs of the whole world and of all false Christians who change it with their perverted Order and maintain that it is untrue.

First then, Christ says, 'Go into all the world and preach the Gospel of all creatures [*aller creaturen*].' Here the Lord shows how man shall come to the knowledge of God and himself, namely through the Gospel of all creatures. But we must first of all learn and know what is this 'gospel of all creatures'. For, God have mercy, the whole world is utterly ignorant of it, and it is also never preached in our age. And though it be preached and spoken by the poor in spirit, despised of the world [*die der welt veracht*], as it should be, to those to whom it is revealed, yet to the soft and carnal men, especially the hireling preachers, who none the less boast that they preach the Gospel, it is the very greatest folly and fanaticism, and those who so preach are railed at as the most scandalous false prophets and lying spirits. Ah well, they have their little day, and, as Paul has so well said, the word of the cross is foolishness to them that are perishing; but to those who shall be saved (that is, us) it is the power of God.

In the 'Gospel of all creatures' is nothing else signified and preached than simply Christ crucified, but not Christ alone as Head, but the whole Christ with all members, this is the Christ which all creatures preach and teach. The whole Christ has to suffer in all members, and not as our Scribes preach Christ (who nevertheless want to be the best, as we hear daily from them), that Christ as the Head has borne and accomplished everything. But then what happens to the members and the whole body in which the suffering of Christ must be fulfilled? Of this Paul bears witness, when he says, 'I rejoice in my suffering, for I fulfil what is lacking in the suffering of Christ in my body'. And therefore, in a short time, which has already begun, they must with their wisdom be turned into fools, for it is God's good pleasure through foolish, silly and fanatical preaching, as the clever ones call it, to save those who believe it, though these rage against it never so much. So they must in a short time, for all their wisdom and pride, give way to the poor in spirit who, as Paul says, are simply fanatics to them. Now this you are to understand with diligence, my dearly beloved brethren, and mark the word which Christ calls 'the Gospel of all creatures' [*das evangelion aller creaturen*]. For it is not here to be understood as though the Gospel is to be preached *to* the creatures, cats and dogs, cows and calves, leaves and grass, but as Paul says, the 'Gospel which is preached to you, in all creatures'.[1] This he also shows when he says that the eternal power and divinity will be perceived when a man truly recognizes it in the creatures or works from the creation of the world.[2] So I say and confess that the Gospel according to the commandment of Christ, as Christ and his apostles preached it, has not been preached in our day, and those who set up to be the best, are ignorant of what the Gospel of all creatures is about. It is hidden from them and sealed, because they do not seek the pure and simple glory of God, but their own belly-glory. And if you tell them about it, they deride it and say it is 'fanaticism and sophistry'. So mark closely, my dearly beloved brethren, what this 'Gospel of all creatures' is, and what Paul means when he says, 'The Gospel which is preached to you in all creatures'.

Thus it is nothing else, as he expounds it in another place, than a power of God which saves all who believe in it. But if a man will understand and confess God's eternal power and divinity, or his invisible being, by the works or creatures from the creation of the world, he must then mark and consider how Christ always showed the kingdom of heaven and the power of the Father to the common

[1] Col. 1:23. Vg: 'quod praedicatum est in universa creatura' (Er. 'apud universam creaturam'); ML: 'unter aller kreatur'
[2] Rom. 1:20

'OF THE MYSTERY OF BAPTISM'

man in a creature, through a parable, through handicrafts, in all manner of works with which men are occupied. He did not direct the poor man to books, as now our senseless scribes do, but he taught them and showed them the Gospel by means of their work, the peasants by their field, seed, thistle, thorn and rock.[1] In the prophets God says men are not to sow amongst thorns, but are first to clear the ground, plough it or turn it up, and then plant afterwards. The power of God, as it is shown us here, is God's work towards us, that God's power must be exercised towards us, as the work of the peasants towards the field.[2] This Christ shows with the field, and Paul says 'you are God's husbandry'. As the peasant does with his field, before he sows seed in it, so does God also with us, before he plants his Word in us, that it may grow and bear fruit. He teaches the gardener the Gospel from his trees, the fisherman from his catch, the builder from his house, the goldsmith by the testing of his gold, the housewives from their dough, the vine-dresser by his vineyard, vine and shoots, the tailor by the patching on an old garment, the merchant by the pearls, the reaper by the harvest, the woodcutter by the axe laid to the tree, the shepherd by his sheep, the potter by his pottery, the steward and the bailiff by their accounts, the pregnant woman by her childbearing, the thresher by his winnowing fan, the butcher by his slaughtering.[3] Paul illustrates the body of Christ in and through a human body, and so Christ always preached the Gospel of the Kingdom of God by the creatures and in parables and without a parable he did not preach to them. And so David says 'I will open my mouth and speak in parables'.[4]

From such parables men are diligently to mark how all the

---

[1] Müntzer, 'Protestation oder Entbietung' (Franz, p. 233): 'Got selbern dein unkraut, disteln und dorner aus deinem fruchtbaren lande, das ist aus deinem hertzen, reutet'; *Fürstenpredigt* (Franz, p. 252): 'Drumb bleibet der acker des wort Gottis voll disteln und dörnen'; 'Von dem gedichteten Glauben' (Franz, p. 222): 'lest die dorn und diteln stehn ... das man pfele yn die erde damit stosse'.

[2] cf. 'Von dem gedichteten Glauben' (Franz, p. 218): 'so wenig wie der agker one die pflugschare vormagk vormanigfeldigten weytzen *zu* tragen'

[3] Abundant Scriptural references accompany this list.

[4] Ps. 78:2: Vg has 'parabolis', ML has 'Sprüche'.

creatures have to suffer the work of men, and come through the suffering to their end, for which they were created,¹ and also how no man can come to salvation, save through suffering and tribulation which God works in him,² as also the whole Scripture and all the creatures show nothing else but the suffering Christ in all his members.³

That is why the whole of the Scriptures is described simply through creatures. And therefore did God give the children of Israel to understand his will through creaturely and ceremonial works, and announced, preached, and described them through Moses. God commands that oxen, sheep, he-goats, rams, and bullocks shall be sacrificed. Through Isaiah he testifies that he does not will such, as he says, 'the sacrifice of bulls, the blood of sheep, calves and goats have I not chosen', and through David he says, 'I will not take any bullock out of thy house, nor he-goats out of thy folds'. Therefore God's commandment does not consist in the letter [*red*] but in the power [*kraft*] which the Spirit gives, and the spiritual force of such commandment will always hold good for men – that man is in relation to God as such sacrifice is in relation to men. That is why David sacrifices to God a burnt offering of rams, oxen and goats, and offers a calf for himself. Such ceremonial sacrifices are therefore signs and witness that men are to offer themselves as living sacrifices. Accordingly God commands [Lev. 11, Deut. 14] that men shall eat clean animals, the [*spiritual*] force of which is that men are to give themselves to God to suffer the will of God, as such animals have to suffer our will, and he forbids the eating of unclean beasts, the [*spiritual*] force of which is that we are not to keep company with impure men, who are compared with such animals. For it is written [Acts 10:15] there is nothing unclean and all is good. These ceremonies point out what is the will of God, and are intended for us as truly as for the children of Israel.

---

¹ a doctrine of 'ends' which is scholastic.

² cf. Müntzer's letter to Christoph Meinhard, 30 May 1524 (Franz, II, No. 49, p. 402): 'yhr müst lernen durch das leyden Gottes werk'

³ cf. Müntzer's 'Hochverursachte Schutzrede' (Franz, p. 324): 'Die gantze heylige schrifft saget nit anderst (wie auch alle creaturen aussweysen) dan vom gecreützigten sone Gottes, ... den leydenden son Gotes, ...'

'OF THE MYSTERY OF BAPTISM'

That is why Christ always spoke through parables, and these consist not in the speaking, but in the power and the meaning. All animals are subject unto man; if a man needs one he must first prepare, cook and roast it, and the animal must suffer. So it is with God and man: if God is to make use of us or enjoy us, we must first be justified by him, and cleansed within and without: inwardly from desire and lust, outwardly from all improper behaviour and misuse of creatures. The peasant sows no corn amongst thistle, thorns, sticks and stones, but he first weeds them out and then sows afterwards. So does God with us: he sows his Word not in a man who is full of thistles or thorns or has desire and affection only towards creatures; that anxiety about bodily welfare which God forbids, must first be rooted out. The builder does not make a house out of whole trees, but first cuts them down and then fashions them as he wills, and afterwards makes a house out of them. In this way we are to learn God's Work and will towards us, which is as a man behaves with a house before he lives in it, which house (Paul says) we are.

Man is often called a tree in the Scriptures: if he is to be turned into a house he must be cut off from the world with all lusts. Then as on a tree one branch sticks out, now in one direction and now in another, so is it too with the desires of men, one branch stretches towards possessions, another towards wife and children, a third towards money, a fourth towards fields and lands, to pomp and temporal honour.

Therefore all the works which we accomplish with the creatures should be our Scriptures which we closely mark. For the whole world with all creatures is a book, in which is to be seen in act all those things which are read in the written book. For all elect men from the beginning of the world until Moses have studied in the book of all creatures, and have taken knowledge of it by reason, as it is written from nature by the Spirit of God in the heart, because the whole law is expressed in creaturely works. And all men are in this wise concerned with the creatures, as the Law shows, even the heathen who have not the law of Scripture, and yet do the same things which they do who have the Scriptural Law. The Law of Scripture prescribes how a man must kill a beast before it is offered to God, and only after this was it eaten; even so do the heathen who have the law of nature, and who eat no animal alive. So we must first die to the world and live in God.

In the Law there is a lamp trimmer beside the lamps, and thus also do the heathen with their lights, and so on in almost all other ceremonies and commandments. That is why Moses illustrates his book with such ceremonies of the creatures of which he reminds men and warns them to seek out and study the will of God in them. As therefore the Law is inscribed in all creatures and shown forth there, we read it in our daily work. In this book we are occupied daily,[1] and the whole world is full, yes, full of the will of God so expressed, of which our own hearts bear witness if we keep them from the coarsening of worldly disorder and lust, and so men can perceive the invisible being and eternal power of God in the works of the creatures, and see how God works with men and prepares them for the end of their perfection which can only take place through the Cross of suffering according to his will. That is why all creatures are subject to man, to rule over them, and as the whole Bible is written in terms of all creatures, so Christ too spoke, or preached and declared, the 'gospel in all creatures' in a parable, as he himself did when he preached it to the poor. So he did not point them to the chapters of a book, as our Scribes do, for all that a man can show through the creatures is all confirmed [?: the original is *beweiset*] in the Scriptures, and Christ needs no Scriptures except for the sake of the Scribes, to convince them with it. When the gospel in all creatures is thus preached according to the commandment of the Lord, and man is brought thereby to understand that reason in a natural and real way is included in his own works which he does over and in the creatures, in which he acknowledges God's will towards him, and gives himself into joyful obedience to Christ, he sees that no man can be saved in any other way than by suffering the will of God in body and in pain, as it may please God.

And so a man says he believes that so it must be with him and with all men who wish to be saved. From such hearing comes the next part of the divine Order, when Christ says, 'Whoso be-

---

[1] On the similarity between this remarkable passage and Raymund of Sabunde's *Theologia naturalis* tit. ccxi, 'Liber creaturarum . . .', see p. 343 above

lieveth...'. Though a man may be instructed about the Gospel in all things or creatures, so that he hears and believes that this really is true, yet this is not enough; for this a man can very well point out and prove to all men. The third part of the divine Order must also follow, which Christ says: 'and is baptized, shall be saved'.

Here Baptism must come and be joined to the two first parts that a man may take the pledge [*verwillige*] to bear and suffer all that will be laid upon him from the Father through Christ, and determine from the heart to adhere to the Lord, and to renounce the world and moreover receive the sign of Baptism to a covenant of his resolve [*bund der verwilligung*] before a Christian congregation [*gmain*] which has received the covenant from God, and in the name of God, has power and authority to divide it out [*auszutailen*] to all[1] those who desire it from their hearts as the Lord says, 'What you bind on earth shall also be bound in heaven'.

But no man ought to be received into such fellowship and incorporated in it, unless he has first heard and learned the Gospel and believes simply what he has heard and has willingly accepted it [*darein auch verwilligt*]. For this covenant is a willing resolve [*ein verwilligung*] [to put oneself] under the obedience of Christ, with an exhibiting of divine Love towards all brothers and sisters in the Lord with body, life, goods and honour, and indifference to what the world may evilly say of him. Yes, but where are these Christians? They are a little flock [*heuflein* =? handful]. And if in these people [*gmein* =? congregation] there were only two or three, that would not matter, if Christ is in the midst as a witness, for in the mouth of two or three witnesses is the truth confirmed. Such a man will always be assured through Baptism, that he is an accepted child of God, a brother or sister of Christ, a member of the Christian Church [*gmain*] and of the body of Christ, because with a true heart he has dedicated himself [*verwilligt*] to such a union according to the will of God. For God commands his saints to assemble, who take more account of the covenant than of all sacrifices, and he will not have the offering of goats but a thank-offering, in which each offers his body as a willing sacrifice for justification, as Paul says,

[1] This could read 'allen' or 'allein'; if the latter, then the translation should read: 'to those alone who desire it...'

and believes God will not leave him in necessity but save him out of all his troubles when he is brought into tribulation.

Such a faith, though it is not perfect and is untried, will he none the less impute to him for righteousness, until he is justified and proved as gold in the fire. The Baptism which follows preaching and faith is not the real essential [*recht wesen*] through which a man becomes godly, but is only a sign, a pledge [*bund*], a parable and a memorial of the dedication [*verwilligung*] which reminds a man daily to expect the true Baptism, of which Christ speaks, the water of all tribulation, through which the Lord cleanses, washes and justifies from all fleshly lusts, sins and impure works and behaviour, because such a man has seen that no creature can justify itself and come to its final being [*entlichen wesen*] without man, to whom it is subject, and so no man can justify himself and reach his end, that is, come to salvation except this happen through the work of God in the Baptism of all tribulation, displayed and exercised upon man by God, to whom alone man is subject for his justification. Therefore, if a man is to be justified by God so he must hold himself passive before God as his Master, that he may accomplish his work in him, so God will bring it to pass, as David says 'Commit thy way unto the Lord, and hope in him, and he will bring it to pass'.[1]

So this water of all tribulation is the real essence and power of Baptism, in which a man is submerged into the death of Christ. This Baptism was not first instituted in the time of Christ, but it was from the beginning, and in it all the Elect Friends of God from Adam until now have been baptized, as Paul shows. So Christ received this covenant [*bund*] from the Father in Jordan, and thereby testified that he was under obedience to the Father, to show love towards all men, even unto death, and as an example, since he himself had the water of tribulation showered upon him richly from the Father. And so the sign and the essence of Baptism are to be sharply distinguished. The sign or covenant of Baptism, the Christian congregation [*gmain*] extends through a faithful minister [*diener*] as Christ received from John. The real Baptism comes afterwards, which God gives through the waters of all tribulation, and again in the comfort of the Holy Ghost. In this Baptism God allows nobody

[1] Ps. 37:5 (ML)

'OF THE MYSTERY OF BAPTISM'

to drown, as it is written: 'He leads into hell and out again: he kills and makes alive'; with this Baptism the Lord must baptize afterwards. And so whosoever would be a disciple of the Lord must also be baptized, and be purified in the Spirit through the bond of peace into the one body; so God makes his own blessed and worthy, and it all happens by means of this covenant of rebirth and the renewal by the Holy Ghost through faith, which God works through his great mercy, that we should be justified by the same grace and be heirs of eternal life according to hope. And so a man shall be washed, sanctified, purified and born again, and become part of a blameless people [*gmain*] before God, and not as the present-day Swiss Christians have set up with their grasping and covetous Scribes. But 'like people, like priest'.[1]

That is why the worthy David asked that God would wash him and cleanse him from his sins, and so he too was graciously heard by God, as we read, when he found himself in the water of all tribulation and cried to the Lord for help in and out of such a depth of the abyss, and was brought up again, and his sins destroyed, and he was made alive in Christ. So too Paul exhorts his brethren to suffer as they have seen in him; for the Kingdom of God does not consist in speech or in outward things, but in power, and therefore is the Gospel not a speech [*red*] but a power of God, which is given by God alone and makes a man entirely new from his mouth and heart and in all behaviour and bearing. So it is a thoroughly wicked Gospel which the world and our most learned preachers are occupied with, for they do not make people better but only worse, as I leave all Christian brethren in the Lord to judge. But blessed are they who hear the Word of God and keep it. A lamb of Christ hears the voice of his Master and fears it: but whoso hears and doeth not, is a fool and will never be just, but he who tries to come to God without the righteousness which counts before God, he casts out the very means, which is suffering or the cross of Christ, yes, Christ crucified himself, as now the whole world does, which suffering they cannot escape for all that. For without the Son who is given in discipline, no man cometh to the Father. Whoso would reign with God must be ruled

---

[1] quoted (from Isa. 24:2; Hos. 4:9) by Müntzer in 'Ausgedrückte Entblössung' (Franz, p. 295) with 'pfaff' for 'priest'; ML has 'Priester'.

by God. Whoso will do the will of God must renounce his own, whoso will find somewhat in God must by so much lose himself. The whole world nowadays prates about liberty and yet sticks fast in the bondage to the flesh all the time, will give up nothing, but keeps on asking for more. O how cleverly do they cover up. And so they all say, 'A man must abide in his calling'. If that is so, why did not Peter remain a fisherman, Matthew a publican, why did Christ tell the rich young ruler to sell all and give to the poor? If it is right for our preachers to keep so much, then the young ruler was right too, to keep what possessions he had. O Zacchaeus, why did you give up your property so easily – according to our preachers you would have done better to stick to it, and still been a good Christian. Oho, comrades, how do you like that? Can't you smell arrant knavery? Ah well, the Lord is at hand who will judge you.

A true genuine Friend of God, who daily waits on the Lord and hopes comfortably in him, will have his heart strengthened so that under the Cross he will be able to bear the will of God. All that such a man suffers is called the sufferings of Christ and not ours, because we are with Christ one body in many members, united and bound together in the bond of charity. Therefore, Christ receives such men to be his own body, and says, 'Who touches you, touches the apple of mine eye', and further, 'What you do to the least of mine, you have done unto me'. For the sufferings of Christ must be fulfilled in each member until the sufferings of Christ be complete. For as Christ the lamb is slain from the foundation of the world, so also will he be crucified until the end of the world that the body of Christ may be made perfect according to the length, breadth, depth and height in the love of Christ which passeth knowledge, that he may be filled with all the fulness of God.[1]

Under such suffering and such a Cross of the rightly constituted Baptism, is a man made sure of his faith, justified and proved like gold in the fire, through which honest faith will be revealed out of God's goodness and mercy, when a man after all suffering and tribulation is comforted anew in the Holy Ghost, and then will he be ready for the Lord and usable in all good works. There is no other way for man, for the Truth shall be revealed inviolable.

[1] cf. Müntzer, 'Ausgedrückte Entblössung' (Franz, p. 298)

'OF THE MYSTERY OF BAPTISM'

The faith which a man obtains by hearing will be imputed for righteousness, until a man is justified and purified under the Cross, for then will such a faith be conformed [*gleichformig*] to the faith of God, and one with Christ. Out of such a faith the just man then lives, and therefore this 'Initial Faith' must be clearly distinguished. God's faith is always true, just, unchanging, as he has promised. Our faith is in the beginning like silver still in the ore, full of dross, unproven, but still to be counted as genuine silver until it is proved, when all that is impure is cleansed away That is why the apostles say, 'We believe, help thou our unbelief'. Oh, well may our belief in the beginning be compared with unbelief, as a man soon discovers in the testing of justification, when he too often finds in himself neither faith nor trust, and is so utterly shut up in unbelief that he thinks he is cast away from the Lord. There nothing can comfort him, yea, all creatures are in vain, as also David said, 'my soul will not be comforted'. And in another place he says, 'I am cast out from before thine eyes'.[1] So a man is shut up in the abyss of hell. Christ calls this the sign of Jonah the prophet. Then nothing can or may comfort him save him alone who led him hither, and this he must wait for, until he comes with his comfort through the Holy Ghost, and then will a man be so full of rejoicing that he forgets all about the desires, joys and honours of all the world, and counts them all but dung. So a man comes back from the depths of hell and gains joy and courage in the Holy Ghost. This justification counts before God, and it does not come from an unproved faith, for an untried faith can do no more than stretch out towards righteousness, but he must first be prepared and then justified.

But the whole world is scared of justification, as of the devil, and would gladly buy itself off with a feigned [*erdichten*] faith and yet will not come to justification.

Such righteousness is not proclaimed by their preachers, for they themselves are enemies of the Cross and of righteousness. They only seek their own honour and what serves their belly-God. So God works his righteousness on us through the suffering of the Holy Cross which he lays on every man, and the faith of God will be

---

[1] not ML. This whole passage is surely reminiscent of Luther's descriptions of 'Anfechtung'?

revealed to our faith according to his promise, that we may believe that God is true and will make good his faith in ours. Then all the lusts which we have received through the creatures are rooted out and broken to pieces. So will the world's yoke of all sins be thrown off, so that the world no longer reigns, but Christ. Then the Law of the Father will be completed through Christ in us as in his members. Then there is a desire and eagerness to do the will of God in true obedience. To such is his burden light and his yoke sweet and everything possible that before was impossible. Then a man might very well say, Christ has extinguished my sins. But whoso will not put himself under the chastening of the Lord, but cleaves to the lusts of the world, will be overtaken by great shame and suffering, and surrounded by it, and though in such suffering he cry out to God, God will not hear him, but scorn him through his members. So will all God-fearing men seek their comfort from the Lord and he will save them out of all tribulation. So help us God (through the bath of rebirth).[1]

Now follows the essence of true Baptism:[2]

Now we shall speak further about the baptism or rebirth [*widergeburt*] which is not an outward sign that Christ shows, but a bath of the soul to wash and rinse it free from all the lusts and desires of the heart. It is a mortifying and purging from all those lusts and disobedience which set themselves within us against God and incite us against him. As in the days of Noah God did with the ancient world, when through the deluge he swept away evil and washed it away from the earth, as also happened to Pharaoh with his Egyptians in the baptismal bath of the Red Sea, when they sank like lead to the bottom. The whole world, with Noah and his household, Pharaoh and all his men, with the whole of Israel were put in the same baptism, but they did not suffer the same fate, or use it in the same way. The wicked went in, but came not out again because weighed down with creaturely lusts, they sank of their own accord to the bottom, could neither let go of themselves nor of the creatures, but of their own accord went on living for ever in lust and love of creatures. That is why they persecute the elect, who do not cling to such

[1] The phrase in parentheses is omitted in the *Kunstbuch*.
[2] The whole of the following section is omitted from the *Kunstbuch*.

'OF THE MYSTERY OF BAPTISM'

things as they do, but who wish to swim out, and try unceasingly like Peter to reach the shore or landing place, that they may escape the wild billows of this world and come out of the water of all tribulation and conflict on to firm land, because they see that God is stretching out his hand and wants to help them. So Baptism is to those who walk in a renewal of life, not a submersion and drowning, but rather a joyful rescue from the billows and waves, the movements of our own desires.

Among such we once lived so readily, and this turbulence is the struggle of the spirit with the flesh, which is in men. In this conflict, if the desire of the flesh, lust, movement, attraction and opposition are to be stilled, pacified, overcome, then the sweet waters, that is the lust and desire of the flesh, must contrariwise and in equal measure become harsh and bitter through the movement of the divine righteousness in purging these things, since they were previously sweet in the creature, not because they came from God, but because our own nature inclined us to them. Then a great tumult arises in the conscience between the flesh and the spirit. Oh, how narrow at this point is the way which leads to life, when, through dying to the old man, one must turn to a new life in God which is the rebirth in Baptism. Here anxiety and trembling and shuddering overtake a man like the pangs [*angst*] of a woman in childbirth. When God brings such waters through the soul, it must be borne patiently until a man is made to understand and taught and born at peace in our world from all stumbling of the flesh. Then a man becomes, in the patient waiting of his time [*langen weil*], in the acceptance of the hand of God, a ready and prepared throne and dwelling place of God.[1] As now the troubled waters become clear, the bitter sweet, the violent calm and still, the Son of God appears on the waters, reaches out a hand, takes him from the billows and lets him see that it is by his Truth that he has opened up our darkness, and hidden the living waterway in us to lead us from the world of sinful, earthly men into eternal life. The waters which press on the soul are temptation, trouble, anxiety, trembling and worry – so then Baptism is suffering. So also was Christ straitened in his

[1] see p. 284 above; this reference to Ps. 93 is intelligible only in the light of Thomas Müntzer's own version (see also Franz, pp. 267–8).

Baptism before it was made perfect by his death. For true Baptism is nothing less than a fight with sin the whole life through... and so the waters of contradiction wash the soul from all lascivious and lustful defilement and attachment. The Baptism of John with water is incomplete, can free nobody from sin, for it is only a figure, a preparation and type of the real Baptism in Christ. Therefore it behoves us to be baptized in Christ after another manner, for Christ himself accepted Baptism in a figure, of which he was to bring the real essence, in himself. So Christ had first to be baptized as an example for us, so that all should come true in him. For in the death of Christ we are all incorporated as members in the likeness of his death, that is put under a sign[1] as Paul says to the Romans: 'you are all baptized into the baptism of Christ, that is into the death of Christ, that henceforth we may look to Christ and that we may receive the true baptism from the Father.' Christ comes to John's baptism that he may humble himself beyond all other men, and he took unto himself our proud nature which had fallen away from God, and brought it under God once again through baptism in which he showed that every man must be baptized into a new creature, in the mortifying of our evil, disobedient, and insolent nature in order to wash away all sin and human properties as Paul says: you who are baptized into Christ have put on Christ. So shall all who died in Adam be made alive in Christ. But he who refuses this Baptism remains for ever in the death of Adam. Therefore Baptism is a lifelong fight with sin, to the death. Who now finds Pharoah behind him, that is all persecution, tribulation, anxiety and necessity, and before him the Red Sea, that is the helplessness of all creatures, and thinks he is abandoned by God and finds nothing to look for than death, he is and abides in the real Baptism for he has put himself under the sign [*verwilligt*] to God and his people or men. This Baptism the world now shuns utterly and completely. That is why the Baptism of this present world is sheer knavery by which the world deceives itself and denies Christ. They do not want Christ to do his work in them, and to allow the place where he would dwell to be swept clean. Thus all is perverted and there is no longer a true Judgement in the earth about the mystery of the divine command-

[1] 'verwilligt'

ment. Yes, we all want to find Christ and to boast about it. But we none of us want to suffer with him. Yes, if God's spirit were given in worldliness and the pomp of the world, the world would be full of Christians. But Christ hides under the cover of flesh and will not be seen by observation other than through suffering and in infinite resignation [*gelassenheit*] in which he showed himself and shows to all his brethren; so that a man must first find God's goodness there, and this is the highest degree of the divine righteousness, the beginning of divine mercy. Then is a man brought into conformity with Christ, united with the crucified Son of God, and he is completely joined with us in one body. Then a man lives no longer, but Christ. That is why Christ says, whoso would be my disciple and learns God's way [*kunst*] and will, must first let himself be disciplined by the Father on account of disobedience, and hang the Cross round his neck as Christ did, and fulfil the will of the Father by means of suffering, as long as this is his lot, and afterwards do God's will by means of action. In no other wise will Christ consider a man as his brother, nor the Father a man as his son.

Christ crucified has many members in his body and yet there is no member but bears his work or suffers or is put [*verwilligt*] to suffering after the example of the Head. Without this means nobody knows Christ who will be known in no other way, for this is the power of the Father which makes us well pleasing to him. This suffering he calls baptism, in which he suffers no brother or sister to sink, or be destroyed, but rather that they may be made good in it, cleansed from all blemish, and made ready to receive the good things of God, that all may be well with them hereafter through knowledge of the divine will.

The whole world is angered and offended at the weakness of Christ and yet none can reach the sweet Son of God unless he tastes first what is bitter in justification. That is why the life of Christ is so bitter, his teaching is so lofty, his person so simple and terrible that you may say that blessed is he who is not offended in Christ.

But where there is little lust a man does not stay long in the waters of tribulation for these waters become pure, clear, refreshing and lovely, transparent so that a man can accept the spirit of God in all fulness, that he may perform the will of God. But that we, like him, must be put under obedience to the Father, comes about in this way, that we through him and in him lay on to him the sin which is in ourselves, for sin had no part in him according to his own person, but on account of our sin he was troubled in the highest degree and his soul most terribly.

Matthew and Luke describe Baptism in fire and spirit and John with water and spirit, while Mark describes neither fire nor water. What Matthew and Luke call fire is the spirit of God and that is what John means by water with the Holy Spirit and thus they all agree together. Water and fire in the Scriptures mean temptation, the sea is the world, fire and water cleanse all things, there is a cleansing of all things in time, either through water or through fire. What is weak and unable to bear fire will be purged with water from impurity, what is hard as gold, silver, copper, iron, tin, will be melted in the fire and purged from dross. Therefore, God's spirit pictures to us water and fire as things opposed (concerning which reason is included in the works of the creatures and brought under the obedience of Christ), for just as water takes away impurity and fire destroys all dross, cleanses and refines from all accretions, so also does the power of God in working the Truth through the suffering of all tribulation, and whoso will not hear the voice of God in the water, must hear it in the fire. God meets us in manifold temptation that thus lust may be driven out from us, and in renunciation [*gelassenheit*] of the whole world he does his work, that he may help us and use us for his work, just as a goldsmith does not use impure gold for his work until it has been first through the fire and is purged and cleansed of all impurity, and what comes through the fiery trial purged will be pure and good. That is why God commands all disobedience to be cast into the fire, and changes its spirits into flames of fire. So he savours the smell of fire, and gives his commandments from fire, and he calls himself a consuming fire which devours all things and is jealous. So he will have no strange fire in his house for a burnt sacrifice and a smoke offering. All living creatures expound this saying about water and spirit, for their earthly body is first conceived and born in water. But were they to remain in water they would be drowned and putrefy.

So Baptism has had its time and goal and age just as our first birth has its goal and time and also its age, and so all the creatures will be born through water to their essence and perfection and without baptism may not live a complete life or be blessed. But it is the present world, with its infant baptism, which is a sheer human invention without the word and command of God, a deceiving of the simple and a wicked shaming of the whole of Christendom, an archknave's cloak of all the godless, for in the whole of Scriptures there is not a single sentence which can be brought to prove their case. Indeed, so groundless is it that they must all hold their silence, however much they may dissemble. According to the word of Christ, and in the light of the Scriptures, nobody should be baptized unless he can, through a burning fidelity, establish his faith and trust. This sign of Baptism, where it is received, points to the true Baptism of suffering which follows, as we have said, without which nobody may be saved. But the false infant baptism is not only unnecessary but it is the very greatest hindrance to the Truth.

INDEX

Aarau conference, 41
Abraham, 122, 192, 220, 293. *See also* purgatory
Adam, 194, 286, 287, 352, 369, 390, 396
Adelmann, Bernard, 13, 15, 16, 21, 65, 75, 83, 85
Adelmann, Conrad, 13, 15, 75
Aesop's Fables, 252, 257
Agricola, Johann, 5, 165f., 212, 276 *n. 2*
Albert, abp of Mainz, 89, 222f., 238
Albert, Count of Mansfeld, 228, 238, 242
Aleander, 17, 88
Alexander de Villa Dei, xxii, 3
Allstedt, xiii, 132, 185–221, 224, 227, 228, 239, 242, 246, 298–302, 314, 336 *n. 2, 3*, 341, 352; Liturgy, 207, 314–23, 342. *See also* Müntzer, T.: liturgy of
Alstatt, 149
Altomünster, 14, 16, 17, 28, 39
Amerbach, Johann, xvii, 150
Amsdorf, Nicholas, 51, 60, 90, 100
Anabaptists, xxi, xxii, 13 *n. 4*, 24, 27, 39, 40 *n. 1*, 41, 43, 45–6, 81, 118 *n. 1*, 4, 139, 157, 172, 181, 233f., 249f., 271, 299, 331, 333, 335, 336 *n. 3*, 352, 370, 371, 372. *See also* Swiss Brethren
Anfechtung, Luther on, 254, 280, 393 *n. 1*; Müntzer on, 175, 179, 220, 280, 282f., 286, 310, 338ff.

Annaberg, 79–80
Anne, St, devotion to, 79, 165
anti-clericalism, 93–4, 95–6, 128–9, 134, 144, 148 *n. 2*, 150, 151, 232, 338
apocalyptic, Anabaptist, 335; Huth, 333, 335f.; Le Fèvre, 326; Müntzer, 177ff., 202f., 205, 228, 254ff., 270, 277 *n. 2*, 298f., 302ff., 305, 326, 329
Apostles' Creed, xix, 366
Appenzell, 358
Apuleius, 217, 253, 292
Aquinas, xxii, 7 *n. 3*, 49 *n. 3*, 51 *n. 1*, 117
Aristotle, xviii, 4, 11, 62, 342; Luther on, 55, 59f., 61; Karlstadt on, 66, 76; Vadianus on, 362
Artickelbrief, 232 *n. 1*, 235 *n. 1*
Articles, Twelve, 232 *n. 1*
Aschersleben, 159
assurance, Müntzer on, 179, 202, 270
astronomy, Vadianus and, 361, 376
atonement, doctrine of, 37; eucharist and, 143; Müntzer on, 194, 340
Augsburg, xiv, 6 *n. 2*, 13, 15, 65, 67f., 136, 377
Augustinianism, 68, 71, 73, 81, 92, 113, 124, 367
Augustine, St, bp of Hippo, xviii, xxi, 7, 11, 12 *n. 1*, 22, 49 *n. 1*, *n. 3*, 55, 56, 57, 58, 59, 60, 61, 63, 73, 82, 117, 192, 251, 253, 260, 264, 267, 273, 277 *n. 2*, 287, 304, 313

INDEX

authority, Biblical, 83; Conciliar, 82, 83, 98; Church, 82; Christ's, 20, 82f.; congregational, 138, 139; episcopal, 128; papal, 81, 84, 121, 128, 138, 366, 381

Bach, J., 153
Baden, 28f., 31, 372
Bader, 268, 302, 335
Baptism, 23, 28, 32, 38, 41, 80–1, 114, 137, 209f., 212, 268, 272, 275, 295f., 321–3, 331ff., 339, 340f., 345f., 370, 371–2, 379–99
Baptists, 323
Barge, Hermann, 50 *n. 1–2*, 66 *n. 1*, 68 *n. 1*, 69 *n. 1*, 70 *n. 1*, 71 *n. 1*, 75 *n. 4*, 76, 77 *n. 2*, 80, 80 *n. 1*, 84 *n. 1–3*, 85 *n. 1, 3*, 86 *n. 1–3*, 87 *n. 1*, 90, 91 *n. 1–3*, 92 *n. 1 and 3*, 93 *n. 1*, 95 *n. 2, 4*, 96 *n. 1–2*, 97 *n. 1*, 98 *n. 1*, 99 *n. 1, 2*, 101, 102, 103, *n. 1–3*, 105 *n. 3*, 112 *n. 1, 2*, 113 *n. 1*, 115 *n. 2*, 123 *n. 1*, 132 *n. 2*, 134 *n. 2*, 135 *n. 2*, 142, 143 *n. 1*, 144 *n. 1*, 147, 152
Bäring, G., 226 *n. 1, 4*
Bäring, H., 335 *n. 1*, 336 *n. 2*, 338
Barlow, William, 131, 141, 147 *n. 2*
Barnes, Robert, 297
Barnim, Duke of Pomerania, 69
Basil, St, the Great, bp of Caesarea, xviii *n. 1*, xxii, 11, 12 *n. 1*, 16, 253
Basle, xiii–xiv, xviii, xxi, 3, 4f., 8, 9, 10, 13, 17, 18, 20, 23, 24, 25, 28, 30, 31f., 33, 34, 35f., 37, 38f., 39–42, 43, 45, 135 *n. 1*, 136f., 149f., 346, 374
Bataillon, M., xx *n. 1*
Bauch, G., 50 *n. 1*
Bauer, K., 50 *n. 1*, 52 *n. 2*, 60 *n. 1*
Bayer, Christian, 90, 94, 97, 98, 102, 107
Beginning (*Ankunft*), 278, 280, 283, 331, 338
Behr, Peter, 198 *n. 3*

Bender, Harold S., 139 *n. 1*, 157 *n. 1*, 335 *n. 1*, 345
Benedictus, 309, 321
Berlepsch, Sittich von, 225, 240
Berlichingen, Götz von, 233
Bern, 30, 332, 359, 373, 379 *n.*; Colloquy at, xx, 31, 33, 372; Reform in, 42
Bernard, St, of Clairvaux, 7, 59, 73–4, 255
Berneck, mountain, 376
Bertschi, Markus, 30
Bible. *See also* individual books in separate index
Bible, authority of, xvii, xxii, 29, 57, 60, 66, 72, 75, 81, 82, 83, 84, 86, 98, 366, 367; classes, 368, 371, 372, 377–8; collections of antitheses in, 215 *n. 2*, 271, 334; German, Luther, M., 88, 338; Karlstadt, and, 72–3, 75, 76, 80, 81, 82, 103, 117; liturgical use, 306–23; Müntzer and, 164, 180, 215, 259ff., 265ff., 272ff., 298f., 306–23, 325f.; New Testament, Karlstadt, on, 83, 96; New Testament, Vadianus, J., 377; Old Testament, Karlstadt, on, 83, 131; 'open', 76; Pentateuch, 83; preaching and—*See* preaching: Bible and; scholarship, and, xviii, 60–1, 62, 76, 144–5, 152; theology, and, xviii, xix, xxii, 61, 76
Bibra, 226, 333, 335f., 351
Biel, Gabriel, 51 *n. 1*
bigamy, suspicions of, 114, 131
Bild, Veit, 13, 23
Billicanus, Theobald, 8
Bilney, Thomas, xix, 297
Bizet, J. A., 118 *n. 4*
Bloch, E., 157 *n. 2*
Bockelson, Jan (John of Leiden), 268, 302
Böhme, Jakob, 285 *n. 2*
Böhmer, Heinrich, 158, 170 *n. 1*

402

INDEX

Bonhoeffer, Dietrich, 121, 248
Bonorand, C., 357 *n. 1*, 360 *n. 2*, 366 *n. 1, 2*
Book of Common Prayer, 271
Book of the Poor in Spirit, The, 256, 267
'Book of Seven Seals and Judgements', 271
Bosch, Hieronymus, 307 *n. 3*, 348
Böschenstein, Johannes, 62
Boswell, James, 368
Bothanus, Jerome, 30, 43
Bourignon, Antoinette, 120
Brandt, O. H., 174 *n. 1*, 199 *n. 2*, 212 *n. 2*, 259 *n. 2*, 284 *n. 7*, 336 *n. 2*
Brendler, G., 159 *n. 1*, 221 *n. 1*
Brenz, John, 4, 8, 21, 25
Breughel, Pieter, the Elder, 348
breviaries, 306, 308
Brigittines, 14, 16, 17
Brixius, Germanus, 34
Brooks, Peter, 26 *n. 4*
brotherhoods, abolishing of, 98, 102
Brück, Gregory, 94, 131, 201
Bruges, embassy to, 13 *n. 4*, 14, 377
Bucer, Martin, 8 *n. 3*, 18, 19 *n. 2*, 25, 27, 31, 33, 40, 41–2, 43, 45, 137, 139, 144, 148, 207, 254, 272, 302, 323, 335, 374
Bucer, Wibrandis, 8 *n. 2*, 33, 44
Büchner, Georg, 243
Budingen, Eberhard von, 237f.
Bugenhagen, Johann, 149, 153, 200, 322
Bulgarius. *See* Theophylact, abp of Achrida
Bullinger, Heinrich, 148, 150, 157, 233, 247, 249, 335, 374
Bultmann, Rudolf, 288
Bunyan, John, 145, 333
Burckhardt, Paul, 40 *n. 1*, 151 *n. 1*
Bürer, Albert: Wittenberg Movement, 95 *n. 1*
Burgauer, Benedict, 366, 370
Burghley, William Cecil, Lord, 377

Burns, Robert, 123
Buschmann, John, 184

Cabbala, 5
Cajetan, Jacopo, Cardinal (Tommaso da Vio), 13, 67, 207
Calvin, John, xxi, 5, 19, 32, 38, 40, 45, 148
Cambridge, Hymnal, 309 *n. 2*; Reformers, 297; University, 61
canon law, 55, 60, 253
Capito, Wolfgang, xviii *n. 4*, xxi, 8 *n. 3*, 31, 33, 59, 66, 72, 94 *n. 1*, 95 *n. 1*, 106, 137, 139, 335
Capreolus, John, 49, 57
Cassian, John, 59
celibacy, 92
censorship, 111–12, 116, 131, 201, 206, 214, 226–7, 336 *n. 2*. *See also* Nuremberg, Diet of: press censorship
chalice, restoration of, 92
Christ, Jesus of History and the Gospels, 288, 348, 365; conformity with, 255, 267, 285–92, 297, 327; fulfiller of the Law, 213, 330f.; Head and members, 211, 287, 305, 383; Incarnation, 214, 216, 220, 285, 289f., 297; righteousness of, 264, 275; 'sweet' and 'bitter', 193, 211, 255, 290; teaching of, 261, 278, 290, 347f.
Christmas, collects, Müntzer's version, 320; hymns, 311–13
Christology, Karlstadt and, 59, 68, 119, 123, 129, 144–5; Müntzer and, 164, 288ff., 295, 297 *n.*, 328, 331, 340; Vadianus and, 374
Chrysostom, John, St. *See* John Chrysostom, St
Church, doctrine of, 31, 66, 81, 287, 290f.; Müntzer and the, 177f., 202, 273
Cicero, 57

403

INDEX

civil government, Luther, M., on, 200, 247f., 254, 260, 300
Claji, Nicasius, 66–7, 79 *n. 1*
Clark, J. M., 118 *n. 4*
Clementine Homilies, xviii *n. 1*
Cochlaeus, Johannes, 172 *n. 1*
Coct, Anémone de, 21
Coleridge, Samuel Taylor, 366
Colet, John, Dean of St Paul's, 5, 16, 24, 104
collects, 320–1
Cologne, 49, 56
Colonna, Aegidius, 56
Colossians, letter to, 43
commandments, 137
communion in both kinds, 86, 92–3, 95, 96, 97–9, 101, 106, 108, 319, 372—*See also* eucharist: communion; of the sick, 321
Complutensian Polyglot, xx
concomitance, doctrine of, 92
confession, auricular, 17, 39, 99, 319; congregational, 26, 315
Confirmation, 271f.
conscience, 152, 213, 218, 263, 281, 283, 319
Constance, 31, 53 *n. 1*, 179, 374
Copenhagen, 115
Copernicus, xviii
cosmology, 361, 363
Cospus, Angelo, 360
Covenant, Divine, 196, 205f., 220, 260, 262, 299, 314
Covenanted associations, 204, 205f., 208, 239, 292 *n. 3*, 299, 300f.
Cranach, Lukas, xv, 68, 360
Cranmer, Thomas, xxi, 26 *n. 4*, 45, 84; liturgy of, 275, 306, 307, 308, 313, 314, 323; Müntzer and, 307 *n. 2*; Vadianus and, 374
Cratander, xvii, 19, 33
Creation, 124, 260, 292–3, 384–5
creeds, xix, 316, 321, 366
Cromwell, Thomas, xxi

Cross, sign of, 318 *n. 1*; theology of, 59, 68, 81, 130, 164, 248, 282, 328, 381ff., 388, 391ff.
Cusa, Nicholas of. *See* Nicholas, of Cusa
Cyprian, St, bp of Carthage, xviii *n. 1*, xxii, 11, 12 *n. 1*, 59
Cyriacus, St, offices for, 305–6
Cyril, St, bp of Alexandria, 11, 33, 34

Daniel, 202f., 261, 262, 268
David, King, 244, 336, 380, 385, 386, 390, 391, 393
Decretals, Luther, M., and, 56, 60
Denck, Hans, 24, 118 *n. 1*, 4, 152, 215 *n. 2*, 226, 227, 256, 266 *n. 6*, 327, 332, 333, 334
Denifle, Heinrich, 302
Denmark: Karlstadt, A., preacher, 87, 89
'Descent into Hell', 366
Deuteronomy: Karlstadt, A., 105
devil: Karlstadt, A., 118, 128–9
devotio moderna, 327
Dickens, A. G., 147 *n. 2*
Diocletian, Emperor: persecution, 306, *n. 2*
Dionysius, the Areopagite, 12 *n. 1*, 68, 125, 255, 294
discipline: church: reformed, 38–42, 45
'divine ordering'. *See* Ordnung
divorce: Basle ordinance, 38
Donatus, Aelius, 3
Dorlandus, Petrus, 342 *n. 3*
Dostoevski, Feodor Mikhaïlovitch, 120
Douglass, E. J. D., 4 *n. 2*
dreams and visions: Karlstadt, A., 112, 122, 184; Le Fèvre, 326; Müntzer, 202f., 269f., 325
Drechsel, Thomas, 100–1, 166, 182
dualism. *See* Letter *v*. Spirit
Dugmore, C. W., 25 *n. 2*

INDEX

Du Museau, Morelet, 21
Duns Scotus, John, 49 *n. 3*, 51, 55, 71, 117
Dürer, Albert (Albrecht), xv, 96, 169

Easter, 12–13, 130, 313
Ebernburg, castle, Oecolampadius, J., at, 18
Eck, Andreas, 363, 373, 376
Eck, John, 11, 15, 28, 29, 32, 59 *n. 1*, 65–79, 80 *n. 3*, 82, 83, 165, 252–3
Eckhart, meister, 277 *n. 2*, 327
Edward VI, King of England: Reform, 105, 148
Egli, E., 109 *n. 2*, 359 *n. 2*
Egranus, Johannes Sylvius: conflict w. Müntzer, 163–8, 170f., 179, 183, 186, 187, 191, 203, 265, 272, 326; in Zwickau, 160ff.
Eichsfeld, 240f.
Eichsfeld, Cistercian monastery at, 222
Eilenburg: Electoral consultation, 107
Eilenburg: Zwilling, G., 107
Einsiedel, Hugo von, 107–8
Eisenach, 108, 133, 200, 239
Eisleben, 212; mysticism, 120
Elect, the: Anabaptists, 387, 390, 394; Müntzer, T., and, 192, 213, 214, 257, 263, 267, 270, 283f., 285f., 291, 305, 310, 313, 314, 316, 317
Elijah, 178, 203, 218, 260, 268, 303
Elizabeth I, Queen of England, 105, 148, 189
Elizabeth, St, of Schönau, 258
Ellenbog, N., 9 *n. 4*
Elliger, Walther, 158, 188 *n. 3*, 284 *n. 3*, 309, 342
Elsterburg, 170; archdeacon of, 160 *n. 3*
Emmen, Ambrosius, 224
Emser, Jerome, Karlstadt, A., and, 75
ends: doctrine, 386
Engels, Friedrich, 157 *n. 2*, 231 *n. 1*

Enzenberg, Hans von, 222
epistles: liturgy, 316
Erasmians, Psalter and, 306
Erasmus, Desiderius, xvii, xviii *n. 1*, 63, 159 *n. 1*, 160, 215 *n. 2*, 253, 272, 364; antitheses in Scripture, 334; Basle departure, 38; biblical studies, 60–1, 83—*see also* Greek; Hebrew; Bible: New Testament, *etc.*; church music, 106; correspondence, 4; Eck, J., and, 59 *n. 1*; eucharistic doctrine, 24, 25, 26, 142; Farel, William, and, 21; Greek scholarship, 8; Hebrew scholarship, 8; humanism, 5, 55; John Chrysostom on Acts, and, 35; Karlstadt, A., and, 59, 81, 82, 83, 117, 124; Latin scholarship, 8; Latomus, against, 17; Luther, M., and, 21, 59; Müntzer, T., and, 251, 252, 326; Oecolampadius, J., and, xxii–xxiii, 19, 20, 21, 33, 34, 44; patristics, and, xxii, 11, 11 *n. 5*, 44, 61; Peutinger, Margaret, and, 14; 'philosophy of Christ', 348; Plato, and, 142; St Gall, 375; saints: invocations, 104; vows to, 92; Tunstall, C., and, 35; Vadianus, J., 365, 366, 367, 375; Valla, L., xx; works: *Augewählte Werke*, 11 *n. 2*; *Colloquies*, 44; *Exhortation to the study of Scripture*, 252; *Method of theology*, 76; *New Testament*, xix, 9–10, 20, 83, 365; *Ratio seu Methodus compendio perveniendi ad veram theologiam*, 11; ed. of Jerome, 9 vols, 1515–16, 10; ed. of Valla, L., *Adnotationes*, xx
Erfurt, 49, 51, 61, 68, 70, 74, 97, 182, 184, 225, 238, 249, 321, 335 *n. 2*
Ernest, bp of Magdeburg, 159
Ernest, Count of Mansfeld, 189f., 200, 221, 228, 238, 241ff., 300, 314, 329, *n. 2*

INDEX

eschatology: Müntzer's, 183, 202f., 209, 299f., 335
Etienne, H., 326 n. 4
Eucharist: Liturgy, 26, 28, 32, 38, 99, 101, 108, 134, 139, 142, 143, 147, 188, 245, 264f., 288f., 289 n. 4, 296-9, 313-22; Doctrine, 23-7, 44, 81, 87, 91, 96-9, 106, 141-53, 317-19, 370
Eusebius, 177f., 202, 253, 291
evangelicals: general refs, xxii, 28; Basel-Land expulsions, 31; Basle: armed band, 1529, 36
evil: creation, Karlstadt, A., 117, 118 n. 1
excommunication: Reformed, 38-9, 45; Roman, 39; Karlstadt, A., 88
Eyb, Gabriel von, bp of Eichstätt, 65

Faber, John (Catholic prosecutor), 7, 29, 34, 234
Fabricius, Johann Albert, 172 n. 2
faith, Anabaptists, and, 380-1, 390, 391, 392-3, 399; Karlstadt, A., and, 59, 81, 103; Luther, M., and, 59, 137, 152-3; Müntzer's view of, 186, 190ff., 202, 209ff., 214ff., 263ff., 274f., 280ff., 285, 305, 314, 320, 331, 339f., 345; Spalatin's Eleven Questions to Müntzer, 190f.; Vadianus, J., on, 367, 376, 377; 'Initial Faith' 393; *see also* justification by faith; and works: Reformers, and, 23
family worship, 123, 124-5, 129, 369
Farel, William: Basle, 21
Fast, Heinold, 157 n. 1, 234 n. 3, 332 n. 1
fasting: communion, 99
Fathers, xvii, xx, 10-12, 16, 58, 314, 342 n. 3; Alexandrian, 11; authority of, 20, 29, 57; Cappadocian, 12, 19; Greek, xxiii, 12, 42, 44; Latin, 42; Müntzer, 326

Fear of the Lord, 202, 215, 268f., 271 n. 2, 276-9, 328
Feldkirchen, Bartholomew, 56, 60, 62, 67
Fellmann, Walter, 118 n. 1, 334 n. 2
Fife, R. H., 70 n. 1
fire, baptism and, 398-9
Fisher, John, bp of Rochester, xxi, 35
Florence, 5, 24, 37
Florentine Academy, 5, 360
Florus, Lucius: Roman History, 361
Foxe, John, xxi n. 2, xxii, 9
Fraenkel, Peter, xvii n. 1
Franciscans, 79, 159, 164, 252, 263
Franck, Sebastian, xx, xxi n. 1, 152, 215 n. 2, 271
Franconia, 49, 136, 231
Frankfort on the Oder: University, 159, 251
Frankenhausen, 157, 185, 237-50, 321, 335, 336 n. 2-3, 345, 346, 351
Franz, Günther, 159 n. 2, 3, 160, 161, n. 2, 163 n. 1, 2, 164 n. 1, 166 n. 2, 170 n. 1-4, 171 n. 1, 3, 172 n. 3, 174 n. 1, 175 n. 1, 182 n. 1, 184 n. 1-4, 6, 187 n. 1, 188 n. 1, 3, 189 n. 1, 190 n. 1, 191 n. 1, 197 n. 2, 198 n. 1, 200 n. 1, 201 n. 2, 203 n. 1, 204 n. 2-3, 205 n. 1-2, 206 n. 2, 209 n. 1, 212 n. 1-2, 213 n. 1, 215 n. 1-2, 216 n. 1-3, 217 n. 1-2, 218 n. 1, 219 n. 1, 220 n. 1, 224 n. 1, 225 n. 1, 226 n. 2, 227 n. 1-2, 229 n. 2, 231 n. 1, 233 n. 1, 235 n. 3, 239 n. 1-2, 241 n. 2, 245 n. 1, 249, 251 n. 2, 252 n. 1-3, 5, 253 n. 1, 4-6, 255 n. 1, 257 n. 1, 259 n. 3-5, 260 n. 1-2, 261 n. 2, 263, n. 1-6, 264 n. 1, 265 n. 2, 266 n. 1-9, 267 n. 2-12, 268 n. 1-7, 269 n. 1-7, 270 n. 1-5, 273 n. 1-4, 274 n. 1-2, 275 n. 1-2, 276 n. 1, 277 n. 1-2, 278 n. 1-3, 5, 279 n. 1-5, 280 n. 1, 3-7, 281 n. 1-9, 282 n.1 -2, 283 n. 1-7, 284 n. 1-7, 285 n. 1-3,

INDEX

286 *n. 1–5*, 287 *n. 1–4*, 288 *n. 1, 3–4*, 289 *n. 1–3*, 290 *n. 1–2, 4*, 291 *n. 1–5*, Franz *n. 1–3*, 293 *n. 1–2*, 294 *n. 1–3, 4*, 295 *n. 1–3*, 296 *n. 1–3*, 297 *n. 1*, 301 *n. 1–4*, 305 *n. 1*, 306 *n. 1, 3*, 307, *n. 3* 313 *n. 1*, 326 *n. 1–3*, 329 *n. 2, 4–5*, 331 *n. 1, 2*, 336 *n. 2, 3*, 339 *n. 1, 2*, 340 *n. 1*, 347 *n. 1*, 385 *n. 1, 2*, 386 *n. 2, 3*, 391 *n. 1*, 392 *n. 1*

Franz, V., 101 *n. 2*, 134 *n. 3*

Frederick, Elector of Saxony, called the Wise, 51–3, 67, 74–5, 88f., 94–9, 100–2, 107–9, 112 *n. 2*, 132–6, 185, 189f., 196ff., 227f., 233, 238, 259 *n. 2*, 261, 300, 329 *n. 1*

free will, 21, 56, 70 *n. 2*, 71 *n. 2*, 73, 118, 252, 304

Freiburg, 364

Freistat, Hans von, 171

Freudenberger, Theobald, 6 *n. 2*

Freys, E., and Barge, H., 116 *n. 2*, 118 *n. 2, 3*, 137 *n. 1, 2*, 138 *n. 1*, 143 *n. 1*, 147 *n. 2*

Friedmann, Robert, 157 *n. 1*, 335 *n. 1*

'Friends of God', 254f., 257, 276, 291, 310, 315, 338, 392

Frisia, 149

Frobenius, Johannes, xvii, 8, 11 *n. 5*

Frohse, 159, 305

Froude, J. A., 9 *n. 3*

Fuggers, family, of Augsburg, 15

Fulda, 235, 238f., 240

fundamentalism, 322

Furcheim, John, 79

Gall, St, 358

Gans, Michael, 170

Gansfort, Wessel, 115 *n. 2*, 142, 183

Gardiner, Stephen, bp of Winchester, 16

Garrard, Thomas, xxi

Gayer, Florian, 233

Gehofen, Matern von, 243, 245

Geiler, John, of Kaysersberg, 4

Gelassenheit (resignation), 57, 69, 85 *n. 2*f., 113, 116, 118 *n. 4*, 119, 120, 123, 128, 248, 256f., 264, 284, 299, 327, 338, 398

Geneva: reformers at, 21, 198

George, Duke of Saxony, 68, 70, 74, 88–91, 107, 199, 204, 221, 222, 225f., 237, 238, 240, 244, 300

Gerard of Borgo San Domino: *Eternal Gospel of Joachim*, 257

Gerbel, Nicholas, 9–10

Gerdes, Hayo, 104 *n. 1*, 124, 254 *n. 2*

German Knights, 222, 237; Mass, 314–20

Gerson, Jean Charlier de, 7, 57, 82, 251, 327

Geyerfalk, Thomas, 30

ghosts, 151. *See also* poltergeist haunting

Gideon, 244, 260, 303

Gilson, E., 71 *n. 2*

Glareanus, Heinricus (Loriti), 35, 36, 371

Glatz, Kaspar, 135 *n. 1*

Glitzsch, Konrad, 81, 101, 113, 114

Gloria in excelsis, 315

Glov, Achatius, 253

Goebke, Hermann, 159 *n. 1, 4*, 184 *n. 6*

Goertz, H. J., 277 *n. 2*

Goeters, J. F., Gerhard, 24 *n. 3*

Goetz, Walter, 18 *n. 3*

Gorce, D., xvii, *n. 1*, 11 *n. 1, 2, 4*

Goslar, 225

'Gospel of all creatures', 261, 278, 290, 334, 344, 346–53, 383

gospels: liturgy, 26, 316

Grace, 56, 58, 63, 66, 69, 70 *n. 2*, 71, 73, 74, 76, 367

Grebel, Conrad, 138 *n. 1*, 139 *n. 1*, 152, 157 *n. 1*, 234, 322–3, 345f., 362, 363, 364, 367, 371–2

407

Grebel, Martha. *See* Vadianus, Martha
Greek (language), xix, xxi, 8, 12, 51, 61, 144–6, 159, 259, 337, 360
Greenslade, S. L., xvii *n. 1*
Gregorian chant, 105–6, 306, 308
Gregory I, Pope, called the Great, 59, 103
Gregory Nazianzen, St, 11, 12 *n. 1*, 14–16, 253, 303
Gregory, of Nyssa, xviii *n. 1*, xxi, 12 *n. 1*, 16
Gregory of Rimini, 49 *n. 3*, 51, 57
Greving, J., 65 *n. 1*, 66 *n. 2*
Grisar, Hartmann, 302
Gritsch, E. W., 117 *n. 1*, 262 *n. 1*, 288 *n. 2*
Grünewald, K., 255 *n. 2*
Grynaeus, Jacob, 49 *n. 1*
Grynaeus, Simon, 43, 150
Guggisberg, K., 31 *n. 2*
Günther, Count von Schwarzburg, 233 *n. 1*
Günther, Franz, 164, 183, 251 *n. 2*, 252, 306
Günther, G., 221 *n. 1*
guilds, 31, 32
Guyon, Mme, 120

Haferitz, Simon, 185, 197
Haina, 332
Halberstadt, 159; breviary, 308
Halle, 159, 184, 221
Halley's Comet, 361, 376
Handel, George Frederick, 153
Haner, John, 27
Hartenstein, Stefan, 243, 245
Hätzer, Ludwig, 24, 152
Haug von Juchsen, 250, 351–2
Hausmann, Nicholas, 147, 170, 172 *n. 3*, 175 *n. 1*, 181, 186f., 188, 259 *n. 2*
Hebrew (language), xix, xxi, 5, 8, 9, 13, 61, 72, 144, 159, 259, 309
Hedio, Kaspar, xviii

Hegau, 231, 240
Hegesippus, St, 177, 178, 253, 291
Heidelburg, 3–5, 8, 59, 65, 136 *n. 1*
Heilbronn, 3
Heldrungen, 241, 245ff.
Helmann, Sebastian: Karlstadt, A., 91, 93 *n. 3*
Henry VIII, King of England, 147 *n. 2*; University reform, 61
Henry, of Brunswick, 243
Hermann, Rudolf, 6 *n. 2*, 188 *n. 3*
Hermas, xviii *n. 1*, 258
Herrgott, Hans, 214
Hertzsch, Erich, 121 *n. 1*, 123 *n. 1*, 125 *n. 1–3*, 127 *n. 1*, 134, *n. 2*, 137 *n. 2*, 138 *n. 1*, 144 *n. 2*, 148 *n. 2*
Herzog, J. J., 3 *n. 1*
Hess, John, 91
Hesse, 231
Hilary, St, Bp of Poitiers, xviii *n. 1*, xxii, 11
Hildegard, St, of Bingen, 254, 258, 327
Hillerbrand, Hans J., 227 *n. 2*, 229 *n. 2*, 250
Hinrichs, Carl, 158, 185, 189 *n. 2*, 196 *n. 2*, 197 *n. 1*, 198 *n. 1*, 199, 200, 201, 204 *n. 1*, 206, 207, 247
Hippolytus, St, 188
Hiskold, Matthew, 79
Hochrütiner, Laurence, 40, 371
Hodejovsky, Jan, 171
Hoen, Cornelius, 23, 142
Holbein, Hans, the younger, xv
Holborn, Hajo, 11 *n. 2*
Holl, Karl, 158, 263, 345 *n. 2*
Höltzel, Hieronymus, 227
Holy days, 123, 128–9
Holy Spirit, 59, 122, 144–5, 164, 176, 179f., 186, 210, 263, 265–72, 273, 314, 315, 317, 325, 367, 372, 379, 387, 391, 392, 393, 397–8
holy water: Karlstadt, A., on, 80–1, 91, 142

INDEX

Hooker, Richard, xxii, 148, 153
Höss, Irmgard, 90 *n. 1*, 95 *n. 4*, 106 *n. 1*, 190, 191 *n. 1*, 279
Hours, Books of, 306
Hubmaier, Balthasar, 24, 26, 40 *n. 1*, 157 *n. 1*, 234f., 332, 333
Huguenots, 248
Hugwald, 234
humanism, xvii, xxi, xxii, 5, 13, 34, 60, 61, 62, 71, 75, 151, 251, 252f., 254, 326, 327, 360
humanists, lay, 377
humanitarianism, Reformation and, 105
Husa, Václav, 170 *n. 1, 4*, 171, 172, *n. 1, 3*, 174, 181
Huss, John, 83
Hussites, 92, 202, 258f., 276, 326
Huth, Hans, 81, 215 *n. 2*, 226, 244, 250, 270f., 295, 331–46, 332 *n. 4*
Hutten, Ulrich von, 109
hymns, 26, 125–6, 128, 188, 195, 207–8, 309, 310, 311–13, 316, 320–3

iconoclasm, 32, 36–7, 370, 371, 373
idolatry, 118 *n. 1*, 103, 138
images, 32, 36–7, 38, 101, 102–4, 105, 111, 114, 124, 136, 138, 139, 147–8, 357, 367, 372, 373
Imitation of Christ, 120–1
Incarnation, eucharist and, 144–7
Index librorum prohibitorum, 343
indulgences, 58, 63, 65, 66, 69, 70, 79–80, 89, 106, 160, 254
infant baptism, 40 *n. 1*, 139 *n. 1*, 181, 210, 275, 295f., 333, 345, 371, 399
Ingdstadt, 15; University, 13
Initiation, Christian, 276, 280, 285
inspiration, 76
Irenaeus, St, bp of Lyons, xviii *n. 1*, 29, 42, 285, 288
Iserloh, E., 8 *n. 1*

Jacobs, Henry Eyster, 93 *n. 2*

Jäger, C. F., 70 *n. 1*, 72 *n. 1*, 73 *n. 1*, 2, 75 *n. 4*, 80 *n. 1*, 84 *n. 1*, 123 *n. 1*, 124
Jansen, Cornelius, 71
Jauchsen, Jorg von, 250
Jena, 109, 116, 121–2, 131, 135–6 and 135 *n. 1, 3*, 142 *n. 2*
Jeremiah, 178, 214, 261; commentary ascribed to Joachim da Fiore, 257, 326
Jerome, St, xviii *n. 1*, xxi, 10, 11, 12 *n. 1*, 14, 59, 60, 73, 76, 82, 83, 253, 367
Jewell, John, bp of Salisbury, xxii
Jews, 39, 328, 329
Joachim da Fiore, 257, 326, 327
Joachimsthal, 79, 162, 164, 167, 168, 171
John XXI, Pope (Petrus Hispanus), 3, 61
John, bp of Lübeck: Book of Hours, 306
John Chrysostom, St, xviii *n. 1*, xxii, 11, 12, 18, 20, 34, 35, 43, 113
John, Elector of Saxony, 114, 132–3, 196–7, 200
John Frederick, Elector of Saxony, 133, 181, 199–200
John, of Damascus, xviii, 16
John the Baptist, St, 193, 214f., 217, 267, 268, 303, 381 *n. 3*, 390, 396
John the Evangelist, St, 398
Johnson, Samuel, 368, 376
Jonah, 187, 282, 339, 393
Jonas, Justus, 52, 86, 90, 91, 94, 96, 100, 102, 107, 141, 149, 187, 322
Jordan, W. K., 105 *n. 2*
Josiah, 203, 205, 262
Judas Iscariot: allegory, 7, 141
justification by faith, 20, 23, 68, 76, 95, 165, 211, 262f., 265, 275, 345, 381, 389–90, 392–4, 397
Justin, Martyr, St, 266

Kähler, E., 49 *n. 1*, 56 *n. 3*, 57 *n. 1*, 58 *n. 1*, 59, 60 *n. 4*, 69 *n. 1*

Kantzenbach, F. W., xxii *n. 1*
Karlstadt, Andrew Rudolf Bodenstein von, xiv, xviii, 7, 11 *n. 3*, 47–153, 159, 200, 201, 251, 255, 381 *n. 2*; anabaptists, 250, 352; Baptism, 345f.; Eck, J., and, 28, 252; eucharistic doctrine—*See* Eucharist: doctrine; Grebel, 345f.; Gregorian chants, 306; Müntzer, T., 182, 184, 187, 188, 214, 252, 256f., 273, 296 *n. 3*, 298, 305, 326; mystical language, 276; preaching, 207; sevenfold gifts of the Spirit, 270; *Theologia Germanica*, 327; Thomism of, 330 *n. 1*; Urbanus Rhegius, 331; vocation, 350; Wittenberg, 168, 182, 183; Andrew: works: *adversus disputationem et Pomerani argumenta librum edunt et prelo committent*, 149 *n. 1*; *Against the old and new Popish Mass*, 147–8; *Auslegung und Erläuterung*, 69; *Bedingungen*, 83–4; *Dialogue . . . of the abominable and idolatrous. Misuse of the Blessed Sacrament . . .*, 144–7; *Defensio contra D. Johannis Eckium monomachiam*, 68; *Distinctions*, 50; *Farrago Rerum Theologicarum*, 142 *n. 1*; *The Intentions*, 50; *Letter against the inept and ridiculous invention of John Eck*, 75; *Missive von der allerhöchsten Tugend Gelassenheit*, 85f.; *Of Holy Water and Salt*, 80; *Of the anti-Christian misuse of the Bread and Cup of the Lord*, 146 *n. 1*; *Of the Papal Holiness*, 84; *Of the Priesthood and Sacrifice of Christ*, 142; *On the Adoration and Reverence for the signs of the New Testament*, 96; *On the Words of God, and with what sincerity and plainness they ought to be preached*, 75; *Open letter about the very highest virtue of resignation*, 85f.; *Theses*, 65–6; *Von Vormögen des Ablas, wider bruder Franciscus Seyler parfuser ordens*, 80; *What Books are Biblical*, 83; *Whether it can be shown from holy scripture that Christ . . . is in the sacrament*, 143

Karlstadt, Andrew, jun., 134 *n. 3*
Karlstadt, Anna, 100, 132, 136, 151
Karlstadt, city of 49, 136 *n. 1*
Kawerau, Peter, 149 *n. 1*
Keble, John, 12 *n. 2*, 343f.
Keller (Cellarius), Ludwig, 8 *n. 3*, 33, 56
Kemberg, 149
Kessler, David, 369
Kessler, Johannes, 109, 368–78
Kessler, John, jun., 369
Kierkegaard, Sören Aabye, xv, 55, 248, 287, 304
Kingdom of God: Anabaptists on, 384–5, 391; suffering, 91, 97
Kirchner, Hubert, 161
Klassen, H., 332 *n. 3*, 345 *n. 2*
Klettgau, 231, 240, 346
Knaute, Ziliax, 197, 199
Knepper, J., 4 *n. 1*
Knox, John, 18, 358, 361
Köditz, Hanna, 298 *n. 2*
Köhler, Walther, 23 *n. 1*, 24, 25 *n. 1*
Kohls, E. W., 302
Kolde, Th., 56 *n. 3*
Könneritz, Heinrich von, 79
Koopmans, J., xix *n. 1*
Koran, 210, 253, 328
Kosmincki, E. A., 157
Krug, 249
Krump, Balthasar, 240
Krump, (Krumpe) Bartel, 198 *n. 3*, 240

Lactantius, 12 *n. 1*
laity: eucharist and, 144–5; theological study and, 366
Lambert, Francis, Franciscan of Avignon, xxi

INDEX

Landeen, 255
Lang, A., 123 *n. 2*
Lang, John, 57, 59–60, 61, 75, 321–2
Lang, Matthaeus, abp of Salzburg, 183
Langensalza, 240
Langweil, 213, 218, 257, 283–4, 327, 338, 341
Lasco, John a: liturgy of, 323
Latimer, Hugh, bp of Worcester, 4, 32, 302 *n. 2*
Latin (language), xix, 8, 51, 61, 159, 163, 259f., 332 *n. 4*, 337
Lau, Franz, 158
Lauds, 307, 308
Law, 192, 212f., 226, 228, 265 *n. 1*, 269, 277f., 280, 288, 293, 294, 330; and Gospel, 59, 103, 124, 130, 137–8, 153; and liberty: Karlstadt, A., 147–8; and love: Karlstadt, A., 137–8; and Spirit: Karlstadt, A., on, 58, 59, 126–7—*see also* of Moses, 148, 386ff.; of nature—*see* nature, law of
lay initiative, 152; ministry, 378
Lebe, Hans, 170
Lebrixa, Antonio, xx
lectureships, English Puritan, 6
Lee, Edward, 10
Le Fèvre, Jacques, d'Etaples, xvii, xviii *n. 1*, xx, xxii, 4, 11, 24, 62, 327; Müntzer, T., 326; *Liber trium virorum et trium spiritualium virginum*, 326; *Quincuplex Psalterium*, xx
Le Fèvre, Pierre, 258
Leff, G., 49 *n. 3*
legal studies: Calvin, J., 5; Karlstadt, A., 52–3, 82; Vienna University, 363
legends, liturgical use of, 306
Legge, J., Wickham, 307 *n. 1*
Leipzig: Karlstadt, A., and, 56, 68, 69; St Thomas's, 70; University, 159, 251

Leipzig Disputation, 1519, 68–74, 77, 101; Luther, M., in, 68, 69, 70, 72, 77, 227, 253; Müntzer, T., 81, 253
Leo, Pope, the Great, 12 *n. 1*
Leo X, Pope, 85, 186
Lessons: liturgy, 307, 309, 316
Letter *v.* Spirit: Karlstadt, A., and, 59, 124
Letters of the Obscure Men, xix
liberty: Christian, 20, 28, 124, 125, 148, 152–3, 367
libraries: Basle: Dominican, 20; Cuspinianus, 360; Munich, 14 *n. 2*, 3; Müntzer, T., 252–3; Oecolampadius, J., 16, 17; Peutinger, C., 13–14; Reuchlin, J., 5, 8; Rhenanus, B., 11 *n. 5*; St Gall: abbey, 262, 358, 362; St Gall: Stadtbibliothek, 367, 374 *n. 2*; Tübingen: University, 8; Vadianus, J., 377
Liestal: Oecolampadius, J., at, 43
linen trade: St Gall, 358, 359
Litany: sick and dying, 28
Littell, F. H., xxii *n. 1*
liturgical reform: Karlstadt, A., 87, 147; Lang, J., 207; Luther, M., 188; Müntzer, T., 188f., 195f., 207, 253, 267, 275, 287 *n. 1*, 288, 291, 296f., 299, 305–23; Oecolampadius, J., 26 liturgy: history, 308, 314; uses, various, 319; *see also* Allstedt liturgy; baptism; Benedictus; Bible: liturgical use; breviaries; Bucer, Martin: liturgy of; collects; epistles: liturgy; Erfurt: Service Books; eucharist; gospels: liturgy; gradual; Hours, Books of; hymns; Lasco, John a: liturgy of; Lauds; legends; lessons; Lord's Prayer; Luther, Martin: liturgical experiments; Magnificat; Mass; Mattins; Müntzer, T., liturgy of; Müntzer, T., works: *Deutsch*

411

Evangelisch Messze; nocturns; Nunc dimittis; prayer; processions; Psalms; Roman liturgy; silence; Te Deum; vernacular liturgy; versicles and responses; vespers; Vigils; visitation of the sick

Loewenstein, counts of, 233

logic: reform, and, 60; Scotist, 62; Thomist, 62

Lohmann, Annemarie, 158, 170 *n.1*, 173, 259, 306

Lollards, 142, 276, 298

Lombard, Peter, xviii, xxii; Augustine, St, and, 49 *n. 3*; Luther, M., and, 55, 56; *Sentences*, 60

Lord's Prayer, 318, 321

Lortz, J., 70 *n. 3*, 71

Lösche, D., 221 *n. 1*

Louvain, university, 17; humanism, and, 60

Lübeck, John, bp of, *see* Hours, Books of

Lukas, Brother, leader of Hussite Church of the Brethren, 181

Luke, St, 366, 398

Lull, Raymond, 327, 342 *n. 3*

Lupinus, Peter: biblical authority, and, 60; patristics, and, 60

Luthard, Johannes, 30

Luther, Martin, xiii–xiv, xviii–xix, xxii, 85, 86, 93 *n. 2*, 108–9, 141, 152–3, 159, 189, 226, 252, 346 *n. 1*; Amsdorf, N., and, 51 *n. 1*; '*Anfechtung*' and Anabaptists, 393 *n. 1*; Aquinas, Thomas, St, and, 50 *n. 1*; Augustine, St, and, 49 *n. 3*, 55, 56, 57, 58, 59; Augsburg, and, 13, 67, 68; Bible: German, 88; Bible: Hebrew, 109; Bible: liturgy, 128; biblical studies, 55, 60, 61, 63; Hebrews, 60, 63; Romans, 63, 192 *n. 1*; Old Testament, 104; Pentateuch, 83; Psalms, 187, 212 *n. 3*; Brück, G., 132 *n. 1*; Cajetan, J., and, 13, 67; Canon law and, 60; Cassian, J., edition of, 253; catechism, 128; Catholic opinions about, 29; church music, 106; civil government, 200, 205 *n. 1*, 206, 247f., 254, 260, 300; Councils, 179; Cross theology, 58, 68, 328; Decretals and, 56, 60; Denmark proposal, 87; Eck, J., and, 11, 13, 15, 28, 65, 66, 67, 74–5, 82; Egranus, J. S., 165, 168; election, doctrine, 164; Erasmus, D., and, 21, 33, 59; eucharistic doctrine, etc., 23, 24, 25, 42, 93, 95, 96, 99, 142–3, 147–8, 318; excommunication, 83; exegesis, and, 25; faith and, 59, 109, 119, 192 *n. 1*, 282, 285, 328; Frederick, *Elector*, and, 67, 89, 99, 108–9, 132, 135–6, 169, 190; *Gelassenheit*, 85 *n. 2*; Glatz, K., 135 *n. 1*; Gregory Nazianzen, St, 303; Hebrews, lectures on, 260; humanists, and, 13, 55; Huth, H., 332 *n. 4*; hymns, 128, 195, 311–12; images, 147–8; impeachment and arrest, 63, 67, 81, 82; imprisonment—*see* Luther, Martin: Wartburg: Castle; indulgences, 58, 63, 65, 66, 69, 80, 89; Jena, 109; 135–6; John Frederick, Duke, 133; justification by faith, 165, 275; Karlstadt, A., and, 49 *n. 1*, 50 *n. 2*, 51 *n. 1*, 55–6, 57, 58, 63, 66–70, 72, 75, 76, 77, 79, 81, 82, 89, 90, 93, 95, 103, 110, 111, 112, 113, 117, 121, 123–4, 127, 131–2, 134, 137–8, 141, 147–8, 149, 150, 152, 183; Karlstadt, Anna, 151; Lang, J., and, 59–60, 61; Law and Gospel, 59, 109, 124, 147–8, 153, 277; legal studies, 5; Leipzig Disputation, 68, 69, 70, 74–5, 77; liturgical experiments, 188, 308, 323; logic and, 60; Lombard, P., and, 55;

INDEX

Marburg conference, 42; marriage and, 33, 92, 100; Masses: private, 95–6; Marxist history, 158; Melanchthon, P., 90, 93, 100–1; ministry, 122 *n. 1*; Müntzer, T., 24, 137, 160, 168, 174f., 179, 183, 184, 186ff., 194, 195, 198, 199, 202, 203, 207, 214, 219, 224, 227f., 231, 247, 250, 253f., 259, 262, 264f., 269, 274 *n. 1*, 275f., 282, 283, 285, 291 *n. 3*, 294, 299, 303, 304, 305, 307, 322, 381, *n. 3*; music, 153, 308; mysticism, 121; natural law, 124, 292; Nominalism, 51, 55; Oecolampadius, J., 13, 17, 19, 21, 22, 23, 32, 42; Orlamünde, 134; Papal Bull, 15, 21, 88, 89; patristics, xxii, 11 *n. 3*, 55, 60; Peasant's war, 205 *n. 1*, 232ff., 242; penitence, 63; Peringer, D., 118 *n. 1*; philosophy and, 4, 55, 56, 60; prayer, 132; preaching, 125, 127–8, 133, 134, 182; preaching: lay, 123; Psalms, 309; reform programme, 88, 90, 109, 151; relics and, 57, 80, 108; religious orders, 252; Roman primacy and, 69; Sabbatarianism, 124, 127; saints' cults and, 104–5; scholasticism and, 55, 60, 61; Scheuerl, C., and, 61; sermons, 1518–20, 252; sermons, 1522, 109, 182; Spalatin, G., and, 61, 67, 97, 112 *n. 1*, 131–2; statues and pictures, 103–4; Staupitz, J., and, 56; suffering, 91; Sunday: Christian, 124–5; Tauler, J., 255; temptation (*Anfechtung*), 280; *Theologia Germanica*, etc., 252–3; Thomism and, 51 *n. 1*; Thuringian tour, 133; Turtfetter, J., and, 51, 60; usury, 126 *n. 3*; Vadianus, J., 365, 367, 374; vocation, on, 122 *n. 1*, 302–3, 350; Vows (clerical and monastic), 92, 96, 101; Wartburg: Castle, 88, 108, 142 *n. 1*, 182; will, human and God's, 117; Wittenberg: Augustinian Canons, 101, 109, 137; Wittenberg, Parish church: murals, 141; Wittenberg: sermons, 109, 134, 137–8, 182; Wittenberg: town, 90, 108, 110; Wittenberg: University, 52, 55–63, 66, 67, 88; Wittenberg Movement, 88f., 90ff.; Word of God, 266; works: *Against the Heavenly Prophets*, 103–4, 124, 147–8, 279 *n. 3*; *Against the murdering hordes of peasants*, 243; *Appeal to the Christian Nobility*, 80, 84, 175; *Appeal to the . . . German Nation*, 76; '*Asterisks*', 65; *Babylonish captivity*, 254; *Concerning Monastic vows*, 95–6; *Concerning the ministry*, 122 *n. 1*; doctrine, 80 *n. 2*; *Exposition of the Epistle to the Romans*, 192 *n. 1*; *Liberty of a Christian man*, 254; *Ninety-five theses*, 80 *n. 2*; *Of Civil Authority*, 254; *Of the Abrogating Private Masses*, 95; *Open letter concerning the rebellious spirit*, 227; *Open letter to the rulers of Saxony*, 206; *Operationes in Psalmos*, 125 *n. 4*; *Resolutions*, 1519, 82; *Table Talk*, 255 *n. 3*, 276 *n. 3*; *Von Ordnung Gottesdienstes in der Gemeinde*, 188; *Von Weltlicher Obrigkeit*, 200; *Vorlesung über den Hebräerbrief*, 274 *n. 3*; Weimar edition, 97 *n. 2*; Worms Diet, 67, 169; worship, pattern, 128

Lutheranism: Karlstadt, A., and, 152; Reformation, and, 149, 153; mysticism, 121

Lutherans, 226

Lutheran tradition, xiv, 105, 139

Magdeburg: bishops. *See* Ernest, Bishop of Magdeburg

INDEX

Magdeburg: riots, 36
magic: medieval 'blessings', and, 80
Magnificat, 309
Mainz, Albert, abp of. *See* Albert, abp of Mainz
Mainz: indulgences, 106; Peasants' War, 231
Mallerbach, 196–8, 200, 300
Manuel, Nicholas, 29
Marbach: Vadianus' family, 365
Marbeck, Pilgram, 342, 352, 377
Marburg: Eucharistic Colloquy, 42, 141, 149, 201
Marius, Augustinus: Basle: Münster: preacher, 30, 35
Mansfeld, 120, 185, 198f., 221
Mantz, Felix, 346, 353
Marius, John, 361
marriage: Basle ordinance, 38; clerical, 91, 106, 114 *n. 1*—*see* also celibacy; (clerical) Feldkirchen, Bernhard, 91; (clerical) Jonas, Justus, 100; (clerical) Karlstadt, A., 87, 100; (clerical) Müntzer, T., 182; (clerical) Vadianus, J., 364–5; monks, 91—*see also* celibacy; Oecolampadius, J., and Rosenblatt, W., 32; service, 321; Westerburg, G., and Von Mochau, 114; widows, 91
Martinians, xiii
Martyr, Peter: eucharistic doctrine, 27
Marxism, xiv, 36
Mary, Virgin: baptism, 296; Karlstadt, A., 116; Müntzer, T., 196–8, 214f., 296; soteriology, 116, 161
Mass: revised order, 18, 28, 99, 101, 114. *See also* Eucharistic: liturgy; (Roman) Canon, 318 *n. 1*; (Roman) communicants, 28, 97–8; (Roman) Karlstadt, A., 138; (Roman) Kyries, 315 *n. 2*; (Roman) and, Müntzer, T., and, 183, 306, 308, 315, 318 *n. 1*, 319; (Roman) private, 87 *n. 1*, 93, 94, 95; (Roman) Reformers and, 23, 30–1, 35, 36, 92–3, 94, 95, 96, 97, 98, 142–3, 372; (Roman) sacrifice, 142–3; (Roman) St Gall, 357; (Roman) St Gall abolition, 372; (Roman) Wittenberg petition, 98; reduction of, 106–7; (Roman) Zürich Disputation, 367
Mathematics: study of, 61, 360, 361
Mattins, 307, 308, 314, Advent, 308–9
Mauersberg, H., 18 *n. 3*
Maximilian, Emperor, 358, 360
Meaux: Oecolampadius, J., and, 21
Mecenseffy, G., 250, 335 *n. 1*, 338
Mechtild, of Hackeborn, 120, 258
medicine: Vadianus, J., 361, 363, 364–5, 375
Mehl, O. J., 158 and *n. 1*, 305 *n. 1*, 306 *n. 1*, 308, 313 *n. 1*, 321 *n. 2*
Meinhard, Christopher, 212, 235, 277, 347 *n. 1*, 386 *n. 2*
Meissen: Bull against Karlstadt, A., 83; episcopal visitation, 106
Melanchthon, Philip, 157, 166, 200, 252, 335; clerical marriage, 91, 100; Drechsel, T., 100–1; eucharistic doctrine, 42, 92, 94, 95, 99; Feldkirchen, Bernhard, 91; Huth, H., 332 *n. 4*; John, St, 368; Karlstadt, A., and, 63, 86, 100, 111, 132 *n. 2*, 150; Kessler, J., 368; Leipzig disputation and, 69; library of, 8; Luther, M., and, 21, 93, 95–6; Marburg conference, 42; Müntzer, T., 167, 172, *n. 3*, 179, 182, 183, 184, 187, 194, 247, 265, 326, 327, 328; Oecolampadius, J., and, 4; patristics, xvii *n. 1*, xxi; Peasants' War, 232f.; Reuchlin, J., and, 5, 62; Spalatin, G., 100–1; Storch, N., 100–1; Stübner, M., and, 100–1, 113, 166,

414

170, 181; theses of, 172 *n. 3*, 173f.; Vadianus, J., 365, 366; Von Einsiedel, H., 107; Wittenberg Movement, 93, 94, 95, 97ff.; Wittenberg town council, 98, 102; Wittenburg University and, 61, 62, 89; Zwilling, G., 94; works: *Loci Communes*, 169, 254

Mennonites, 157, 335

Merseburg: episcopal visitation, 106, 111

messianism, 305, 323

Methodism, 287; Müntzer and, 270

Methodist Revival, 120

Merx, Otto, 185 *n.1*, 221 *n. 1*, 225 *n. 2*

Meusel, A., 157 *n. 2*

Meyer, C., 332 *n. 3*, 335 *n. 4*, 336 *n. 1*

Milt, Bernhard, 357 *n. 1*, 375 *n. 2*

Mochau, Anna von.

modes: Peregrinus, 316

Moeller, Bernd, xiv, 18 *n. 3*, 53 *n. 1*, 255 *n. 3*

Mohammedanism: Müntzer's theology compared with, 304

Möller, W., 226 *n. 3*

monasticism: abolition, 105; Müntzer, T., 161; Vadianus, J., 375

monks: apostasy, 101, 106; deposition and Anabaptists, 381

Montaigne, Michel de, 342 *n. 3*

More, Sir Thomas, 14, 377; family worship, 128; heretics and, 13 *n. 4*; humanism: Catholic, xxi, 5, 16; Peutinger, C., 13; religious orders, 16; saints: invocation, 104

Mörli, Wiborata, 371

Mosellanus, Petrus: humanism, 252; Leipzig disputation and, 70–1

Moses, 148, 192, 240, 278, 293, 330f., 349, 386, 387, 388

Movement (*Bewegung*), 218, 280–3, 328, 331, 338, 339, 340

Mozarab use, 319

Mühlhausen, 298 *n. 2*; Müntzer in, 221–9, 235, 237f., 240ff., 252 *n. 1*, 302, 336 *n. 2, 3*, 352

Müller, Karl: Wittenberg Movement, 90, 98 *n. 2*, 102

Müller, Konrad, 366 *n. 1*

Müller, L., 379 *n. 1*

Müller, Lydia, 172 *n. 3*, 173, 331, 332 *n. 1, 2*, 333 *n. 2*, 334 *n. 1, 3*, 337, 338, 339 *n. 3*, 351 *n. 2, 4*

Müller, Nikolaus, 91 *n. 4*, 93 *n. 3*, 94 *n. 1–2*, 95 *n. 1, 3, 4*, 96 *n. 1, 2*, 97 *n. 1*, 99 *n. 1*, 101 *n. 1, 3*, 107 *n. 1, 2*

Münster, 335

Münster, Sebastien, 8, 374

Müntzer, Thomas, xiv, 157–353; Anabaptists, 139 *n. 1*; anticlericalism, 93–4; Drechsel, T., 100; *Fürstenpredigt*, 134; Grebel, C., 139 *n. 1*; Karlstadt, A., and, 81, 101, 112, 113, 134; Law of Moses, 148; library, 252–3; liturgies of, 195, 305–23, 342—*see also* Allstedt liturgy; Lotter, M., and, 70; Luther, M., 137, 325, 326, 327, 328, 330, 381 *n. 3*; Mass, 134; Meinhard, C., 386 *n. 2*; mysticism, 113, 117 *n. 1*, 118; Oecolampadius, J., and, 24; penitence and, 68; Prague, 112; Psalms, 395 *n. 1*; Storch, N., 100; temptation—*see* Anfechtung: Muntzer, T., Thome M., 100; works: *Ausgedruckte Entblossung*, 226, 274, 336 *n. 2*, 391 *n. 1*, 392 *n. 1*; *Covenant Sermon*, 205f., 300; *Deutsch Evangelisch Messze*, 313–20; 322; *Expressed exposure of false faith in an untrue world*, 213ff.; *Hochverursachte Schutzrede*, 227, 342, 386 *n. 3*; *Order and account of the German Services recently established at Allstedt through the Servants of God*, 314–21;

INDEX

Prague Manifesto, 174–5, 188 n. 3, 190, 259, 270, 282, 291, 294, 296 n. 3, 303, 329, 330; *Protestation oder Entbietung*, 209ff., 339 n. 2, 385 n. 1; *Sermon before the Princes*, 201ff., 227f., 261f., 291 n. 3, 300, 334, 339 n. 1; *Von dem gedichteten Glauben*, 191, 274, 285, 385 n. 2

Murner, Thomas, 29, 227

Musculus, Wolfgang, xxi

music: church, 105–6, 153, 305 n. 1, 306, 308, 309, 316–20, 357–8; Vadianus, J., and, 363; Vienna University, 361

Mutz (Mucius), 364, 365

Myconius, Oswald: Basle, 150; Karlstadt, A., 150; Vadianus, J., and, 362

Myers, Frederic William Henry, 279 n. 3

mysticism: German, 7, 14, 117 n. 1, 118 n. 4, 151, 254, 284—see also *Gelassenheit*; (German) Karlstadt, A., and, 69, 113, 116, 118–19, 120–3, 124, 127–9, 152, 255ff.; (German) Müntzer, 254ff., 261, 266, 277 n. 2, 327; (German) Oecolampadius, J., and, 14; (German) Staupitz, J., and, 7, 56; vocabulary, 276, 338f.

Näf, Werner, 357 n. 1, 359 n. 1, 360 n. 2, 3, 361 n. 1, 362 n. 1, 363 n. 1, 364 n. 1, 366 n. 2, 373 n. 1, 2, 374 n. 1, 2, 375 n. 1

natural law: Luther, M., 124; Müntzer, 302

natural reason: Müntzer, 263, 293–5

natural theology, 277f., 292f., 337, 343f., 387–8. See also theology of nature

nature: biblical allegory and teaching, 384–5

nature, law of: Luther, M., 148; Müntzer, 292–3, 299

Naumburg, bp of, 106, 164

Naundorf nuns, 196

Nebuchadnezzar, 122, 202, 203, 286

Neocaesarea: St Basil's hospital, Oecolampadius, J., sermon at, 15

Neo-Thomists: Luther, M., and, 50 n. 1

Neuenburg: Basle chapter and, 36

Neuser, W., 332 n. 3, 333 n. 2

Neustadt: Luther, M., preaching, 135

Newman, John Henry, Cardinal, xxii, 303f.

Newton, Sir Isaac, 377

Nicholas, of Cusa, 5, 7, 251, 253, 278 n. 4, 294, 327, 328

Nicolsburg, 351 n. 4; Anabaptist debates in, 333

Nipperdey, T., 262 n. 1

Nocturns, 306, 308

nominalism, 82; Luther, M., and, 51, 55; Trutfetter, J., and, 51

Nordhausen, 160, 184, 207, 221, 225

Nunc dimittis, 319

Nuremberg: Cranmer, T., in, 307 n. 2; humanists, 13; Müntzer, T., 226–7, 336 n. 2; preacherships, 6 n. 2; Scheurl, C., in, 57, 61

Nuremberg, Diet of, 107–8, 131, 195; press censorship, 131

Obermann, H. A., 49 n. 3, 57 n. 1, 142 n. 1

Ochsenfart, 111

Ockham, William, xxii, 3, 8 n. 1, 49 n. 3, 51, 342 n. 3

Oecolampadius, Aletheia, 33, 44

Oecolampadius, Eusebius, 33, 36, 44

Oecolampadius, Irene, 33, 44

Oecolampadius, Johannes Hausschein, xvii, xviii n. 4, xxi, xxii, 1–46, 327; death of, 150; Karlstadt, A., 139, 149; Luther, M., and, 75; Müntzer, T., 187, 227, 234, 298;

416

works: *Canonici Indocti* (with Adelmann bros.), 73; *De genuina verborum Domini: 'Hoc est corpus meum' juxta vetustissimos authores expositione liber*, 25; *De reducenda excommunicatione*, 38; *De risu paschali*, 12; *Liturgy*, 28; *On the harmful and fruitful winds which blow in the garden of the soul*, 14; *True Easter Joy*, 13; *The Wise Virgin*, 14
Oecolampadius, Wibrandis. *See* Bucer, Wibrandis
Of the Mystery of Baptism, authorship of text of, 331–46, 379 *n. 1*, 379–99
Of true and false penitence, 56
Öhringen: preachership, 6 *n.* 2
Oporinus, Johannes, 8, 9
Orange, Council of, 71
'Order.' *See Ordnung*
Ordinance of the City of Wittenberg. *See* Wittenberg: Ordinance of the City . . .
Ordnung, 294, 330, 339, 347, 380, 382; baptism, 383, 389
organs: Karlstadt, A., 106
Origen (Adamantius), xviii *n. 1*, xxii, 11, 12 *n. 1*, 59
Orlamünde: anticlericalism, 134; Glatz, K., 134–5; Glitzsch, K., and, 101; Karlstadt, A., and, 52, 81, 101, 111–30, 132–6, 137 *n. 2*, 195; Luther, M., 135–6
Osiander, Andrew, 226, 262, 307 *n.* 2
Østergaard-Nielsen, H., xix *n. 1*
Oswald, Matthias, 364–5
Oxford Movement, xvii, 12
Oxford University: Greek study, xxi; Hebrew study, xxi; patristics at, xxi–xxii; reform, 61

pacifism: Müntzer, T., 323
Padua: University: Vadianus, J., 362–3

Papal Bulls: Luther, M., 88, 89
parables, 385, 387
Paracelsus, Philippus, 375–6
paraphrases: Müntzer, T., 309
Paris: Anabaptists and, 381; humanists, 4; University, 26, 51, 62, 70, 74
Passion: eucharist, 96
Passiontide: Müntzer's office, 310
Patriarchs: Luther and, 260; Müntzer and, 203, 216, 260
patristics: xvii, xviii, xxii, 10–12, 21, 29, 33–4, 44–5, 58; biblical studies and, 60, 61, 66, 82; eucharistic doctrine and, 25, 42; Müntzer, T., 177, 251, 253, 266, 298; Vadianus, J., 365
patristic studies: Wittenberg: University, 59–60, 65
Paul, Apostle: 103, 106, 117, 122, 138, 176–8, 213, 266, 286 *n. 3*, 287–8, 297–8, 306–7, 314, 315, 316, 322–3, 339, 348, 349, 366, 367, 380, 383, 384, 387, 389–91, 396
Peasants' War, 24, 32, 134, 148, 151, 207, 208, 231–5, 237ff., 301, 335, 371
Pelagianism: Eck, J., and, 71, 73; Karlstadt, A., and, 74; Luther, M., and, 55
Pelagius: Augustine, St, against, 57
Pelargus, Ambrosius, 30, 32
Pellican, Conrad (Kürschner), Hebrew studies, 8; leaves Order, 17; professor at Basle, 19
Pelt, Hans, 171
penance: abuses, Oecolampadius, J., on, 17
penitence, 45, 56, 63, 66, 68, 69
Pentecost: Müntzer's office, 320–1
people of God: Anabaptist view, 383; worship, 305
Peringer, Diepold: Nuremberg sermon, 118 *n. 1*

Perkins, William, 71, 287
Peter, Apostle, St, 203, 289, 350, 379, 392, 395
Peters, R., xvii *n. 1*
Petrus, Hispanus. *See* John XXI, Pope
Petry, L., 61 *n. 1*
Petry, R. C., 118 *n. 4*
Peutinger, Conrad, xviii, 9 *n. 4*, 12 *n. 1*, 13, 19, 128, 359, 366, 377
Peutinger, Constance, 14
Peutinger, Felicitas, 14
Peutinger, Margaret, 14, 366
Pfeiffer, Heinrich, 222ff., 226, 235, 238f., 241f., 245, 336 *n. 2*
Pharaoh: baptismal type, 394, 396
philanthropy. *See* poor relief
Philip, Landgrave of Hesse, 42, 222, 225, 237, 238, 243, 246, 249
Philip I, Landgrave of the Rhine Palatinate, 5
Philip, Margrave of Baden: Oecolampadius, J., dedication to, 33-4
pictures: churches, 101-4, 114, 138, 196ff.
pietism: Müntzer, T., 272, 287; Staupitz, J., and, 56
Pilatus, Mount, 362-3
Pirckheimer, Willibald, 13, 16, 21, 26, 75, 83, 85, 359, 366, 377
plague: Basle, 151; St Gall, 364-5
Plato: influence on Erasmus, 142; influence on Gansfort, 142; influence on Karlstadt, A., 124, 142; influence on Muntzer, 217, 253, 286 *n. 2*, 292, 294f., 302
Pleissenberg Castle: Leipzig disputation and, 70-74
Pollich, Martin, of Mellerstadt: Wittenberg: University, 50-1, 55
Polman, P., xviii *n. 2*
poltergeist haunting: Karlstadt, A., 135 *n. 1*, 151
poor relief: Karlstadt, A., 105
Popes: appeals to, 52

Prague: Müntzer in, 112, 169-84, 188, 286, 329 *n. 2*
prayer: Karlstadt, A., 105, 129; Kessler, J., 378; Luther, M., 132; Müntzer, T., 313, 315, 320; Vadianus, J., 378
preachers: Basle synods of, 38; Reichsregiment demand for, 106
preacherships: medieval, 6-7
preaching: Anabaptist warnings, 380-4, 391, 392; Bible and, xviii-xix, 30, 75, 76, 107, 122-3, 125; Brigittine Order and, 16; cathedrals, 6 *n. 2*; Karlstadt, A., 75, 76, 107, 108, 123-6, 132, 138; lay, 123, 378; Luther, M.—*see* Luther, Martin: preaching; Müntzer, T., 315, 316-17, 323; popular, 12; St Gall, 370, 378; scholasticism and, 76; Thuringia, 133-4; vocation, 122; Wittenberg, 98, 106; Zwilling G., 106
predestination, 57, 58, 118 *n. 1*, 367
Pregner, Wilhelm, 120 *n. 1*
priesthood: doctrine: of all believers, 20, 84, 95, 113, 123, 369; Mass, 143-5; Müntzer, T., 320
printing: invention, xvii, 200, 201, 254; scholar printers, 8—*see also* individual names
processions and processionals, 306, 313
prophets: false, 134
Prosper, St, of Aquitaine, Oecolampadius, J., on, 21-2
Protestants: eucharistic doctrine, 147-8
Psalms: Augustine's exposition, 277 *n. 2*; Luther's exposition, 187, 212; Müntzer, T., 212, 259 *n. 5*, 260, 268, 272, 395 *n. 1*; Vadianus, J., 377; Vulgate, 309; (liturgy) Basle, 32; (liturgy) Cranmer, T., 306; (liturgy) Erasmian view, 306;

(liturgy) Karlstadt, A., 114, 306; (liturgy) Luther, M., 309; (liturgy) Müntzer, T., 307, 308–9, 315, 316–17, 320, 321, 322–3

purgatory: Burgauer, B., 370; Karlstadt, A., 114–15; Müntzer, T., defends, 183; Pirckheimer, W., 366; Westerburg, G., 115

purging: inward: baptism and, 394; Karlstadt, A., on, 122–3

Puritan legalism, 148; literature, 127; tradition, 76, 128, 138

Puritanism, 152, 214, 272, 276; England, 71, 123, 124, 138, 152, 353; Germany: Karlstadt, A., 90, 104, 105, 112, 123, 152; music, 105; Reformation and, 109; Zwingli, U., 104

Quedlinburg, 159

radicalism, 24, 113, 118 *n. 4*, 122–3, 127, 129, 149, 314, 322, 371, 372, 379–99

Ratcliffe, F. W., 338 *n. 1*, 341

Ratisbon, 377

Ray, John, 377

Raymond, of Sabunde, 253, 254, 278, 327, 342ff. and *n. 3*, 388 *n. 1*

Red Sea: baptismal type, 394, 396

redemption: saints' cults and, 104

Reformation: authority, 89; civic, 139; English liturgy, 307; eucharistic controversy, 141; Puritanism and, 109; radicalism, 115 *n. 1*, 139; Roman Catholicism and, 357; Swiss, 153

Reformed tradition, xiv, 76, 105, 139

Reformers, English, xxii, 26 *n. 4*, 45, 104, 142; French, 21; German, 13, 50; Swiss, 94, 104

Reichart, Hans, 198 *n. 3*

Reichsregiment, 1522, 106, 107

Reinhard, Martin, 79 *n. 1*, 87, 115–16; *Acta Ienensia*, 135 *n. 3*

Reinhart, Maurice, 170

relics: Annaberg, 79–80; Karlstadt, A., and, 57, 79–80; Luther, M., 57, 80, 108

Rembrandt, 45

'remembrance': eucharist, 146–7

Renaudet, A., 11, 326 *n. 4*, 327 *n. 1*, 342 *n. 3*

renunciation: Karlstadt, A., 124

res and *signum*, 81

Resurrection: eucharist, 96, 147; neglect, 130

Reuchlin John, xxiii, 4, 5, 8, 10, 50, 51, 62, 252, 365

Reval, I. S., 342 *n. 3*

revelation: Müntzer and, 186, 193, 203, 258, 263, 266, 269, 331, 340

Reyss, Johann, 6 *n. 2*

Rhau, George: Mass in 12 parts, 70

Rhegius, Urbanus, xxi, 323, 326, 330, 331, 332 *n. 2, 4*, 350

Rhenanus, Beatus, xvii, xviii *n. 1*, 11 *n. 5*, 95, 327 *n. 1*, 365

rhetoric, 360, 362

Rinck, Melchior, 250

Rinn, Hermann, 136 *n. 1*

Ritter, G., 8 *n. 1*

Rode, Hinne, 23, 142

Römer, Hans, 249–50, 335, 336 *n. 3*

Rörig, F., 18 *n. 3*

Roman liturgy: varieties of, 307

Rome, 65; critics of, 13; pilgrimage: Karlstadt, A., and, 52–3; primacy: Luther, M., and, 69

Roth, F., 332 *n. 3*, 333 *n. 2*

Roth, P., 36 *n. 1–3*, 37 *n. 2*

Roth, Stephen, 160, 161

Rothenburg, 148

Rückert, Hirsch, 274 *n. 3*

Rückert, Nick, 185, 196, 199, 201

Rühel, John, 242

Rütiner, John, 376

INDEX

Rufinus, 12 *n. 1*
rulers, attitude to, Bucer, M., 40, 41-2, 45; Calvin, J., 40, 45; Müntzer, T., 197, 202ff., 228, 245ff., 254, 260, 292, 300

Saale, river valley, xiii, 52, 113, 115, 133, 135, 136, 153
Saaz, 170 *n. 1*, 4, 172
Sabbath, 123-30
Sacraments, 125, 142, 141-8, 151
Sagrena, 100
St Anthony: hermits, 94
St Gall: Abbey, 357, 358, 372, 373, 374, 376; (Abbey) library, 262, 358, 362, 374; Academy of Vadianus, 366; Anabaptists of, 249, 370, 371; Biblical lectures, 38, 366, 368, 370, 371, 372; Christian civic league, 372; civil authority, 358-9, 371, 373; council, 364, 368, 370, 371; Erasmus, D., 375; Grebel, C., 371; images, removal of, 372, 373; Kessler, J., 368-70, 377-8; linen trade, 358, 359; magistrates, 368, 371; Münster, 357-8; Reformation, 367, 370-4, 377; Reformers, xiv, xxi, 357, 375; St Laurence church, 358, 371-2; St Leonard's nunnery, 371; School: Kessler, J., master, 378; Stadtbibliothek: Vadianus MS., 366 *n. 2*, 367, 374 *n. 2*, 377; students of, 109; Synod, 1530, 373; Vadianus, J., 357-9, 362, 364-78; Zürich and, 373
Saints: invocation: humanists on, 104; (invocation) Karlstadt, A., 118 *n. 1*; (invocation) Oecolampadius, J., 20; (invocation) Peringer, D., 118 *n. 1*; offices for, 306; Shrines: English, 104; vows to, 92
Saints' days; Karlstadt, A., 128-9; Müntzer, T., 306
salt: baptism: Müntzer, T., 321;

consecrated: Karlstadt, A., on 79, 91, 142
salvation: damned and, 114-15; Müntzer's doctrine, 202, 212, 214, 263ff., 273, 275-6, 278 *n. 3*, 286, 289 *n. 1*, 292f., 303, 331; 'Of the Mystery of Baptism', 383, 386, 388, 390-1; 'plan of', Karlstadt, A., 127
Salza, 225, 237, 240, 243
Salzburg, 231
Sam, Conrad, 42
sanctification: mysticism, 119, 127, 130
Sangerhausen, 204, 241, 242
Savonarda, Girolamo, 37
Saxony: liturgical experiments in, 188
Scheel, Otto, 255 *n. 3*
Schenck, George, 116
Scheurl, Christopher, 13, 50, 57, 61, 65, 66
Schiemer, Leonard, 250, 351f.
Schiff, O., 184 *n. 5*
Schlaffer, Hans, 250, 337, 351f.
Schleupner, 214
Schmalkaldic League, 198, 207
Schmidt, Martin, 191, 254, 265
Schmolk, Benjamin, 125-6
Schoch, R., 109 *n. 2*, 359 *n. 2*
Scholasticism, xviii, 11, 57-61, 71, 74, 144, 360
Schönewerthe, 204
Schott, Hans, 249
Schubert, Friedrich Hermann, 136 *n. 1*
Schürpf, Augustine, 62
Schürpf, Jerome, 60
Schürpf, Johannes, 363
Schugger brothers, 372
Schulz, K., 305 *n. 1*
Schwäbish Hall: preachership, 6 *n. 2*
Schwarz, W., xx *n. 2*, 5 *n. 1*
Schweinfurt, 136 *n. 1*
Schwenckfeld, Caspar, 374, 377

INDEX

Schwiebert, E. G., 61 *n. 1*, 3, 67 *n. 2*, 70 *n. 1*
Scotism, 49 *n. 3*, 51
Scotists: 62, 70
Scotus, Duns. *See* Duns Scotus
'Scribes': Anabaptist polemic, 380, 381, 382, 383, 385, 388, 391
Sectarianism, 153, 319
Sedulius: hymn, 311
Sehling, Emil, 305 *n. 1*, 313 *n. 1*
Seidemann, J. K., 166 *n. 1*, 167 *n. 1*
Seidler, Jacob, 91
Septuagint, 309
'Servants of God', 314
Servetus, Michael, 42
Seuse, Heinrich. *See* Suso, Henry
Seven Seals, 270f., 333
seven spirits of God, 129
Seven Words: allegory, 7
Sevenfold gifts of the Holy Spirit, 179, 270f., 283
Sevenfold purging and sprinkling, 129
Seyler, Francis, 79-80
Sickingen, Franz von, 18
Siena: University: Karlstadt, A., at, 53
Silence: liturgy, 26, 318
Sitter, river: baptisms in, 371
Sleep: death and, 115
Smend, Julius, 18 *n. 1*, 305 *n. 1*, 321 *n. 2*, 322, 323
Smirin, M. M., 157, 158, 161, 172 *n. 3*, 173, 231 *n. 1*, 235 *n. 1*, 294
Sobek, Burian, 171
Spalatin, George Burkhardt, xviii, 90 *n. 1*, 95 *n. 1*; Karlstadt, A., and, 53, 57, 58, 63, 75, 86, 92, 131; Luther, M., and, 61, 63, 67, 75, 77, 100-1, 112 *n. 1*, 131-2; Müntzer, 187, 190f., 195, 198, 279 *n. 3*, 282; preaching, 106; Reichsregiment, 106; Wittenberg Movement, 95, 96; Zwickau prophets, 100-1

Spiritual Franciscans, 257, 327
Spittelmayer, Ambrosius, 332 *n. 2*
Spitz, L. W., 4 *n. 1*, 360 *n. 1*
Sprinkling, 176, 180, 218, 261, 269, 271, 296 *n. 3*
Stadtler, Ulrich, 299
Stachelin, E., 3 *n. 1*, 7, 32 *n. 2*, 35 *n. 1*, 38, 44
Stähelin, Wolfgang, 60
Stainpeis, Martin, 363
Staupitz, Johannes, 85 *n. 2*, 251, 327; Augustinianism, 56 *n. 3*, 57; Karlstadt, A., and, 49 *n. 3*, 56, 57, 58, 113; mysticism, 119; Oecolampadius, J., and, 7
retirement, 55; Thomism, 56; Wittenberg Reformation and, 56; works: *Libellus de executione eterne predestinationis*, 57
Stayer, James, 249
Stein, Wolfgang: usury, 126 *n. 3*, 133, 195, 200
Steinmüller, 161 *n. 2*, 162 *n. 2*
Stephen, St, 157, 167
Stolberg, 158, 159, 185, 188, 209, 242, 341
Stolberg, Maria von, 184 *n. 6*
Storch, Nicholas, 114, 100-1, 144, 166, 170, 173, 181-2, 259
Strabo, Walafrid: *Hortulus*, 362
Strasbourg, xiv, xviii, xxi, 4, 19 *n. 2*, 25, 28, 31, 32, 41, 42, 114, 116, 136 *n. 1*, 137, 250, 335, 352
Strauss, Johann, 126 *n. 3*, 133, 195, 200, 232, 239, 305
Strobel, G. T., 203 *n. 1*, 255, 258
Studer, Christopher, 376
Stübner, Balthasar, 198 *n. 3*
Stübner, Mark (M. Thome), 100-1, 166, 170, 172, 174, 181-2, 187, 276 *n. 2*
Stupperich, R., 172 *n. 3*
Stuttgart, 5
suffering, 114, 383-4, 385-6, 392, 398

421

Sunday, 123–7, 130—*See also* sacraments
Suso, Henry, 7, 118 *n. 4*, 127, 255f., 326
Swabia, 25
Swabian league, 233
Swiss Brethren, 138 *n. 1*, 139 *n. 1*, 234, 250, 322–3, 346, 352, 371
Swiss Confederacy, 358, 372
Switzerland, 234, 250
symbolism. *See* eucharist: doctrine
Symmen, Nicholas, 115–16

Taborites: influence on Müntzer, 228, 259
Tartaret: study of, 61
Tauler, Johann, 7, 57, 68, 85 *n. 2*, 113, 115, 117, 127, 137, 161, 165, 251, 255f., 258, 265 *n. 1*, 267, 270, 277 *n. 2*, 285, 286 *n. 2, 5*, 290, 326f., 338, 352
Tavard, G. H., 5 *n. 1*, 80 *n. 3*
Te Deum, 310
Teilhard de Chardin, 377
Temptation. *See Anfechtung*
Ten Commandments, 111
Tertullian, xviii *n. 1*, xxii, 11 *n. 5*, 12 *n. 1*, 25, 253, 365
Tetzel, John, 66–7
Thebouthis, 178 *n. 1*
Theologia Germanica, 68, 113, 116, 117 *n. 1*, 118 *n. 1, 4*, 119, 127, 128, 252–3, 256, 286 *n. 2*, 327
theology, political: Müntzer's, 298–302
theology, social: Müntzer's, 298–302
theology of nature: Anabaptists, 385–8; Müntzer, T., 325–31
Theophylact, abp of Achrida, 20, 34
Thome, Mark. *See* Stübner, Mark
Thomism, 49, 51, 117
Thomists, 49–51, 56, 62, 73, 113
Thuringia, 133, 135–6, 196, 198, 201, 227, 231ff., 237ff., 301

Tiburtius, 164–5
Timavus, river, 362
time: 'waiting time', 127, 129
Tirol, 231
Torgau, 52
transubstantiation: Reformers, and, 23, 143
Trent, Council of, 71, 307
Treyer, Jacob, 41
Trieste, 362
Trithemius, abbot of Sponheim, 5
Trinity: doctrine of, 288ff.
Trittenheim. *See* Trithemius
Troeltsch, Ernst, 262, 325
Trutfetter, Jodocus, 51, 60
truth, unity of, 376
Tübingen: University, 8
Tunstall, Cuthbert, bp of London, xxi, 35
Turks, 178f., 199, 329 *n. 2*
Tyndale, William, 281

Uhlstädt, 53
Ulm, 42, 43, 232
Ulrich, Duke of Württemberg, 90, 233
Ulrich, the Smith, 232
Ursula, St, 258
Ursula, Sister, 255, 326
Usury, 16, 32, 126
Utenheim, Christopher, von, 45
Utraquists, 169, 171

Vadianus, Dorothy, 365
Vadianus, Joachim, *of St Gall*, 4, 357–78; baptism and, 345; Bern Colloquy, 31; Luther, M., and, 254; works: *Brevis indicatura symbolorum*, 366; *Chronicles of Abbey of St Gall*, 374; *The Cockfight (Gallus pugnans)*, 362; *Collectanea in Acta Apostolorum*, 366–7; *De Poetica*, 362; *How to deal with the Plague*, 365; ed of Pomponius Mela and *scholia*,

362; *Six Books of Aphorisms*, 374; ed. of Strabo's *Hortulus*, 362
Vadianus, Martha, 364, 374
Valla, Laurentius, xx, 251, 252, 365, 366, 367
vernacular: liturgy, 18, 26, 99, 101, 108, 114, 147, 296, 306–23, 342
versicles and responses, 306, 307–9
Verwunderung, 227ff., 282, 296
Vespers, 307, 308, 314
vestments, 98, 99, 105
Vienna: humanists, 4; plague, 363; school of poetry and mathematics, 360; University, 60, 61, 359–61, 363
Vigils: 98, 321
visions: vocation and, 122
visitation of the sick: order for, 28, 38
Vocation, 121–2, 268, 302f., 325–6, 377
Volkerode: conference at, 1523, 225
Vows: monastic: Luther, M., 92, 96, 101
Vulgate, 144, 309

Waldensians, 276
Waldshut, 231
Walker, D. P., xxii *n. 4*, 11 *n. 5*
Wappler, P., 160 *n. 4*, 259 *n. 2*, 276 *n. 2*, 332 *n. 2, 4*, 333 *n. 1*, 335 *n. 2*
Warbeck, Veit: John Frederick, Duke, 133
Warmuth, Peter, 198 *n. 3*
Wartburg: Castle, 88, 169, 172 *n. 3*, 182
water: significance of, 81
Watt, Hugh von, 359
Watt, Leonard von, 359, 365
Watt, Melchior von, 363
Watts, Isaac, 309 *n. 2*
Webb, C. C. J., 342 *n. 3*
Weilner, I., 255 *n. 2*
Weinsberg, 3, 6, 8, 12, 13, 16, 32–3, 233
Weischenfelder, Martin, 332 *n. 2*

Weissensee, 241
Werra, 239
Wesley, Charles, 272, 281 *n. 1*, 289 *n. 1*
Wesley, John, 252, 290 *n. 4*, 328
Westerburg, Gerhard, 23, 79 *n. 1*, 114–16, 188, 346
Wetter, Wolfgang, 366
Whole and the Parts, Müntzer's doctrine of, 176, 260, 267, 286 *n. 5*, 287, 294f., 329f., 347 *n. 2*, 382 *n. 1*
Wiechert, Friedrich, 308
will, divine, 116–17, 119, 122, 123, 267, 386ff., 392, 394, 397; human, 66, 71, 73, 74, 76, 117, 119
Williams, G. Huntston, xxi *n. 1*, 115 *n. 1, 2*, 118 *n. 1, 4*, 139 *n. 1*, 158 *n. 1*, 201, 250 *n. 1*, 291 *n. 3*, 299 *n. 1*, 323 *n. 1*
Wimpfeling, Jacob, 4, 7, 8
Winkworth, Catherine, 125–6
Wisdom, divine, 256, 260, 379, 381
Wishart, George, 18
Wittenberg, 88, 94, 108–9, 134, 137–8, 142, 365; Anabaptists and, 381; Augustinian Canons, 93, 94, 96–7, 99–100, 101, 109, 134, 137–8, 182; Common Chest, 102; Karlstadt, A., and, 83, 146, 152; liturgical reform, 188; Masses reduced, 106–7; Ordinance of the City . . ., 101–2, 108, 110; parish churches, 90, 98, 107; preaching, 107–8; Zwickau prophets in, 167, 168, 181f., 183f., 276 *n. 2*
Wittenberg: All Saints, 101, 107; Chapter, 90, 94, 95, 98, 99, 107–8, 195–6; choristers, 106; Elector and, 51, 90, 94, 95, 107; Karlstadt, A., 95, 107, 112, 113, 121
Wittenberg: Castle church: Jonas, J., 96; Karlstadt, A., and, 51–2, 53, 57, 107; Orlamünde living, 114, 132

INDEX

Wittenberg Concord, 1536, 374
Wittenberg: Franciscans: unrest, 97; Karlstadt, A., and, 51
Wittenberg Movement, 160, 350; Karlstadt, A., 90ff.; Müntzer, T., 185, 200, 202, 214, 221, 260, 272, 325–6, 328; radical theology, 334
Wittenberg: Parish Church, 96, 99, 101, 107, 111; murals, 141
Wittenberg: town council, 90, 97, 98, 99, 102, 107; *Ordinance of the City...*, 101
Wittenberg: University, xviii, xxi, 87, 166, 251 *n. 1*; Augustinianism, 59–60, 61, 65, 118; biblical studies, 59; Böschenstein, and, 62; canon law, 52; Eilenburg Consultation, 107–8; Elector and, 51, 97, 98, 107; exodus from, 106 *n. 1*; eucharist, 99–100; Greek professorship, etc., 62; Hebrew professorship, etc., 13, 62; Karlstadt, A., 66–7, 90, 111–14, 116, 121, 131–2, 136, 150; attack on, 23; teacher at, 49–53, 58, 89; Kessler, J., 368, 369; Könneritz family, 79; Leipzig disputation, and, 68–77; Luther, M., 52, 53, 55–63, 66, 67, 88, 89, 90, 108–9, 113; Melanchthon, P., and, 61, 62, 63, 89, 170; Orlamünde living, 114, 132, 136; patristic studies, 59–60, 65; Reformation, 90; syllabus reform, 60–62, 65; Wittenberg Ordinance, 102; Zwilling, G., 94
Witzleben, Frederick von, 204
Wohnung Gottes: Müntzer, 284
Wöhrdt, Peasant of. *See* Peringer, Diepold
Wolf, E., 56 *n. 3*
Wolfenbüttel: Müntzer's liturgy at, 322 *n. 2*
Wolfgramm, E., 174 *n. 1*
Word of God: Anabaptists, 372, 391; Luther, M., 266; Müntzer, T., 265ff., 272ff., Vadianus, J., 367, 377
Work of God: Anabaptists, 380, 386–7; Müntzer, T., 202, 213, 267, 269, 277ff., 294f., 315, 316, 339
worker-priesthood: Karlstadt, A., 121
works, doctrine of, 63, 66, 71, 73, 74, 80 *n. 2*, 119
Wörlitz: Karlstadt, A., 112, 114, 120
Worms: Diet of, 67, 86ff., 167, 169, 195, 227, 231, 303; Edict of, 88–90
Wray, John. *See* Ray, John
Württemberg, 3, 231 *n. 2*; Ulrich, Duke of—*see* Ulrich, Duke of Württemberg
Wycliffe, John: influence on Müntzer, 202, 228, 258

Yoder, John: works: *Die Gespräche zwischen Täufern und Reformatoren in der Schweiz*, 40 *n. 1*

Zacchaeus, 350, 392
Zacharias, 214f., 284
Zeiss, Hans, 185, 187, 189, 191, 194, 196, 197, 199, 201, 204ff., 212 *n. 2*, 265, 295, 299, 300, 330
Zili, Dominicus, 366, 371
Zinck, Heinrich, 6 *n. 2*
Zschäbitz, G., 157 *n. 2*, 250, 335 *n. 1, 4*
Zürich, xiv, xviii, xxi, 28; Bullinger, H., 374; Catholic party, 31; Christian civic league, 42, 372; Disputation, 1st, 1523, 367; Disputation, 2nd, 1523, 367; edict on scriptural preaching, 30; 'Gospel of all creatures', 352, 353; Grebel, C., 371; iconoclasm, 371; Karlstadt A., 137, 149–50; magistrates, 32, 40, 367; prophesyings, 38; St Gall and, 358, 373, 374; Vadianus, J., 364, 367; Zwingli, U., and, 38, 41

INDEX

Zug, Diet of, 370

Zwick, Johannes: Constance, 53 *n. 1*

Zwickau, 93–4, 157, 159 *n. 3*, 160ff., 163–9, 170ff., 225, 250, 252, 259, 300; prophets, 113, 166, 168, 173, 181ff., 186–8, 190, 195, 259, 270, 276

Zwilling, Gabriel, 93, 94, 96, 107

Zwingli, Ulrich, 152, 244, 249, 262; Anabaptists and, 40 *n. 1*, 371–2; Bern Colloquy, 31; Christian Civic League, 198; death of, 43, 150; Eck, J., and, 28, 29; eucharistic doctrine, 23, 24, 26, 27, 44, 142, 298; exegesis and, 25; Gansfort, W., and, 142; Grebel, C., 138 *n. 1*, 370; heresy charge, 30; infant baptism, 40 *n. 1*; Karlstadt, A., 137, 139, 148, 149; liturgical reform, 32, 308; Luther, M., 253–4; Marburg conference, and, 42; music, 105; Oecolampadius, J., and, 13, 21, 24, 26, 28, 32, 43, 44, 45; Peasants' War, 232; statues and pictures, 104; Vadianus, J., 366, 367, 373; Zürich disputations, xviii *n. 4*, 20; Zürich influence, 38, 41

INDEX OF BIBLE REFERENCES

Chapters and verses are those of the Authorized Version.

OLD TESTAMENT

Genesis, 20, 32, 260, 275, 344; 1, 124; 15, 213; 33, 240
Exodus 23, 219
Leviticus 11, 386
Numbers 15, 228; 19, 180, 218, 261, 271, 279, 296; 19:19, 269; 30, 92
Deuteronomy 7, 240, 243; 14, 386
Judges, 237
I Kings 8, 228
II Kings 22–3, 205
Job, 32, 260
Psalms, 85, 107, 125 *n. 4*, 187, 212, 259 *n. 5*, 260, 268, 272, 275, 277 *n. 2*, 307–9; 1, 261; 5, 284; 19, 212, 260, 269, 277f., 294, 331, 339; 31, 213; 37:5, 390; 43, 313, 315 *n. 1*; 49, 219; 51, 309, 316; 63:3, 310; 67, 309; 68, 261; 69, 321; 78:2, 385 *n. 2*; 79, 228; 93, 188, 212, 260, 278 *n. 3*, 284, 309, 341f., 395; 93:5, 341; 110, 309; 118, 295; 119:94, 56; 128, 321; 140, 310
Song of Solomon (Song of Songs), 14; 5, 120
Ecclesiastes, 11
Isaiah, 261; 11, 261; 11:2, 270, 271f.; 22:22, 315; 24:2, 391 *n. 1*
Jeremiah, 32, 176f., 180, 214, 257, 326; 1, 261; 17:5, 299; 20, 261; 23, 273; 31, 299
Lamentations, 32
Ezekiel, 32, 180, 214, 261; 13, 261; 47:1, 313
Daniel, 32, 190, 225; 2, 202; 7, 228
Hosea, 32; 4:9, 391 *n. 1*
Amos, 32, 261
Obadiah, 32
Jonah, 32, 187, 282
Haggai, 32
Zechariah, 32, 112
Malachi, 32, 101

APOCRYPHA

Wisdom, 260, 380
Ecclesiasticus, 73, 260; 1:14, 339; 15:14–19, 73

NEW TESTAMENT

Matthew, 9, 32, 34; 3, 321; 3:13ff., 398; 5, 229, 261; 10, 261; 11:12, 91; 13, 217; 16, 193; 16:19, 389; 21:13, 381 *n. 2*; 23, 261; 28:19, 20, 383, 388–9
Mark, 43, 163; 1, 398; 4, 285; 11:17, 381 *n. 2*; 16, 163; 16:15, 43, 334, 337, 347
Luke, 279; 1, 207, 213ff., 226f., 262, 289, 336; 1:46–55, 309; 1:68ff., 309; 3:21ff., 398; 6, 329; 12, 321; 16:1ff., 264; 17:13, 319; 19:46, 381 *n. 2*; 22:19–20, 144–7

INDEX OF BIBLE REFERENCES

John, 32, 261; 1:29ff., 398; 2, 321; 3:5, 210; 5:24–9, 321; 5:39, 379; 7, 268, 280; 8:44, 117–18; 10, 289; 13:5–10, 81; 16, 297

Acts, 122, 138, 261, 269, 301, 366, 379; 2, 122; 2:15, 17, 329; 10, 216, 328; 10:15, 386; 12, 367; 26, 261

Romans, 63, 396; 1, 293; 1:16, 37; 1:20, 337, 347 n. 2, 384 n. 2; 2, 331; 2:12, 228; 4, 213; 6, 371; 7, 164, 331; 8, 176, 200, 228, 270; 10, 266; 13, 190, 197, 202f., 216, 228, 247, 300

I Corinthians 1, 97, 261; 2, 380; 7:17, 264f.; 10:16, 143; 13, 86, 295, 329; 14, 177, 261, 320

II Corinthians 3, 176; 5, 297

Galatians, 68, 75

Ephesians 4, 329; 5, 261, 320; 5:19, 323

Philippians, 2, 264; 3, 285

Colossians, 43, 261; 1, 295; 1:23, 337, 347 n. 2, 384 n. 1; 3:16, 323

II Timothy 3, 213; 3:1, 339

Hebrews, 32, 60, 63, 124, 260

James, 80, 80 n. 2, 82

I John, 20, 35; 3:6–9, 398

Revelation, 190, 228, 261; 5, 261, 270; 6, 228